AF600372

Horizons of Difference

SUNY series in Gender Theory

Tina Chanter, editor

Horizons of Difference

Rethinking Space, Place, and Identity with Irigaray

Edited by

Ruthanne Crapo Kim, Yvette Russell, and Brenda Sharp

Cover image: "Horizon," Rebekah Pryor, 2017, mixed media on cotton rag; used by permission of the artist.

Published by State University of New York Press, Albany

Printed in the United States of America

For information, contact State University of New York Press, Albany, NY
www.sunypress.edu

Library of Congress Cataloging-in-Publication Data

Names: Crapo Kim, Ruthanne, editor. | Russell, Yvette, editor. | Sharp, Brenda, editor.
Title: Horizons of difference : rethinking space, place, and identity with Irigaray / edited by Ruthanne Crapo Kim, Yvette Russell, Brenda Sharp.
Description: Albany : State University of New York Press, [2022] | Series: SUNY series in Gender Theory | Includes bibliographical references and index.
Identifiers: ISBN 9781438488455 (hardcover : alk. paper) | ISBN 9781438488479 (ebook)
Further information is available at the Library of Congress.

10 9 8 7 6 5 4 3 2 1

Contents

Figures

Abbreviations

Works by Irigaray

Books

BEW *Between East and West: From Singularity to Community*. Translated by Stephen Pluháček. New York: Columbia University Press, 2001. (Originally published as *Entre Orient et Occident. De la singularité à la communauté* [Paris: Grasset, 1999].)

BNW Luce Irigaray and Michael Marder, eds. *Building a New World. Luce Irigaray: Teaching II*. Basingstoke: Palgrave Macmillan, 2015.

C *Conversations*. With S. Pluháček and H. Bostic, J. Still, M. Stone, A. Wheeler, G. Howie, M. R. Miles and L. M. Harrington, H. A. Fielding, E. Grosz, M. Worton, B. H. Midttun. London: Continuum, 2008.

DB *Democracy Begins between Two*. Translated by Kirsteen Anderson. New York: Routledge, 2000. (Originally published as *La democrazia comincia a due* [Turin: Bollati-Boringhieri, 1994].)

EP *Elemental Passions*. Translated by Joanne Collie and Judith Still. New York: Routledge, 1992. (Originally published as *Passions élémentaires* [Paris: Minuit, 1982].)

EPQ *Everyday Prayers. Prières quotidiennes*, bilingual edition. Nottingham: University of Nottingham and Paris: Maisonneuve & Larose, 2004.

ESD *An Ethics of Sexual Difference*. Translated by Carolyn Burke and Gillian C. Gill. Ithaca, NY: Cornell University Press, 1993. (Originally published as *Éthique de la différence sexuelle* [Paris: Minuit, 1984].)

FA *The Forgetting of Air: In Martin Heidegger*. Translated by Mary Beth Mader. Austin: University of Texas Press, 1999. (Originally published as *L'oubli de l'air. Chez Martin Heidegger* [Paris: Minuit, 1983].)

IB *In the Beginning, She Was*. London: Bloomsbury, 2013.

ILTY *I Love to You: Sketch of a Possible Felicity in History*. Translated by Alison Martin. New York: Routledge, 1996. (Originally published as *J'aime à toi. Esquisse d'une félicité dans l'histoire* [Paris: Grasset, 1992].)

IR *The Irigaray Reader*. Edited by Margaret Whitford. Oxford: Basil Blackwell, 1991.

JTN *Je, tu, nous: Towards a Culture of Difference*. Translated by Alison Martin. London: Routledge, 1993. (Originally published as *Je, tu, nous. Pour une culture de la différence* [Paris: Grasset, 1990].)

KW *Luce Irigaray: Key Writings*. London: Continuum, 2004.

LD *Le langage des déments*. Approaches to Semiotics, 24. The Hague: Mouton, 1973.

ML *Marine Lover: Of Friedrich Nietzsche*. Translated by Gillian C. Gill. New York: Columbia University Press, 1991. (Originally published as *Amante marine. De Friedrich Nietzsche* [Paris: Éditions de Minuit, 1980].)

PP *Le Partage de la parole*. Special lecture series 4. Oxford: European Humanities Research Centre, University of Oxford/Legenda, 2001.

S *Speculum: Of the Other Woman*. Translated by Gillian C. Gill. Ithaca, NY: Cornell University Press, 1985. (Originally published as *Speculum. De l'autre femme* [Paris: Éditions de Minuit, 1974].)

SG *Sexes and Genealogies*. Translated by Gillian C. Gill. New York: Columbia University Press, 1993. (Originally published as *Sexes et parentés* [Paris: Éditions de Minuit, 1987].)

SGL *Sexes and Genres through Languages, Elements of Sexual Communication*. Translated by Gail Schwab and Katherine Stephenson. New York: Routledge, 2007. (Originally published as *Sexes et genres à travers les langues, Éléments de communication sexuée* [Paris: Grasset, 1990].)

SN *To Speak Is Never Neutral*. Translated by Gail Schwab. London: Continuum, 2002. (Originally published as *Parler n'est jamais neutre* [Paris: Éditions de Minuit, 1985].)

SW *Sharing the World*. London: Continuum, 2008.

T Irigaray with Mary Green, eds. *Teaching*. London: Continuum, 2008.

TBB *To Be Born: Genesis of a New Human Being*. Basingstoke: Palgrave Macmillan, 2017.

TBT *To Be Two*. Translated by Monique M. Rhodes and Marco F. Cocito-Monoc. New York: Routledge, [1994] 2001. (Originally published as *Être deux* [Paris: Grasset, 1997].)

TD *Thinking the Difference: For a Peaceful Revolution*. Translated by Karin Montin. London: Continuum-Routledge, 1994. (Originally published as *Le Temps de la différence. Pour une révolution pacifique* [Paris: Libraire Générale française, Livre de poche, 1989].)

TS *This Sex Which Is Not One*. Translated by Catherine Porter with Carolyn Burke. Ithaca, NY: Cornell University Press, 1985. (Originally published as *Ce sexe qui n'en est pas un* [Paris: Éditions de Minuit, 1977].)

TVB *Through Vegetal Being: Two Philosophical Perspectives*. With Luce Irigaray and Michael Marder. New York: Columbia University Press, 2016.

WD Luce Irigaray and Sylvere Lotinger, eds. *Why Different? A Culture of Two Subjects*. Translated by Camille Collins et al. New York: Semiotext(e) Foreign Agent Series, 2000.

WL *The Way of Love*. Translated by Heidi Bostic and Stephen Pluháček. London: Continuum, 2002. (The original text, *La voie de l'amour*, is not yet published in French.)

Articles and Chapters

AB "The Age of the Breath." Chap. 14 in *Luce Irigaray: Key Writings*, edited by Luce Irigaray, translated by Katja van de Rakt, Staci von Boeckman, and Luce Irigaray, 165–170. London: Continuum, 2004. (Originally published as *Le temps du soufflé* [Rüsselsheim: Christel Göttert Verlag, 1999].)

AC "Animal Compassion." In *Animal Philosophy*, edited by Matthew Calarco and Peter Atterton, 195–201. London: Continuum, 2004.

BB "Beginning with Breathing Anew." In *Breathing with Luce Irigaray*, edited by Emily A. Holmes and Lenart Škof, 217–226. London: Bloomsbury 2013.

BMH "Between Myth and History: The Tragedy of Antigone." In *Interrogating Antigone in Postmodern Philosophy and Criticism*, edited by S. E. Wilmer and Audrone Zukauskaite, 197–211. New York: Oxford Press, 2010.

BTE "Being Two, How Many Eyes Have We?" With Catherine Busson, Jim Mooney, Heidi Bostic, and Stephen Pluháček. Translated by Luce Irigaray. *Paragraph* 25, no. 3 (2002): 143–151. (Originally published as *À deux, nous avons combien d'yeux?* [Rüsselsheim: Christel Göttert Verlag, 2000].)

BTI "Beyond Totem and Idol, the Sexuate Other." Translated by Karen I. Burke. *Continental Philosophy Review* 40 (2007): 353–364.

D *Dialogues: Around Her Work*. Edited by Luce Irigaray. Special issue *Paragraph* 25, no. 3 (November 2002). A collection of essays on Irigaray's work by C. Bainbridge, H. Bostic, M. J. García Oramas, L. Harrington, M. Joy, K. Kukkola, A.-C. Mulder, S. Pluháček, H. Robinson, J. Still, F. Trani, L. Watkins, and A. Wheeler; each essay is followed by questions from L. Irigaray.

EBU "The Ecstasy of the Between Us." In *Intermediality as Inter-esse. Philosophy, Arts, Politics*, edited by Henk Oosterling, Hugh Silverman, and Ewa Plonowska Ziarek, 45–55. Lanham: Lexington Books/Rowman & Littlefield, 2011.

EM "Ecce mulier?" In *Nietzsche and the Feminine*, edited by Peter Burgard, 316–331. Charlottesville: University Press of Virginia, 1994.

EST "Entering a Space and a Time in the Feminine." In *La dona, metamorfosi de la modernita*, edited by Gladys Fabre, exhibition catalogue, 353–355. Barcelona: Fundation Joan Miró, 2004.

EW "Equal to Whom?" In *The Essential Difference*, edited by Naomi Schor and Elizabeth Weed, translated by Robert L. Mazzola, 63–81. Bloomington: Indiana University Press, 1994. (Originally published as "Égales à qui ?" *Critique* 43 [1987]: 420–437.)

FC "The Fecundity of the Caress: A Reading of Levinas, *Totality and Infinity*, 'Phenomenology of Eros.'" In *Feminist Interpretations of Emmanuel Levinas*, edited by Tina Chanter, 119–144. University Park: Pennsylvania University Press, 2001. (Also appearing in Richard A. Cohen, ed., *Face to Face with Levinas*, 231–256 [Albany: State University of New York Press, 1986].

Originally published as "La fecondité de la caresse. Lecture de Lévinas *Totalité et infini*, section IV, B, 'Phénoménologie de l'éros,'" in Luce Irigaray, *Éthique de la différence sexuelle* [Paris: Éditions de Minuit, 1984]. See: **ESD** supra.)

FH "A Future Horizon for Art?" Translated by Jennifer Matey. *Continental Philosophy Review* 36 (2003): 353–365. (Originally published as "Un horizon futur pour l'art?" *Compara(i)son: An International Journal of Comparative Literature* [January 1993] 107–116.)

HCW "How Can We Live Together in a Lasting Way?" In *Luce Irigaray: Key Writings*, translated by Alison Martin, Maria Bailey, and Luce Irigaray, 123–133. (The original text, "Comment habiter durablement ensemble?," was given as a lecture at the International Architectural Association of London, November 2000.)

HM "How to Make Feminine Self-Affection Appear." In *Two or Three or Something: Maria Lassnig and Liz Larner*, exhibition catalogue, 36–67. Graz: Kunsthaus Graz am Landesmuseum Joanneum, 2006.

I "Interview: Cultivating a Living Belonging." Luce Irigaray interviewed by Emily Anne Parker. *Journal of the British Society for Phenomenology* 46, no. 2 (2015): 109–116. https://doi.org/10.1080/00071773.2014.963345.

NL "A Natal Lacuna." Translated by Margaret Whitford. *Women's Art Magazine* 58 (May–June 1994): 11–13. (Originally published as "Une lacune natale," *Le Nouveau Commerce* 62–63 [1985]: 39–47.)

ODS "And the One Doesn't Stir without the Other." Translated by Helene Wenzel. *Signs* 7, no. 1 (1981): 56–59. (Originally published as *Et l'une ne bouge pas sans autre* [Paris: Éditions de Minuit, 1979].)

OCH "Où et comment habiter?" *Cahiers du Grif* 24 (March 1983): 139–143.

PC "Perhaps Cultivating Touch Can Still Save Us." *Substance* 40, no. 3, issue 126 (2011): 130–140.

PI "To Paint the Invisible." Translated and interviewed by Helen Fielding. *Continental Philosophy Review* 37 (2004): 389–405.

PTO "The Path Towards the Other." In *Beckett after Beckett*, edited by Stan Gontarski and Anthony Uhlmann, 39–51. Gainesville: University Press of Florida, 2006.

QEL "Questions to Emmanuel Levinas." In *The Irigaray Reader*, edited by Margaret Whitford, translated by Margaret Whitford, 178–189. (Originally published as "Questions à Emmanuel Lévinas, Sur la divinité de l'amour," *Critique* 522 [1990]: 911–920.)

SFO "Starting from Ourselves as Living Beings." *Journal of the British Society for Phenomenology* 42, no. 2 (2015): 101–108. https://doi.org/10.1080/00071773.2014.963346.

SH "Sharing Humanity." In *Deconstructing Zionism*, edited by Santiago Zabala and Michael Marder, 169–180. London: Bloomsbury, 2013.

TBA "To Begin with Breathing Anew." In *Breathing with Irigaray*, edited by Lenart Škof and Emily A. Holmes. London: Bloomsbury Academic, 2013.

TDF "Towards a Divine in the Feminine." In *Women and the Divine: Touching Transcendence*, edited by Gillian Howie and J'annine Jobling. Basingstoke: Palgrave Macmillan, 2009.

TLR "Thinking Life as Relation: An Interview with Luce Irigaray." With Stephen Pluháček and Heidi Bostic. In *Conversations*. London: Continuum, 2008.

TMH "Toward a Mutual Hospitality." In *The Conditions of Hospitality. Ethics, Politics, and Aesthetics on the Threshold of the Possible*, edited by Thomas Claviez, 42–54. New York: Fordham University Press, 2013.

TR "The Return." In *Rewriting Difference: Luce Irigaray and "the Greeks,"* edited by Athena Athanasiou and Elena Tzelepis, 259–272. Albany: State University New York Press, 2010.

WCD "Why Cultivate Difference?" *Paragraph* 25, issue 3 (2002): 79–90.

WO "What Other Are We Talking About." In *Encounters with Levinas*, edited by Tom Trezise. New Haven, CT: Yale University Press, 2004.

Introduction

Ruthanne Crapo Kim, Yvette Russell, and Brenda Sharp

In *An Ethics of Sexual Difference* Irigaray pens a line that is evocatively incomplete—"difference is at *least* two." Irigaray's project has been a steady insistence that we have yet to emerge from a cultural metaphysics of the One and that two remains at the brink until difference at the level of the sexuate is cultivated and politicized. In this edited volume of writing on or inspired by the work of Luce Irigaray, we feature a series of contributions from two annual proceedings of the Luce Irigaray Circle by scholars who are committed to the generative project envisioned by Irigaray's work and to contributing to the process of thinking difference as at least two. The circle met at the University of Winchester in the United Kingdom in 2017 for a conference entitled A Sharing of Speech: Scholarship on or Inspired by the Work of Luce Irigaray. In 2018 it met again at Brock University in St. Catharines, Canada, for a conference whose theme, "Horizons of Sexual Difference," inspired the title of this anthology.

This book follows on from a rich tradition of scholarly and collaborative edited volumes on Irigaray, many of which are featured in SUNY Press's catalogue.[1] While several of these volumes (and others) on Irigaray attend to the diverse complexity of Irigaray's move from sexual to sexuate difference, her capacious challenge to androcentric thinking,[2] and the diversity of projects that result from her writing,[3] this volume features scholarship that attempts to push the scope of Irigaray's work beyond its horizon. In so doing, this volume offers twelve essays informed and inspired by Irigaray's complex and nuanced critique of Western philosophy, culture, and metaphysics and her call to rethink our relationship to ourselves and the world through sexuate difference.

Included are original and innovative readings of urgent and diverse topics, such as trans feminist theory, feminist legal theory, film studies, critical race theory, social-political theory, philosophy of religion, environmental ethics, philosophical aesthetics, and critical pedagogy. Some texts speak directly to matters with which Irigaray has explicitly engaged, such as divine women (Barker), ecological ethics (Kim), and Heidegger's ontological legacy (Sares). Others foray into topics where Irigaray has chosen not to venture, such as white supremacist miscegenation (Hom), speculative evolutionary theory (Dahiya and Murtagh), and trans misogyny and feminine identities (Colman). The essays, as an ensemble, shift from a critique of the One to a conceptual reimagining of what "at least two" could bring about culturally, spiritually, aesthetically, and materially; they seek to venture toward that expanded horizon of possibility. We present these chapters under topical headings and the varying essays in each part include those that enlarge, challenge, and push Irigaray's claims, and others that transform and broaden the force of her theorization.

Space, Place, and Identity

The chapters in this volume take up the paramount themes within Irigaray's oeuvre of space, place, and identity in contemporary and cross-disciplinary ways. We suggest that these thematic tropes clarify the prescient urgency of sexual difference to theorize what is at stake if we fail to examine the diversity of topologies and morphologies foregrounded by Irigaray's work. The themes guide an intersectional and embodied analysis that responds to urgent demands for safe spaces that targeted bodies require, seats at the table for excluded others, and a language to articulate identity and difference.

In *An Ethics of Sexual Difference*, Irigaray urges us to rethink space and time, particularly the association between space and the feminine; additionally, she challenges the function of women's bodies as containers, serving as a place for place.[4] By theorizing sexual difference via the language usually considered the domain of the natural sciences, Irigaray reveals the sexualized discourse that overdetermines how we encounter space-time relation and find our places within its fabric and folds. An underthought contribution of her work is the relationship between natural science and the politics of identity and this volume seeks to fill that lacuna.

The authors of this volume use the convergent themes of space, place, and identity to investigate the promise and possibility of Irigarayan terms and theories, including locomotion, containment, the interval, the negative, desire, morphology, as well as racial, trans, and posthuman identities.

Space and place take twin precedent throughout this volume and reconceptualizations of space often infer a necessary and ongoing reconfiguration of place. For example, in Michael Lucas's essay on Irigarayan theory in studio practice, Lucas uses Irigarayan principles of intersubjectivity and the interval to instruct his students toward reconceptualizing their mediated perceptions of objects, rethinking how students analyze the planes, texture, and scope of an artistic installation. Wesley Barker's essay on eros and the cross of vertical and horizontal direction signified by the two lips within the body dismantles binaries between sacred and secular space, allowing morphological difference to guide reconceptualizations of eros.

With a different set of disciplinary concerns, M. D. Murtagh and Annu Dahiya's work in the discipline of philosophy of science suggests a sexual difference analysis regarding containment of the universe, primordial wombs, matrices, and the gradient of hydraulic flow. By scrutinizing the sexual underpinnings of the terminology and its described function in origins theory, both scholars engage an evocative notion of space-time and the places necessary for place to exist, while eliciting ongoing curiosity regarding the maternal tropes that convey containment and origins.

Identity and the markers of inclusion and exclusion are carefully considered in works such as Athena Colman's essay on trans identities and Yvette Russell's analysis of rape with a nuanced case study of cultural difference and sexual violence. Sabrina Hom and Mary Rawlinson's contributions consider the implication of racial purity, miscegenation, and anti-blackness—themes often elided in Irigaray's explicit work. Rather than understanding sexual difference theory to be antagonistic or irrelevant to such conversations, the work of these scholars reveals both the limits of Irigarayan theory and its ongoing potential to contribute toward a thick feminist analysis that queries law, art, and culture.

We suggest that throughout this volume, complex and complicated renderings of these thematic tropes bring together the disciplines of natural philosophy with nuanced sociopolitical accounts of being human, and in the case of James Sares and Ruthanne Crapo Kim's essays, more than human. Sexual difference is both a unifying thought, bringing together disparate groups, and also one that insists that the fragmented, nonunitary, and wounded subjectivities that have persisted and subsisted within the regime of phallic sameness can inform us on how we negotiate space, find place, and transform identity. In the following, we delineate the subtopics included in the volume and introduce the essays in the volume in more detail.

Trans Identities and Sexual Violence

In the first essay of the volume, Athena V. Colman puts Irigaray into conversation with Judith Butler and trans theorist Talia Mae Bettcher. Danielle Poe's earlier work on Irigaray and the trans body foregrounds the way sexual/sexuate difference theory can engender thinking on sexual identity beyond Irigaray's corpus and remain influenced by her generative work.[5] Colman extends these insights, mobilizing Irigaray's pertinacious critique against the logics of sameness while revealing a profound heterogeneity of trans subjectivities and identities that refuse to figure these bodies as abject or exceptional. In "Tarrying with Sexual Difference," Colman develops Talia Mae Bettcher's analysis of the responses often proffered to the inclusion of transwomen with the category of *woman*. Reading Bettcher with Judith Butler on gender performativity, and Irigaray's ontological argument for sexual difference, Colman argues that both Butler and Irigaray offer valuable explanatory frameworks for understanding trans-identification as ontological in its claim to reality *and* performativity. In so doing, Colman works to reconcile meaningfully the experience of "realness" as a sexed being that trans sociopolitical scholars argue for, without fixing a universal or abstract notion that grounds this reality or relying on a blunt psychic self-reporting. Instead, Colman returns to the phenomenological tradition that reveals the foregrounding of reality in a metaphysics of a relation prior to one's birth into the world, or movement from the container or the womb to the container of a post-Cartesian world. Irigaray's theorization of morphology is helpful insofar as it specifies the relational and spatiotemporal conditions in which these containers dwell and explains lived experience as both valid and intersubjectively woven with ecological, genealogical, and linguistic layers.

In the second essay of this part, Yvette Russell considers the place of erotic transformation in Irigaray's work, in light of Russell's own work on rape and rape law. Russell reflects on the failure of law in the area of sexual crimes against women, focusing on Irigaray's constructive project to imagine a new mode of resistance to rape and rape culture that, until now, has remained unthought. Russell argues that sexuate difference provides a path that links the feminist critique of rape law to a framework for resistance, one that reveals why erotic transformation must form a central part of any revolutionary feminist political agenda to end rape. In working toward such an erotic transformation of subjecthood and desire feminists might be able to pose an alternative vision of heterosexuality in which the scaffolding that supports the cultural coherence of rape is destroyed. To take seriously Irigaray's claim is to grapple sociolegally with a plural form of thinking and being that engenders an erotic transformation the structure itself is unable to codify. Both Colman and Russell's essays challenge sexual sameness and its undoing as a condition for just inclusion and representation, invoking a demand for difference that can attend to material and transcendental differences.

Sexuate Ontology

The second part of the book shifts the focus to sexuate ontology, offering speculative insights about the origins of life and the gradient of water flow in early hydraulic movements (Dahiya) and the conditions prior to the explosion of the universe and our present space-time (Murtagh). James Sares's essay closes the part with an ambitious analysis of how Irigaray's work can ontologically inform the inquiry surrounding transhumanism. This part features close readings of Irigaray's work through the disciplinary lenses of biology, physics, and technology, contributing significant evolutionary analyses that works like Elizabeth Grosz's *Becoming Undone*,[6] Astrida Neimanis's *Bodies of Waters*,[7] and Deboleena Roy's *Molecular Feminisms*[8] agitate and foreground.

In *An Ethics of Sexual Difference*, Irigaray calls attention to how the biological sciences have been slow to study the permeability of membranes, a reservation she directly correlates with the female and maternal sexual imaginary. Dahiya, in "The Conditions of Emergence: Irigaray, Primordial Wombs, and the Origins of Cellular Life," examines how the concept of *womb* in contemporary origins of life research coalesces with, and can potentially reframe, the relation between matter and life within feminist theory. Dahiya concentrates on research that theorizes the origins of cells by considering how the environmental conditions of the Ancient Earth may have facilitated their emergence. This research suggests that cellular life required semipermeable compartmentation, or inorganic wombs, to initially form. Disentangling "womb" from cis-female bodies, Dahiya contends that the far-from-equilibrium hydro-logics of primordial inorganic wombs dissolve a binary relation between matter and life, instead reframing this relation as a difference in degree rather than a difference in kind in the context of the latter's emergence.

M. D. Murtagh, in "Irigaray's Extendable Matrix: Cosmic Expansion-Contraction and Black Hole Umbilical Cords," takes up Irigaray's urging to rethink space-time—at the level of the Copernican revolution—given the critique of sexual difference theory. Murtagh's chapter facilitates a preliminary dialogue between sexual difference and cosmology, investigating the query: What contains the container of the universe itself? Murtagh explicates how Irigaray's work brings into focus the conditions that engender the universe prior to the Big Bang. Murtagh presses into the multiverse hypothesis, utilizing the insights of Stephen Hawking, Martin Rees, and Alan Guth in order to draw attention to the filial language all three deploy as they use words such as *embryo*, *offspring*, *child*, and *baby* to describe the universe as an emergent phenomenon of something Other. Murtagh suggests a failure to recognize a primordial "place" for the emergent universes to appear and highlights the occlusion of a relational theory of cosmic gestation. Murtagh suggests, "A multiverse theory of fundamental reality, however, would resolve the contradiction by pointing to an even more fundamental maternal origin or ground out of which they both emerge; that which remains absent and unthought." Murtagh turns to Irigaray's essay "Place, Interval" in *An Ethics of Sexual Difference* in order to elaborate how her early essay foreshadows key notions of locomotion, gravitational attraction, and cosmic expansion through the lens of sexual difference.

James Sares provides an account of sexual ontology, grounded in and responsive to Irigaray's philosophy, which focuses on the question of possibility. He considers the scope of ontology in terms of the "negativity" of sexuate beings, whereby one sex or sexuate morphology does not exhaust all that that one being is or *can be*. Sares goes on to consider how understanding sexuate difference as a structure of being brings about "positive" possibilities for sexuate beings to develop in their singularity. With particular focus on the human being, he argues that these principles develop a sexual ontology that recognizes how sexuate difference structures being through determinate limits while also engendering possibilities for its development and for new expressions of life.

Divine Women

The third part of the book focuses on another topic familiar to Irigarayan scholars—divine women. However, the writers featured here bring fresh and innovative readings of the ecstatic and erotic, which Irigaray argues we must rethink to transform categories like the sacred and ordinary and, importantly, the function of woman in these ascriptions. Using text and film, these chapters trace the crisscrossing of word and flesh, evocatively situating Irigaray's enduring analysis.

In "A Theology of Lips: Beyond the Wounding of Desire" Wesley Barker focuses on Irigaray's mimetic use of the feminine in her attempt to "speak" feminine desire through the language of lips. Barker is interested in the intersection of Irigaray's writing with religious language and Christian theology, in particular. Within the saying and unsaying of feminine desire vis-à-vis her mimetic use of fleshy language, argues Barker, Irigaray's writing evokes a territory at the limits of philosophy—a space that explicitly invites an exploration of religious language. The chapter concludes by reading Irigaray's invocation of lips crossing in *An Ethics of Sexual Difference* to shift focus away from the association of desire with either penetrative wounding or impenetrable touching, and toward a notion of desire as a continuous incarnation of the ambiguities of eros found in the generative slippage between flesh and word.

In her contribution to the volume, Tessa Nunn examines two films, *Hail Mary* by Jean-Luc Godard and Anne-Marie Miéville's short film *The Book of Mary*. In her analysis of these films Nunn proposes an Irigarayan viewing practice in which spectators search for representations of maternal genealogies and relationships among autonomous women, thereby affirming positive representations of the female gender, even when films fail to offer such images. Nunn argues that such a practice enables viewers to celebrate and enjoy women in relation and communion with one another, while also exposing the gaps in films that normalize a reductive representation of women as objects.

Rethinking Race and Sexual Difference

While Irigaray's work has called for a rethinking of subjectivity that imbricates other aspects of lived experience, scholars like Mary K. Bloodsworth,[9] Stephen Seely,[10] Rachel Jones,[11] and Rebecca Hill[12] have mapped structures of racism and colonialism with sexual difference theory, advancing the relevance of multiple differences without reinstating hierarchical comparison. The authors of this part expand upon these prior readings of Irigaray's work and bring into focus prescient political turmoil such as the rise of white nationalism, practices of miscegenation, and the summarily dismissive volley of "fake news" that conceal a sameness of critical race consciousness.

Sabrina L. Hom's chapter "White Supremacist Miscegenation: Irigaray at the Intersection of Race, Sexuality, and Patriarchy" explores the relevance of Irigaray's philosophy to understanding the role of patriarchy in resurgent white nationalist movements. According to Hom, feminist analyses must not take the white nationalist focus on racial purity at face value but need to account for the fact that white nationalist leaders frequently engage in interracial sexuality, even as they argue for the preservation of an endangered white race. Although patriarchy is ostensibly focused on the maintenance of white purity, the responsibility of maintaining purity is placed on white women's bodies, while white men are afforded unfettered access to nonwhite women. Hom argues that Irigaray's account of the patriarchal exchange in women and the exploitation of women's reproductive capacities provides an accurate description of the role of white women in white patriarchy but fails to account for racial differences between women. Hom argues that Irigaray's analysis can be expanded and enriched by putting it into dialogue with the work of black feminist scholars who have elucidated the role of race in the sexual economy. Together, these approaches offer an analysis of "white patriarchy" that scripts different but related roles for white and nonwhite women in the sexual and reproductive economy. The double action of white patriarchy to produce both pure white legitimate lineages and also to produce highly profitable but unacknowledged, racially impure lineages, explains the phenomenon that Hom calls "white supremacist miscegenation."

In her contribution to the volume Mary C. Rawlinson explores the genre of noir crime fiction, arguing that it proves particularly pertinent to the possibility of justice in the era of "fake news," false narratives, and growing social inequity. Philosophical narratives of equality elaborated in the law of property prove equally impertinent in a world where the very institutions meant to protect the vulnerable instead serve increasingly to exploit them, while concentrating wealth and privilege in elite zones of security at their expense. In her investigation of noir crime Rawlinson observes that Irigaray's critique of philosophical fictions of equality under globalization calls for a rethinking of justice and new narratives of political solidarity. Rawlinson argues that Frank Miller's neo-noir graphic novel and film *Sin City* offer just such an account of the possibility of justice and solidarities across difference in a world of structural injustice.

Environments of Relational Difference

This final part engages Irigaray's attention to the environment, which includes the material, social, and cultural environs of living and learning. The first chapter (Kim) coalesces around themes of ecological ethics and Irigaray's recent publications that reinforce her insistence that sexual difference theory isn't an anthropocentric critique, but one with a substantial force that can guide our thinking about all of life.[13] The next chapter (Lucas) speaks to Irigaray's ongoing interest in built environments and how lived space can cultivate respect between beings. Architectural philosophers Peg Rawes and Andrea Wheeler have developed Irigaray's work in this area at length[14] and Lucas's chapter includes an investigation of their considerations with the wave of new materialists influencing design and studio practices. The part concludes with the specific sociopolitical environment of Belfast, Northern Ireland, and an Irigarayan methodology that the author forwards to sustain peace and reduce political strife (Merrick).

In her contribution to the volume Ruthanne Crapo Kim traces Irigaray's sexuate ecological ethics through a conversation with ecofeminist Val Plumwood and biocentric deep ecologist Freya Matthews. Kim focuses on Irigaray's conceptualizing of self-affection, breath, and her critiques of artificial life, as they relate to environmental thinking. She argues that by situating Irigaray's self-affection as a poiesis of human making, Irigaray can be read as calling for a safeguarding against a fabricated, unified world where the environment serves as a neutered backdrop. In this way, Kim draws from Irigaray a normative ecological ethics that urges humans to relate in difference to other beings to share the diversity of worlds we inhabit.

Michael Lucas's contribution to the volume is a reflection on his own pedagogical practice in the architectural studio in conversation with Irigaray's work on language, air, breath and the "third space." Lucas reads Irigaray alongside Graham Harman on flattened ontologies and argues that students benefit from being involved in a sexuate, embodied, and inductive practice of encounter and discovery in the process of design and making, beyond mere idealist/object form and weak critical functionalism.

Situated firmly in Belfast, Northern Ireland, Ciara Merrick provides a lyrical rumination on Irigaray, breath, and the processes of peace making. The making of alternative horizons in and through peace requires, argues Merrick, a return to elemental and ontological commitments. Irigaray's work provides the path to such a return. Merrick puts Irigaray into conversation with philosopher Erin Manning to draw out an embodied relationality of movement to think anew Irigaray's "to-be" of bodily becoming. Merrick recalls a year of fieldwork in Belfast during which she implemented an Irigarayan inspired methodology of breath as an active and sensing participant researcher. Merrick calls for a conception of peace from within an alternative horizon in which the body is always in becoming and always moving with breath.

In conclusion, we acknowledge the labor required to organize scholarship and scholars, the grant monies generously given, and the profound artistry in word, image, and performance that no volume can justly represent. We acknowledge the two annual meetings of the Irigaray Circle, the first organized by the Institute for Theological Partnerships at the University of Winchester in the United Kingdom (2017) and the second by the Department of Philosophy at Brock University in St. Catharines, Canada (2018). We are grateful to many members of the Irigaray Circle and beyond who provided thoughtful and generous peer review of the chapters included in this volume, and who are committed to creative and supportive feminist scholarship. Thank you to Rebekah Pryor for generously donating an image of her beautiful artwork Horizon (2017), which adorns the cover of this volume.[15] Thanks finally are due to Luce Irigaray, whose work seems endlessly generative and nourishing in these uncertain times. It is our hope that this volume continues the flourishing dialogue that she started.

Notes

1. Maria C. Cimitile and Elaine P. Miller, eds., *Returning to Irigaray: Feminist Philosophy, Politics, and the Question of Unity* (2006); Elena Tzelepis and Athena Athanasiou, eds., *Rewriting Difference: Luce Irigaray and "the Greeks"* (2010); Mary C. Rawlinson, Sabrina L. Hom, and Serene J. Khader, eds., *Thinking with Irigaray* (2011); Mary C. Rawlinson, ed., *Engaging the World: Thinking after Irigaray* (2017); Gail M. Schwab, ed., *Thinking Life with Irigaray: Language, Origin, Art, Love* (2020).

2. See, for example: Serene Khader, "Introduction: The Work of Sexual Difference," in *Thinking with Irigaray*, ed. Mary C. Rawlinson, Sabrina L. Hom, and Serene J. Khader (Albany: State University of New York Press, 2011), 1–9.

3. See further: Luce Irigaray, Introduction to *Luce Irigaray Teaching*, ed. Luce Irigaray with Mary Green (London: Continuum, 2008), ix–xi; Gail M. Schwab, Introduction to *Thinking Life with Irigaray: Language, Origin, Art, Love* (Albany: State University of New York Press, 2020), 3–24.

4. Luce Irigaray, *An Ethics of Sexual Difference*, trans. Carolyn Burke and Gillian C. Gill (Ithaca, NY: Cornell University Press, 1993), 7, 40.

5. Danielle Poe, "Can Luce Irigaray's Notion of Sexual Difference Be Applied to Transsexual and Transgender Narratives?" In *Thinking with Irigaray*, 111–130.

6. Elizabeth Grosz, *Becoming Undone: Darwinian Reflections on Life, Politics and Art* (Durham, NC: Duke University Press, 2011).

7. Astrida Neimanis, *Bodies of Water: Posthuman Feminist Phenomenology* (London: Bloomsbury Academic, 2017).

8. Deboleena Roy, *Molecular Feminisms: Biology, Becomings, and Life in the Lab* (Seattle: University of Washington Press, 2018).

9. Mary K. Bloodsworth, *In-Between Bodies: Sexual Difference, Race, and Sexuality* (Albany: State University of New York Press, 2007).

10. Stephen D. Seely, "Irigaray between God and the Indians: Sexuate Difference, Decoloniality, and the Politics of Ontology," *Australian Feminist Law Journal* 43, 1 (2017): 41–65.

11. Rachel Jones, "Philosophical *Métissage* and the Decolonization of Difference: Luce Irigaray, Daniel Maximin, and the Elemental Sublime," *Journal of Aesthetics and Phenomenology* 5, no. 2 (2018): 139–154.

12. Rebecca Hill, "The Multiple Readings of Irigaray's Concept of Sexual Difference," *Philosophy Compass* 11, no. 7 (July 2016): 390–401.

13. Luce Irigaray BTE; TVB; I.

14. See Peg Rawes, *Irigaray for Architects* (Abingdon: Routledge, 2007); Andrea Wheeler, "Architectural Issues in Building Community through Luce Irigaray's Perspective on Being-Two," in *Luce Irigaray: Teaching*, edited by Luce Irigaray with Mary Green (London: Continuum, 2008), 61–68.

15. *Plane + Horizon*, Rebekah Pryor, https://www.rebekahpryor.com/plane-andhorizon, accessed November 29, 2021.

Bibliography

Bloodsworth, Mary K. *In-Between Bodies: Sexual Difference, Race, and Sexuality*. Albany: State University of New York Press, 2007.

Cimitile, Maria C., and Elaine P. Miller, eds. *Returning to Irigaray: Feminist Philosophy, Politics, and the Question of Unity*. Albany: State University of New York Press, 2006.

Grosz, Elizabeth. *Becoming Undone: Darwinian Reflections on Life, Politics and Art*. Durham, NC: Duke University Press, 2011.

Irigaray, Luce. *An Ethics of Sexual Difference*. Translated by Carolyn Burke and Gillian C. Gill. Ithaca, NY: Cornell University Press, 1993.

Irigaray, Luce. Introduction to *Luce Irigaray Teaching*, edited by Luce Irigaray with Mary Green, ix–xi. London: Continuum, 2008.

Hill, Rebecca. "The Multiple Readings of Irigaray's Concept of Sexual Difference." *Philosophy Compass* 11, no. 7 (July 2016): 390–401.

Jones, Rachel. "Philosophical *Métissage* and the Decolonization of Difference: Luce Irigaray, Daniel Maximin, and the Elemental Sublime." *Journal of Aesthetics and Phenomenology* 5, no. 2 (2018): 139–154.

Khader, Serene. "Introduction: The Work of Sexual Difference." In *Thinking with Irigaray*, edited by Mary C. Rawlinson, Sabrina L. Hom, and Serene J. Khader, 1–9. Albany: State University of New York Press, 2011.

Poe, Danielle. "Can Luce Irigaray's Notion of Sexual Difference Be Applied to Transsexual and Transgender Narratives?" In *Thinking with Irigaray*, edited by Mary C. Rawlinson, Sabrina L. Hom, and Serene J. Khader, 111–130. Albany: State University of New York Press, 2011.

Seely, Stephen D. "Irigaray between God and the Indians: Sexuate Difference, Decoloniality, and the Politics of Ontology." *Australian Feminist Law Journal* 43, no. 1 (2017): 41–65.

Neimanis, Astrida. *Bodies of Water: Posthuman Feminist Phenomenology*. London: Bloomsbury Academic, 2017.

Rawes, Peg. *Irigaray for Architects*. Abingdon: Routledge, 2007.

Rawlinson, Mary C., ed. *Engaging the World: Thinking after Irigaray*. Albany: State University of New York Press, 2017.

Rawlinson, Mary C., Sabrina L. Hom, and Serene J. Khader, eds. *Thinking with Irigaray*. Albany: State University of New York Press, 2011.

Roy, Deboleena. Molecular Feminisms: *Biology, Becomings, and Life in the Lab*. Seattle: University of Washington Press, 2018.

Schwab, Gail M. *Thinking Life with Luce Irigaray: Language, Origin, Art, Love.* Albany: State University of New York Press, 2020.

Tzelepis, Elena, and Athena Athanasiou, eds. *Rewriting Difference: Luce Irigaray and "the Greeks."* Albany: State University of New York Press, 2010.

Wheeler, Andrea. "Architectural Issues in Building Community through Luce Irigaray's Perspective on Being-Two." In *Luce Irigaray: Teaching*, edited by Luce Irigaray with Mary Green, 61–68. London: Continuum, 2008.

Part I

Trans Identities and Sexual Violence

Chapter One

Tarrying with Sexual Difference

Toward a Morphological Ontology of Trans Subjectivity[1]

Athena V. Colman

> A concrete philosophy is not a happy one. It must stick close to experience, and yet not limit itself to the empirical but restore to each experience the ontological cipher which marks it internally.
>
> —Maurice Merleau-Ponty, *Signs*

With the emergence of trans studies, which has sought to theorize trans embodiment, trans subjectivities, and identities in their multiplicity, it would seem that Luce Irigaray's positing of the question of sexual difference as *ontological* difference has been outstripped by the specificity of the phenomenon she sought to attend to: embodied sexuate difference.[2] Thus, on the face of it, bringing Irigaray's thought of sexual difference to a consideration of trans subjectivity and embodiment may seem passé or even regressive. However, the trans embodiment Irigaray's formulation of sexual difference putatively excludes has in fact reignited, rather than extinguished, the very question of sexual difference. The very term *transition* implies a transition *from* female to male or male to female, and even those who reject the notion of transition in favor of "gender fluidity," or gender variance, are inevitably embroiled in the ways by which the very notion of transition has become a new ordering principle of coherence and a norm of trans identification. For example, on some views, it remains more intelligible to claim that one's transition is a matter of access to medical technologies; such that even if one's access to resources cannot accomplish the goal of transitioning, at the very least one's desire should.

The recent phenomenon of *transsexual separatism*, which is characterized by "transsexuals—particularly those who have undergone genital reconstruction and who choose not to disclose their trans history—[and who] see themselves as non-consensually subsumed under the transgender umbrella"[3] asserts a difference within trans discourse, which is often articulated at the register of a reinvestment in—or attempt to depart from—claims about sexual difference. Rather than lay the question of sexual difference to rest, trans discourses rehearse many of the hierarchized binary oppositions theorized by feminist thinkers decades ago. As Julia Serano's work explicates, there is an assumption of the inferiority of women and femininity operative in many instances of transphobia, particularly against trans women. Her analysis of transmisogyny extends feminist insights: "In a male-centered gender hierarchy, where it is assumed that men are better than women and that masculinity is superior to femininity, there is no greater perceived threat than the existence of trans women, who despite being born male and inheriting male privilege 'choose' to be female instead."[4] The clarity of Serano's account illustrates how much transmisogyny gains its conceptual coherence from the fundamental problematic of sexual difference. And so, it would seem that for a while longer, we must tarry with the question of sexual difference.

This essay enacts that tarrying by remaining with the ontological stakes of the question of sexual difference. On the one hand, it is clear that from at least one perspective, trans embodiment and subjectivity remain an insoluble problem for Irigaray's account of sexual difference; namely, that the ontological elaboration of sexual difference is unable to respond *at the level of ontology* to trans identities. To clarify, on this view, trans embodiment and subjectivity is not so much aberrant as it is unintelligible on its own terms and so can only be understood as derivative of the larger question of sexual difference. On the other hand, it is also clear that the same problematics of sexual difference, which Irigaray elucidated so long ago, remain operative in trans discourses and enacted in the reality of the violence of transphobia, especially violence against trans women.[5] Indeed, it would seem that trans women are excluded from Irigaray's thought of sexual difference at the same time as they are subject to an amplification of the violence of its cultural absence.[6]

In what follows, I read Irigaray with Talia Mae Bettcher, in order to first show how trans discourses that make ontological claims about trans subjectivity often reiterate the larger problematics of sexual difference. I then argue this reading illuminates the necessity of returning to the question of an ontology of sexual difference. While Irigaray's prioritizing of sexual difference risks reduplicating violence against alterity in its sexuate expression, I argue her unique thinking of the relational ontology of sexual difference, in particular, her account of morphology and the relational context of birth, provides resources for thinking trans embodiment and identification in terms of sexual difference. Such an elaboration may open up accounts of trans subjectivities that respond to the "epistemic violence"[7] of their theorization, avoiding the reduction of trans bodies to being the repository of nonnormative (abject) embodiment and countering tendencies to view trans embodiment in abstraction, or as "a universal (visible) trans subject."[8]

Posing the Question: Irigaray and Butler

In the philosophical consideration of sex/gender, we can productively stage two accounts that seem opposed: the claim of sexual difference in Irigaray's philosophy and Judith Butler's theory of gender performativity.[9]

Irigaray's thought works to retrieve sexual difference from the oblivion of its assumption. That is to say, the everyday appearance of sexual difference is at the same time the site that covers over the very erasure of this difference. Although it appears that sexual difference is everywhere, for Irigaray, this covers over the culture of sexual *indifference* it reinscribes. In order to illustrate the possibility of thinking this difference, Irigaray's rereading of the history of Western thought points to the exclusion of the feminine and its associated cognates of woman, female, and so forth; demonstrates how the Western symbolic is dependent upon the support of the feminine (e.g., for her unrecognized labor in social reproduction) at the same time as it depends upon her negation; and reconsiders moments in this history where the question of sexual difference *almost* appears on the horizon of Western thought. Irigaray points to these seminal moments in the history of philosophy where the feminine almost enters the symbolic (e.g., Diotima's speech in Plato, sexuality in Freud, etc.) but in the end is used to erect the symbolic that bars her entry into any symbolic.

The call for a feminine symbolic is not simply a claim about recognition. Women, or the feminine, cannot be recognized in the current symbolic as the very logic that subtends its meaning requires her absence or negation as a subject. Thus, our task cannot be one of further inclusion of women in the present symbolic but must be, more radically, the realization and creation of an entirely distinct feminine symbolic. This requires that the very question of sexual difference appears on our horizon of meaning, that is, that asking the question of sexual difference becomes central to human life and culture. Our task, then, is to think through the question of sexual difference.[10] Since we do not, according to Irigaray, have access to the notion of "two" sexes in our present symbolic, we must seek ways in which to construct and recover a feminine imaginary. To be clear, Irigaray's call to reach through the *appearance* of difference to the *actuality* of difference does not recall or fall prey to the classic philosophical problematic of an appearance/reality divide: sexual difference does not hide beneath particulars or in another metaphysical realm waiting to be rescued by untethered reason. Irigaray is more radical—sexual difference is the actuality we cover over every day. If we are to reach an understanding of true difference, sexual difference, we must undermine what appears to be differentiated. Irigaray claims the recovery of the feminine requires an attentiveness to the *perception* of difference. The problem is that representation reduces perception to sensation. "The logic of Western culture ends in a substitution of representation for perception."[11] For Irigaray then cultivating a culture of perception is central to the development of our capacities to attend to and support a culture of two, of two imaginaries and the irreducible interval between them, which is difference as such.

The other dominant account of sex/gender is Judith Butler's account of gender performativity, where sexual difference is not ontologically primary but is a discursive inscription constituted by the "stylized repetition of acts"—"regulatory practices," or later, what she will qualify as "citationality," which both constrain and produce gendered subjectivity. Her brilliant transposition of Foucault's *dispositif* (disciplinary apparatuses) finds gender a regulatory norm that governs the way we produce ourselves as subjects.[12] Despite the notorious difficulty of her texts, I believe the capture of the theory of performativity lies in the power of what, retrospectively, seems painfully obvious: that if gender were "natural" or ontologically primordial, why are gender ideals never achievable; and how, if we are ontologically feminine or masculine, could we ever fail to achieve—or not measure up—to what we already are? Indeed, for Butler, the moment of failure in normative gender success, seen for example in so-called masculine women (butch) or feminine men, are sites of incoherence (underwritten by associated discursive practices such as compulsory heterosexuality) that do not illustrate the exception to the rule of normativity but rather show us the rule itself—our own constant failure to make permanent the gender to which we nonetheless never measure up and are never adequate to. Notably, neither moment in this putative opposition between performativity and "primordial" ontological difference seems to accommodate trans subjectivities. Here a crucial caveat is needed: there is no *universal* trans subject or trans experience. To emphasize the point, it is worth quoting Nihils Rev and Fiona M. Geist again here, "[There is a] tendency among researchers, writers, and activists to assume a universal (visible) trans subject. This tendency frequently makes particularities of trans experience vanish into abstraction."[13] To posit a universal trans subject negates the phenomenological and feminist work that has led us to attend to experience in its location, history, and specificity in the first place.

Bettcher: Two Models of Trans Embodiment

In her attempt to find a theoretical account adequate to her own trans experience, in her words an account that "justifies" or secures her claim to be a woman, Talia Mae Bettcher discerns two available models operative in explaining and justifying claims about trans embodiment and identity: the "trapped in the wrong body" model and the "beyond the binary" model.[14] The "trapped in the wrong body" model views trans experience as arising from the "misalignment between gender identity and the sexed body."[15] (She notes that trans politics often appeals to both accounts.) Bettcher identifies two versions of the "trapped in the wrong body" model. The weaker version of this argument is that "one is born with . . . [a] medical condition" and through "corrective" medical intervention one "*becomes* a man or a woman."[16] The stronger version of this argument asserts an identity between gender identity and "real sex,"[17] that is, if one identifies as a woman one *is* a woman. As Bettcher notes, beyond the overall danger of pathologizing trans embodiment, there are problems with the "trapped in the wrong body" model. The claim that trans experience is the result of a physical misalignment cannot be secured on its own terms. Sex determination is made in relation to multiple features: chromosomal, gonadal, hormonal, genital, among others. Moreover, as Bettcher argues, the stronger version of the argument, namely, that one *really is* a man or a woman prior to sex reassignment surgery, suffers from the problem of legitimizing that one aspect of the self—gender identification—should outweigh all other aspects (the gonadal, chromosomal, hormonal, etc.). In other words, what can be appealed to in order to justify the claim that one's entire body is "defective while the internal sense of self is not"?[18]

On Bettcher's view, the second model, "beyond the binary," is also inadequate. The inevitable touchstone of this model is the assumption that gender is cultural. In Butler's famed words, "sex itself is a gendered category."[19] On this view, trans experience is the site of the *failure* of gender performance, illustrating gender was always a social construction. However, Bettcher indicates, thinkers Jay Prosser and Vivian Namaste have argued this view does not reflect the lived experience of trans people "for whom gender identity seems impervious to cultural modification."[20] Furthermore, as both Bettcher and Serano indicate, the "beyond the binary" model cannot give an account of how, for example, a trans woman can be subject to both sexism, that is, violence inflicted upon her insofar as she is a woman, at the same time as being subject to the violence of transphobia, that is, violence inflicted upon her insofar as she is deemed not to be "woman enough" (i.e., not passing as a "real" woman).

Parenthetically, I think one could add a third model, which embraces insights from both accounts and suggests a physiological basis for the differences of multiple sexes (where that physiology, in turn, is already culturally influenced). Such theories for the most part surreptitiously borrow justification from contemporary scientific theories that describe a multiplicity of sexes and sex expression across chromosomal, hormonal, and gonadal registers. These theories speak of a number of sexes, or a continuum of sexes, or of a multiplicity of sexes.[21] However, the taxonomy of these biochemical admixtures, which vary from claims about multiple-but-discrete sexes to a sex continuum or gender spectrum, still posits a sex before there is anyone to be sexed, and cannot give an account of trans embodiment on its own terms—as it is not necessarily the case that self-identification directly corresponds or lines up with any of these multiple physiological aspects. The argument against such a model is not with the scientific research or empirical findings as such, but rather to point to the more fundamental assumptions already at play in such endeavors. To clarify, such accounts cannot speak to the preoccupation and concern with sex and gender that demarcate, initiate, and frame such scientific endeavors in the first place. Indeed, these theories of sex and gender are often entirely foreign to phenomenological and lived accounts of trans experience.

Thematizing the Issue

Returning to Irigaray and Butler in light of Bettcher, we can summarize the problem: if sex or gender is ontological difference, then in either case it would seem that the trans person is deluded, or, they are refusing to align to what is real, which again would suggest that they are deluded.[22] Yet, if we take what accounts for a gender identification as an always-already self-identification of being a man or woman, despite the experience of always having been in "the wrong" body, then, on Irigaray's view, the fact that we do not have a culture of sexual difference by which the sense (or meaning) of this gender is symbolically available to *identify with* in the first place means trans identifications with the "opposite" sex are, by extension, masculine identifications.

An instructive (if skewed) hedging of Irigaray's view may further the point here. If trans identification can be explained as access to a primordial apprehension, or access to this fundamental difference, then it follows that the trans woman would have epistemic privilege as to what the currently absent or excluded feminine culture may look like. If this is so, then, arguably, we could inquire as to why transitions that are marked by the disciplinary regime of "passing" are unevenly demanded of trans women as opposed to trans men. Here it would seem that Butler's gender performativity is crucial. However, more fundamentally, if we accept Butler's view then given that gender is this "repetition of stylized acts of gender," how could someone who has been repeating these acts ever have had the sense that their identification is other than the "congealment" of these acts, that is, what could the trans experience, embodiment, and identification meaningfully be? Despite showing difficulties with our broad strokes of both positions, it may nonetheless be the case that trans identification is *ontological in its claim to reality* (à la Irigaray) and it is *performative in its realization* (à la Butler).

But how can we provide a deeper account that accommodates both of these insights? Furthermore, the disclaimer that there is no universal trans subject is itself a claim, which both suggests heterogeneity (difference) at the same time as appealing to the legitimacy of a claim to a general category (identity). As the emergence of transsexual separatism has shown, if the experience signified by those who experience or identify with trans embodiment marks both those who invest in a claim to gender identity (e.g., I am a woman in "reality," I am just in the wrong body) as well as those who claim to be outside of the binary, then how can we have a meaningful account that not only acknowledges and supports—with equal weight—the claim to actually be a woman or man at the same time as have that same theory support with equal weight the claim to be outside of both? Problematically, with the exception of Butler's—the limitations of which we have already shown—such accounts assume an ontological stability to gender and a concomitant epistemic privilege of identity with a secondary assumption of its coherence over time or its stability, namely, that because I know means I will *always* know. Such a suggestion would entail a privileged place of epistemological access to subjectivity. How do we account for possible differences between the nature of embodiment and the inscription of the psychic register that both Irigaray and Butler question—but ultimately reassert—in their accounts of subjectivity and subjectivization? How do we accommodate the importance of epistemic privilege (in other words, take people at their word that they are who they say they are) at the same time as providing a coherent account adequate to the phenomena of gender that does not make trans people the abject others to gender? I suggest that to take claims of both being beyond the binary and trapped in the wrong body seriously, we need to provide an account of gender that is not the reassertion of a subject equidistantly distributed between psyche and soma. We require an account where the cut through, what we call the historical, imaginary, and corporeal is not the same, or even the self-same. What is required is a thinking that offers an account for all of these differences *in terms of their differences*.

In what follows, I want to first mobilize Irigaray's intransigent critique of the logic of sameness in order to demonstrate how her thought contributes to situating what is required of a transfeminist thinking;

second, I suggest an extension of Irigaray's thought on morphology and relational ontology, which might gesture toward a thinking of trans subjectivities and identities, without figuring trans embodiment as abjection or exception.[23]

In developing resources for transfeminist thought, we can return to Bettcher in light of Irigaray's critique of a culture of sameness, or a culture of sexual indifference. Bettcher's elaboration of the "beyond the binary" model provides an entry into considering the fundamental problematic of the oppositions that masquerade as difference, which Irigaray's thought has continually thematized and deconstructed. The obvious problem with the "beyond the binary" model is that it depends on identity being defined against what it is not, reasserting the necessity for the binary it asserts it overcomes. However, more to the Irigarayan point, "beyond the binary" is *not* beyond the two: since there is not yet a culture of two subjects, the binary in question is in fact the articulation of masculine sameness that shores itself up through the appearance of difference. Moreover, the specious singularity of the indefinite "beyond" falls prey to an "auto-logical" solipsism insofar as it denies its origins in another, and so again suffers from an underlying conceptual reversion to an abstract universalism that its very claim of specificity denies, where "the plural of the one would be the multiple before being the two."[24]

As we have seen, for Bettcher the "trapped in the wrong body" model cannot be justified on its own terms. On the face of it, for Irigaray, this model might be read as particularly strange, again especially for a trans woman, since she argues that there is no culturally available feminine subjectivity for the trans woman to identify with in the first place. And yet, given that Irigaray will claim that sexual difference can be recovered and cultivated in its ontological availability—*precisely because it is ontological*—the trans woman's identification with the feminine might in fact support Irigaray's claim of the ontology of sexual difference. The difficulty here becomes a cautionary reminder of Irigaray's own thought: we must not abstract the ontological to a metaphysical ideality but return it to the concrete richness of embodied experience. Our epigraph from Merleau-Ponty guides us here: we must "stick close to experience" without limiting ourselves to the empirical "but restore to each experience the ontological cipher which marks it internally."[25] Turning to Irigaray's clarification of sexual difference in terms of the morphology of the body and the relational position of birth helps us to do just this.

Morphology and the Relational Position of Birth

> Living beings, insofar as they are alive, are a becoming. They produce form. No becoming is morphologically undifferentiated, even if its source is chaotic.
>
> —Luce Irigaray, *To Speak Is Never Neutral*[26]

Irigaray retrieves morphology as relational form, intending its resonances to both the morphological study of biological forms as well as the linguistic study of morphology in language. As Hilary Robinson notes, morphology, "the relationship between forms" rather than a "deterministic analysis of forms in themselves," is an approach found in studying both biological and linguistic forms.[27] In biology, morphological studies are focused on forms in *relation* to each other rather than to an ideal model, exemplary specimen, or origin. Unlike anatomy, which is static, the relational approach of morphology resists teleological accounts of biological change, as well as any original or ideal comparator external to the relation between the forms being studied. In linguistics, morphology centers on the morpheme, the smallest material expression of meaning in language. Irigaray's mobilization of morphology, a study of forms in relation across biology and linguistics is akin to a Möbius strip of the body and language, nature and culture, and shows not only their inextricability (cutting through the binary that reifies them) but also their ontological articulation. A clue to this articulation can be traced in Irigaray's analysis of the disappearance of the middle voice of ancient Attic Greek, a disappearance she suggests is a loss of a morphological form.[28] She argues that the lost middle voice "conveys both activity and passivity . . . [and] express[es] a process of self-affection, and even of reciprocity, that neither simple active nor passive forms could convey."[29] Irigaray specifies self-affection "outside the economy of the pair of opposites,"[30] which is not an oscillation or an "alternation" of these two.[31] As a reciprocity beyond self-reflexivity, self-affection as a morphological form, self-affection entails a "modality . . . possible both 'to be' and 'to let be, two modes of being . . . time and space can unite with one another from a bodily experience.'"[32] Self-affection ensures a noncoincidence within the subject that allows the subject to become, again. According to Irigaray, this notion of self-affection cannot be interpreted through categories of traditional culture[33] and must be distinguished from autoeroticism, as it is the "dwelling" or "living frame, starting from which we enter into relations with ourselves, with the other(s), and with the world."[34] This self-affection is marked by recovering our "sensibility and sensuousness,"[35] which would be to wrest our own bodily relation from a representational symbolic that erects itself on the very negation of cultivating that perception. In this way, we must recover becoming from its hypostatization in the concepts of the masculine symbolic, as well as from the ways embodiment has been circumscribed to a dislocated correspondence of its parts to a sensation governed by that same symbolic, which is an anatomization bereft of thought since "we have learned a code and not because we observe reality."[36]

The cultivation of perception requires time and is a process in contrast with the current situation in which the child is "induced" to recognition rather than "initiated into perceiving by itself."[37] If there is no cultivation of perception through self-affection as the "living frame" of our relations, then "a culture of ourselves as living beings, is still lacking."[38] The distinction between sensation and perception recalls this distinction between: anatomy, which enforces a model that precedes and codifies the meaning of all bodies before they emerge; and, morphology, which is a gesturing toward the indissolubility of meaning in the materiality of its expression.

For Irigaray, "birth is distance before any form, or more exactly, it constitutes the entry into a morphology."[39] If there is no form prior to birth, then birth is a nonteleological event that makes all other events possible. In a culture of sexuate indifference, birth signifies the teleological completion of the anatomical structures that will organize and guarantee that same telos understood as an outcome of birth as a single event. This reduction of birth to a telos, or an original form (an arche—a form *before* form), is the negation of maternal origins.[40] Here we must be cautious to grasp the ontological nature of the claim in its radical reconstrual of spatiality and temporality. Irigaray's reclamation of birth highlights her relational notion of spatiality realized with temporality: it is distance before form and dwelling. Resonant with her critique of the history of Western thought, which denigrates space for time or reduces space to time altogether, Irigaray recovers birth from accounts that reduce it to the movement from one container (the mother) to another container (the Cartesian space of the world). She spatializes the embodied relationality of the morphological where it is never severed from temporal becoming. "Our genus is the first particular dwelling, the architecture or morphology of which opens up to meeting the other, others, and building a collective dwelling."[41] Again, Irigaray has always demarcated the notion of birth in contradistinction to reproduction (which always relies on reproducing a said genealogy and not a new advent of being in its becoming). Irigaray would seem to develop the argument that birth cannot be reduced to the biological (even as the biological conditions it) since that would be to reduce human becoming to a teleological form, which posits being *prior* to the emergence of any being. This reduces human becoming to the accomplishment of some predetermined end or form, which obviates the possibility of human cultivation at all. Birth makes possible the distance that engenders morphological emergence.

What is important here is a rereading of nature where sexed subjectivity is not read as a teleological outcome. The retrieval of birth from its reduction to reproduction recasts its creative possibilities and instills it in its relational structure. Birth is the discontinuity that allows our connection. Birth has a debt beyond its social construction, and because the debt is to a time I cannot remember, or master in my memory, it is a latency that allowed me to become. This recovery of birth in its actuality is also the recovery of a nonteleological reading of desire, central to Irigaray's thought. "Desire reminds us of the non-representable nature of origin: our own, that of the other and that of the world."[42] In other words, all subjects have a mother from whom they were born and a moment that initiates all other moments—their birth—that allows them to be. To be a subject is to take up a relation to this birth. On Irigaray's view there are two basic relations: identifying or not identifying with the mother. In her words,

> Male and female identity cannot be reduced to physical differences that are more or less visible in their forms and effects. Sexed identity implies a way of constituting subjectivity in relation to the world, to the self, and to the other, that is specific to each sex. This specificity is determined in part by corporeal characteristics as implying a *different relational attitude*.[43]

While there may be morphological styles that express this relation, Irigaray does not claim these are anatomical styles. Nonetheless, these styles, of course, cannot be abstracted from the sensible specificity of their arising. Hence, the morphological is the *bodily as relation in relation*. This relation cannot be held in abstraction, as self-chosen, because that would imply an identity before the other, which supported that identity in coming to be. In this sense, it may be that sexual difference should be understood ontologically as a priority that allows relation to any identity, including those we subsequently discover and become as ourselves.

As has been argued, the becoming of the morphological is rooted in its relational position to birth, as the nonteleological discontinuity that allowed it to emerge and become its own being.[44] In this way, the morphological is the body in relation and as such is not a structure of meaning but a sensible movement of meaning in relation, which structures and restructures experience. Form is always form in relation, which is why for Irigaray sexuate identity is always relational identity. In this way, sexual difference *really is the possibility of relation*. Reconceived in terms of Irigaray's notion of birth, futurity itself is sensible in birth; birth is the sensible contouring of futurity (whether or not the subject is able to take it up in cultivation), pointing to a beyond that never abolishes the here.[45]

The difficulty of thinking difference, which does not collapse back into the same difference, that is, the otherness of the same, returns us to the rigor of Irigaray's thought: "The choice is not found in duality or non-duality"[46] and is "beyond sameness and otherness—a reserve of the relation-between."[47] When elaborated through the facets of relational identity, including morphology and the relational context of birth, sexual difference is clarified as a way of thinking that "escap[es] the physiological or cultural imperative of genealogy."[48] To reiterate, in pointing to morphological becoming rather than anatomical correspondence, Irigaray is able to recover an ontological notion of birth, which resists teleological or biologically deterministic views of sexuate embodiment. In other words, in her turn to the morphology of the body, she "escapes" a reduction to the physiological while at the same time returning to an embodied thinking that recovers the body in its sensible actuality. This thought enables Irigaray to figure sensible sexuate embodiment where materiality is never extracted from its meaning or expression. Her resuscitation of "sensibility and sensuousness," resists a reification of materiality to either: an inert substratum of matter—as if the mud of a golem awaiting the words to write its meaning into being, or, an overdetermined materiality, an élan vital, or an absolute immanence, where sexuate difference is simply one layer, or an appearance, of its determination. Neither being nor becoming—both sensible and transcendental—this relational identity

> contests the cleavages sensible/intelligible, concrete/abstract, matter/form, living/dead. *It also refuses the opposition between being and becoming*. . . . Relational identity considers the concrete identity which is always identity in relation.[49]

The point is not to insert or include women, or the feminine, into the current symbolic hierarchy, nor to revalorize the body or matter. Rather, Irigaray calls for us to recognize the morphology that subtends Western thought/philosophy at the same time as focusing on the importance of the question of sexual difference in order to bring it into view as a meaningful *question* for our time. It cannot be that *one* person thinks beyond this problematic. Her attention to subjectivity, to birth and relationality, means that any thought must be embedded in the relationality of the body from whence it was initiated. This is a relationality with a space for singularity to breathe. "This needs a being with oneself free from representation or knowledge already determined—a repose in oneself of breath, of energy, without any intention or plan."[50]

Transphobia and Transmisogyny as a Function of Sexual *In*difference

With Irigaray's morphological thought in mind we can see that the "trapped in the wrong body" model of trans subjectivity falls prey to an implicit empiricism, telos, or arche, which fails the ontological cipher. Trans subjectivity highlights the question of morphology in all embodied subjectivity. Morphology exceeds any static notion of embodiment in its temporality and ontology of relationality. Rather, trans embodiment and subjectivity illuminate the ontology of sexuate difference, which is never reducible to any one aspect of physiological inflections or symbolic uptakes of the relational and lived embodied subject and identity we all are. This view of sexual difference is only a problem for a masculine symbolic, which can only assert an abstract universal if there is a particular body over which to assert itself. Again, the problem is that we keep looking to the body of the individual as if it should duplicate the model of the universal in an atomized (and anatomized) form. However, if we understand relationality as embodied, then the morphological can be thought with the ontological and in terms of its emergence (and continual reemergence) in birth, rather than with the anatomical where questions of ontology are totally eclipsed.[51]

Thinking birth and the morphological situate Irigaray's critique of sameness in such a way as to illuminate the problem of transphobia, and particularly transmisogyny. The sameness or oneness that dominates transphobic discourses is a function of a culture of sexual indifference. The need to search for either a definition of sex or a sensation of sexed difference, rather than a relational perception of a sexuate other, "representation anaesthetizes perception"[52] of the other in her irreducible otherness. This is to have the appearance of two, which are really two self-sames, that is, to reduce the two to one. To take difference seriously allows multiple iterations of the form of the feminine, which is itself an "open form."

To take the irreducibility of difference seriously is to allow the morphological and ontological to cultivate ourselves and move a deadened sensation that cuts us off from others into a culture of perception that apprehends actuality. This model of sameness finds "relations" as an abstraction in an epistemic violence that duplicates a logic of the same, which disciplines our sexed identity instead of providing a framework for its cultivation. In this way, Irigaray's unceasing critique of the masculine, monosexual symbolic, and her intransigent disclosure of its pervasive replication, especially where the *appearance* of difference covers over the possibility of its emergence in form, is a powerful analysis in which to address transphobic and transmisogynist discourses.

Such a reading of Irigaray enables us to see that transphobia and transmisogyny point to a culture that lacks a relation to the sensible and covers over the morphological with anatomical models that negate the actuality of our relational becoming. The morphological attends to the body in its specific becoming, which takes the physiological seriously but acknowledges its changing, and its changing in relation to the self, the other, and the world. In avoiding the dangers of reductive accounts of biological determinism, we must not occlude the biological inflections that are available in phenomenological experiences. Indeed, if sexuate difference were entirely an effect of culture (or a history of gender expressions) then the very critique that sexual difference has been covered over by a monosexual culture could not arise. Here Irigaray can be read as resonant with some trans discourses: the realization of sex at the ontological level is not reducible to a particular history but always has relational traces in that history. It stakes itself on a claim not entirely determined by the conditions that one finds oneself in. This understanding is consistent with Irigaray's psychoanalytic influences: I do not first identify with myself (as if I were something that preceded the world into which I was born). I always, at first, identify with an Other (even when that other is the other of myself). Thus, my process of self-identification is always about my histories of identification. This means that there is something in relation that preserves the possibility of other ways of relating (including of the self to the self).

But what does this mean for thinking trans embodiment and subjectivity? I think that despite some of the ways that Irigaray clearly cannot think trans embodiment or subjectivity, the ethical insight to attend to the actual otherness of our possibilities can move us toward ways that help us think identity-in-and-as-relation, alongside claims to self-identity and self-determination. Indeed, many claims about what trans "really is" enact territorial strategies and repeat versions of the autonomous, masculine subject criticized so long ago by feminists such as Irigaray. The point is not one of simple criticism: our blind drive to "solve" identity betrays a fragility and an intolerance to process, ambiguity, and indeterminacy. The desire to have "found" out, or have affirmed who or what we are, once and for all, betrays a thwarting of the labor of the negative that sexuate difference (and life) demand. The turn to feminine morphology for new forms of thought must be about new forms of relation and self-relation, including self-affection. Sexual difference in this way, may be considered the first difference that allows any differentiation at all. This means that there is something in relation that preserves the possibility of other ways of relating (including of the self to the self). It resists the ideality of a telos of femininity, while restoring its actuality and calling for its cultivation. Irigaray's emphasis on culturation and cultivation means that sexuate embodiment is not an immediacy, fully available to sensation: It is the marker and remarking of the first difference that allowed me to be. We are not self-founding; we are a *difference with a legacy to differentiation*. The very history of being able "to be" was not my self-creation—even if it is that from which I am able to create myself. "That which is sexed is linked to perception, to its specific imaginary creation."[53]

Conclusion: In the Beginning, She Is

> Be what you are becoming . . .
> Of course, no woman has the morphology of another.
>
> —Luce Irigaray, *This Sex Which Is Not One*

Transphobia and transmisogyny find a concrete form in the frequently encountered question: "Are trans women really women?" This question exposes the operative assumptions in a so-called feminist thought that raises such a question. This repetition of phallocentrism implies representation before perception, or a model in advance of a sexuate being to which a woman must be adequate, that is, it implies that a woman is an instance of a type. Irigaray's rigorous critique of these very assumptions can be mobilized for a transfeminist thinking. In resisting dead anatomical models of sexuate embodiment for "a woman's phenomenological elaboration of the auto-affection and auto-representation of her body,"[54] Irigaray's thought enables a thinking of femininity beyond anatomy to a morphological becoming, which is inextricable from the perceptual specificity of subjects. In this way, trans feminine subjectivity is feminine subjectivity in a poiesis of her own forms of becoming held in relation. The self-affection through which trans feminine subjectivity speaks/iterates/becomes her body reveals "the way the body and its morphology are imprinted upon imaginary and symbolic creations."[55]

Trans feminine subjectivity inscribes the actuality of her feminine subjectivity through a cultivation of perception that is generative of form(s). In so doing, she moves beyond the immediacy of sensation in a self-affection that cultivates her sexuate subjectivity. (Our assumption that cultivation is "natural" or painless is already critiqued in Irigaray's work.) To extend this reading, trans feminine subjectivity indexes embodiment acting upon itself in a retrieval of perception not possible in representation. Far from being unintelligible or aberrant, on this view, trans feminine subjectivity and embodiment point beyond a reduction of the sexuate to the immediacy of sensation to an *ontology* of sexual difference. For this reason, Irigaray will link self-affection to "the possibility of different perceptions and creations."[56]

Read in this way, transphobia and transmisogyny may signal a contempt for the trans body that acts on itself, bringing itself into being in self-affection and in the labor of the negative. Such a profound grappling with sexuate difference might trouble the passivity of an unquestioned and unthought immediacy through which monosexual culture continues to stifle and dominate sexuate life. Careful not to duplicate this domination, Irigaray cautions that the retrieval of perception might only be practiced as a "sort of negative ontology . . . deconstructing what it represents for ourselves until we return to its living singularity."[57]

Thinking morphology through relational ontologies, I suggest figuring sexuate subjectivity *in relation* resists discourses that hierarchize differences and sever the sexuate from the actuality of the living subject. The morphological is always self-relation, relation to other and relation to worldedness (including its violence). This consideration helps us rethink Irigaray's imaginary and symbolic of feminine genealogy, which, as relational, always includes the sensible specificity of those relations. In this way, we could also trace a possible path for us to begin to see the ways in which Irigaray's morphological thought opens up the inscription of the land, peoples, histories, and so forth, within a relational ontology, wresting the very world from its reduction to cartographical legacies of representation that deaden life.

Notes

1. The use of "tarrying" in this essay's title is an invocation of Hegel's use of the term in the preface to *Phenomenology of Spirit*, and signals Irigaray's own relation to Hegel in her own debt to the "negative," as will be indicated in the conclusion. This use is also meant to signal the methodological import of staying with the difficulty of a thought, such as sexual difference, at its limit and as limit. "But the life of Spirit is not the life that shrinks from death and keeps itself untouched by devastation, but rather the life that endures it and maintains itself in it. It wins its truth only when, in utter dismemberment, it finds itself. It is this power, not as something positive, which closes its eyes to the negative, as when we say of something that it is nothing or is false, and then, having done with it, turn away and pass on to something else; on the contrary, Spirit is this power only by looking the negative in the face, and tarrying with it. This tarrying with the negative is the magical power that converts it into being. This power is identical with what we earlier called the Subject, which by giving determinateness an existence in its own element supersedes abstract immediacy, i.e., the immediacy which barely is, and thus is authentic substance: that being or immediacy whose mediation is not outside of it but which is this

mediation itself." G. W. F. Hegel, *Phenomenology of Spirit*, trans. A. V. Miller (Oxford: Oxford University Press, 1977), 19.

2. I proffer a disclaimer about the use of terms to refer to trans subjectivities, trans identities, and trans embodiment in this essay. The experiences of those who claim the prefix of "trans' " in their self-understanding or identification cannot be collapsed into an uncontested group identity. Nevertheless, despite its perils, I will use the terms *trans subjectivity*, *trans embodiment*, and *trans identifications* in the broadest sense—signifying a claim of their imbrication in each other without offering any unified account of that imbrication. This multi-imbricated sense attempts to specify a *dilation* of "trans" in order to acknowledge differences in trans experiences and discourses, including, but not limited to, differences articulated by transsexual people, transgender people, and people who are gender-variant or genderqueer but who also identify as trans. I deploy this initial imprecision not simply for pragmatic reasons (where the alternative would be a listing of identities, which no matter how exhaustive would nevertheless be exclusionary), nor because I assume there is no meaningful distinction between these terms; but rather because I want to suggest that a thinking that meaningfully accounts for these differences, *in terms of their differences*, has yet to be fully elaborated. I take this essay to be only one part of what such an elaboration would require. In this same way, this essay is only addressing trans feminine subjectivity.

3. Talia Mae Bettcher, "Trapped in the Wrong Theory," *Signs: Journal of Women and Culture* 39, no. 2 (2014): 384.

4. Julia Serano, *Whipping Girl: A Transsexual Woman on Sexism and the Scapegoating of Femininity* (New York: Seal Press, 2007), 15.

5. The fact that trans women of color are even more likely to be victims of violence cannot be directly accounted for in Irigaray's thought, if at all.

6. It is not at all a marginal point that what I call the exclusion-amplification problem owes its legacy to blood more than insight. This problematic can only emerge as a problem for thought because of the ongoing history of violence against the bodies and lives of trans women.

7. Viviane Namaste, "Undoing Theory: The 'Transgender Question' and the Epistemic Violence of Anglo-American Feminist Theory," *Hypatia* 24, no. 3 (2009): 11.

8. Nihils Rev and Fiona Maeve Geist, "Staging the Trans Sex Worker," *Transgender Studies Quarterly* 4, no. 1 (February 2017): 113.

9. The fraught conceptual couple "sex/gender" (a quasi-graphism of feminist thought) both demarcates the historical emergence of gender as a concept in feminist thought, as well as signifies subsequent and ongoing debates about the meaning or validity of this very distinction. In brief, early theories of gender challenged the dominant claim of "biological determinism": the view that one's body as biologically construed, that is, as biologically female or male,

corresponds to—or determines—one's feminine or masculine traits, and one's social role. The concept of gender arises as a way to mark the social off from the biological and draw attention to the ways in which the biological division of the sexes is an effect of the social. With regard to Irigaray, the unavailability of this distinction in French, particularly when translating sex/gender cognates, that is, male/female, masculine/feminine, among others, is often taken to signal the incommensurability or irrelevance of this distinction for Irigaray. However, Tina Chanter points out that Irigaray's later work uses the terms *sex* and *gender*, signaling Irigaray's concern with precisely this relation (*An Ethics of Eros: Irigaray's Rewriting of the Philosophers* [New York: Routledge, 1995], 172). From an Irigarayan vantage point, I understand the question of the sex/gender distinction to be an exemplar, or a symptom, of *a culture of sexual indifference*. In this respect, I necessarily use these terms without precision in what follows. For others on the sex/gender distinction in relation to Irigaray, see: Alison Stone, *Luce Irigaray and the Philosophy of Sexual Difference* (Cambridge: Cambridge University Press, 2006), 30 and 112; and, Margaret Whitford, *Luce Irigaray: Philosophy in the Feminine* (London: Routledge, 1991), 7–8.

10. Irigaray ESD, 5.

11. Irigaray IB, 15.

12. Judith Butler, "Performative Acts and Gender Constitution: An Essay in Phenomenology and Feminist Theory," *Theatre Journal* 40, no. 4 (1988): 519–531; Judith Butler, *Gender Trouble: Feminism and the Subversion of Identity* (New York: Routledge, 1999 [1990]); Judith Butler, *Bodies That Matter: On the Discursive Limits of "Sex"* (New York: Routledge, 1993).

13. Rev and Geist, "Staging," 113.

14. Bettcher, "Trapped," 383–384. I am rehearsing Bettcher's perspicacious account of these two models without the benefit of her substantial and careful response as well as the richness of her subsequent analysis, which is beyond the purview of this essay.

15. Bettcher, "Trapped," 383.

16. Bettcher, "Trapped," 383, emphasis original.

17. Bettcher, "Trapped," 383. Bettcher notes this view is sometimes referred to as *native identity*.

18. Bettcher, "Trapped," 386.

19. Butler, *Gender Trouble*, 11.

20. Bettcher, "Trapped," 385.

21. The most well-known account of this view can be found in the work of Anne Fausto-Sterling. See her *Sexing the Body: Gender Politics and the Construction of Sexuality* (New York: Basic Books, 2000).

22. I note the violence of this pathologizing, and its legacy is not a past that has passed by.

23. For the groundwork that has been laid in beginning to think of Irigaray's thought for transfeminism see: Danielle Poe, "Can Luce Irigaray's Notion of Sexual Difference Be Applied to Transsexual and Transgender Narratives," in *Thinking with Irigaray*, ed. Mary C. Rawlinson, Sabrina L. Hom, and Serene J. Khader (Albany: State University of New York Press, 2011), 111–128; Gayle Salamon, *Assuming a Body: Transgender and Rhetorics of Materiality* (New York: Columbia University Press, 2010).

24. Irigaray WD, 160.

25. Maurice Merleau-Ponty, *Signs*, trans. Richard C. McCleary (Evanston, IL: Northwestern University Press, 1964), 57.

26. Also see: "The female has yet to develop its own morphology" in Irigaray SG, 180.

27. Hilary Robinson, "Approaching Painting through Feminine Morphology," *Paragraph* 25, no. 3 (2002): 93.

28. Notably, Irigaray also refers to this as a "loss of the sensible transcendental" in Irigaray IB, 146.

29. Irigaray IB, 147.

30. Irigaray TR, 263.

31. Irigaray TR, 271.

32. Irigaray TBB, 49.

33. Irigaray I, 111.

34. Irigaray I, 110.

35. Irigaray I, 110.

36. Irigaray BTE, 144. In Rachel Jones's words, "The concept of morphology thus provides Irigaray with a language of sensible forms with which to counter both Plato's transcendent Forms of Ideas and the image of maternal matter as simply form-less. Instead, this matter gives the Forms a new form by allowing them to be translated into sensible configurations." *Irigaray: Towards a Sexuate Philosophy* (Cambridge: Polity Press, 2011), 60.

37. Irigaray TBB, 63.

38. Irigaray TS, 57.

39. Irigaray NL, 13.

40. Irigaray calls for form "without telos or arche." Irigaray S, 229.

41. Irigaray TBB, 4.

42. Irigaray TBB, 72.

43. Irigaray KW, 177.

44. Irigaray also tied birth to a "morphé in continual gestation. Movements ceaselessly reshaping this incarnation." Irigaray ESD, 193.

45. In Irigaray's words, "the material, the situation, the subjects and their relationships bring about different morphologies in a state of becoming." Irigaray WD, 42.

46. Irigaray TBT, 59.
47. Irigaray IB, 7–8.
48. Irigaray BTE, 150.
49. Irigaray WD, 159–160, emphasis mine.
50. Irigaray TBB, 41.
51. This reading of Irigaray may help us respond to interpreters who rightly worry about the erasure or discounting of trans subjectivity in her thought. However, the argument could be made that her call to cultivate bodily becoming toward a culture of sexuate difference in the inscription of sexuate limit and in relation is what the trans person takes on. This is akin to Danielle Poe's insight that "transexual and transgender narratives can also help us better understand Irigaray's insistence that corporeality is indispensable for cultivating sexual difference." "Luce Irigaray's Notion," 111.
52. Irigaray TBB, 72.
53. Irigaray SG, 163.
54. Irigaray JTN, 59.
55. Irigaray ESD, 68.
56. Irigaray SG, 164.
57. Irigaray TBB, 62.

Bibliography

Bettcher, Talia Mae. "Trapped in the Wrong Theory." *Signs: Journal of Women and Culture* 39, no. 2 (2014): 383–406.

Butler, Judith. *Bodies That Matter: On the Discursive Limits of "Sex."* New York: Routledge, 1993.

Butler, Judith. *Gender Trouble: Feminism and the Subversion of Identity*. New York: Routledge, 1999 [1990].

Butler, Judith. "Performative Acts and Gender Constitution: An Essay in Phenomenology and Feminist Theory." *Theatre Journal* 40, no. 4 (1988): 519–531.

Chanter, Tina. *An Ethics of Eros: Irigaray's Rewriting of the Philosophers*. New York: Routledge, 1995.

Hegel, G. W. F. *Phenomenology of Spirit*. Translated by A. V. Miller. Oxford: Oxford University Press, 1977.

Jones, Rachel. *Irigaray: Towards a Sexuate Philosophy*. Cambridge: Polity Press, 2011.

Merleau-Ponty, Maurice. *Signs*. Translated by Richard C. McCleary. Evanston, IL: Northwestern University Press, 1964.

Namaste, Viviane. "Undoing Theory: The 'Transgender Question' and the Epistemic Violence of Anglo-American Feminist Theory." *Hypatia* 24, no. 3 (2009): 11–32.

Poe, Danielle. "Can Luce Irigaray's Notion of Sexual Difference Be Applied to Transsexual and Transgender Narratives." In *Thinking with Irigaray*, edited by Mary C. Rawlinson, Sabrina L. Hom, and Serene J. Khader, 111–128. Albany: State University of New York Press, 2011.

Rev, Nihils, and Fiona Maeve Geist. "Staging the Trans Sex Worker." *Transgender Studies Quarterly* 4, no. 1 (February 2017): 112–127.

Robinson, Hilary. "Approaching Painting through Feminine Morphology." *Paragraph* 25, no. 3 (2002): 93–104.

Salamon, Gayle. *Assuming a Body: Transgender and Rhetorics of Materiality*. New York: Columbia University Press, 2010.

Serano, Julia. *Whipping Girl: A Transsexual Woman on Sexism and the Scapegoating of Femininity*. New York: Seal Press, 2007.

Stone, Alison. *An Introduction to Feminist Philosophy*. Cambridge: Polity Press, 2007.

Stone, Alison. *Luce Irigaray and the Philosophy of Sexual Difference*. Cambridge: Cambridge University Press, 2006.

Whitford, Margaret. *Luce Irigaray: Philosophy in the Feminine*. London: Routledge, 1991.

Chapter Two

Rethinking Feminist Resistance to Rape

Irigaray and Erotic Transformation

Yvette Russell

Introduction

There has traditionally been only sparse dialogue between legal scholars and the work of Luce Irigaray; with few exceptions,[1] sustained treatment of Irigaray *on* law and Irigaray *and* law has been hard to find. Legal research that has fruitfully engaged with Irigaray does so almost exclusively with the first phase of her corpus and broader engagement with her project is rare.[2] In my own research I have tried to put Irigaray's work into conversation with criminal law. Specifically, I trace Irigaray's project through rape law and practice in the courtroom to try to reveal what I argue is the law's continuing complicity in sexual crimes against women, despite the claims of many legislatures and criminal justice actors that they are doing all they can to "deal with" the problem.[3]

In this chapter I reflect again on the broad failure of law in the area of sexual crimes against women with a focus on Irigaray's constructive project to tease out avenues for resistance to rape and rape culture that much feminist sociolegal analysis leaves untouched. I argue that sexuate difference provides a path that links the feminist critique of rape law to a framework for resistance, one that reveals why erotic transformation must form a central part of any revolutionary feminist political agenda to end rape. With reference to the important anthropological work of Christine Helliwell,[4] I claim that feminist anti-rape praxis must encompass the goal of fostering subject-subject relations in which the transcendence of the other in their sexuate oneness is preserved and respected. In this way, we might pose an alternative vision of heterosexuality in which the scaffolding that supports the cultural coherence of rape is destroyed.

Rape and Rape Law

Feminist legal scholars have long had to reckon with the scourge of sexual violence against women and the seeming ambivalence of state and legal actors to its ubiquity. The history of feminist legal rape scholarship in several Western jurisdictions over the last forty years is notable, however, because it reveals in many ways some of the most successful examples we have of feminist partnering with the state. Many jurisdictions have seen the wholesale enactment of feminist-championed reforms to laws and public policy in and around sexual violence with the aim of putting best practice into action and enshrining feminist values into law. However, as these reforms have been implemented over the last forty years it has become clear that there has been little to no real improvement in "successful" criminal justice outcomes for complainants.[5] In England and Wales, for example, and while there has been a year-on-year increase in reporting of rape and other sexual offenses to police, there has been a marked decrease in successful criminal justice outcomes, measured in prosecutions and convictions. Analysis of recent statistics issued by the Home Office in the United Kingdom shows that rape is now one of ten offenses in England and Wales where the chances of cases reported to police resulting in criminal prosecution have fallen to approximately 1.5 percent, the lowest rate ever recorded.[6] In the London Metropolitan area, the largest police district per capita in the United Kingdom, a review of 501 cases of rape reported to police in April 2016 found that only fifteen of those cases (or 3 percent) resulted in conviction.[7] These stark figures have led a number of commentators to reiterate a long repeated feminist refrain that rape is a crime, more often than not, committed with impunity.[8]

There is a broad body of feminist work over the last forty years that catalogues and attempts to explain the collective failure of most Western legislatures to stem the rising tide of sexual violence within their respective jurisdictions, or to deliver something approximating justice to its victims and the community. Some scholars argue that this failure is attributable to a coalescence of institutional, policy, and legal negligence around which tangible material reform can be made to improve outcomes.[9] Others contend that the legal environment is suffused with and beholden not only to the sexist attitudes of those who operate the levers (attorneys, police, prosecutors, judges) but also to laypeople on juries upon whom the burden of determining guilt in the few rape cases that get to court rests.[10] It is these attitudes that militate against successful criminal justice outcomes by activating "rape myths"[11] that deny a complainant credibility, thus perverting the good intentions of the letter of the law. Others still query the presumptions underpinning rape laws themselves, interrogating concepts like "consent" and arguing that if we are to fully grasp why sexual violence remains so impervious to reform initiatives, we must look critically at the interest of law and legal institutions in maintaining the status quo.[12]

In my own work, and with reference to Irigaray's diagnosis of the void at the heart of Western metaphysics, I attempt to reveal what goes unspoken in a lot of feminist sociolegal and doctrinal discussion of rape law and practice. The law, I contend, has a particularly pernicious investment in the erasure of woman as a singular sexuate subject because she represents a plural form of thinking and being and is thus a fundamental challenge to the unitary logic that lends legal discourse its coherence.[13] If the law is to truly fathom the harm of rape, the conception of personhood upon which it relies must be freed from its symbiotic tie to property. Within such a conceptual framework the value of the harm of rape to women—and, therefore, the likelihood a case will proceed through the criminal justice system—depreciates the farther away the facts of a case are from the classic "real rape" scenario.[14] This is because the wrong of rape is conceived as an invasion or appropriation of property (the body) without consent. In cases where the perpetrator is a former intimate, or where there is little evidence of serious bodily injury, the "damage" to the person is harder to recognize. Irigaray explains the logic that supports this phenomenon eloquently in *Sharing the World*: "In love, the gaze often remains fascination, enchantment, occasionally rape and possession. Why is it that the other who looks at me during or after loving can injure me? He looks at an object, not at a subject."[15] The law replicates this objectified gaze toward women who come before it for justice in the aftermath of sexual violence.

With reference to Irigaray's work on "virginity" I try to think about how sexuate personhood, and thus the harm of rape to law, could be conceived of otherwise.[16] In Irigaray's formulation, virginity is not limited to its phallocratic meaning regarding the status of the hymen; rather, it connotes "the opening of a transcendental space in the relation to self and to the other."[17] For women to realize their own virginity requires cultivating a spiritual interiority of one's own, "capable of welcoming the word of the other without altering it."[18] In so doing, it also implicates a broader moral and physical integrity and inviolability.[19] Within the dominant liberal legal framework the self, conceived as property in the person or as an object, fundamentally alienates subjectivity within a possessive paradigm. To think the person as virgin is to think along a plane of horizontal transcendence in which the relation with the other involves the recognition of autonomy as an expression of a particular and inviolable sexuate belonging. To conceive of the self in such a way means that the harm of rape can be seen more readily as a crime that damages the whole of a person's being, and possibilities for becoming. Approaching the question of rape in this way involves an attempt to think *through* sexuate difference, and to displace the ruling symbolic order in which the masculine morphology dictates the boundaries of sexuate identity and of desire.

Louise du Toit's work is also important to highlight here because she too has made important interventions into the feminist canon on rape by drawing fruitfully on the work of Irigaray, among others.[20] It is simply impossible within the current masculine symbolic order, argues du Toit, to understand rape as a violent erasure of women's sexual subjectivity because that order, fundamentally and systematically, denies and undermines women's sexual subjectivity. Du Toit attempts to think a feminine sexuate subjectivity that has the potential to alter power relations in a way that might provide a path toward a rape-free society.[21] In her reading, this first requires the restoration of the maternal voice with a new symbolics to represent the maternal body[22] and the (re) introduction of the feminine divine.[23]

Du Toit shows how the obliteration of the maternal voice and objectification of the maternal body are foundational aspects upon which the project of undermining feminine sexuate subjectivity proceeds.[24] Notions of truth and representation come to reinforce this original forgetting of the material foundation upon which life proceeds, thus covering over the maternal debt; "if everything can be reduced to an abstract masculine-universal origin, men would owe women nothing."[25] Within the Order of the Same created by this original forgetting, all that is radically other must be erased so that the masculine dream of self-engendering can be perpetuated. An attempt to locate the lost and erased (m)other is, therefore, crucial in creating the conditions for the emergence of sexuate subjectivity because without her, the feminine remains mired within a masculine fantasy.[26] The resurrection of the mother as goddess is important too, Du Toit argues, to address the matricide at the heart of the monosexuate symbolic order.[27] Such a spiritual or divine intervention is necessary to forge a genre, space, or "imaginary domain"[28] in which women may engender their own becoming: "the goddess is the most significant 'other' needed to give women *their* world."[29]

In attempting to rehabilitate the maternal in its material and spiritual capacity as central to the feminine imaginary, Du Toit does not seek to reify the masculine projection of woman as mother in service to the phallocratic order in which sexual difference is reduced to mere reproductive difference. Rather, this exercise is concerned with tracing the psychic consequences of that projection, and of trying to think about how sexuate identity might be developed with reference to a different imaginary. Thinking through these elements, though they may appear largely removed from an agenda to resist rape, is essential to the feminist anti-rape project because they provide the building blocks for imagining an alternative and independent sexuate subjectivity that is not reducible to a neutral universal, or an aberration of that universal, and one that is coded as inherently rapable.

Du Toit's and my own earlier work is focused primarily, therefore, on tracing rape and rape law to the second phase of Irigaray's project. To this end it attempts to think the feminine as subject, to better conceive of the harm of rape and to challenge dominant legal conceptions that fail to capture the complex nature of that harm. In what follows I want to extend these analyses to try to draw on the third phase of Irigaray's project. That is, to consider the cultivation of carnal desire in intersubjectivity, or the generation of the conditions for erotic transformation in which we might contemplate the end of rape. Irigaray's thought reveals avenues by which desire through difference can be thought without resort to a reproduction of the hom(m)osexual symbolic order in which the law functions as a gatekeeper of (a)sexuate being and in which rape culture flourishes. This type of thinking is crucial for the feminist anti-rape project, I contend, because it illustrates the importance of situating resistance to rape within a broader revolutionary feminist agenda.

Rethinking Feminist Resistance to Rape

Feminist sociolegal work often involves theorizing resistance to rape as immanent critique within the boundaries of existing legal frameworks and discourse. That might comprise rethinking concepts like sexual autonomy or consent or calling for law reform to minimize the pernicious effects of "rape myths" and other prejudicial modes of thinking on criminal justice actors. In contrast, the most developed body of feminist philosophical work that considers the question of resistance argues for the need to reimagine embodiment and, in particular, women's embodiment, away from its current state as passive, weak, and violable.[30] Strategies like self-defense training for women are proposed, for example, with the purpose of encouraging women to embody a new and more radical motility, one which resists its designation as rapable.[31] Elsewhere I have criticized this latter body of scholarship for neglecting the importance of sexuate difference as crucial not only to understanding rape culture but to what is required to oppose it.[32] A focus on self-defense training as a strategy to resist rape is flawed, I contend, because it seeks the reconstitution of woman's embodiment from within an existing paradigm that has been constructed without reference to women's morphology, sexuality, or desire. I argue instead that if critical rape scholars are to truly contemplate the end of sexual violence against women, they must prioritize erotic transformation as part of a revolutionary feminist political agenda more broadly.

A significant component of the third phase of Irigaray's work has been addressed to consider the conditions under which erotic transformation might occur and what sexuate relations between men and women might look like where subjectivity is imagined beyond the One. Sexuate rights form part of this agenda,[33] and are supplemented by careful musing on how one might approach the other as corporeal being in intersubjectivity. It is clear that this requires a cultivation of an ethics of horizontal transcendence toward the other, or to that which I cannot consume, possess, or appropriate. The implications of such a mode of being (and Being) are so radical they will necessarily require "a different discourse, a different logic, a different relation to perfection."[34] Irigaray spends a lot of time considering the cultivation of a space, or interval, in and through which one might contemplate the transcendence of the other. It is through such a space that two worlds might open and be in relation with one another, and which might "give birth to a third world as work in common and space-time to be shared."[35] Crucially, the interval preserves a place of transcendence through respect for different needs that contemplate a "place of possible alliance."[36] The will to possess the other corresponds to a "solipsistic dream which forgets your consciousness and mine do not obey the same necessities."[37] The desire to grasp and capture the other precludes the possibility of transcendence in which there exists another subjectivity beyond my immediate senses or contemplation.[38] In this way, "it is not a matter . . . of sharing a common transcendence but of elaborating the between-two as a site of cultivation of the transcendental reality born from the attraction in difference."[39]

It is through such transcendental difference that the "becoming of a dialectic of two subjects in their alterity" can move away from circularity in which mastery of the whole in possession is no longer the desired end point.[40] A movement instead between two different Beings, says Irigaray, is animated by an energy that enlivens "the process [but] does not separate off from the body that it transforms and transfigures[,] as a thinking is elaborated that recognizes it as the sources and dwelling of Being."[41]

> This other, and the relation with them that corresponds to a part of me, can never be definitively subjected to negativity. It is rather a pretension to an Absolute founded upon my own identity that must accept the negative as marking an unsurpassable limit with regard to the existence of the other in their difference.[42]

In thinking through a new ethics of touch Irigaray emphasizes the importance of conceiving carnality in the context of a "between us" that is reflected by an equilibrium in nature and in language:

> How can I speak to you: find the words, discover the tone, touch you without losing myself? To touch you and thus exist beginning from the two. The listening which permits you to be makes it possible for you to hear me. Between us is created a

> field of life's vibrations intersected with those of the universe. United to the earth and to the sky, we are supported by our horizontality, sustained by it, by us. This force protects our equilibrium: despite gravity, we are lifted slightly above the ground, while remaining faithfully on the earth.[43]

That "between us" is necessary to be able to cultivate sensible perception, in which we can fundamentally reimagine desire, affectivity, and touch outside the matrices of possession and objectification that currently dominate carnal ethics. By living in "a night of the senses" in which language and its truth functions as our only perception,[44] our relationship to the other is "reduced to sensation, to simple affect, the other, even if he is active, becomes an object, losing his qualities as subject."[45] Perception should not become a means of appropriating the other, says Irigaray; instead it must be "cultivated for itself, without being reduced to a passivity or to an activity of the senses."[46] Desire remains trapped within instinct if it has not been worked through in the relational context in which it arises.[47] The caress, therefore, must unfold "as an intersubjective act, as a communication between two, a call to an in-stasy in us and between us, and not to an ecstasy outside of us."[48] The process that unfolds "between us" is the basis for a new carnal ethics but is also a model for relations with the other more generally:

> To consider a cultivation of desire as a new manner of establishing an amorous stability, possibly at the level of the family and community, requires reaching another stage of our human becoming—one in which the relations with the other as other are an essential dimension. Appropriation, property, possession, on which the family, indeed society, were based, must then be overcome thanks to a mutual respect between different subjectivities.[49]

In the final section of this chapter, and with reference to the important anthropological work of Christine Helliwell,[50] I attempt to illustrate how the existence of two unique and sexuate subjects might provide the path toward the erotic transformation required to create a rape-free society and why, therefore, thinking that difference as a component to a new carnal ethics is an important element of the feminist anti-rape project.

Sexuate Difference as a Path to Erotic Transformation and the End of Rape

In a compelling article published in the journal *Signs* in 2000, Christine Helliwell recounts her time as a participant observer within the Dayak community of Gerai in Indonesian Borneo.[51] Helliwell opens with an account of an event that occurred during her time living with the tribe in September 1985. Helliwell awoke one morning to hear a group of women laughing and talking loudly and excitedly about something that had occurred the previous night. A young woman of the tribe had awoken with a start in the freestanding house that she shared with her elderly mother, sister, and young children to find a man attempting to climb into bed with her. The woman responded to the man's actions by getting up and pushing him violently backward until he became tangled in her mosquito net. Eventually freeing himself, clothes askew, he fled into the night with the woman in pursuit yelling his name and screaming abuse in his direction; the commotion woke many of the surrounding neighbors.

Helliwell recounts her shock and indignation at the women's obvious amusement at the story, particularly given what they were describing was, to Helliwell at least, clearly an attempted rape. Speaking to the woman involved, Helliwell again expressed her outrage at what she characterized as a sexual assault and questioned the woman's reaction. The woman's response forms the basis for Helliwell's subsequent analysis and bears repeating in full:

> Her anger was palpable, and she shouted for all to hear her determination to exact a compensation payment from the man. Thinking to obtain information about local women's responses to rape, I began to question her. Had she been frightened? I asked. Of course she had—Wouldn't I feel frightened if I awoke in the dark to find an unknown person inside my mosquito net? Wouldn't I be angry? Why then, I asked, hadn't she taken the opportunity, while he was entangled in her mosquito net, to kick him hard or to hit him with one of the many wooden implements near at hand? She looked shocked. Why would she do that? she asked—after all, he hadn't hurt her. No, but he had wanted to, I replied. She looked at me with puzzlement. Not able to find a local word for rape in my

> vocabulary, I scrabbled to explain myself: "He was trying to have sex with you," I said, "although you didn't want to. He was trying to hurt you." She looked at me, more with pity than with puzzlement now, although both were mixed in her expression. "Tin [Christine], it's only a penis," she said. "How can a penis hurt anyone?"[52]

In the two years Helliwell spent with the Dayak, she heard of no other instances of sexual assault or violence. In fact, she says, when she questioned men and women about sexual assault their responses ranged "from puzzlement to outright incredulity to horror,"[53] leading her to characterize the community as "rape free."

Helliwell describes the relations between men and women in Gerai as egalitarian in many respects but highlights aspects which could easily be described as unequal, particularly with respect to the civil or community roles of men and women. Men are described by the Gerai as "higher" than women and this manifests itself in their greater speaking roles in community meetings, their monopoly on legal expertise, the degree of formal authority they hold over their wives, and the greater weight their evidence is accorded in a moot.[54] Despite these seemingly inegalitarian characteristics of Gerai life, this superior authority and status, says Helliwell, does not manifest itself as a power to dominate and control women sexually.[55]

Helliwell goes on to analyze this particular cultural state with reference to what she reads as a particular Gerai understanding of men and women reliant not on an inherent and immutable notion of *difference*, but on *sameness*.

> In Gerai, men and women are not understood as fundamentally different types of persons: there is no sense of a dichotomized masculinity and femininity. Rather, men and women are seen to have the same kinds of capacities and proclivities, but with respect to some, men are seen as "more so" and with respect to others, women are seen as "more so." Men are said to be braver and more knowledgeable about local law (*adat*), while women are said to be more persistent and more enduring. All of these qualities are valued.[56]

Crucially, says Helliwell, the ability to nurture and care, seen in Western culture as a feminine quality, is attributed to men and women equally in Gerai. These differences in conceptualizing personhood are linked inextricably to work and specifically to the role of rice production in sustaining the individual and community.[57]

The notion of the "good life" for the people of Gerai, says Helliwell, is the same for all members of the community and marked by the wish for a successful and bountiful rice harvest and the desire to raise healthy children. This life is dependent on a particular notion of partnership between men and women in which their respective capacities for certain types of work are not assumed by a rigid division of labor, but do involve the acknowledgment that "men are much better at men's work, and women are much better at women's work."[58] This illustrates, in Helliwell's reading, not a stress on "radical difference" but on "identity between men and women."[59]

This emphasis on identity extends, says Helliwell, to sex and sexuality. Men and women are said by people of the community to both menstruate, to both be capable of lactation, and, indeed, to both have the capacity for pregnancy and childbirth (though women are said to normally carry out this work as they are "better" at it).[60] This demonstrates, says Helliwell, "the community's stress on bodily identity between men and women."[61] Furthermore, Helliwell found that in Gerai the way in which men and women's sexual organs were conceived was essentially the same.

> When I asked several people who had been to school (and hence were used to putting pencil to paper) to draw men's and women's respective organs for me: in all cases, the basic structure and form of each were the same. One informant, endeavoring to convince me of this sameness, likened both to wooden and bark containers for holding valuables (these vary in size but have the same basic conical shape, narrower at the base and wider at the top). In all of these discussions, it was reiterated that the major difference between men's and women's organs is their location: inside the body (women) and outside the body (men). In fact, when I pressed people on this point, they invariably explained that it makes no sense to distinguish between men's and women's genitalia themselves; rather, it is location that distinguishes between penis and vulva.[62]

In line with the emphasis on sameness, says Helliwell, is the conceptualization in Gerai culture of the sex act itself. This is seen "as an equal coming together of fluids, pleasures, and life forces," which is said to lead to the conception of a fetus created through "the mingling of equal quantities of fluids and forces from both partners."[63] The sex act can only occur through a mutually reciprocated "need" between partners, without which the balance required to complete the act would be lacking.[64]

> The sexual act is understood as preeminently mutual in its character, including in its initiation. The idea of having sex with someone who does not need you to have sex with them—and so the idea of coercing someone into sex—is thus almost unthinkable to Gerai people. In addition, informants asserted that any such action would destroy the individual's spiritual balance and that of his or her rice group and bring calamity to the group as a whole.[65]

What this illustrates, according to Helliwell, is not the coming together of two different bodies as in Western culture, but "it is the similarity of the two bodies that allows procreation to occur."[66] Helliwell does concede that while the emphasis is on "identity, mingling, balance and reciprocity" the Gerai do have a strong sense of the importance of women and men as conjugal pairs that "fit" together and have complementary "life forces."[67] This life force is conceived as the spiritual essence that animates the person and gives the person life, which is also said to be true of all other elements of the universe. While the Gerai "stress sameness over difference" they do, nevertheless, see their life forces "oriented differently." This again, explains Helliwell, relates primarily to the respective roles of each in the rice production cycle of the community, as opposed to their biology.[68] Helliwell concludes that the Gerai have no conception of genital dimorphism upon which most Western feminist analyses of rape proceed, nor any regulatory regime of heterosex in the Foucauldian sense against which gendered bodies are produced and sexed.

Returning to the event that prompted her analysis, Helliwell attributes the origins of her reaction to the events to her "girling" within her own culture, in which she learned to fear acquisitive, aggressive male sexuality and to protect her own passive, vulnerable sexuality. The Gerai woman, by contrast, had no fear of sexual violence when awoken by a male intruder "because in the Gerai context 'girling' involves the inscription of sexual sameness, of a belief that women's sexuality and bodies are no less aggressive and no more vulnerable than men's."[69]

The impetus for Helliwell's critique of some feminists' reliance on sexual difference to explain the phenomenon of the rape of women by men seems to be influenced by an intersectional feminist critique of radical feminism and its universalizing tendencies, and her desire as an anthropologist to trouble the radical feminist assumption of the cultural ubiquity of rape. In this sense, Helliwell does not appear to be aligning herself in her desire to challenge feminist reliance on difference to explain rape with the radical urge to erase sexual difference and hence, the source of women's oppression. Rather she is interested in thinking about how "the practice of rape inscribes such differences."[70] In this way, her project is very much in keeping with the inquiry in my own work about the way in which rape *law* inscribes difference. However, Helliwell's conception of sexual difference seems to be limited to biological difference, or difference as it is conceived in the dominant symbolic; what Irigaray would call "sexual *in*difference." This fails to capture the notion of sexual difference as *morphological*. This distinction is important because the morphology of difference does not stop at the body's surfaces but considers the social and psychical context of the body's coding in culture. I say this not as a criticism but because I think in Helliwell's observations there is the potential to read a clear morphology of sexuate difference in the culture and society of the Gerai. I argue that such a reading illustrates how thinking difference as sexuate is crucial to feminist anti-rape theory and praxis.

Certainly, Helliwell's research suggests that there is no prediscursive coding of bodies as masculine or feminine, as in Western discourse, and, in this sense, there is not the immediate dimorphism that then dictates a specific type of gendered performance. However, from Helliwell's observations, men and women are still distinguished in this culture by their morphology. As she says, men and women have different values that are not seen hierarchically but as necessary for balance. This comes through most clearly, in my view, in the idea of the complementary "life forces," which, as Helliwell described it, is very much an energy coming from an individual's unique and uniquely different sexuate being. The presence of the life force and the esteem in which it is held, not as a generic "good" or "worth" of each community member but as an ultimately unknowable alterity of the sexuate individual, also indicated a space, or horizontal transcendence, between the two in which neither could consume the other but in which the creation of the energy required to sustain and generate life was nurtured. The complementarity thus does not refer to a collapsing of the one into the other, which Irigaray warns against; rather, it connotes a mutual coming together of two in radical alterity, which nonetheless, preserves a space "between us." The life force, as Helliwell describes it, forms the basis of a subjecthood different in respect of each being, which in turn generates alternative knowledges, practices, and values.

Reading Helliwell's observations psychoanalytically it is possible to discern almost immediately the apparent absence in this community and culture of the phallus as the mediating signifier. There is no sense in which the penis is coded as a weapon and the vagina as lack or hole, or a single dominating standard against which value is attributed. In other words, there is not a sense in which women are conceived as double, defective, or opposite of man, man being the standard against which all difference is judged.

Helliwell reads as evidence of sameness the Gerai's description and drawing of their genitals as essentially similar, "hav[ing] the same basic conical shape, narrower at the base and wider at the top." This was likened by participants "both to wooden and bark containers for holding valuables,"[71] which had important significance in the Gerai culture as the receptacles for containing their life source, rice, and also connoting the containing womb and the value placed on nurturing and caring. This receptacle seems to take on the role in this reading of an alternative signifier, analogous to Irigaray's two lips,[72] which mediates the Gerai desire for the good life and moderates their intersubjective relations that appear to be entirely free of any kind of coercive sexuality, as we understand it.

Helliwell's mesmerizing description of the sex act, as recounted to her, seemed to all but preclude the physical possibility of rape; it would, at least, be impossible to translate the Gerai notion of a mutual coming together of bodies, reciprocating their shared need, into the framework of permissible sex implicitly prescribed by most Western legislatures. In other words, there is simply no sense in which one party acquires the consent of another party who is inherently passive. As Helliwell puts it, "Sexual intercourse and conception are viewed as involving a mingling of similar bodily fluids, forces, and so on, rather than as the penetration of one body by another with a parallel propulsion of substances from one (male) body only into the other, very different (female) one."[73] While there is clearly not equality in this society in the way in which we perceive it in the liberal West (men are generally considered "higher" than women), this "formal inequality" does not also mean that men dominate and control women through their sexuality.

It is not my intention, with this brief recounting of Helliwell's observations some thirty years ago, to present this community as an unproblematized utopia that holds all the answers to the feminist fight against rape. However, I do think that Helliwell's research is instructive in illustrating the relationship between what I have characterized in my reading of it as the presence of two singular sexuate identities and an erotic order in which heterosexual desire is radically other, linked here to reciprocal need and to community well-being and balance. These aspects of embodied sexuate being in the Gerai community are important in explaining why, as Helliwell contends, it is "rape free." What I argue we can draw from Helliwell's observations, then, is important data about the prevention of rape and also about the type and nature of cultural change that is required for that discussion to be meaningful. The prevention of and resistance to rape is not just about prohibitive laws that fix the iteration of the sex act and of sexed bodies, nor is it about the reconstitution of women's bodies as ready to fight off rape. It first requires an ethics of subject-subject relations that can be read in Irigarayan terms as a form of respect for the absolute otherness of that which I cannot consume. Thinking through and working toward generating these conditions must therefore form a central part of feminist anti-rape theorizing and praxis.

Conclusion

Feminist scholars have long had to reckon with the question of how best to reconcile the contradictions that law and legal institutions present in the fight against sexual violence. In my own work I have tried to hold the law to account for the claims it makes about itself and what it is doing to "deal with" the rape problem. In this chapter I have argued that if we are to better understand law's failures in respect to sexual violence we have to be able to imagine where we want to be beyond the confines of legal logic. Feminist resistance to rape cannot stop, therefore, with prohibitive laws but must encompass careful attendance to the development of an ethics of subject-subject relations in which different sexuate subjectivities are enabled to flourish in their own singularity. The third phase of Irigaray's project is useful here because it provides the path toward a revolution in carnal ethics through which we might think the erotic transformation required to end rape. Through a reading of Christine Helliwell's anthropological study of a society in Indonesian Borneo that she labeled "rape free" I suggested we can see evidence of two embodied and singular sexuate identities existing within an erotic order in which heterosexual desire is linked not to possession and objectification, but to reciprocal need and to community well-being and balance. In this way, we can perhaps see the scope of the feminist anti-rape project that faces us with all its complexity and the depth of the work that is required to resist and prevent it.

Acknowledgments

Thank you to two anonymous reviewers for very generous readings of a draft of this chapter and to Ruthanne Crapo Kim for her patience.

Notes

1. See: Gail Schwab, "Women and the Law in Irigarayan Theory," *Metaphilosophy* 27, no. 1–2 (1996): 146–177. See also Penelope Deutscher, *A Politics of Impossible Difference* (Ithaca, NY: Cornell University Press, 2002), 42–55, for an excellent consideration of sexuate rights.

2. See: Maria Drakopoulou, "Of the Founding of Law's Jurisdiction and the Politics of Sexual Difference: The Case of Roman Law," in *Jurisprudence of Jurisdiction*, ed. Shaun McVeigh (Oxford: Routledge Cavendish, 2007), 45–72; Alain Pottage, "A Unique and Different Subject of Law," *Cardozo Law Review* 16 (1994): 1161–1204; Alain Pottage, "Recreating Difference," *Law and Critique* 5, no. 2 (1994): 131–147; Peter Goodrich, *Languages of Law: Logics of Memory to Nomadic Masks* (London: Weidenfeld and Nicolson, 1990); Peter Goodrich, *Oedipus Lex: Psychoanalysis, History, Law* (Berkeley: University of California Press, 1995). Irigaray herself characterizes her work into three distinct, but interrelated, phases as follows:

> The first part of my work amounts to a criticism of the Western tradition as constructed by a single subjectivity, a masculine subjectivity, who has elaborated a logic and a world according to his own necessities. In the second part, I try to indicate mediations which permit a feminine subjectivity to emerge from the unique and so-called neutral Western culture, and to affirm herself as autonomous and

> capable of a cultivation and a culture of her own. The third part of my work is devoted to defining and rendering practicable the ways through which masculine subjectivity and feminine subjectivity could coexist, enter into relation without submitting or subjecting the one to the other, and construct a world shareable by the two with respect for their own worlds. (Irigaray C, 124)

3. Yvette Russell, "Thinking Sexual Difference through the Law of Rape," *Law and Critique* 24, no. 3 (2013): 255–275; Yvette Russell, "Woman's Voice/Law's Logos: The Rape Trial and the Limits of Liberal Reform," *Australian Feminist Law Journal* 42, no. 2 (2016): 273–296.

4. Christine Helliwell, "'It's Only a Penis': Rape, Feminism, and Difference," *Signs: Journal of Women in Culture and Society* 25, no. 3 (2000): 789–816.

5. What constitutes "success" in the context of criminal justice and sexual violence is contested. There is increasing evidence from research with rape victim/survivors that the outcomes that the criminal justice system offers do not necessarily accord with what they feel is owed to them as justice (see: Judith Herman, "Justice from the Victim's Perspective," *Violence against Women* 11, no. 5 (2005): 571; Amanda Konradi, *Taking the Stand: Rape Survivors and the Prosecution of Rapists* (Westport, CT: Praeger, 2007); Clare McGlynn, "Feminism, Rape and the Search for Justice," *Oxford Journal of Legal Studies* 31, no. 4 (2011): 825–842; Clare McGlynn, Nicole Westmarland, and Nikki Godden, "'I Just Wanted Him to Hear Me': Sexual Violence and the Possibilities of Restorative Justice," *Journal of Law and Society* 39, no. 2 (2012): 213–240; Jennifer Temkin, *Rape and the Legal Process* (Oxford: Oxford University Press, 2002). Here, however, I am referring to success in the terms that the criminal justice system measures itself against: numbers of cases prosecuted and convictions achieved. As feminists working on sexual violence and law have long acknowledged, there is often a cost to investing too much hope in the "siren call of law" (see: Joanne Conaghan, "The Siren Call of Legal Reason," in *Law and Gender* [Oxford: Oxford University Press 2013], 199–240; Maria Drakopoulou, "Feminism and the Siren Call of Law," *Law and Critique* 18, no. 3 [2007]: 331–360). These costs include the "capture" of feminist-led reforms by state and political apparatuses, which then use them to justify the increased use of state violence disproportionately against poor and racialized communities. See further: Kristin Bumiller, *In an Abusive State: How Neoliberalism Appropriated the Feminist Movement against Sexual Violence* (Durham, NC: Duke University Press, 2008).

6. Owen Bowcott and Caelainn Barr, "Just 1.5% of All Rape Cases Lead to Charge or Summons, Data Reveals," *Guardian Online*, July 26, 2019, https://www.theguardian.com/law/2019/jul/26/rape-cases-charge-summons-prosecutions-victims-england-wales, accessed February 5, 2020.

7. Mayor of London and Office for Policing and Crime, *The London Rape Review: A Review of Cases from 2016*, July 2019, https://www.london.gov.uk/sites/default/files/london_rape_review_final_report_31.7.19.pdf, accessed February 5, 2020.

8. See, for example, Catharine A. MacKinnon, *Men's Laws, Women's Lives* (Boston: Harvard University Press, 2005). See also Joan Smith, "To Understand Violent Men, Talk to the Women Who Know Them," *Guardian Online*, August 1, 2019, https://www.theguardian.com/commentisfree/2019/aug/01/violent-men-women-criminal-justice, accessed February 5, 2020.

9. See, for example: Liz Kelly, Jo Lovett, and Linda Regan, *A Gap or a Chasm: Attrition in Reported Rape Cases* (London: Home Office Research, 2005); Wendy Larcombe, "Falling Rape Conviction Rates: (Some) Feminist Aims and Measures for Rape Law," *Feminist Legal Studies* 19, no. 1 (2011): 27–45; Catharine A. MacKinnon, *Feminism Unmodified* (Cambridge: Harvard University Press, 1987); Catharine A. MacKinnon, *Towards a Feminist Theory of the State* (Cambridge: Harvard University Press, 1989).

10. See, for example: Clare Gunby, Anna Carline, and Caryl Beynon, "Alcohol-Related Rape Cases: Barristers' Perspectives on the Sexual Offences Act 2003 and Its Impact on Practice," *Journal of Criminal Law* 74, no. 6 (2010): 579–600; Anna Carline and Clare Gunby, " 'How an Ordinary Jury Makes Sense of It Is a Mystery': Barristers' Perspectives on Rape, Consent and the Sexual Offences Act 2003," *Liverpool Law Review*, 32, no. 3 (2011): 237–250; Louise Ellison and Vanessa E. Munro, "Of 'Normal Sex' and 'Real Rape': Exploring the Use of Socio-sexual Scripts in (Mock) Jury Deliberation," *Social and Legal Studies* 18, no. 3 (2009): 291–312; Louise Ellison and Vanessa E. Munro, "A Stranger in the Bushes, or an Elephant in the Room? Critical Reflections upon Received Rape Myth Wisdom in the Context of a Mock Jury Study," *New Criminal Law Review* 13, no. 4 (2010): 781–801.

11. Joanne Conaghan and Yvette Russell, "Rape Myths, Law, and Feminist Research: 'Myths about Myths'?," *Feminist Legal Studies* 22, no. 1 (2014): 25–48; Hannah Frith, "Sexual Scripts, Sexual Refusals and Rape," in *Rape: Challenging Contemporary Thinking*, ed. Miranda Horvath and Jennifer Brown (Devon: Willan, 2009), 99–124; Nicola Gavey, *Just Sex? The Cultural Scaffolding of Rape*, second ed. (New York: Routledge, [2005] 2019).

12. Rosemary Hunter and Sharon Cowan, eds., *Choice and Consent: Feminist Engagements with Law and Subjectivity* (London: Routledge, 2007); Nicola Lacey, *Unspeakable Subjects: Feminist Essays in Legal and Social Theory* (London: Hart, 1998); Ngaire Naffine, "Possession: Erotic Love in the Law of Rape," *Modern Law Review* 57, no. 1 (1994): 10–37; Russell, "Woman's Voice/Law's Logos."

13. Russell, "Woman's Voice/Law's Logos."

14. Russell, "Thinking Sexual Difference," 265. The term *real rape* was brought into common parlance by Susan Estrich, who used it to refer to the

perception of hierarchies among different "types" of rapes. *Real rape* usually refers to a rape that occurs outside, by a stranger, with a weapon, that is particularly violent, leaves evidence of trauma on the body, and where the victim complains quickly and is a "good" victim, that is, not drunk or promiscuous. Susan Estrich, *Real Rape* (Cambridge: Harvard University Press, 1987).

15. Irigaray SW, 42.

16. Russell, "Thinking Sexual Difference," 267–269.

17. Irigaray C, 12.

18. Irigaray KW, 152.

19. Irigaray KW, 206–207.

20. Louise du Toit, *A Philosophical Investigation of Rape: The Making and Unmaking of the Feminine Self* (New York: Routledge, 2009).

21. Du Toit, *A Philosophical Investigation of Rape*, 181.

22. Du Toit, *A Philosophical Investigation of Rape*, 166–181.

23. Du Toit, *A Philosophical Investigation of Rape*, 189–191.

24. Du Toit, *A Philosophical Investigation of Rape*, 154–166.

25. Du Toit, *A Philosophical Investigation of Rape*, 157.

26. See further: Irigaray C, 31–32.

27. Du Toit, *A Philosophical Investigation of Rape*, 189.

28. Drucilla Cornell, *The Imaginary Domain: Abortion, Pornography and Sexual Harassment* (New York: Routledge, 1995).

29. Du Toit, *A Philosophical Investigation of Rape*, 189–190.

30. See Ann J. Cahill, *Rethinking Rape* (Ithaca, NY: Cornell University Press, 2001); Ann J. Cahill, "In Defense of Self-Defense," *Philosophical Papers* 38, no. 3 (2009): 363–380; Gavey, *Just Sex?*; Nicola Gavey, "Fighting Rape," in *Theorizing Sexual Violence*, ed. Renee Heberle and Victoria Grace (New York: Routledge, 2009), 96–124.

31. Cahill, *Rethinking Rape*, 201–202.

32. Yvette Russell, "Theorizing Feminist Anti-Rape Praxis and the Problem of Resistance," *Signs: A Journal of Women in Culture* 46, no. 2 (2021): 465–488.

33. Irigaray JTN, 86–89; TD, 60–62; ILTY, 132.

34. Irigaray WL, 9.

35. Irigaray WL, 10.

36. Irigaray TBT, 19.

37. Irigaray TBT, 14.

38. Irigaray TBT, 20.

39. Irigaray SW, 60.

40. Irigaray WL, 100.

41. Irigaray WL, 100.

42. Irigaray WL, 100–101.

43. Irigaray TBT, 14.

44. Irigaray TBT, 22.

45. Irigaray TBT, 40.
46. Irigaray TBT, 43.
47. Irigaray SW, 4.
48. Irigaray TBT, 23.
49. Irigaray SW, 59.
50. Helliwell, "It's Only a Penis."
51. The community comprised approximately seven hundred individuals.
52. Helliwell, "It's Only a Penis," 790.
53. Helliwell, "It's Only a Penis," 798.
54. Helliwell, "It's Only a Penis," 799.
55. Helliwell, "It's Only a Penis," 799.
56. Helliwell, "It's Only a Penis," 800.
57. Helliwell, "It's Only a Penis," 800.
58. Helliwell, "It's Only a Penis," 802.
59. Helliwell, "It's Only a Penis," 802.
60. Helliwell, "It's Only a Penis," 802.
61. Helliwell, "It's Only a Penis," 803.
62. Helliwell, "It's Only a Penis," 803.
63. Helliwell, "It's Only a Penis," 803.
64. Helliwell, "It's Only a Penis," 808.
65. Helliwell, "It's Only a Penis," 808.
66. Helliwell, "It's Only a Penis," 803.
67. Helliwell, "It's Only a Penis," 804.
68. Helliwell, "It's Only a Penis," 805–806.
69. Helliwell, "It's Only a Penis," 810.
70. Helliwell, "It's Only a Penis," 795.
71. Helliwell, "It's Only a Penis," 803.
72. Irigaray TS, 205–218.
73. Helliwell, "It's Only a Penis," 804.

Bibliography

Bowcott, Owen, and Caelainn Barr. "Just 1.5% of All Rape Cases Lead to Charge or Summons, Data Reveals." *Guardian Online*, July 26, 2019. https://www.theguardian.com/law/2019/jul/26/rape-cases-charge-summons-prosecutions-victims-england-wales. Accessed February 5, 2020.

Bumiller, Kristin. *In an Abusive State: How Neoliberalism Appropriated the Feminist Movement against Sexual Violence*. Durham, NC: Duke University Press, 2008.

Cahill, Ann J. "In Defense of Self-Defense." *Philosophical Papers* 38, no. 3 (2009): 363–380.

Cahill, Ann J. *Rethinking Rape*. Ithaca, NY: Cornell University Press, 2001.

Carline, Anna, and Clare Gunby. "'How an Ordinary Jury Makes Sense of It Is a Mystery': Barristers' Perspectives on Rape, Consent and the Sexual Offences Act 2003." *Liverpool Law Review* 32, no. 3 (2011): 237–250.

Conaghan, Joanne. *Law and Gender*. Oxford: Oxford University Press, 2013.

Conaghan, Joanne, and Yvette Russell. "Rape Myths, Law, and Feminist Research: 'Myths about Myths'?" *Feminist Legal Studies* 22, no. 1 (2014): 25–48.

Cornell, Drucilla. *The Imaginary Domain: Abortion, Pornography and Sexual Harassment*. New York: Routledge, 1995.

Deutscher, Penelope. *A Politics of Impossible Difference*. Ithaca, NY: Cornell University Press, 2002.

Drakopoulou, Maria. "Feminism and the Siren Call of Law." *Law and Critique* 18, no. 3 (2007): 331–360.

Drakopoulou, Maria. "Of the Founding of Law's Jurisdiction and the Politics of Sexual Difference: The Case of Roman Law." In *Jurisprudence of Jurisdiction*, edited by Shaun McVeigh, 45–72. Oxford: Routledge Cavendish, 2007.

Du Toit, Louise. *A Philosophical Investigation of Rape: The Making and Unmaking of the Feminine Self*. New York: Routledge, 2009.

Ellison, Louise, and Vanessa E. Munro. "'Sex' and 'Real Rape': Exploring the Use of Socio-Sexual Scripts in (Mock) Jury Deliberation." *Social and Legal Studies* 18, no. 3 (2009): 291–312.

Ellison, Louise, and Vanessa E. Munro. "A Stranger in the Bushes, or an Elephant in the Room? Critical Reflections upon Received Rape Myth Wisdom in the Context of a Mock Jury Study." *New Criminal Law Review* 13, no. 4 (2010): 781–801.

Estrich, Susan. *Real Rape*. Cambridge: Harvard University Press, 1987.

Frith, Hannah. "Sexual Scripts, Sexual Refusals and Rape." In *Rape: Challenging Contemporary Thinking*, edited by Miranda Horvath and Jennifer Brown, 99–124. Devon: Willan, 2009.

Gavey, Nicola. "Fighting Rape." In *Theorizing Sexual Violence*, edited by Renee Heberle and Victoria Grace, 96–124. New York: Routledge, 2009.

Gavey, Nicola. *Just Sex? The Cultural Scaffolding of Rape*, second ed. New York: Routledge (2005) 2019.

Goodrich, Peter. *Languages of Law: Logics of Memory to Nomadic Masks*. London: Weidenfeld and Nicolson, 1990.

Goodrich, Peter. *Oedipus Lex: Psychoanalysis, History, Law*. Berkeley: University of California Press, 1995.

Gunby, Clare, Anna Carline, and Caryl Beynon. "Alcohol-Related Rape Cases: Barristers' Perspectives on the Sexual Offences Act 2003 and Its Impact on Practice." *Journal of Criminal Law* 74, no. 6 (2010): 579–600.

Helliwell, Christine. "'It's Only a Penis': Rape, Feminism, and Difference." *Signs: Journal of Women in Culture and Society* 25, no. 3 (2000): 789–816.

Herman, Judith. "Justice from the Victim's Perspective." *Violence against Women* 11, no. 5 (2005): 571–602.

Hunter, Rosemary, and Sharon Cowan, eds. *Choice and Consent: Feminist Engagements with Law and Subjectivity*. London: Routledge, 2007.

Kelly, Liz, Jo Lovett, and Linda Regan. *A Gap or a Chasm: Attrition in Reported Rape Cases*. London: Home Office Research, 2005.

Konradi, Amanda. *Taking the Stand: Rape Survivors and the Prosecution of Rapists*. Westport, CT: Praeger, 2007.

Lacey, Nicola. *Unspeakable Subjects: Feminist Essays in Legal and Social Theory*. Oxford: Hart, 1998.

Larcombe, Wendy. "Falling Rape Conviction Rates: (Some) Feminist Aims and Measures for Rape Law." *Feminist Legal Studies* 19, no. 1 (2011): 27–45.

MacKinnon, Catharine A. *Feminism Unmodified*. Cambridge: Harvard University Press, 1987.

MacKinnon, Catharine A. *Men's Laws, Women's Lives*. Cambridge: Harvard University Press, 2005.

MacKinnon, Catharine A. *Towards a Feminist Theory of the State*. Cambridge: Harvard University Press, 1989.

Mayor of London and Office for Policing and Crime. *The London Rape Review: A Review of Cases from 2016*, July 2019. https://www.london.gov.uk/sites/default/files/london_rape_review_final_report_31.7.19.pdf. Accessed February 5, 2020.

McGlynn, Clare. "Feminism, Rape and the Search for Justice." *Oxford Journal of Legal Studies* 31, no. 4 (2011): 825–842.

McGlynn, Clare, Nicole Westmarland, and Nikki Godden. "'I Just Wanted Him to Hear Me': Sexual Violence and the Possibilities of Restorative Justice." *Journal of Law and Society* 39, no. 2 (2012): 213–240.

Naffine, Ngaire. "Possession: Erotic Love in the Law of Rape." *Modern Law Review* 57, no. 1 (1994): 10–37.

Pottage, Alain. "Recreating Difference." *Law and Critique* 5, no. 2 (1994): 131–147.

Pottage, Alain. "A Unique and Different Subject of Law." *Cardozo Law Review* 16 (1994): 1161.

Russell, Yvette. "Theorizing Feminist Anti-Rape Praxis and the Problem of Resistance." *Signs: A Journal of Women in Culture* 46, no. 2 (2021): 465–488.

Russell, Yvette. "Thinking Sexual Difference through the Law of Rape." *Law and Critique* 24, no. 3 (2013): 255–275.

Russell, Yvette. "Woman's Voice/Law's Logos: The Rape Trial and the Limits of Liberal Reform." *Australian Feminist Law Journal* 42, no. 2 (2016): 273–296.

Schwab, Gail. "Women and the Law in Irigarayan Theory." *Metaphilosophy* 27, no. 1–2 (1996): 146–177.

Smith, Joan. "To Understand Violent Men, Talk to the Women Who Know Them." *Guardian Online*, August 1, 2019. https://www.theguardian.com/

commentisfree/2019/aug/01/violent-men-women-criminal-justice. Accessed February 2020.
Temkin, Jennifer. *Rape and the Legal Process*. Oxford: Oxford University Press, 2002.

Part II

Sexuate Ontology

Chapter Three

The Conditions of Emergence

Irigaray, Primordial Wombs, and the Origins of Cellular Life

Annu Dahiya

Introduction: Life's Matrix

It is often assumed that because the emergence of life began with single-celled organisms, and since single-cellular organisms can reproduce asexually, that concepts associated with reproduction in the human or mammalian realm, such as womb, gestation, and birth, have no bearing on life's origins. This essay considers how the concept of "womb" in contemporary origins of life research has the potential to reorient how we theorize the emergence of cellular life from matter. I argue that novel ways to understand the origins of life emerge when concepts that have long been explored within feminist theory—embodiment, gestation, and birth—frame and guide scientific research. I concentrate on a particular strand of origins-of-life research, one that uses the far-from-equilibrium thermodynamics of inorganic wombs to destabilize a binary and hierarchical relation between life and matter framed through the lens of activity and passivity, respectively. Instead, the relation between these two terms in the wombs operating in deep-sea vents is one where these semipermeable compartments are thought to provide the complex thermodynamic and chemical conditions for cellular life to begin, somewhere between 4.4 and 3.8 billion years ago.[1] In doing so, the relation between matter and life can be rethought from a difference in kind to a difference in degree in the context of the latter's initial emergence from matter.

Throughout the essay, I link contemporary origins-of-life research with Luce Irigaray's philosophy of sexual difference, paying close attention to moments in her corpus where she meditates on the biological sciences. I place Irigaray's nuanced intuitions concerning biology alongside contemporary origins-of-life research in order to demonstrate how they surprisingly confirm each other's intuitions on the conditions of emergence for life. I substantiate Irigaray's discernments regarding the "mechanics" of fluids, the potential of disequilibrium, and the importance of the "permeability of membranes" by outlining how her ideas are affirmed in geochemically rooted origins of life research, which theorizes the emergence of cellular life in and through the far-from-equilibrium hydro-logics of semipermeable inorganic wombs. I use hydro-logics here as a rhetorical play on hydrology, the scientific study of the movement and flow of water on the Earth. Such a hydro-logics would not perpetuate a phallocentric logic of sameness that operates through binary oppositions. It would instead be a *contiguous* logic of relation where beings "touch on one another, without merging into one"—a kind of logic that not only coincides with the "mechanics" of fluids but can also "represent the co-existence of irreducibly different beings."[2]

My goal in this essay is not to present a holistic overview of the contemporary origins-of-life research (though the strand I detail later, which centers around what is known as alkaline vent theory, or AVT, continues to gain attention and critical appraisal by the wider scientific community). Instead, I trace how *certain* geochemically informed strands of origins-of-life research coalesce with Irigaray's writings.[3] It should be noted that origins-of-life research is a largely speculative field due to its central object of study. That being said, the ways in which the relation between matter and life are framed in the latter's emergence should be of critical concern to feminist theorists, as this relation can either rely on a sexed hierarchy, where life animates dead matter, *or* alternatively, can reimagine the relation between these two terms that signals the development of an alternative formulation of both matter and life. The question of where we come from is one that we cannot but ask. Indeed, for Irigaray, acknowledging our origins—where we come from, what makes us possible, what and where we may have once gestated within—is an utmost ethical concern because it signals a debt to the maternal that we can never repay.

The etymological roots of "matrix" originate in the maternal. Irigarayan scholar Irina Aristarkhova argues "matrix" and "maternal" are so deeply intertwined that "matrix is 'ground zero'; it is *the* origin; it is that original *place*/space of generation and becoming."[4] Aristarkhova reminds us that matrix's "connection to origin and generation was etymologically embodied in one of its oldest usages—'a pregnant animal.'"[5] In its earliest Latin uses, "matrix" refers to both "pregnant animal" and "breeding female" as well as to *mater*, the root of "matter" and "mother." "Matrix" subsequently begins to coincide with "womb" by the first millennium CE.[6] A matrix can be defined as "a place or medium in which something is originated, produced, or developed; the environment in which a particular activity or process begins; a point of origin and growth."[7] Furthermore, matrix is "a supporting or enclosing structure."[8] Thus, this concept is marked with "female," "mother," "womb," "structure," "medium," as well as a point of origin.

This essay foregrounds the relation between "maternal" and "womb" while simultaneously disentangling this gestational, generative space from cisfemale human embodiment. While maternal wombs are most often associated with cisfemale bodies, using the hydro-logics of inorganic wombs, I reframe the "maternal" in a thoroughly prehuman, nonanthropomorphic evolutionary sense. Collapsing "womb" and "maternal" with cisfemale bodies risks an anthropomorphization of embodiment more generally, as human cisfemale bodies invented the concept of neither birth nor womb. Rather than an anthropomorphism of the natural world, theorizing the gestation of all of cellular life in an inorganic womb shifts us away from the idea that life evolutionarily began by birthing itself, thereby challenging the idea of autonomy—a kind of self-birthing that requires no "other"—as what can explain life's origins.

Defining "exactly" what life "is" is a notoriously difficult task that continues to be debated in origins research and the philosophy of science. In this essay, I do not locate the concept of "life" exclusively within *cellular* life, and I also do not provide a strictly delineated definition of what life "is." While I focus here on the conditions that generated the possibility of *cellular* life, in an ontological register, life always exceeds its cellular forms. Constricting life to only mean cellular life is often a conceptual (though not universal) maneuver in origins-of-life research, but I argue such a move is theoretically problematic—it self-creates problems that *then* seem and indeed become insurmountable. For one thing, whenever life is strictly defined and located, there are always bound to be exceptions.[9] Furthermore, according to Irigaray, defining what life "is" is a phallocentric framing of the concept of life. In *This Sex Which Is Not One*, Irigaray writes that "the question 'what is . . . ?' is the question—the metaphysical question—to which the feminine does not allow itself to submit."[10] In other words, defining what life "is" is a phallocentric approach because it freezes and solidifies a concept that is fundamentally about becoming, flux, and creative evolution. Life is too creative, too open to transformation, for any strict definition to solidly define it.

That being said, the particular *feature* of cellular life that concerns me here is how it is a far-from-equilibrium thermodynamic process. My wager is that this thermodynamic complexity could have only initially been birthed by an inorganic matrix that provided the same thermodynamic gestational conditions. As such, I put Irigaray in conversation with contemporary origins research to provocatively suggest that the complex thermodynamic processes within cellular life were only able to come into being by gestating in far-from-equilibrium inorganic wombs. In doing so, I foreground the question of embodiment as the conditions of emergence for life: perhaps life is such a complex process that it, even at the level of a single cell, involves a kind of thermodynamic ingenuity that could not *initially* be *self*-made or sustained.

In what follows, I understand cellular life as a process that requires "compartments separated from their surroundings that spontaneously multiply with energy gleaned through self-contained, thermodynamically favourable redox reactions."[11] Redox reactions are a specific kind of chemical reaction of critical importance within biological systems, in which there is a flow or "transfer of electrons from an external donor to an available acceptor."[12] Batteries involve redox chemistry as do the most fundamental thermodynamic features of cellular life. I think about the specific, unceasing chemistry cells perform to harness energy in order to stay alive in order to speculate how the origins of these complex biochemical processes may have been first engendered by the Earth's geochemistry. Though this can lend itself to thinking about the origins of cellular metabolism quite seamlessly, due to limitations of space, I will use Irigaray and origins research to outline how primordial inorganic wombs could have provided *the conditions of emergence* for cellular metabolism, and subsequently genetics, rather than directly focusing on these questions themselves.[13]

I begin the essay by juxtaposing two hypothetical environmental settings that have had key roles in theorizing the origins of life: prebiotic soup and deep-sea vents. I contend that origins research around deep-sea vents works in tandem with Irigaray's marking of fluidity and far-from-equilibrium thermodynamics as concepts that cannot be adequately understood or represented using phallocentrism's "ruling symbolics."[14] Following this, I concentrate on origins research that theorizes how primordial wombs could have fulfilled two key conditions for cellular life to emerge: first, the compartmentation they provide could solve what is known as the concentration problem in origins research; and, second, the far-from-equilibrium geochemical processes that generated these semipermeable wombs could also provide the geochemical gradients for the beginnings of redox chemistry (which is a fundamental energy harnessing process that occurs across cellular membranes) to come into being, thereby providing the conditions for the birth of biochemistry.

Geochemistry as the Conditions of Life

A single cellular life form (such as a bacterium) is an evolutionary invention in the most profound sense: it maintains a difference between self and other, a tremendous feat that requires complex electrochemical differences in the form of gradients to be actively maintained at its membrane. A concentration gradient can be defined as a difference in concentration of something (such as a hydrogen ion) on either side of a boundary (like a membrane); this difference is replete with potential energy that can be used to drive cellular work, and thus could not be further from a static, "lifeless" wall. In fact, a cell that ceases to maintain a chemical and electrical heterogeneity between itself and its environment is no longer a cell but rather a dead remnant of something that was once living. The far-from-equilibrium complexity sustained across single-cellular membranes raises the question in origins-of-life research of how this thermodynamic intricacy came about. Is it possible for one to self-make such a heterogeneous boundary between self/other, particularly, if there cannot be a "self" without this boundary? If the emergence of cellular life requires the invention of such a far-from-equilibrium boundary to drive chemical processes, before there is genetics to code for such membranes, can such an activity be self-created? Or can it only be generated if it first gestates in an *other*, perhaps a complex, aquatic milieu or environment, which is also far from equilibrium?

Since the 1920s, "primordial soup" or "prebiotic broth" theory has been the most prominent scenario for the origins of life.[15] According to this theory, "UV radiation provided the energy to convert methane, ammonia and water into the first organic compounds in the oceans of the early Earth. In the absence of life forms to consume them, these molecules accumulated to the concentration of a 'hot dilute soup,'"[16] making the ancient ocean a nutritive broth for the first living forms to devour. Prebiotic broth speculations assume a heterotrophic origin of life. As the prefix *hetero* implies, a heterotroph needs to obtain food and energy (in the form of organic compounds) from an exterior source. In heterotrophic scenarios of the origin of life, then, the first living entities were provided "sustenance" (reduced carbon compounds) in the ancient oceanic broth. It was only *after* they fully consumed their original nutritional sources of carbon that these hypothetical living entities developed *auto*trophic ways to generate organic carbon compounds from inorganic sources such as carbon dioxide.

In order to generate and further transform the prebiotic components of life, heterotrophic scenarios often center around chemical reactions that no form of extant cellular life (as far as we know) uses. For this reason, many biologists are skeptical of heterotrophic theories due to the large gap they generate between the chemistry that life required at its onset and what it continues to use today.[17] Furthermore, heterotrophic origin scenarios are often incompatible with what is known about the geology and geochemistry of the infant Earth given how they often seem to require conditions that were unlikely to have existed. They also have a much less specific (perhaps *un*specific) idea of the particular environment in which life might have begun (often somewhere in the ancient sea or tidal zones). One of the most pressing problems "soup" theories have difficulty answering concerns how the "broth" is at thermodynamic equilibrium. Once the particular chemical precursors of interest have initially reacted from their initial external input or "spark" of energy, they cease to further react and complexify. The reason the chemical precursors are "reluctant to react further in a soup is that they are at thermodynamic equilibrium."[18] A system operating *at thermodynamic equilibrium* fails to provide the energetic conditions that the emergence of cellular life requires, for such a system is devoid of the disequilibria needed to sustain the ceaseless chemistry we understand as life. Instead of cellular emergence requiring a singular "spark" of energy, the far-from-equilibrium thermodynamics it requires signals that "what life needed was not some harsh and problematic source of energy like UV radiation (or lightning), but a continuous and replenishing source of chemical energy."[19]

In contrast to a "prebiotic soup" and heterotrophic origin of life, autotrophic theories suggest life was able to generate its own sources of organic carbon and energy since its inception. Autotrophic scenarios tend to posit very specific material and environmental conditions for life's emergence. They are most often set in deep-sea hydrothermal vents. Since their discovery in 1977, deep-sea hydrothermal vents have become important sites for theorizing the origins of life because of how they fundamentally reframed scientists' understanding of where and how life could exist. Researchers found aquatic life ranging from small bacteria, feeding on natural sources of sulfur, to plant and animal life. Because plate tectonics theory predicted the existence of hydrothermal vents, scientists were most surprised about the entire living ecosystems existing around the vents rather than the actual vents themselves.

Before witnessing hydrothermal vents sustaining life and entire ecosystems through geochemical energy, scientists assumed that all life requires photosynthetic energy from the Sun to exist. Microbes are the primary producers of the food web of vent ecosystems. They perform chemosynthesis for their metabolic needs, harnessing and converting geochemical energy into organic compounds. Photosynthesis and chemosynthesis are similar in that they are both processes where inorganic sources of carbon (like CO_2) are transformed into organic carbon (biomolecules that are energetic sources, in other words, food). Photosynthesis uses the Sun's energy to drive this reaction, while chemosynthesis uses chemical energy generated from the Earth's own geothermal and geochemical reserves. While the process of chemosynthesis was known since the late nineteenth century, it "was considered to play no significant, quantitative role in the carbon cycle of the photosynthetically dominated Earth's surface. . . . The biogeochemical significance of chemosynthesis emerged only upon discovery of deep-sea hydrothermal vent systems"[20] where an alternate production of organic carbon from inorganic sources became apparent. The recognition of how microbial life could harness the intense amounts of geochemical energy available at these sites thus spurred intense speculation on how similar vents themselves could have been "chemically 'reactive' hatcheries for the origins of life."[21]

The environmental setting, available energy, and particular chemical materials for life's emergence directly affects our conception of LUCA, the last universal common ancestor of life before its first major evolutionary divergence into the lineages of archaea and bacteria. LUCA is the theoretical organism and space between "nonliving" and "life." We have no direct access to LUCA—there are no "fossils" of it for us to study. Instead, the nature and characteristics of LUCA are reconstructed based on logical inferences, especially using phylogenetic analysis, a technique greatly enhanced by contemporary digital genomic databases. Though many aspects of LUCA continue to be debated, there is wide consensus that in addition to a working metabolism, LUCA possessed some sort of genetic code (though the details of *which* genes are still actively being debated) as well as a ribosome (a molecular machine that synthesizes proteins across cellular life).[22]

A key insight regarding LUCA, one that I will later connect to primordial wombs, can be ascertained by thinking about archaea and bacteria as the two most ancient prokaryotic lineages of life. (The third domain of life—eukaryotes—include plants and animals such as humans. Eukaryotes are evolutionary descendants of an ancient symbiotic merger between archaea and bacteria that occurred *only* 2.7 billion years ago and thus are irrelevant to our theorizing LUCA here.[23]) Archaea and bacteria have universal bioenergetics yet different membrane compositions. Despite their membrane bioenergetics being universal, their respective phospholipid membranes "are *fundamentally different*."[24] In other words, though the bioenergetic reactions that occur across their membranes are the same and the orientation of their membranes are congruent (they have a hydrophilic exterior and hydrophobic interior), the actual chemical architecture of bacterial and archaeal membranes themselves vastly differ.[25] This similarity in their bioenergetics combined with their vastly differing membrane composition suggests that LUCA did not have a "true" cellular membrane itself, for if it did possess a "true" cellular membrane, such an important aspect of life would have likely been conserved in its two major evolutionary offspring.

A possible connection between LUCA's membrane chemistry and the early Earth's geochemistry emerges in recent phylogenetic research. An in-depth 2016 study concludes that LUCA was an autotroph that was "only half-alive" in the sense that it was "dependent upon geochemistry."[26] Reconstructing LUCA's "microbial ecology,"[27] in other words "how and where LUCA lived,"[28] researchers argue that LUCA inhabited a thermophilic hydrothermal setting. In addition, LUCA possessed an ATP-synthase, an enzyme (or biological catalyst) that can "harness ion gradients for energy metabolism."[29] As a microscopic rotary machine, ATP-synthase generates adenosine triphosphate, or ATP, the "energy currency" of cellular life. It does this by harnessing the potential energy of the proton (or hydrogen ion) gradient at its boundary by coupling the (thermodynamically favored) entrance of a proton into LUCA with the chemical reaction that generates ATP from ADP (adenosine diphosphate) and a phosphate group. Despite having an ATP-synthase, however, LUCA does *not* seem to have proteins that *generate* this proton ion gradient *itself*. Researchers infer that this "paradox" could be reconciled if LUCA lived in an environment that provided proton gradient in situ.[30] In short, and in feminist theoretical terms, one could say that LUCA's "ability to use but not generate ion gradients" points to alkaline hydrothermal vents as its primordial gestational site.[31]

In contrast to black smoker vent systems,[32] alkaline hydrothermal vents are "off axis vents" in that they do not sit right on top of zones of tectonic activity but rather a few kilometers away. These vents are formed through a process called *serpentinization* in which water seeps deep into the ocean floor below sea level into the Earth. In doing so, water chemically transforms the particular kinds of rock it touches, turning subsurface ultra-mafic rocks (which have low silica content) such as olivine into a new kind of rock called serpentinite. In addition to newly formed serpentinite, serpentinization generates hydrogen gas (H_2) that is dissolved in an alkaline fluid. This reaction is exergonic (it releases heat), which results in the products of serpentinization traveling back up to the surface of the Earth (at the bottom of the ocean). When these fluids flow back up to the ocean floor, a gradient is formed between the alkaline-rich H_2-bearing, relatively warm (90 to 100° C) exhaled water interfacing with the cooler, more acidic ocean water. This fluid gradient is continuously maintained in an alkaline vent system for the duration of its existence (which can extend up to 150,000 years). The first alkaline vent system occurred in 2000.[33] It was found deep in the Atlantic Ocean "about 2,300 miles east of Florida on the Mid-Atlantic Ridge, one of the world's largest undersea mountain ranges"[34] and had massive implications for geochemically oriented origins-of-life research.

One of the most remarkable things about alkaline vents is how the gradient between the "exhaled" alkaline, warm water and the cooler, more acidic exterior ocean *mirrors* the chemical gradient that cellular life maintains at its boundaries against its exterior environment. While a fully evolved cell can maintain this chemically charged polarity itself through the ion pumps within its cellular membranes, the question of how this chemical gradient first arose in a world *before* the advent of genetics to code for pumps was an anomaly.

Given how the chemical gradient naturally formed in alkaline vent systems is similar to the chemical differentiation cellular life actively maintains within itself, how does a nonliving geochemical gradient evolve into a biochemical gradient of a cell? The answer lies in how the hydrological flow of water generates a chemical gradient as well as a physical compartmentation that is "semipermeable." Alkaline hydrothermal vents create the possibility for a living topology not only because of the fluid gradient they create but also because of how they produce microscopic compartments or "inorganic pores." These microscopic "holes" are distinct from each other but still permeable to water and the movement of dissolved ions, especially tiny hydrogen ions (H^+).

While the modern-day alkaline vents found in 2000 consist of towering carbonate chimneys (which also have semipermeable compartmentation or womblike properties), analogous vent systems on the early Earth would be vastly different in their chemical makeup. Four billion years ago, the ancient oceans were replete with dissolved iron (due to the lack of oxygen in the early atmosphere), making the alkaline vent systems generate iron sulfide (FeS) chimneys.[35] These microscopic iron sulfide holes provided the far-from-equilibrium semipermeable compartmentation necessary for cellular life to begin. Because of the constant movement of water and gradient between alkaline fluids meeting the ocean water, the inside of these pores are hot H_2-rich alkaline fluids while the outside is cooler and acidic. These pores are significant because they actually exhibit the polarity of modern cells, which are also more alkaline in their interior. In other words, they *mime* the topology of living cells because of the gradient difference between inside and outside. An autonomous living cell, *once it is formed*, maintains this gradient on its own by microscopic pumps in its cell membrane (by actively pumping protons [H^+] out to keep itself alkaline on the inside).

Remembering back to how archaea and bacteria have different membrane compositions but universal membrane bioenergetics, this strange difference makes sense if one takes into account that the last common universal ancestor out of which they both arose *already had a redox and chemical gradient* that was established through the movement and friction between two different fluid flows. In simpler terms, the first form of life, LUCA, had derived its proto-semipermeability by depending "on natural proton gradients"[36] for the energy needed to drive carbon metabolism (the chemical changing of inorganic carbon such as CO_2 into organic carbon such as CH_4) in its ancient protein pumps. The shift from a direct dependence on proton gradients to autonomous cellular existence (autonomous in the sense of regenerating this gradient between inside and out *oneself*) in the distinct lineages of archaea and bacteria resulted in different membrane phospholipids and ion pumps *that enabled them to ceaselessly* (re)create a chemical and topological gradient between self and other.

Semipermeable Compartmentation, or, the Hydro-logics of Iron Sulfide Wombs

> *The Biological Sciences* have been slow to take on certain problems. The constitution of the placenta tissue, the permeability of membranes, for example. Are these not questions directly correlated to the female and maternal sexual imaginary?
>
> —Luce Irigaray, *An Ethics of Sexual Difference*

In *This Sex Which Is Not One* and *An Ethics of Sexual Difference*, Irigaray outlines two key elements that intuit the thermodynamic milieu life needs to initially emerge. The first concerns the "mechanics" of fluids, which embody a logic that cannot be adequately grasped within a phallocentric representation of Nature.[37] She writes,

> Now if we examine the properties of fluids, we note that this "real" may well include, and in large measure, *a physical reality* that continues to resist adequate symbolization and/or that signifies the powerlessness of logic to incorporate in its writing all the characteristic features of nature. And it has often been found necessary to minimize certain of these features of nature, to envisage them, and it, only in light of

> an ideal status, so as to keep it/them from jamming the works of the theoretical machine.[38]

Before turning to how this may pertain to the emergence of life, let me add an additional thought from Irigaray. In *An Ethics*, she experiments with whether "female sexuality" can be represented via a scientific model:

> If a scientific model is needed, female sexuality would perhaps fit better with what Prigogine calls "dissipatory" structures, which function through exchanges with the exterior world, which proceed in steps from one energy level to another, and which are not organized to search for equilibrium but rather to cross thresholds, a procedure that corresponds to going beyond disorder or entropy without discharge.[39]

Like Irigaray, my interest in this passage is not to define and solidify female sexuality. Rather, I am interested in how the logic of "female sexuality" *cannot* be adequately thought through a logic of solids. Such a logic may be able to represent a static, already-made object but is incapable of incorporating the forces that generate novelty in the world. The latter would require an alternative logic, one that moves within and is made possible by disequilibrium; one that generates entropy in order to create new processes, and through this how new ways of being and existing become contingent on disequilibrium itself. Female sexuality could align with such a logic because it would never remain the same "one" thing but would always be open to becoming more, something unknown that could not be predicted in advance—in effect, a creative process that would embrace entropy and the arrow of time. Coined by Nobel Laureate Ilya Prigogine (in a paper written with Grégoire Nicolis) in 1967,[40] a dissipative structure is a nonequilibrium structure that "must necessarily 'feed' on fluxes of matter and/or energy (thus, on external constraints) that permanently maintain the system far from equilibrium. They can only exist in open systems."[41] A dissipatory or dissipative structure is a particular spatiotemporal organizational state that arises within a dissipative process that is an open system exchanging energy and matter with its environment. "Dissipative structures are generated and maintained through irreversible processes that continuously generate entropy."[42]

A dissipatory structure instead would be a better model for female sexuality because of its desire to cross thresholds and its contingency upon larger dissipatory processes, to not be afraid or stumped by disorder. This scientific model of "female sexuality"—in how it moves beyond "entropy without discharge"—affirms the second law of thermodynamics. If, according to the second law of thermodynamics, the entropy of the universe must always be increasing, in a spatially bounded yet permeable system, "it is only the irreversible processes taking place *within* the system [rather than the flow of matter/energy the system exchanges with its environment] that effect the entropy of the universe."[43] Such a "structure" can only be maintained by a continuous flux of energy. It therefore is contingent on disequilibrium.

The necessity to theorize disequilibrium is also at the center of geochemically rooted origins research. On this, two researchers write:

> *What precisely is a "disequilibrium"?* When a quantity of matter and/or energy ("M/E") can exist within a spatially bounded system in two alternative states (necessarily equal in all relevant conserved quantities) those states will form a disequilibrium (a "gradient") if and only if they differ in their entropy content . . . a disequilibrium is therefore fundamentally defined by the condition that the two alternative states differ in entropy content, i.e., in microstate multiplicity. . . . Discussions of bioenergetics almost always have "energy" center stage and running the show—albeit energy suitably discounted (in "its ability to perform work") by the 2nd law tax. But this, in our view, is misleading. Energy doesn't drive processes—or become "consumed" or "used" in their occurrence. Disequilibria (via their dissipation) alone are to blame for why—and how—things happen (and not just in the processes of life).[44]

Geochemically rooted origins-of-life research argues that life's beginning required something *other than* stable equilibrium. In geochemical terms, "equilibrium is death."[45] If the chemical processes that mark extant life require nonequilibrium, then perhaps those that brought it into being do as well: "The question remains of how a solution at equilibrium can start doing chemistry. Put another way, once autoclaved, a bowl of chicken soup left at any temperature will never bring forth life."[46] A prebiotic soup stockpiled with ingredients, even if it is heated, cannot generate life. Geochemistry *becomes* biochemistry when chemical disequilibrium operates in tandem with the hydro-logics of a womb.

According to Irigaray, the unconscious of science affects "the research goals that science sets, or fails to set for itself."[47] The seeming neutrality of the subject of science becomes evident if one pays attention to how certain questions and topics are continually elided and ignored within an avenue of research. The constitution of the placenta tissue, though it is also a profound mediating relation, refers to mammalian animal gestationality. Because it is a much later evolutionary event after the initial emergence of single-cellular life, it is not my focus here. Instead, I will focus on origins research that surprisingly agrees with and affirms Irigaray's contention that the "problem" of the *permeability of membranes* has not significantly been addressed in biology. I will track how the permeability of membranes directly concerns the maternal, extending all the way back to the birth of cellularity. Though it is unlikely that they read her work, two scientists, William Martin, a microbiologist, and Michael J. Russell, a geochemist, echo Irigaray's diagnosis of how the question of the membrane is constantly eschewed in an article that theorizes the origin of cells.

According to Martin and Russell, origins-of-life research overfocuses on concocting the "right mixture of self-replicating molecules."[48] A strict focus on the "right kind of stuff" makes the question of how that "stuff" was first enveloped in a membrane (the hallmark of all cellular life) recede out of focus. If genes code for membranes, Martin and Russell argue that the question of how the first replicating systems *encased themselves* (without needing something that encased them) is a concern that is consistently not addressed:

> Getting the universal ancestor into the membranous or other cloak that it has to have at some time under all models for the origin of life and the origin of cells poses seemingly insurmountable problems. In models for the origin of cells, the *membranes that surround living systems*—under whatever chemical premise and if they are addressed at all—*just seem to come from thin air*, and the ultimate contents of cells so derived have to arise as a free-living cytosol that needs to get inside, even in well-argued cases.[49]

The second-class status of the "membrane problem" in this epistemological framework is directly at odds with the actual evolution of life. The authors seek to rectify a glaring issue in origins research that has been created through an overwhelming focus on the origins of genetics and code, which often results in ignoring how membranes and their permeability first arose and thus overlooks a fundamental feature of life: the principle of semipermeable compartmentation. Martin and Russell state that "the principle of semipermeable compartmentation from the aqueous environment is even more strictly conserved than the universal genetic code, because there are rare deviations from the universal code."[50]

One reason semipermeable compartmentation, or more concisely, a *womb*, is a requirement of life is that it directly addresses what is known as the "concentration problem" in origins research: how did the preorganic precursors of life remain in close enough proximity to further react and complexify in the ancient Hadean ocean?[51] Without any boundary, these precursors would have diffused far away from one another in the ancient expansive ocean, most likely never to chemically react again. In the middle of the last century, the idea of "surface catalysis," in which certain inorganic compounds such as clay, rocks, and metals provide a catalytic *surface* for prebiotic reactions to occur upon, attempted to address the concentration problem.[52] Simply providing an energetic surface for prebiotic reactions to occur, however, is not enough: "a fundamental drawback to the surface catalysis model is that once two molecules have reacted on a surface, they diffuse away into the Hadean ocean, never to react again."[53] Over and above simply a surface, spatiotemporal structures that have specific forms of interiority and semipermeability are crucial. For researchers such as Martin and Russell, "containment"—a "dead" characteristic often associated with the "feminine"—was a fundamental requirement for the emergence of cellular life.

The semipermeable compartmentation that primordial wombs could provide in emergence of cellular life is not solely an enclosed space where the precursors of life can continually react and complexify. The material enclosures Martin and Russell spotlight also provide a far-from-equilibrium geological milieu that strangely parallels extant cellular life in terms of the temperature, pH, and ion gradients they generate. Semipermeable containment and bioenergetic chemistry are fundamentally interlinked: *the beginning of membrane chemistry requires a boundary*. Any possibility of a resolution of this problem can only appear if one first thinks through the realities of unicellular membranes themselves.

If the beginnings of cellular life coincide with the invention of biochemistry, the differences between inorganic chemistry and biochemistry are such that the latter can emerge if it is "coupled to an external disequilibrium"[54] that can drive the reactions of life. The specific kind of geochemical disequilibria found at alkaline hydrothermal systems generates an "'abiotic' womb."[55] In a speculative theoretical piece on submarine alkaline vents, Russell and Elbert Branscomb, a theoretical physicist, theorize that

> perhaps it was literally the deep bosom of the ocean whose coddling Hadean embrace and uniquely fecund far-from-equilibrium geophysical distempers "transcended" chemistry in exactly the required biological ways and thereby leapt the key initial barrier to giving birth to life (and thoughtfully did so in a womb safely tucked away from, amongst other things, the especially ruinous horrors of the Hadean's UV radiation [that bombarded the surface of the early Earth]).[56]

These "dissipative processes that indirectly produce chemically specific, pro-biological, 'trans-membrane' gradients of both redox and ion-concentration types" makes them "the [thermodynamic] drivers of life's emergence."[57] In this origins scenario, iron sulfide wombs generated from the hydrothermal exhalation of metallic and sulfide rich waters are *semi-permeable compartments that preexist membranes, and in doing so, create the possibility of their existence by providing (porous) boundaries and disequilibria that can drive the reactions of life necessary for the birth of biochemistry into being.*[58] If life, in its initial cellular emergence, is not different in kind from far-from-equilibrium matter, the gestational space of alkaline vents closes the gap for this embryological unfolding.

Conclusion: What Life Shares with Matter

For Luce Irigaray, "an ethics of sexuate and sexual difference is the basis of an ecological ethics."[59] In her essay "Starting from Ourselves as Living Beings," Irigaray outlines how dominant Western, Eurocentrically derived forms of language regarding life bear "witness to an intention of mastering" rather than "a desire to coexist with respect for the differences between" living beings.[60] This impulse for mastery rather than coexistence that respects the sexuate alterity of the other manifests in the words we have to comprehend life:

> We really have not a lot of words to express a coexistence in life itself. . . . We lack words to express this universal sharing between us, a sharing that unites us on this side and beyond every definite culture, civilization, and even species, and the expression of which would be crucial to achieving an ecological ethics. All the living beings are more interrelated, whatever their difference(s), than our discourses let us assume, a deficiency which does not contribute toward the respect for our common belonging and for the environment that is necessary to it.[61]

This essay extends Irigaray's grounding of an ecological ethics generated from a philosophy of sexuate difference by theorizing the emergence of life from matter between 4.4 and 3.8 billion years ago.[62] If "our" (biological) discourse hides what all life shares, then in the spirit of Irigaray, I hope to remind us what all life shares at its origins: the debt it owes to a maternal milieu that preexisted and conditioned the possibility of its emergence. In the geochemically rooted origins research I have highlighted here, the emergence of cellular life becomes a highly probable statistical inevitability rather than an improbable occurrence. This rhetorical transformation signals an epistemological and ontological reframing of the relation between matter and life. At the origins of cellular life, the relation between matter and life shifts from a difference in kind to one of degree. The hydro-logics of primordial inorganic wombs engender these rhetorical, epistemological, and ontological shifts, thus offering us a way to fundamentally reorient how we understand the nature of life and its capacity to be engendered by and to further generate difference.

Origins research that thinks in tandem with the logic of a womb and a nonanthropomorphic concept of the "maternal" brings us closer to understanding one of the most pressing and enduring questions we, as human beings, have been asking about our origins. For Irigaray, to "live maternity" necessitates being "capable of engendering the living endowed with autonomous existence with respect to them."[63] The theoretical absence of research about the first cell membranes confirms Irigaray's assertion that the biological sciences have been negligent on the question of their permeability. The particular kind of matter that characterizes primordial wombs cannot be easily classified as purely "living" or "nonliving" but rather operates in an interval between the two. Irigaray's inkling that the permeability of membranes needs to be a serious question within biological research carries more weight than perhaps she herself was aware. Theories of life's origin that resonate with an Irigarayan philosophy of life understand embodiment as an irrefutable feature for the emergence of cellular life. Cellular life *in utero* gestated in an*other* body—a far-from-equilibrium primordial place "from which and from *where* everything comes."[64] Though it can be and often has been forgotten and ignored in origins research, the constitution of interiority—of a defined yet permeable boundary between self and other, inside and outside—was not an afterthought in the origins of cellular life but rather part and parcel of its emergence from matter. The geochemical disequilibria of these gestational semipermeable spaces provided the conditions for the possibility of life to begin, to germinate until it could maintain the complex thermodynamic conditions itself. The emergence of life is not possible with a "spark of life" running through a passive, fluid oceanic milieu. This model, in which an outside "active" other, a force bringing life (through light), is in fact too thermodynamically weak to explain the complex bioenergetics that are needed to drive the dissipatory structures that can *then* engender the disequilibria that we term "life."

Notes

1. William Martin and Michael J. Russell, "On the Origins of Cells: A Hypothesis for the Evolutionary Transitions from Abiotic Geochemistry to Chemoautotrophic Prokaryotes, and from Prokaryotes to Nucleated Cells," *Philosophical Transactions of the Royal Society of London B* 358, no. 1429 (January 2003): 59–60.

2. Rachel Jones, *Irigaray: Towards a Sexuate Philosophy* (Malden, MA: Polity Press, 2011), 85.

3. For a broad overview of origins-of-life research in the twentieth century, see Iris Fry, *The Emergence of Life on Earth: A Historical and Scientific Overview* (Piscataway, NJ: Rutgers University Press, 2000).

4. Irina Aristarkhova, *Hospitality of the Matrix: Philosophy, Biomedicine, and Culture* (New York: Columbia University Press, 2012), 2, emphasis in original.

5. Aristarkhova, *Hospitality of the Matrix*, 2, emphasis in original.

6. Aristarkhova, *Hospitality of the Matrix*, 12.

7. "Matrix, n.," *OED Online*, June 2017, Oxford University Press, http://www.oed.com.proxy.lib.duke.edu/view/Entry/115057?rskey=VqmYYl&result=1, accessed October 26, 2017.

8. "Matrix, n."

9. On how problems arise when one tries to define and solidify life, see Bich Leonardo and Sara Green, "Is Defining Life Pointless? Operational Definitions at the Frontiers of Biology," *Synthese* 195 (2018): 3919–3946.

10. Irigaray TS, 122.

11. Martin and Russell, "On the Origins of Cells," 63.

12. Martin and Russell, "On the Origins of Cells," 63.

13. My insistence on an ordering that begins with the conditions of emergence from some kind of proto-metabolism that *then* generates genetic systems is based on geochemical- and thermodynamic-oriented origins research that argues "no nucleic acid evolution is possible without a supporting geochemistry, later biogeochemistry and finally biochemistry to provide a steady flow of adequate concentrations of polymerizeable precursors (for example nucleotides) and thus to underpin any sort of replication." Martin and Russell, "On the Origins of Cells," 64.

14. Irigaray TS, 106–107.

15. The "primordial soup" theory was independently proposed by Soviet scientist A. I. Oparin and British geneticist J. B. S. Haldane in two separate (but theoretically similar) papers in the 1920s. See Alexander Ivanovich Oparin, *The Origin of Life* (in Russian) (Moscow: Moscow Worker, 1924) as well as John Burdon Sanderson Haldane, "Origin of Life," *Rationalist Annual* 148 (1929): 3–10. The first book-length English translation of Oparin's work is *The Origin of Life on Earth* (1938).

16. Nick Lane, John F. Allen, and William Martin. "How Did LUCA Make a Living? Chemiosmosis in the Origin of Life," *BioEssays* 32 (2010): 271.

17. Peter Schönheit, Wolfgang Buckel, and William F. Martin, "On the Origin of Heterotrophy," *Trends in Microbiology* 24, no. 1 (January 2016): 12, http://dx.doi.org/10.1016/j.tim.2015.10.003.

18. Lane, Allen, and Martin, "How Did LUCA," 272.

19. Lane, Allen, and Martin, "How Did LUCA," 272.

20. Cindy Van Dover, *The Ecology of Deep-Sea Hydrothermal Vents* (Princeton, NJ: Princeton University Press, 2000), 117.

21. Martin and Russell, "On the Origins of Cells," 63. On early speculations linking hydrothermal vents to the origins of life, see J. B. Corliss, J. A. Baross, and S. E. Hoffmann, "An Hypothesis concerning the Relationship between Submarine Hot Springs and the Origin of Life on Earth," *Oceanologica Acta* 4 (1981): 59–69. Stanley L. Miller and Jeffrey L. Bada, "Submarine Hot Springs and the Origin of Life," *Nature* 334, no. 18 (1988): 609–611, are among the earliest and most well-known critics of this hypothesis.

22. Madeline C. Weiss et al., "The Physiology and Habitat of the Last Universal Common Ancestor," *Nature Microbiology* 1 (2016): 16116.

23. Geoffrey M. Cooper, "The Origin and Evolution of Cells," in *The Cell: A Molecular Approach*, second ed. (Sunderland, MA: Sinauer Associates, 2000), https://www.ncbi.nlm.nih.gov/books/NBK9841/.

24. Victor Sojo, Andrew Pomiankowski, and Nick Lane, "A Bioenergetic Basis for Membrane Divergence in Archaea and Bacteria," *PLOS Biology* 12, no. 8 (2014): e1001926, doi:10.1371/ journal.pbio.1001926, emphasis added.

25. Archaeal and bacterial membranes share a fundamental similarity in how they are amphiphilic: they both have exterior "heads" that are hydrophilic and are attracted to water and the interior "tails" are hydrophobic and have an aversion to water. The amphiphilic structure of both membrane compositions allow for the spontaneous self-organization of a membrane once its chemical components are formed. The chemical composition of bacteria and archaea lipid "tails" differ: archaeal lipids are composed of repeating isoprene units while bacteria lipids use fatty acids. The "heads" have a chemical similarity but are enantiomers (mirror images) of one another and therefore not superimposable. In addition, the bonds that connect the lipid tails to the "head" differ: archaea membrane lipids have chemical bonds called *ether* bonds while bacteria lipids have *ester* bonds. Furthermore, bacterial membranes are "bilayers" while archaeal membranes can be composed of "bilayers" or, in some cases, "monolayers." The monolayer lipid membranes tend to be found in archaea that live in extreme environments.

26. Weiss et al., "The Physiology and Habitat of the Last Universal Common Ancestor," 16116.

27. Weiss et al., "The Physiology and Habitat of the Last Universal Common Ancestor," 16116.

28. Weiss et al., "The Physiology and Habitat of the Last Universal Common Ancestor," 16116.

29. Weiss et al., "The Physiology and Habitat of the Last Universal Common Ancestor," 16116.

30. Madeline C. Weiss et al., "The Last Universal Common Ancestor between Ancient Earth Chemistry and the Onset of Genetics," *PLOS Genetics* 14, no. 8 (2018): e1007518, https://doi.org/10.1371/journal.pgen.1007518.

31. Madeline C. Weiss et al., "The Last Universal Common Ancestor between Ancient Earth Chemistry and the Onset of Genetics," e1007518.

32. Alkaline hydrothermal vents are less well known than deep-sea black smoker vents. The latter exist at the boundaries between tectonic plates of the Earth's upper crust and mantle. Here, water comes into direct contact with magmatic chambers within the Earth and remerges in the ocean at temperatures that exceed 300° C, carrying within it large amounts of black sulfide minerals that create dynamic dark-colored plumes, which give these vent systems their name. Though black smokers are indeed far-from-equilibrium systems, in contemporary origins research, they are generally not considered ideal sites for the emergence of life as organic molecules tend to degrade rather than further complexify at such extreme temperatures. Despite this, Williams and colleagues have proposed black smoker sites as a possible setting for the emergence of life by speculating

on how clays could have acted as *primordial wombs* that shielded developing organic molecules from degrading. Williams et al., however, do not focus on the thermodynamics of these clay inorganic wombs in their hypothesis, which makes their conception of "womb" differ from my focus here. See Lynda B. Williams, Brandon Canfield, Kenneth M. Voglesonger, and John R. Holloway, "Organic Molecules Formed in a 'Primordial Womb,'" *Geological Society of America* 33, no. 11 (2005): 913–916.

33. Geochemist Michael J. Russell predicted the existence of alkaline vent systems as well as their relevance to the origins of life in the early 1990s. See Michael J. Russell, Roy. M. Daniel, Allan J. Hall, and John A. Sherringham, "A Hydrothermally Precipitated Catalytic Iron Sulphide Membrane as a First Step Toward Life," *Journal of Molecular Evolution* 39 (1994): 231–243, doi:10.1007/BF00160147. Russell's ideas were largely viewed as idiosyncratic until alkaline vent systems were discovered in the Atlantic Ocean. His work now is at the center of geochemically oriented origins-of-life research.

34. Sandra Hines, "Lost City Pumps Life-Essential Chemicals at Rates Unseen at Typical Black Smokers," *University of Washington News*, January 31, 2008, https://www.washington.edu/news/2008/01/31/lost-city-pumps-life-essential-chemicals-at-rates-unseen-at-typical-black-smokers/.

35. Martin and Russell, "On the Origins of Cells," 63.

36. Nick Lane and William Martin, "The Origin of Membrane Bioenergetics," *Cell* 151, no. 7 (2012): 1407, https://doi.org/10.1016/j.cell.2012.11.050.

37. Irigaray TS, 106–18.

38. Irigaray TS, 106–107, emphasis in original.

39. Irigaray ESD, 124.

40. Ilya Prigogine and Grégoire Nicolis, "On Symmetry-Breaking Instabilities in Dissipative Systems," *Journal of Chemical Physics* 46, no. 9 (1967): 3542–3550.

41. Radu Balescu, "Ilya Prigogine: His Life, His Work," in *Advances in Chemical Physics: Special Volume in Memory of Ilya Prigogine*, vol. 135, ed. Stuart A. Rice (Hoboken, NJ: Wiley & Sons, 2007), 13.

42. Dilip Kondepudi and Ilya Prigogine, *Modern Thermodynamics: From Heat Engines to Dissipative Structures*, second ed. (West Sussex, UK: Wiley, 2014), 428.

43. Elbert Branscomb and Michael J. Russell, "Turnstiles and Bifurcators: The Disequilibrium Converting Engines That Put Metabolism on the Road," *Biochimica et Biophysica Acta* 1827 (2013): 64.

44. Branscomb and Russell, "Turnstiles and Bifurcators," 63, emphasis in original.

45. Sojo, Pomiankowski, and Lane, "A Bioenergetic Basis for Membrane Divergence," e1001926.

46. Martin and Russell, "On the Origins of Cells," 62.

47. Irigaray ESD, 122.

48. Martin and Russell, "On the Origins of Cells," 63.

49. Martin and Russell, "On the Origins of Cells," 63, emphasis added.

50. Martin and Russell, "On the Origins of Cells," 63. Martin and Russell are aware that viruses complicate the "principle of semipermeable compartmentation." This is not a theoretical oversight, however, but rather an intentional exclusion. This is because although viruses do destabilize the concept of life, they still require semipermeable compartmentation: viruses depend upon cellular forms of life that *are* bounded and semipermeable to replicate. On how viruses complicate the concept of life, see Annu Dahiya, "Before the Cell, There Was Virus: Rethinking the Concept of Parasite and Contagion through Contemporary Research in Evolutionary Virology," in *Transforming Contagion: Anxieties, Modalities, Possibilities*, edited by Breanne Fahs, Annika Mann, Eric Swank, and Sarah Stage (New Brunswick, NJ: Rutgers University Press, 2018).

51. Christian De Duve coined the concentration problem. See Christian De Duve, *Blueprint for a Cell: The Nature and Origin of Life* (Burlington, NC: Neil Patterson, 1991).

52. Günter Wächtershäuser is the primary advocate of surface catalysis. See Günter Wächtershäuser, "Before Enzymes and Templates: Theory of Surface Metabolism," *Microbiology Reviews* 52 (1988): 452–484.

53. Martin and Russell, "On the Origins of Cells," 62.

54. Elbert Branscomb and Michael J. Russell, "Frankenstein or a Submarine Alkaline Vent: Who Is Responsible for Abiogenesis? Part 1: What Is Life–That It Might Create Itself?" *Bioessays* 40 (2018): 1700179.

55. It is interesting to note here that Branscomb and Russell place scare quotes around *abiotic* and not womb. This rhetorical emphasis is different from "primordial womb" in scare quotes in Williams and colleagues, "Organic Molecules Formed in a 'Primordial Womb.'" I read this as Branscomb and Russell striving to expand the concept of womb, making it precede the beginnings of cellular life, while also simultaneously complicating the boundary between "biotic" and "abiotic."

56. Elbert Branscomb and Michael J. Russell, "Frankenstein or a Submarine Alkaline Vent: Who Is Responsible for Abiogenesis? Part 2: As Life Is Now, So It Must Have Been in the Beginning," *BioEssays* 40 (2018): 1700182.

57. Branscomb and Russell, "Frankenstein or a Submarine Alkaline Vent: Part 2."

58. Martin and Russell, "On the Origin of Cells," 65.

59. Irigaray I, 111.

60. Irigaray SFO, 106.

61. Irigaray SFO, 106–107.

62. Martin and Russell, "On the Origins of Cells," 60.

63. Irigaray TLR, 7.

64. Aristarkhova, *Hospitality of the Matrix*, 2, emphasis in original.

Bibliography

Aristarkhova, Irina. *Hospitality of the Matrix: Philosophy, Biomedicine, and Culture*. New York: Columbia University Press, 2012.

Balescu, Radu. "Ilya Prigogine: His Life, His Work." In *Advances in Chemical Physics: Special Volume in Memory of Ilya Prigogine*, vol. 135, edited by Stuart A. Rice, 1–72. Hoboken, NJ: Wiley, 2007.

Bich, Leonardo and Sarah Green. "Is defining life pointless? Operational definitions at the frontiers of biology." *Synthese* 195 (2018): 3919–3946.

Branscomb, Elbert, and Michael J. Russell. "Frankenstein or a Submarine Alkaline Vent: Who Is Responsible for Abiogenesis? Part 1: What Is Life—That It Might Create Itself?" *Bioessays* 40 (2018): 1700179.

Branscomb, Elbert, and Michael J. Russell. "Frankenstein or a Submarine Alkaline Vent: Who Is Responsible for Abiogenesis? Part 2: As Life Is Now, So It Must Have Been in the Beginning." *Bioessays* 40 (2018): 1700182.

Branscomb, Elbert, and Michael J. Russell. "Turnstiles and Bifurcators: The Disequilibrium Converting Engines That Put Metabolism on the Road." *Biochimica et Biophysica Acta* 1827 (2013): 62–78.

Cooper, Geoffrey M. "The Origin and Evolution of Cells." In *The Cell: A Molecular Approach*, second ed. Sunderland, MA: Sinauer Associates, 2000. https://www.ncbi.nlm.nih.gov/books/NBK9841/.

Corliss, J. B., J. A. Baross, and S. E. Hoffmann. "An Hypothesis concerning the Relationship between Submarine Hot Springs and the Origin of Life on Earth." *Oceanologica Acta* 4 (1981): 59–69.

Dahiya, Annu. "Before the Cell, There Was Virus: Rethinking the Concept of Parasite and Contagion through Contemporary Research in Evolutionary Virology." In *Transforming Contagion: Anxieties, Modalities, Possibilities*, edited by Breanne Fahs, Annika Mann, Eric Swank, and Sarah Stage, 42–55. New Brunswick, NJ: Rutgers University Press, 2018.

De Duve, Christian. *Blueprint for a Cell: The Nature and Origin of Life*. Burlington, NC: Neil Patterson, 1991.

Fry, Iris. *The Emergence of Life on Earth: A Historical and Scientific Overview*. Piscataway, NJ: Rutgers University Press, 2000.

Grosz, Elizabeth. *Becoming Undone: Darwinian Reflections on Life, Politics, and Art*. Durham, NC: Duke University Press, 2011.

Haldane, John Burdon Sanderson. "Origin of Life." *Rationalist Annual* 148 (1929): 3–10.

Hines, Sandra. "Lost City Pumps Life-Essential Chemicals at Rates Unseen at Typical Black Smokers." *University of Washington News*, January 31, 2008. https://www.washington.edu/news/2008/01/31/lost-city-pumps-life-essential-chemicals-t-rates-unseen-at-typical-black-smokers/.

Kelley, Deborah. "From the Mantle to Microbes: The Lost City Hydrothermal Field." *Oceanography* 18, no. 3 (2005): 32–45.

Kelley, Deborah S., Jeffrey A. Karson, Donna K. Blackman, Gretchen L. Früh-Green, David A. Butterfield, Marvin D. Lilley, Eric J. Olson, Matthew O. Schrenk, Kevin K. Roe, Geoff T. Lebon, Pete Rivizzigno, and the AT3-60 Shipboard Party. "An Off-Axis Hydrothermal Vent Field Near the Mid-Atlantic Ridge at 30 Degrees N." *Nature* 412 (2001):145–149. Kondepudi, Dilip, and Ilya Prigogine. *Modern Thermodynamics: From Heat Engines to Dissipative Structures*, second ed. West Sussex, UK: Wiley, 2014.

Koonin, Eugene V., and William Martin. "On the Origin of Genomes and Cells within Inorganic Compartments." *Trends in Genetics* 12, no. 12 (December 2005): 647–654.

Jones, Rachel. *Irigaray: Towards a Sexuate Philosophy*. Cambridge: Polity Press, 2011.

Lane, Nick. "Proton Gradients at the Origin of Life." *BioEssays* 39 (2017): 1600217.

Lane, Nick. "Why Are Cells Powered by Proton Gradients?" *Nature Education* 3, no. 9 (2010): 18.

Lane, Nick, John F. Allen, and William Martin. "How Did LUCA Make a Living? Chemiosmosis in the Origin of Life." *BioEssays* 32 (2010): 271–280.

Lane, Nick, and William Martin. "The Origin of Membrane Bioenergetics." *Cell* 151, no. 7 (2012): 1406–1416, https://doi.org/10.1016/j.cell.2012.11.050. Leonardo, Bich, and Sara Green. "Is Defining Life Pointless? Operational Definitions at the Frontiers of Biology." *Synthese* 195 (2018): 3919–3946.

Martin, William, and Michael J. Russell. "On the Origins of Cells: A Hypothesis for the Evolutionary Transitions from Abiotic Geochemistry to Chemoautotrophic Prokaryotes, and from Prokaryotes to Nucleated Cells." *Philosophical Transactions of the Royal Society of London B* 358, no. 1429 (January 2003): 59–85.

Miller, Stanley L., and Jeffrey L. Bada. "Submarine Hot Springs and the Origin of Life." *Nature* 334, no. 18 (1988): 609–611.

Oparin, Alexander Ivanovich. *The Origin of Life*. [In Russian.] Moscow: Moscow Worker, 1924.

Oparin, Alexander Ivanovich. *The Origin of Life on Earth*. Translated by Sergius Morgulis. New York: Macmillan, 1938.

Oreskes, Naomi. 2003. "A Context of Motivation: US Navy Oceanographic Research and the Discovery of Sea-Floor Hydrothermal Vents." *Social Studies of Science* 33(5): 697–742.

Prigogine, Ilya, and Grégoire Nicolis. "On Symmetry-Breaking Instabilities in Dissipative Systems." *Journal of Chemical Physics* 46, no. 9 (1967): 3542–3550.

Russell, Michael J., Roy M. Daniel, Allan J. Hall, and John A. Sherringham. "A Hydrothermally Precipitated Catalytic Iron Sulphide Membrane as a First Step Toward Life." *Journal of Molecular Evolution* 39 (1994): 231–243. doi:10.1007/BF00160147.

Schönheit, Peter, Wolfgang Buckel, and William F. Martin. "On the Origin of Heterotrophy." *Trends in Microbiology* 24, no. 1 (January 2016): 12–25.

Shock, E. L., J. P. Amend, and M. Y. Zolotov. "The Early Earth vs. the Origin of Life." In *Origin of the Earth and Moon*, 527–543. Tucson: University of Arizona Press, 2000.

Sojo, Victor, Barry Herschy, Alexandra Whicher, Eloi Camprubi, and Nick Lane. "The Origin of Life in Alkaline Hydrothermal Vents." *Astrobiology* 16, no. 2 (2016): 181–197. Sojo, Victor, Andrew Pomiankowski, and Nick Lane. "A Bioenergetic Basis for Membrane Divergence in Archaea and Bacteria." *PLOS Biology* 12, no. 8 (2014): 1–12.Van Dover, Cindy. *The Ecology of Deep-Sea Hydrothermal Vents*. Princeton, NJ: Princeton University Press, 2000.

Wächtershäuser, Günter. "Before Enzymes and Templates: Theory of Surface Metabolism." *Microbiology Reviews* 52 (1988): 452–484.

Weiss, Madeline C., Martina Preiner, Joana C. Xavier, Verena Zimorski, and William F. Martin. "The Last Universal Common Ancestor between Ancient Earth Chemistry and the Onset of Genetics." *PLOS Genetics* 14, no. 8 (2018): e1007518. https://doi.org/10.1371/journal.pgen.1007518.

Weiss, Madeline C., Filipa L. Sousa, Natalia Mrnjavac, Sinje Neukirchen, Mayo Roettger, Shijulal Nelson-Sathi, and William F. Martin. "The Physiology and Habitat of the Last Universal Common Ancestor." *Nature Microbiology* 1 (2016): 16116. doi: 10.1038/NMICROBIOL.2016.116.

West, Timothy, Victor Sojo, Andrew Pomiankowski, and Nick Lane. "The Origin of Heredity in Protocells." *Philosophical Transactions of the Royal Society of London B* 372 (2017): 20160419.

Williams, Lynda B., Brandon Canfield, Kenneth M. Voglesonger, and John R. Holloway. "Organic Molecules Formed in a 'Primordial Womb.'" *Geological Society of America* 33, no. 11 (2005): 913–916.

Woese, Carl R., and George E. Fox. "Phylogenetic Structure of the Prokaryotic Domain: The Primary Kingdoms." *Proceedings of the National Academy of the Sciences of the United States of America* 74, no. 11 (1977): 5088–5090.

Chapter Four

Irigaray's Extendable Matrix

Cosmic Expansion-Contraction and Black Hole Umbilical Cords

M. D. Murtagh

> Though of course what unfolds in the womb unfolds in function of an interval, a cord, that is never done away with. Whence perhaps the infinite nostalgia for that first home? The interval cannot be done away with.
>
> —Luce Irigaray, "Place, Interval," in *An Ethics of Sexual Difference*

> From the point of view of the parent universe, the "umbilical cord" of the child universe is indistinguishable from a black hole. The umbilical connection in the child universe would similarly look like a black hole.
>
> —Alan H. Guth, *The Inflationary Universe*

Luce Irigaray's *An Ethics of Sexual Difference* is a philosophical call-to-arms; not least to reconceive a maternal-feminine *subject* irreducible to Man, but to create an entirely new, different *space* and *time*, a feminine *universe*. In this sense, Irigaray challenges future generations to think seriously about the transition to a new age of sexual difference, how it requires "a change in our perception and conception of *space-time*" and "entails an evolution or a transformation of forms, of the relations of *matter* and *form* and of the interval *between*."[1] Following this declaration at the outset of *An Ethics*, the remainder of the book provides a series of critical analyses of various philosophical *universes* within the Western canon: Aristotle's, Descartes's, Levinas's, and others, which Irigaray deems inadequate for the maternal-feminine subject because the materiality of those universes is marked as the maternal-feminine itself.

In spite of her plea for creative (r)evolution, most contemporary scholarship on Irigaray tends toward careful meta-analyses of Irigaray's own texts, readings of her readings that contextualize, reinterpret, and parse the complicated dynamics of her dialogues, critical mimesis, and psychoanalysis of Western thought's unconscious. Still, there remains no response to her call for a new space and time of the maternal-feminine; no cosmology of sexual difference yet exists.

The purpose of this essay, therefore, is to facilitate a precursory dialogue between sexual difference and cosmology, a contemporary, scientific discourse concerned with the nature of our universe, especially the origin and evolution of space and time. In *Speculum of the Other Woman*, Irigaray claims, "The Copernican revolution has yet to have its final effects in the male imaginary."[2] She observes here how the male imaginary continuously recenters itself within an expanding cosmic container in every revolutionary iteration from Copernicus onward. Beginning with the paradigm shift from a geocentric, or "Earth"-centered cosmos, to a heliocentric, or "Sun"-centered one, Man finds a way to remain the center of the universe regardless of how expansive the cosmic matrix becomes: from a tiny solar-system to a full galaxy, from the Milky Way to an intergalactic sea, and from a Big Bang singularity with billions of galaxies to a multiverse within which infinite "Big Bangs" exist. Regardless of how expansive the male imaginary conceptualizes the cosmos to be, the idea of it as a container for him seems to remain pervasive.

The question that stumps the scientific imaginary, then, is: What contains the container itself? Perhaps this question is more aptly situated for metaphysics than for physics, which is why responding to it through the framework of sexual difference is not any more unlikely than through scientific discourse: "We can confidently trace cosmic history back to the first second. The ground gets shakier when we extrapolate still farther back, into the first millisecond."[3] Is there a "multiverse," some hyperspace vacuum, out of which infinite universes—including ours—emerge and develop? If so, what are the *pre*ontological or *meta*physical conditions of this cosmic matrix that precede time and space?

In the late 1970s and early 1980s, a motley crew of physicists and cosmologists became especially interested in this question of the conditions that engender the Big Bang and the ultra-early formation of our universe. These were categorized as "beyond the standard model" because they speculate the context and causation of the Big Bang itself: "The standard model is not the most satisfying theory imaginable of the origin of the universe . . . there is an embarrassing vagueness about the very beginning, the first hundredth of a second or so."[4] Even though theories beyond the standard model focusing on initial conditions are not astronomically observable, they *are* mathematically calculable. For this reason, multiverse theory continues to gain more and more traction among contemporary cosmologists and physicists. The challenge to those who advocate it is to explain *how* universes emerge from the multiverse. Is the multiverse some kind of eternal and infinite vacuum in which self-enclosed universes pop into and out of existence like floating bubbles? Or, does one universe tunnel out of another, out of another, out of another, ad infinitum? Another way to ask this question, in the spirit of Irigaray, would be: Is the multiverse some kind of maternal womb out of which all embryonic universes are birthed? Or, is each universe simultaneously the embryo of one universe and the maternal matrix of another?

In this essay, I draw from a compilation of texts by Stephen Hawking, Martin Rees, and Alan Guth to flesh out what they imagine constitutes the multiverse. All three use terms such as *embryo*, *offspring*, *child*, and *baby* to describe *our* universe as an emergent phenomenon of something Other, some more primordial and encompassing place. None of them, however, intimate that the more primordial multiverse is a "mother," or "maternal" matrix of some sort.[5] There is almost no meditation in the literature on the ways an embryonic universe's capacity for self-making requires the *place* of a dark milieu to develop and grow itself.[6] It seems physicists and cosmologists have not, as of yet, theorized the multiverse as an incorporeal womb out of which baby universes emerge; they have not yet devised a *relational* theory of cosmic gestation.

Historically, scientific method follows from a phallocentric logic wherein entities, from particles to the universe itself, take on corpuscular form: solid, bounded, self-enclosed, autonomous units. Multiverse theory, by contrast, calls for an excess or overflow of this logic, which necessarily surpasses certain inconsistencies in current theoretical and experimental physics. One of the greatest inconsistencies, a relic of this phallic tendency in scientific thought, is that between *general relativity*, which implies the irreversibility of the expansion of space-time, and *quantum mechanics*, in which reversibility is possible. These physical laws appear, on the surface, to contradict each other. A multiverse theory of fundamental reality, however, would resolve the contradiction by pointing to an even more fundamental maternal origin or ground out of which they both emerge; that which remains absent and unthought. To get a sense of how baby universes emerge from a maternal matrix, from a multiverse, would require at least two concessions by phallocentric thinking: 1) that this universe is not something that sparks itself out of nothingness, and 2) that its emergence is not a uniquely singular event; that there might be any number of variant universes like or different from ours, yet another Copernican Revolution. A multiverse, in short, would operate as the maternal origin of both the quantum realm and the fabric of space-time. These seem incompatible in their present manifestations, but in the most fundamental and earliest moments, they are not. To this point, philosopher of sexual difference Rebecca Hill insightfully offers: "For Irigaray, the maternal-feminine is not a concept; she is the very condition of conceptual logic . . . [and therefore] can move beyond the strictures of the infamous law of noncontradiction."[7]

My reading of the three scientists mentioned earlier parallels Irigaray's reading of Aristotle's cosmology in her famous essay "Place, Interval." There, Irigaray reveals Aristotle's concept of place in *Physics* as the condition of his conceptual logic, the maternal-feminine on which his philosophical system rests. Place, unlike the bodies that occupy it, does not have its own origin or capacity for locomotion in Aristotle's system. Through an ethics of sexual difference, Irigaray presses on this aporia of the place of place since it seems to define the cosmos and maternal bodies concomitantly. Following Irigaray, I aim to reconceive the multiverse, a womb of all universes, in this framework of maternal-feminine morphology. I spotlight a number of interrelated scientific theories that offer explanatory accounts for how baby universes form in relation to the multiverse; these include Hawking's primordial black holes, Rees's quantum foam, and Guth's cosmic inflation. The goal is to unveil an unarticulated sexual difference within multiverse theory that reimagines the relation between fundamental physics and cosmology "beyond the standard model." To do this, I split the essay into two main parts.

In the first part, I offer an idiosyncratic reading of the umbilical cord in Irigaray's "Place, Interval." Unlike the womb, placenta, or even mucous membranes, the umbilical cord has not been examined closely. Once cut, the umbilical cord severs the baby from the maternal body, its place of origin. This incites the baby's capacity for *locomotion*, a term Aristotle uses to designate movement from place to place, with its autonomous body. Through the severing of the umbilical cord, one body occupying one place becomes two bodies occupying two places. Still, the body of the child desires and longs to return to its first place: the maternal body. In an interesting parallel, Irigaray notes Aristotle's cosmos is a maternal body within which all the elements are gravitationally attracted to their origin place where they come to rest. In this way, Irigaray makes an important link in Aristotelian logic between nostalgic attraction for one's maternal origin and gravitational attraction.[8] To reimagine place through an ethics of sexual difference, Irigaray calls for a theory of gravitation that extends the matrix itself. This requires a gravity beyond that which moves bodies up and down, front and back, or left and right, in short, what locomotion entails for Aristotle. For the place of place—the cosmos—to become locomotive, a theory of gravitation that expands and contracts place outward and inward is vital. This kind of gravitational *repulsion* gives a locomotion to place where Aristotle's strictly attractive gravitational force privileges only the locomotion of bodies within place.

The second part of this essay examines *how* theories supporting multiverse hypothesis require gravitational expansion, sometimes referred to as "dark energy" or "a cosmological constant," to explain the stretching of space-time constitutive of our universe. The idea that a baby universe grows out of a multiverse requires some generative, expansive force to explain how a tiny, quantum false-vacuum bubble might transverse the gravitational abyss of a black hole's event horizon and proceed to inflate rapidly into its own cosmos at the other end. Here, I make the case that primordial black holes, first theorized by Stephen Hawking, operate as an "umbilical cord" between the multiverse and an embryonic universe such as ours. The point is to address the following question: Does a new philosophy of place emerge from multiverse hypothesis that has the potential to align with Irigaray's reconception of Aristotelian "place" in *An Ethics of Sexual Difference*? The primordial black holes Hawking imagines between a maternal and an embryonic universe exceed the laws of general relativity in an important way. Primordial black holes form by density differentials in the energy of space-time that begin with quantum level fluctuations and continue to amplify as space-time grows, stretches, or expands. Quantum particles are the only entities able to escape the gravitational pull of black holes.[9] In this sense, they offer the possibility of a new model for understanding the origins of our universe. The Big Bang becomes an event in which the umbilical cord, a primordial black hole, is cut, separating mother multiverse from embryo universe. Snipping the cord incites the gravitational expansion of "dark energy" to begin inflating the space-time fabric of our universe. This theory of gravitational expansion is a foil to Aristotle's theory that origin places are necessarily and exclusively attractive sites; place, in his conception, relies on a classical theory of gravity, which only pulls bodies into it rather than one that expands itself outward, leaving place itself empty, immobile, and self-cannibalizing.

Gravitational Differences in Aristotle and Irigaray's Concepts of "Place"

> From at least Aristotle onward, it has been assumed that sexual difference makes no difference when it comes to matters of place and space.
>
> —Edward Casey, *The Fate of Place: A Philosophical History*

In this first section, I turn to Irigaray's "Place, Interval" where she critiques Aristotle's concept of place from *Physics* IV. After recapitulating her critique, I mobilize her method of "reaffirm[ing] the maternal-feminine as the disavowed outside of [t]his project, an outside that functions as the secret foundation of philosophy"[10] in my own examination of multiverse hypothesis. Within the ancient philosophical imaginary, the cosmos itself is reducible to place, a bound container for the elements and their interactions. Irigaray seeks to counter this phallic cosmic structure by using "topological figures of her own, using a range of tropes from the discourses of particle physics, fluid dynamics, [and] the body's materiality . . . to create an alternate imaginary."[11] Responding to Irigaray's ethics for reimagining place, then, is twofold. In reimagining the cosmos in terms that coincide with maternal-feminine morphology, one subsequently forges a new ethical relation in excess of the one in which one thing is merely a container for the other's pleasure, growth, or development. Aligning Irigaray's version of place with contemporary cosmology, therefore, opens the potential for considering how sexual difference "operates in the very structure of the world,"[12] not only in the sexuate bodies within it.

To start, Irigaray's critique of Aristotle's place is just as much a critique of his cosmology as it is of his physics: "Aristotle believes that the universe is eternal, with no end and no beginning to time or motion."[13] There is a *sublunar* realm in which material beings come into and pass out of being. There is also the *superlunary* realm in which "the heavens, mov[e] in perfect circles, eternally and fully predictably."[14] For Aristotle, celestial bodies move in circular motions but they do not change places; instead, they constitute the boundary of cosmic place. This means there is no possibility of place beyond the revolving celestial spheres because there are no bodies beyond celestial bodies. In Aristotle's sublunary realm, by contrast, bodies have "natural" places toward which they move. While these bodies are locomotive, or have the capacity to move from place to place, the places toward which they move are stationary in the sublunar realm for Aristotle. Once a body arrives to its natural place, it comes to rest. Examples of such bodies include the elements: fire, earth, air, and water. While the locomotion of fire and air are directed upward toward the heavens, water and earth move downward toward the center of the Earth to varying degrees. There is a gravitational pull in the elements to move them toward their natural places. Once they arrive, however, they stop moving. For this reason, Aristotle's cosmos is ultimately an enclosed one: "The cosmos [is] not as an empty and endless Space but as an embracing Place, filled to the brim with snugly fitting proper places. The firmament that encircles the world-whole is at once a paradigm for all lesser places and filled with these very same places. Everything, or almost everything, is in place."[15]

In "Place, Interval," Irigaray demonstrates how Aristotle's clear-cut distinctions between place and body do not hold up universally. For Aristotle, place locates a body in space; it is coextensive with the body that occupies it but irreducible to the matter or form of that body. Even though he insists place is inseparable from a body, Irigaray urges that it only "reveals itself as a result of that separability."[16] Place must be separable from the body to the extent that it functions as the condition of locomotion for the bodies that move toward it, or are gravitationally attracted to it. Further, place must be nonexistent, according to Aristotle, because "*if it is itself an existent, it will be somewhere . . . for if everything that exists has a place, place too will have a place, and so on* ad infinitum."[17] So if place exists, it too must occupy a place; but this creates an infinite regress that Aristotle wants to avoid. Therefore, Aristotle ensures the placelessness of place itself by determining that place does not have its own being. He defines it by *lack* of being, which the body comes to fill in occupying it. Irigaray diagnoses Aristotle's assumption of the infinite regress of place as a means to deflect a consideration of a place's own origin. With a cosmos that is a primordial "no-place" whose cause is a placeless unmoved mover, Aristotle strategically precludes the question of where place begins because, for him, it is both nonexistent and unlocomotive anyway.

For Irigaray, Aristotle's distinctions between place and body seem insufficient in accounting for bodies that function as the place of other bodies. The pregnant or gestating body is a prime example. This body complicates Aristotle's claim that two bodies cannot occupy the same place. Rather, it is an extendable place: "both container and extension."[18] The aporia of this body is that it is simultaneously a body *and* a place. It is, therefore, a double place: the place of the fetus and the place of the gestating body, which retains the properties of a body such as an origin in existence and the mobility of locomotion. Hence, if place is *also* a body, a gestating body, then place *can* have an origin and be locomotive. This is an ethical claim for Irigaray: that a body can be the place of another body that emerges from it. It is only by virtue of that body that an emergent body is able to move around to other places within the Place of the cosmos.

Irigaray's insistence in recuperating the characteristics of bodies for defining place boils down to her assertion that the maternal-feminine body *is* place in the Aristotelian philosophical imaginary. The maternal-feminine "container" is "assigned to be place without occupying a place."[19] By em-placing other bodies, this place is systematically denied its own place. As Hill notes, "In his treatise, woman is place for the embryo and for man's penis, but she has no place of her own. When Irigaray says woman is place for herself, she is already speaking in excess of Aristotle's system."[20] Hence, reframing the relation between place and body means reframing woman's relation to herself, to other women, between the sexes, and embryos as well. It also means reframing the cosmos as the place of all places and considering its *own* maternal origins. Aristotle's cosmos is "conceived as a closed vessel, the receptacle for all the elements";[21] it is the containing body or *corps enveloppant* while the elements are contained bodies or *corps enveloppé*. It is only the contained bodies, for Aristotle, that come into existence and move around within the containing body; the container's emergence remains unimagined.

An ethics of sexual difference gives place a place of her own: "If the matrix is extendable, it can figure as *the place of place*."[22] Through the concept of an "extendable matrix," Irigaray coalesces the maternal body with the expansion of the universe. The maternal body is not an "extendable matrix" because it endlessly defers the place of place. It is extendable because it is a place that locomotes: it stretches, grows, folds, wrinkles, produces and gestates other bodies within its own. For place to doubly envelope herself requires a new definition of locomotion; not the rectilinear motion of bodies toward each other in straight lines within a container, but the expansion or dilation of place, of the container, itself. Importantly, however, defining locomotion in this way violates and exceeds the laws of physical motion governing the Aristotelian cosmos:

> Woman, insofar as she is a container, is never a closed one. Place is never closed. The boundaries touch against one another while still remaining open. And can they do so without necessarily touching the boundaries of the bodies contained? There are two touches between boundaries; and these are not the same: the touch of one's body at the threshold; the touch of the contained other. There is also the internal touch of the body of the child, with mother and child being separated by one envelope or several. Within this container the child moves. Is it possible to speak of locomotion? It seems not. Where would the child move to? Toward the place that nourishes him, toward the exit that leads from one place to another place? And again toward that movement of growth within the place?[23]

While Aristotle's model is one of strict containment,[24] Irigaray's "has an oxymoronic structure: it is an open/enclosure."[25] Place remains *without* an ethics of sexual difference so long as it fails to render woman, the cosmos, capable of her own movement and expansion. Reconceiving place in this way implies that it must indeed have its own primordial origin from which it expands outward; its locomotion is its capacity to push the boundaries of itself. This locomotion is obviously distinct from the locomotion of bodies that move *within* the closed container cosmos.

In fact, Irigaray contends that locomotion understood as the extension of place is an issue that has long been forgotten or ignored at the junction of physics and metaphysics: "At issue is the extension of place, of places, and of the relation of that extension to the development of the body and bodies. An issue either forgotten or ignored in the junction of physics and metaphysics, since these two dimensions have been set aside or dislocated, but an issue still alive today."[26] An ethics of sexual difference calls for a cosmos of the extendable matrix, a cosmology that expands space-time itself, an envelope that grows *as* it envelops rather than a closed container or vessel that demarcates and self-encloses movement: a Big Bang theory of the maternal-feminine.

Irigaray and Aristotle do concur that all bodies have a "first" place, or place of origin: "The first place is the maternal body,"[27] Irigaray declares. The origin of each body's place within space and time begins in utero. "In utero," here, extends beyond its usual connotation with human cis-women, it is important to note. In fact, our universe is itself in utero within a multiverse. The "maternal body," whatever its form or magnitude, is simply the condition of possibility for a "big bang," an emergence of some other, each embryo being a cosmos of its own and each cosmos being its own embryo. While Aristotle's cosmos does not have space-time origins, terrestrial bodies within his cosmos, including the elements, do indeed have specific origins in specific places. The place of origin is the body's "proper and primary place,"[28] and the body desires to return toward it. Its locomotion is oriented toward moving closer to this proper and primary place; as though it is being pulled toward it gravitationally: "When separated from place, the [body] feels an attraction to place as a condition of existence."[29] Irigaray identifies the maternal womb as the first, "natural" place of the fetal body in gestation. The economy of desire in a subject's life is, therefore, organized around substituting its return to a maternal-feminine origin, the cosmic basis of phallic desire. A body's attraction toward its proper and primary place is an attraction toward an unacknowledged place of origin: "The masculine is attracted to the maternal-feminine as place."[30] Nostalgia for the womb incites the masculine to substitute his desire for origin with sexual desire: "For Irigaray, everything delimited by place on the Aristotelian model, whether animate or inanimate, is traced with man's nostalgic longing for his first dwelling, the womb; the irrecuperable first dwelling. Irigaray describes this as an umbilical cord that man cannot sever."[31] Severing the umbilical cord allows bodies to move about but also orients the attraction of bodies back toward that place from which they have been severed.

The body's nostalgia for its first place is how Irigaray makes sense of locomotion in Aristotle. She almost posits a proto-theory of gravitational attraction in her reading of place within his cosmos. This nostalgia for first place incites the body's locomotion back toward it as though guided by some gravitational force. This force of gravitational attraction is place's primary function for Aristotle: "that toward which there is locomotion."[32]

> According to Aristotle, such a place would have to be characterized, among other things, by the dimensions of up and down, which are in fact consistently associated with the physical laws of gravitation, as well as with the economy of desire. Place would be directed up or down rather than into expansion-contraction, according to the theory elaborated about it. And to the conception of place which is still and forever Aristotle's.[33]

There is no theory of the expansion or contraction of bodies or their places here. These movements are outside the scope of "locomotion" as Aristotle defines it. Whereas Aristotelian locomotion refers to a body's capacity to move from place to place, Irigaray's redefinition of place through an ethics of sexual difference incites a subsequent redefinition of locomotion. This includes the body's expansions and contractions that implicitly expand and contract the place it occupies; these, too, are gestational and birthing movements. Irigaray articulates that an "up and down" conception of gravity is "still and forever Aristotle's" to signal that her own would call for "physical laws of gravitation" that include "expansion-contraction."[34] Her investment in rethinking the expansion-contraction of place is so that the extendable matrix, the place of origin, becomes locomotive in its own right and can begin to emplace itself in relation to others.

The difference between Aristotle's and Irigaray's conceptions of gravity manifest in the different functions they grant the umbilical cord. In both cases, the cutting of the umbilical cord produces an interval, a gap, a difference so that the maternal and fetal bodies become at least two. In Aristotle's cosmos, the cord produces an interval "that is never done away with."[35] Even though the fetal body detaches from its maternal place, it always desires to return: "The locomotion toward and reduction in interval are the movements of desire"; "the greater the desire, the greater the tendency to overcome the interval while at the same time retaining it."[36] It is the impossibility of overcoming of this desire, of reoccupying the maternal womb, that drives locomotion: "Since desire can eat up place, either by regressing into the other on the intrauterine model or annihilating the existence of the other in one way or another."[37] The interval allows for place to subsist without being cannibalized by the body that grows inside it. Still, the only characteristic of place for Aristotle is that it attracts bodies and orients their locomotion. It is the umbilical cord severing that marks the origin of the autonomous body and directs its locomotion back to its natural place, "when perhaps the infinite nostalgia for that first home"[38] began.

On the other hand, for Irigaray's "place" to become an extendable matrix, the event of the umbilical cord cutting would need to incite a different relation between body and place. She writes: "The umbilical cord push[es] the interval toward and into infinity. The irreducible. Opening up the universe and all beyond it."[39] In opposition to Aristotle's gravitational attraction, Irigaray's place evokes a theory of *reverse* gravity, or gravitational expansion. As the conduit of expansion, the umbilical cord not only grows the body of the fetus in utero but grows the extendable matrix as well. Whereas cutting the umbilical cord marks the interval between a body and its place of origin as it does for Aristotle, contemporary cosmology would mark the event as a "big bang." It is by separating from its maternal conditions through the primordial black hole that a baby universe is able to inflate rapidly from a small quantum fluctuation to a large-scale cosmos like ours with density differentials producing galaxies and clusters of galaxies.

This severing does not limit the expansion of the maternal in any way; the multiverse continues birthing other universes. The umbilical cord cut between the extendable matrix and the fetal body ignites the energy potential of a negative gravitational field. The gravitational energy is negative because it is culled from a reservoir latent in the field itself. Like woman, this negative gravitational field is an extendable matrix. Woman does not desire to statically contain herself, or to close herself off to being the place of others. Instead, she seeks to expand herself constantly from within: "The boundary of the containing body might be the bodily identity of woman, reborn and touched anew by inner communion, and not destroyed by nostalgia for a regression in utero."[40] Irigaray's place operates according to a totally different logic from Aristotle's, and each is contingent on the way the umbilical cord produces a relation between body and place; for Aristotle, it is strictly an attractive lack whereas for Irigaray, it is expansive.

Ultimately, a theory of gravitational repulsion in which place expands is decisive for an ethics of sexual difference. A phallocentric cosmos is one in which gravity is strictly understood as an attractive force, bodies are discrete, and places are containers for those bodies. The theory of an extendable matrix, by contrast, calls for a revolutionary concept of gravity as a matrix that extends itself. This flies in the face of Aristotle's cosmic container in which bodies are pulled toward their proper places, but places themselves have no movement or locomotion. As the origin place of all elemental bodies, the cosmos is an expanding womb: "in some manner a transmutation of earth into heaven, here and now."[41] The containing body "[weaves] the veil of time, the fabric of time, time with space, time in space. Between past and future, future and past, place in place. Invisible. Its vessel? Its container? The soul of the soul?"[42] Irigaray insists on rethinking the cosmic womb through an ethics of sexual difference, "always working to produce a place of transcendence for the sensible [by] accompanying cosmic time. Between man's time and the time of the universe."[43]

Cosmic Umbilical Cords and Fetal Big Bangs

> It is only belatedly, marginally and not without resistances that science has become interested in "the partly-opened," in the "permeability of membranes," in the theory of "fields," in the "dynamic of fluids," in the current programming of discourse, in the "dialogic," etc. Now these objectives have more affinity with the feminine universe.
>
> —Luce Irigaray, "Thinking Life as Relation"

In this second section, I examine an umbrella of theories that postulate the conditions for embryonic or baby universes to emerge from some more primordial multiverse. These encompass the theory of the Big Bang, but also extend to some highly speculative theories that precede and are concomitant with the event itself. These include theories of cosmic inflation, false vacuum bubbles, primordial black holes, and quantum tunneling. Importantly, this arena of speculative physics addresses the fundamental laws of reality that subsequently call for reconciling the laws governing the quantum world and those governing our observable universe. Positing a "complete" theory of cosmic origin and expansion would not be possible without overcoming this aporia, which scientists take to mean developing a theory of *quantum gravity*, what Stephen Hawking claims would be necessary to explain primordial black holes: "The uncertainty principle allows particles to escape from what was thought to be the ultimate prison, a black hole."[44] In short, "one therefore has to find a new theory that combines general relativity with the uncertainty principle [of quantum mechanics]."[45] Very plainly, the conditions for the emergence of space and time cannot be space and time itself. Quantum gravity must therefore play some role in the gestation and formation of this universe. But if its role was pivotal during the formation of the ultra-early universe, why do quantum laws seem incompatible with the gravitational law, even though it is compatible with the laws of other interactions in our universe?

Some fundamental physicists and early-universe cosmologists speculate during the Planck era, approximately 10^{-43} seconds, the universe was so hot and dense that the fabric of space-time itself was made up of quantum fluctuations, frothing like foam, which included many primordial black holes:

> Some theorists believe it is no longer premature to explore what physical laws prevailed at the Planck time, and have already come up with fascinating ideas; there is no consensus, though, about which concepts might really fly. We must certainly jettison cherished commonsense notions of space and time: space-time on this tiny scale may have a chaotic foamlike structure, with no well-defined arrow of time; there may be no timelike dimension at all; tiny black holes may be continually appearing and merging. The activity may be violent enough to spawn new domains of space-time that evolve into separate universes.[46]

Hawking was able to provide a mathematical calculation demonstrating that gravity emits negative energy density particles out of primordial black holes. In other words, primordial black holes defy the notion that all black holes, like Aristotelian place, merely pull massive bodies toward them as they collapse in on themselves. Instead, particles are pushed out, or expelled, from primordial black holes, which means the definition of gravity as strictly attractive is insufficient to account for this phenomenon. This process of quantum tunneling through a primordial black hole, or umbilical cord, is crucial to the process of forming a baby universe.

Sometimes a quantum fluctuation takes the form of a false vacuum bubble, a patch of vacuum characterized by big energy density with negative pressure. This bubble is surrounded by empty space. When the false vacuum bubble goes through the primordial black hole, it inverts or turns the pressure of the bubble inside out: "Once the wormhole develops, a dramatic change takes place—the bubble has turned inside out. Now the region of false vacuum can grow larger and larger without encroaching on the original space. It creates new space as it expands, resembling an inflating balloon."[47] Eventually, the false vacuum bubble grows extremely large and detaches from its parent universe: "forming a new, completely isolated closed universe."[48] According to Alan Guth, this process takes approximately 10^{-30} seconds, and during this time, the baby universe grows or "inflates" by a factor of 10^{25}. It takes the child universe roughly 10^{-37} seconds to detach. The black hole disappears or evaporates within 10^{-23} seconds, and finally when the umbilical cord is completely severed, the "standard" Big Bang theory begins at t=0 seconds.

Stephen Hawking's 1974–1975 papers on primordial black holes posit that black holes are themselves quantum-sized or subatomic, which means they do not follow the same rules as classical black holes. For instance, they *radiate* quantum particles that "leap" or "tunnel" faster than the speed of light, a violation of Einstein's general relativity:

> As a black hole gives off particles and radiation, it will lose mass. This will cause the black hole to get smaller and to send out particles more rapidly. Eventually, it will get down to zero mass and will disappear completely. What will happen then to the objects . . . that have fallen into the black hole? According to some recent work of mine, the answer is that they will go off into a little baby universe of their own. A small, self-contained universe branches off from our region of the universe. This baby universe may join on again to our region of space-time. If it does, it would appear to us to be another black hole that formed and then evaporated. Particles that fell into one black hole would appear as particles emitted by the other black hole, and vice versa.[49]

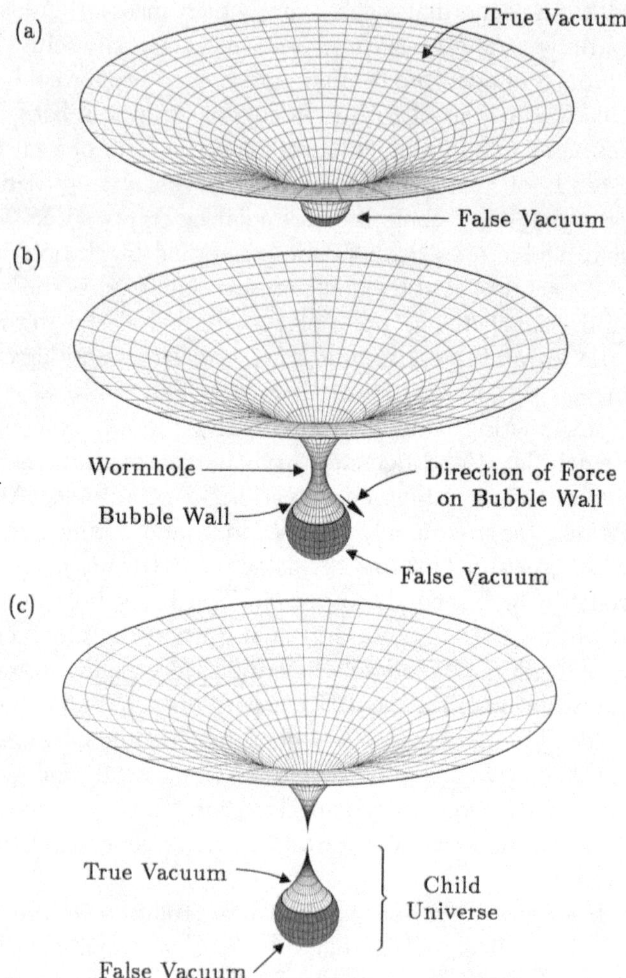

Figure 4.1. Alan H. Guth, "The Creation of a Child Universe," in *The Inflationary Universe: The Quest for a New Theory of Cosmic Origins* (New York: Addison-Wesley, 1997), 262, figure 16.4.

From this, it becomes feasible to imagine that the Big Bang of *this* universe is the result of a small quantum fluctuation that emerged from a primordial black hole. It is possible that our universe is one among an infinite number of universes, of quantum fluctuations, within the multiverse. But how does a tiny, subatomic fluctuation become a universe, such as ours, containing over one hundred thousand galaxies and spanning more than five hundred million light-years?

Martin Rees echoes this question when he asks: "Can the space inside the hole sprout into an entire new universe through a quantum effect?"[50] For this sprout to occur, a quantum fluctuation is not enough to explain how the subatomic evolves into the ultra-large. According to Rees, Guth's inflationary theory provides the answer: "Very early on, the expansion would have been exponentially *accelerated*, so that an embryo universe could have inflated, homogenized, and established the fine-tuned balance between gravitational and kinetic energy when it was only 10^{-36} seconds old."[51] Inflation attempts to explain the "bang" part of the Big Bang: the propulsion of space from quantum uncertainty to general relativity. Prior to the theory of inflation, Big Bang proponents had no explanation for the universe's expansion; they simply took it as given. In this sense, the theory of the Big Bang prior to the hypothesis of inflation was really only a theory of the *aftermath* of the Big Bang. Inflationary theory in unison with primordial black holes opens new avenues for understanding the different capacities of gravity, which exceed the classical Aristotelian or even Newtonian conceptions. Gravity can no longer be confined to the force of attraction, inversely proportional to the square of the distance between two massive objects.

While this definition of gravity works at the cosmic level, it does not hold the same way in the quantum world. By thinking about gravity at the quantum level, it becomes clear that it is not a universally attractive force. It also has the capacity for repulsion or expansion. What's more, it is not only applicable to bodies within space-time but to the movement of space-time itself. Vacuum fluctuations "bubble" into patches of false vacuum: "The false vacuum has a negative pressure which creates a repulsive gravitational field, capable of driving the universe into a period of *exponential expansion* called *inflation*."[52] Thereafter, inflationary theory posits a universe might evolve from an initial seed of vacuum fluctuation by tapping into the reservoir of negative energy from the gravitational field: "No energy is needed to produce a gravitational field but energy is released when a gravitational field is created."[53] The wall of the false vacuum bubble *expands outward* because of the strong negative gravitational repulsion: "One might guess that the gravitational repulsion of the false vacuum would push outward on the bubble wall, so if this repulsion were strong enough, the bubble would start to grow."[54] This false vacuum bubble is surrounded by empty space, or "true vacuum."

The boundary between the true vacuum and the false vacuum bubble is the bubble wall. If gravity and pressure from the true vacuum push inward on the bubble wall, it eventually collapses into another black hole. However, if the false vacuum bubble has a strong initial outward velocity, it creates an indentation in the curvature of space-time, and:

> As the bubble grows the indentation will become deeper. The indentation will continue to deepen, developing a neck, or *wormhole*. Once the wormhole develops, a dramatic change takes place—the bubble has turned inside out. Now the region of false vacuum can grow larger and larger without encroaching on the original space. It creates new space as it expands, resembling an inflating balloon. After the formation of the wormhole, the pressure difference continues to exert a force from the true vacuum toward the false vacuum. Now, however, this forces acts to cause the bubble wall to enlarge! The climax of evolution is shown in the region of false vacuum, with a region of true vacuum attached, disconnects from the parent space [true vacuum], forming a new, completely isolated closed universe [from false vacuum]. It will then continue to enlarge, going through the usual evolution of an inflationary universe. A new universe has been created, and the parent universe is unharmed—universe creation is not a doomsday machine. From the point of view of the parent universe, the "umbilical cord" of the child universe is indistinguishable from a black hole. The umbilical cord connection in the child universe would similarly look like a black hole.[55]

The "umbilical cord" that the false vacuum bubble travels through is the primordial black hole. This allows for the gravitational field to reverse and expand itself out into a new extendable matrix. The umbilical cord gives the gravitational field the capacity to invert, or turn inside-out so that it might expand instead of contract and collapse. The probability that a false vacuum bubble will tunnel through a hole and expand depends on its mass density and initial velocity. The umbilical cord orients the emission of negative gravitational energy within the bubble, which propels its inflation. Guth's theory, therefore, relies on Hawking radiation, which proves that primordial black holes have the capacity to emit quantum particles. As umbilical cords, these black holes tunnel subatomic vacuum bubbles, inciting the rapid "expansion" or "inflation" of the bubble into its own massive universe. These baby universes eventually detach and become self-enclosed, marking their own origin and capacity for locomotion. In a word, gravity's potential becomes even more generative when it is "negative" or expansive rather than "attractive," but this requires a rethinking of the extendable matrix, including its quantum, maternal origins.

Conclusion

Hawking's primordial black holes, Guth's inflation, and related theories attempt to think through the logical gap between quantum mechanics and general relativity to arrive at the underlying conditions of emergence of the universe itself. I link this impulse in contemporary cosmology and fundamental physics to Irigaray's ethics of sexual difference, as a method of unearthing or revealing the feminine-maternal often covered over in phallocentric philosophical and physical theories. Irigaray provides a critique of Aristotle's concept of place in "Place, Interval" that hinges on his claim that place itself has no origin and is nonlocomotive because it functions as the origin and condition of locomotion for bodies. However, I argue it is possible to reimagine place as an extendable matrix by renegotiating what kind of "interval" the umbilical cord generates between place and bodies that emerge from place. A brand new way of thinking the interval emerges in reconceiving the maternal body in line with negative energy potential latent in a gravitational field. Irigaray's ethics of sexual difference asserts the maternal body is the first place, or the place of origin of the fetus. Nonetheless, she resists that this place is merely a container without its own place: an origin and capacity for locomotion through expansion-contraction.

Fundamental physics offers an alternative to Aristotle's *Physics* for thinking the conditions of emergence of place and bodies that brings the maternal universe, or multiverse, to the fore. The occasion for this essay has been to suggest Irigaray's call for a more highly nuanced theory of place aligns with theories that rely on the principle of quantum gravity. This comes out of the way she reads umbilical cords through the physics of an extendable matrix in opposition to Aristotle for whom elemental bodies require gravitational attraction toward their natural place. The umbilical cord as the generator of an interval reorients the relation from gravitational attraction to gravitational repulsion in this reading. For this reason, I contend Irigaray might prefer the primordial black hole umbilical cord that inverts gravity so that it becomes expansive rather than contractive, repulsive rather than attractive. In this way, a baby universe might become its own extendable matrix rather than relying on the multiverse to function as its indefinite place, or container. This is a new and different way of thinking the conditions of Big Bang universes apart from what currently exists in the standard model, which only begins to think about the questions of origin and motion at *t=1* second, effectively erasing any consideration of maternal conditions of emergence in the interval between physics and metaphysics.

Notes

1. Irigaray ESD, 7.

2. Irigaray S, 133.

3. Martin Rees, *Before the Beginning: Our Universe and Others* (New York: Basic Books, 1998), 2.

4. Stephen Weinberg, *The First Three Minutes: A Modern View of the Origin of the Universe* (New York: Basic Books, 1977), 8.

5. See Sean Carroll and Jennifer Chen's 2004 paper titled "Spontaneous Inflation and the Origin of the Arrow of Time," or Christopher Gregory Weaver's *Fundamental Causation* where "a cosmogonic model according to which our space-time is produced by the dynamical activity of a background de Sitter *mother universe* together through a quantum tunneling process." Gregory Weaver, *Fundamental Causation: Physics, Metaphysics, and the Deep Structure of the World* (New York: Routledge, 2018), 22.

6. Elizabeth Grosz, *The Incorporeal: Ontology, Ethics, and the Limits of Materialism* (New York: Columbia University Press, 2017), 237.

7. Rebecca Hill, *The Interval: Relation and Becoming in Irigaray, Aristotle, and Bergson* (New York: Fordham University Press, 2012), 24.

8. Emanuela Bianchi, *The Feminine Symptom: Aleatory Matter in the Aristotelian Cosmos* (New York: Fordham University Press, 2014), 136.

9. "This phenomenon is called 'Hawking radiation,' which is true of primordial black holes as well as classical black holes. When so-called vacuum fluctuations, the spontaneous creation and annihilation of particle-antiparticle pairs from the energy of the vacuum, occur at the event horizon of *any* black hole, one of these particles can end up beyond the event horizon while the other is allowed to escape. It would still feel the gravitational attraction of the black hole but would have enough energy to escape it. Primordial black

holes, created from early universe energy-density fluctuations, are distinct from classical black holes which are formed from the collapse of stars. Primordial black holes no longer exist but might have played a role in the evolution of the early universe. What has a 'negative' gravitation effect is dark energy: a hypothesized field that exerts a negative pressure on space-time to explain why the universe's expansion is observed to be accelerating. If there was only the attractive gravitational force, then the universe might still be expanding from the Big Bang but that expansion would have to be slowing down. However, it is not, which is a puzzle given the ad hoc term 'Dark energy.'" Mark Kruse, personal correspondence.

10. Hill, *The Interval*, 55–56.
11. Bianchi, *The Feminine Symptom*, 120–121.
12. Bianchi, *The Feminine Symptom*, 120–121.
13. Bianchi, *The Feminine Symptom*, 86.
14. Bianchi, *The Feminine Symptom*, 50.
15. Casey, *The Fate of Place*, 71.
16. Irigaray ESD, 37.
17. Irigaray ESD, 34.
18. Irigaray ESD, 37.
19. Irigaray ESD, 52.
20. Hill, *The Interval*, 59–60.
21. Irigaray ESD, 50.
22. Irigaray ESD, 34.
23. Irigaray ESD, 51.
24. Casey, *The Fate of Place*, 325.
25. Casey, *The Fate of Place*, 325.
26. Irigaray ESD, 36.
27. Irigaray ESD, 34.
28. Irigaray ESD, 36.
29. Irigaray ESD, 39.
30. Irigaray ESD, 39.
31. Hill, *The Interval*, 68.
32. Irigaray ESD, 39.
33. Irigaray ESD, 40.
34. Irigaray ESD, 42.
35. Irigaray ESD, 48.
36. Irigaray ESD, 48.
37. Irigaray ESD, 48.
38. Irigaray ESD, 49.
39. Irigaray ESD, 48.
40. Irigaray ESD, 50.
41. Irigaray ESD, 53.

42. Irigaray ESD, 53.

43. Irigaray ESD, 53.

44. Stephen Hawking, *Black Holes and Baby Universes and Other Essays* (New York: Bantam Books, 1993), 73.

45. Hawking, *Black Holes and Baby Universes*, 70.

46. Rees, *Before the Beginning*, 158.

47. Alan H. Guth, *The Inflationary Universe: The Quest for a New Theory of Cosmic Origins* (New York: Addison-Wesley, 1997), 261–262.

48. Guth, *The Inflationary Universe*, 263.

49. Hawking, *Black Holes and Baby Universes*, 110.

50. Martin Rees, *Before the Beginning*, 181–182.

51. Martin Rees, *Before the Beginning*, 167–168.

52. Guth, *The Inflationary Universe*, 331.

53. Guth, *The Inflationary Universe*, 12.

54. Guth, *The Inflationary Universe*, 257.

55. Guth, *The Inflationary Universe*, 262–263.

Bibliography

Aristotle. "Physics IV." In *The Complete Works of Aristotle: The Revised Oxford Translation*, edited by Jonathan Barnes, 783–835. Princeton, NJ: Princeton University Press, 1984.

Aristotle. "On the Heavens." In *The Complete Works of Aristotle: The Revised Oxford Translation*, edited by Jonathan Barnes, 447–511. Princeton, NJ: Princeton University Press, 1984.

Bianchi, Emanuela. *The Feminine Symptom: Aleatory Matter in the Aristotelian Cosmos*. New York: Fordham University Press, 2014.

Carroll, Sean, and Jennifer Chen. "Spontaneous Inflation and the Origin of the Arrow of Time." 2004. hep-th/0410270.

Casey, Edward S. *The Fate of Place: A Philosophical History*. Berkeley: University of California Press, 1997.

Guth, Alan H. *The Inflationary Universe: The Quest for a New Theory of Cosmic Origins*. New York: Addison-Wesley, 1997.

Grosz, Elizabeth. Keynote Address, The Feminist Theory Workshop, Duke University, Durham, NC, March 2007. https://www.youtube.com/watch?v=mwHoswjw5yo.

Grosz, Elizabeth. *The Incorporeal: Ontology, Ethics, and the Limits of Materialism*. New York: Columbia University Press, 2017.

Hawking, Stephen. *Black Holes and Baby Universes and Other Essays*. New York: Bantam Books, 1993.

Hawking, Stephen. *A Brief History of Time: From the Big Bang to Black Holes.* New York: Bantam Books, 1988.

Hawking, Stephen. "Stephen Hawking Discusses Baby Universes, UC Berkeley 1988." Lecture. https://www.youtube.com/watch?v=_SW7I5SBRhs. Accessed October 18, 2018.

Hill, Rebecca. *The Interval: Relation and Becoming in Irigaray, Aristotle, and Bergson.* New York: Fordham University Press, 2012.

Irigaray, Luce. *An Ethics of Sexual Difference.* Translated by Carolyn Burke and Gillian C. Gill. Ithaca, NY: Cornell University Press, 1993.

Rees, Martin. *Before the Beginning: Our Universe and Others.* New York: Basic Books, 1998.

Satz, Helmut. *Before Time Began: The Big Bang and the Emerging Universe.* Oxford: Oxford University Press, 2017.

Tryon, Edward P. "Is the Universe a Vacuum Fluctuation?" *Nature* 246 (December 1973): 396–397.

Weaver, Christopher Gregory. *Fundamental Causation: Physics, Metaphysics, and the Deep Structure of the World.* New York: Routledge, 2018.

Weinberg, Steven. *The First Three Minutes: A Modern View of the Origin of the Universe.* New York: Basic Books, 1977.

Chapter Five

Irigarayan Ontology and the Possibilities of Sexual Difference

James Sares

Introduction

The purpose of this chapter is to develop an account of sexual ontology, grounded in and responsive to Irigaray's philosophy, that is structured around the question of possibility. Following and developing her work, I argue that the importance of possibility for sexual ontology is twofold. First, it indicates a sexuate being's irreducible, hence ontological, relationality to sexuate otherness given the differentiation of its *own* body. Insofar as this differentiation is structured through a greater logic of generational reproduction, a sexually differentiated being refers *in itself* to the sex(es)/form(s) of sexuate morphology that it is not.[1] With the term "sex/form of sexuate morphology," I understand sex expansively in terms of commonly structured morphologies and capacities associated with the potentiality for sexual reproduction, thus particularly in terms of primary sex characteristics but also in terms of secondary sex characteristics.[2] This expansive definition, which I keep open here yet, which one may further specify and refine, allows us to keep in mind a myriad of traits at play in lived, sexuate embodiment. At the same time, I leave open how an individual might embody these differentiated sex characteristics in combinations or developments that diverge from the predominant expressions of a species, understood loosely here in terms of individuals whose properties are commonly structured by a particular genealogy and reproductive logic.[3] Second, a focus on possibility underscores how sexual difference opens multiple potentials, within the determinate—though not deterministic[4]—bounds of distinct sexes/forms of sexuate morphology, for the development of singular beings. Morphological determinateness engenders shared opportunities or tendencies for development at the same time that it allows for differences in actions, relations, and expressions over time and among individuals.

With the resources of Irigaray's philosophy, I argue that sexuate morphology incarnates an ontological condition, in the sense that the beings structured by sexual difference cannot exist or develop outside of a relationality to this structure in the two aforementioned senses. One purpose of this chapter is to shift an understanding of sex from a merely biological discussion about reproductive capacity to one that also engages the ontological dimensions of this materiality, including how it limits and opens possibilities for the development of living beings. As such, I claim that Irigaray's philosophy opens space for examining how sexual difference both structures the relational being of sexuate beings and also brings about dynamic and historically developing relationships and embodiments through its structural determinations.

In what follows, I examine sexual difference as it incarnates an ontological relationality through distinct morphological forms. First, in conversation with Elizabeth Grosz, I consider how one might understand an Irigarayan ontology as grounded in the idea that much of natural life must be thought as irreducibly relational, through the differentiation of sexes/forms of sexuate morphology. This relationality has been understood primarily in terms of how any singular sexuate being cannot exist outside of actual relations to sexuate otherness—reproductive and otherwise—that have engendered its own existence and that enable future generations. Second, in view of new reproductive technologies, I consider sexual difference through the question of possibility in order to extend its ontological significance beyond the immediacy of actual relations with sexuate others, in virtue of a being's *own* differentiated morphology. Third, I consider how sexual difference has more than a merely negative function by describing how it allows the space for development and action. Finally, applying these principles to the human being, I consider in what sense Irigaray takes sexual difference as a condition of subjectivity. I argue that Irigaray's insights open us to possibilities for new forms of embodiment through cultural mediations and technologies in view of the ontological nature of sexual difference.[5]

Being (at least) Two

I begin my analysis by considering how the possibility of sexual difference itself appears in the context of natural history, as a structure of being that contributes to the development and diversification of life. In several texts, Irigaray underscores the connection between sexual difference and the creative development of life. For instance, in *I Love to You*, she writes that sexual difference is the condition of possibility of the "realms of the living," which would not exist in their complexity and diversity without sexual differentiation.[6] Similarly, in *Sexes and Genealogies*, Irigaray writes that sexual difference helps to structure nature's creative evolution across generational cycles, as opposed to a mechanical repetition of the same.[7] Irigaray's expansive view of sexual difference in these texts, and in her recent work like *Through Vegetal Being*, offer possibilities to engage the question of sexual difference in her work beyond the merely human and toward life more generally. Indeed, these texts demonstrate the ways in which sexual difference can be thought as emerging in the course of natural history, as both grounded in life and enabling new forms for life. As Irigaray writes in *To Be Born*, sexual difference "represents a limited structure that life itself gives."[8] While Irigaray writes here of the human being more specifically, such a claim can be expanded to consider how sexual difference structures the development and expression of an array of living beings.

Yet, how might we understand the ways in which nature or life itself "gives" sexual difference? Following Irigaray, Elizabeth Grosz writes that sexual difference lends to the increasingly complex formation of unique and irreplaceable living beings out of their environments.[9] Insofar as organisms actively engage and appropriate their inorganic environments and exist with spatiotemporal horizons, they are able to express, direct, and preserve their singularity. Sexual difference further contributes to these active engagements by positioning living beings in relation to each other, so as to enable possibilities for individual development and generational reproduction. As Grosz indicates in linking Irigaray and Darwin, the capacity of organisms for sexual selection or other kinds of relational engagements with sexuate others *directly* and *directedly* contributes to the diversity of life by enabling organismic populations to better adapt to and creatively transform their environments. Thus, with particular emphasis on the theory of evolution, Grosz underscores how sexual difference introduces greater possibilities for newness and directionality to life, in contrast with the more limited powers of merely asexual reproduction.[10]

From this perspective, Irigaray's philosophical project engages the underappreciated ontological implications of the dependence of much of life on the union of or interval between sexes. Grosz takes the heart of Irigaray's philosophy to be her understanding of the structure of being as irreducibly relational,[11] insofar as the creativity of life is driven by the differentiation of beings in/as (at least) two sexes/forms of sexuate morphology.[12] Following Grosz, Irigaray's philosophy can be read ontologically as staking out a sexuate "mode of being"[13]—emerging in nature and further contributing to natural diversity—that exists through one's irreducible embodied relationality to sexuate otherness. Importantly, sexual difference is not a timeless structure over and above organisms, as if "applied" to them externally. Rather, this difference is always incarnated in the morphologies of singular beings and in the various relations they can form with sexuate others. While the ways that any living being may relate to the structure of sexual difference depend on historical constitution and shift between and within species, all sexuate beings necessarily relate to it in some way, through the structuring of their being according to the differentiation of sexes/forms of sexuate morphology.

Grosz's emphasis on the ontological dimensions of Irigaray's work is important because it brings into view the need to examine relations engendered by sexual difference, both at the level of an organism's genealogies and filiations and at the level of its active engagements with sexuate others. The clearest way that singular beings exist in relation to sexual difference is that most sexuate organisms emerge *directly* from the copulative union of different sexes and rely on making these copulative unions to bring forth new generations.[14] Grosz explicitly warns against reducing sexual difference to a question of reproduction alone, given that it also structures various other kinds of engagements between living beings and their environments.[15]

Nevertheless, neither should we underemphasize the ontological importance of a singular sexuate emerging from the reproductive union of sexes. As Irigaray writes in *To Be Born*—albeit, once more, specifically of the human being—"we have been conceived by two but we are only one, even if we embody something of the two who have conceived us."[16] A more expansive application of this principle to other kinds of natural life underscores the importance of sexual selection and the materiality of reproductive relations by which successive generation takes place. It becomes necessary to consider how singular beings emerge out of embodied relations between different sexes/forms of sexuate morphology, such that any "one" requires unions between sexes in order to exist at all. Indeed, from this perspective, sexual difference is ontological because any singular sexuate being carries with it, in its very singularity, an irreducible relationality to the otherness that has directly engendered it.

Thinking the Possibility of Sexual Difference

My argument for the ontological nature of sexual difference has a slightly different emphasis away from the immediate actuality of relations with sexuate otherness. Grosz's work typifies the natural—and justified—tendency to engage the ontological dimensions of sexual difference in terms of the concrete relations of actually existing beings.[17] Irigaray herself thinks in these terms. While I agree that these actual relations must be examined in order to develop a rigorous sexual ontology, I also want to consider how reproductive technologies may problematize the tendency to focus on these relations *only* in their immediate actuality. In view of technologies like *in vitro gametogenesis*, which has been realized in some animals and appears on the horizon for the human being, there seem to be new possibilities for reproduction no longer requiring copulative unions between different sexes. How would we understand a future in which a sexually differentiated species has been selectively engineered to be only one sex, in accordance with such reproductive technologies? What about cloning technologies that would reduce such a sexually differentiated being to the most radical "one" conceivable? Thinking through these possibilities requires disentwining the ontological nature of sexual difference from the immediacy of reproductive relations—or, indeed, any other immediately present relationships—between sexes. Far from a digression or distraction, consideration of these technologies clarifies the sense in which sexual difference is an irreducible, ontological condition of any sexuate being, regardless of the actual relations it forms with sexuate others.

In the context of Irigaray's philosophy, Stephen Seely has already disentwined the question of sexual difference from a focus on these kinds of actual relations. In conversation also with Simondon, Seely argues that an individual is sexed in "countless" ways given the prepersonal, "virtual" flows that persist in it and contribute to genetic transfers and creative investments between the self and its environments.[18] Yet, such an understanding of sex does not capture the determinate morphological difference with which I am concerned at this stage of analysis. I reject Seely's definition of sex as "the capacity to engage in exchange with another body"[19] because, in my view, this definition is too abstract to understand the unique ontological situation of sexuate being. Such a definition muddies this ontological situation because it allows *all* of life—even asexual bacteria (who indeed conjugate with each other but not via distinct sexes)—to be sexed "virtually." Doubtlessly, transfers between an organism and its environments or even across its own cells contributes to and underlies its development. However, in my view, the ontological condition of sexuate being occurs in an entirely different register based on the determinateness of morphological limitation in relation to sexuate others, especially as they can enable the directed, generational reproduction of life.

In view of this concern for engaging a sexuate being's necessary reference to sexuate otherness, I argue instead for expanding an ontological understanding of sexual difference in terms of *possibility*. A sexuate being carries an irreducible, hence ontological, relationality to sexual difference simply by being differentiated through a reproductive logic referring it to the sex(es)/form(s) of sexuate morphology that this *one* is not. This understanding of sexual difference encompasses the situation of all sexuate life today while extending its ontological nature beyond it, even if technological innovations like cloning would allow for only one sex/form of sexuate morphology of a species to *actually* exist in the world. In other words, a sexuate being is sexuate because its differentiated morphology always already relates to sexuate otherness, and thus is structured/limited by it, regardless of extrinsic circumstances or relations with actual others. Importantly, this kind of ontological negativity—of not being the "All" in relation to an other—has been discussed by Irigaray and has been taken up in the secondary literature.[20] Yet, these accounts tend to focus on the human being and the question of ethical relations with and recognition of *actual* others. In this chapter, I extend this consideration beyond the human and beyond this kind of actuality. Indeed, regardless of whether a sexuate being were "freed" from the immediacy of dependence on reproductive copulation or other relations with sexuate others, sexual differentiation remains essential to that being and thus lies at the heart of its ontological condition, without which its singular existence would be undifferentiated.

Despite this shift to thinking sexual difference in terms of possibility, I again emphasize the importance of examining how relations between different sexes/forms of sexuate morphology actually manifest and structure life. An extension of the ontological significance of sexual difference beyond the immediacy of reproductive (among other) relations between sexuate beings aids in understanding how these beings are always already relationally differentiated through their *own* morphologies. Yet, we are confronted with at least three complications that underscore the importance of considering the actuality of sexual difference in view of these technologies. First, actual relations between sexuate others would remain a *historically* or *genealogically* irreducible condition for those sexuate beings affected by reproductive technologies, such that their singularity could be seen as dependent on these relations in a qualified sense.[21] Second, perhaps sexually differentiated morphologies would remain "actual" in some circumstances and to some degree, for instance, given the need of *in vitro gametogenesis* for artificially produced sperm and egg from stem cells. Third, an account of sexual difference via limits on possible embodiment must consider the ways that these limitations *actually* emerge or are generated in relation to other possibilities. If sexual difference involves the ontological relationality to other sexes/forms of sexuate morphology incarnated by a sexuate being, how is it that this otherness *can* appear in relation to it?

Given these complications, the problem of ontological negativity provokes the concern to examine how sexual difference can bring about actual relations between and among sexuate beings. Examining the emergence of these relations also requires considering how sexual difference can be embodied and developed in various ways by individuals. Indeed, an account of the possibilities of sexual difference must engage not only how beings are structured/limited in relation to sexual difference but also how this limitation opens various potentials for their singular development. As such, I turn to how distinct sexes/forms of sexuate morphology exist in relation to each other and are lived by singular beings open to a variety of expressions.

Sexual Difference and Sexuate Embodiment

As I understand it, the task of a critical sexual ontology is to overcome an understanding of sexual difference that either denies the malleability of sexuate embodiment or the nonarbitrary determinacy of the difference itself. In my view, this can be overcome only if we reconcile the irreplaceability of singular beings with the structural determinateness engendered by sexual difference. As emphasized by Alison Stone,[22] and as recently motioned toward by Irigaray herself,[23] sexual difference can be understood as "framing" determinate limits to and thus establishing different sexes/forms of sexuate morphology, and hence as giving a situation for the individual sexuate being to develop and engage with the world. Insofar as sexual difference organizes morphological forms enabling the reproduction of life itself, singular beings incarnate a determinate structure that transcends their mere individuality. Yet, because sexual difference is incarnated through singular beings rather than existing as something abstractly transcendent to them, sexuate embodiment is not a static or purely identical givenness among individuals, nor must individuals act or develop in relation to their sexuate determinations in precisely the same ways. The expressions of sexuate embodiment are open to development through and with environmental contexts and a being's own singularity, though only as it is structured in relation to the distinct forms of sexuate morphology enabling that organism to emerge as itself.

Irigaray's claim that "life itself" gives the structure of sexual difference underscores the need to do justice to the ways that sexuate beings are nonarbitrarily yet dynamically differentiated according to distinct forms of sexuate morphology. To be sexuate is to be morphologically structured in relation to primary sex characteristics associated with the possibility of generational reproduction, alongside the other morphological traits that follow therefrom. Far from a reductive question of reproductive teleology, however, these traits help to organize the multiplicity of relations an organism develops with its environments and thus structure the lived embodiment of that singular being.

To emphasize once more, and with greater specificity, there is never a pure identity of qualities among singular beings but rather a more or less "coinhabited" relational locus vis-à-vis sexual difference, based on shared morphological determination and limitation yet open to individual differences and developments. Individuals share qualities and can be classified together as such, in relation to sexual difference, without being reducible to one another. While Irigaray does not thematize this issue extensively, there may always be some kind of variation in sexually differentiated characteristics between individuals, including genetics, hormones, (in)fertility/reproductive fitness, or genital appearance. However, these differences are structured through the determinate forms of sexuate morphology organizing the generational reproduction of the individuals of a species that may express some or all of these qualities. As such, doing justice to the complexities of the structure of sexual difference demands comprehensive concern for how sexuation is embodied and lived through a multiplicity of commonalities and differences. Depending on the organism, this comprehensive concern may include engaging how traits may be open to qualitative change and how individuals may relate to the structure of sexual difference in multiple ways over time (including the development or dissolution of certain sexually differentiated qualities or functions). It may also include examining how sexual difference may be expressed in ways that challenge the predominant distribution or development of sexually differentiated characteristics in a species (perhaps, at times, leading to evolutionary divergences and new structures of life).[24]

Regardless of the precise combinations or developments of sex characteristics, however, these characteristics are differentiated in some relation to distinct morphological forms that organize the possibility of generational reproduction. As such, it is necessary to consider their differentiation as structured according to such a relationality. Irigaray often expresses this structure through the language of "the two," which has been a source of significant criticism for its perceived incapacity to engage with sexual difference outside of sexed or gendered binaries. Yet, as I interpret it, the invocation of "the two" functions simply to underscore a minimum of differentiated sexes/forms of sexuate morphology for sexuate beings, rather than a delineation of how these beings must experience and develop their bodies. Given her recent work on the "frame" of sexual difference and her care for exploring the different expressions of sex across organismic life (even the vegetal), it is clear that Irigaray understands a diversity of sexuate expressions to arise from this minimum difference. For instance, fungi have mating types that, although typically not understood as "sexes," involve a minimum morphological difference for generational reproduction; the hermaphroditism of certain plants and animals internalizes a difference of two *within* themselves; and a predominantly dimorphic logic organizes life in "higher" animals. In view of this diversity of organic expression, we can read Irigaray to be concerned with doing justice to how distinct forms of sexuate morphology—not necessarily restricted to only two, for certain species in reproductive logic and certainly for many in actual expression[25]—incarnate an ontological relationality that can be expressed in myriad ways, between and within species.

Accordingly, my interpretation of Irigarayan ontology engages both the determinate structures of sexual difference and also the ways that individuals are open to development with and through these determinations. Recognizing differences in sexuate expression or morphological development at the level of individuals, generations, and species does not require an abandonment of the determinate structures engendering distinct sexes/forms of sexuate morphology. Rather, understanding sexual difference as the "frame" of an individual's singularity maintains both the determinateness that this difference *is* for structuring the possibility of its life and also the ways that it may develop (in relation to) its determinations, as it involves the specificities of the circumstances it engages or in which it finds itself. As I have developed this argument here, achieving this analytic complexity requires distinguishing sexual difference as a structure engendering distinct sexes/forms of sexuate morphology from the dynamic ways that sexually differentiated characteristics, structured in some relation thereto, are developed and distributed in and by singular beings.

I thus agree with other readers who take Irigaray's philosophy to provide opportunities for engaging how the determinations of sexual difference engender dynamic possibilities for singular beings. As Ruthanne Crapo writes, sexual difference "sets forth the general conditions of possibility and impossibility without foreclosing on possible changes, mutations, and transmutations," opening up the space for "real existent individuals" and mandating "the need for every creature to be(come) themselves" as uniquely singular.[26] Crapo invokes readings by Jane Gallop and Margaret Whitford that take Irigaray's emphasis on morphology—specifically for the human being but also more broadly applicable to other organisms—not to stultify the body but instead to engage how its sexuate structuring opens horizons on which one can develop and establish connections with the world.[27] As such, although sexuate embodiment is structured through certain determinate limits distinguishing sexes/forms of sexuate morphology, these limits are not static, unchanging, or unnegotiable. They are not merely a dead, negative imposition but also the space for a "positive" coming-to-be.[28] Following this interpretative strain, avenues are opened for considering how the sexuate body itself may give unique opportunities—though not strict inevitabilities—for action and development based on morphological determinateness. Although I lack space to provide an exhaustive account of how this coming-to-be might manifest, such an account would require consideration of the ways that singular beings engage various relations in dynamic mediation with and through their sexuate determinations.

On the Human Being

To conclude, I consider how sexual difference operates more specifically for the human being, since we are the locus of concern for most of Irigaray's philosophy. While all sexuate life exists with and through the structures of sexual difference, Irigaray underscores the distinction between merely having a sex and cultivating oneself as sexuate, the latter referring primarily to organisms whose growth and reproduction happens "through sexual attraction and relation between two" and "effective connections" with others.[29] A plant may have sexed parts but require various intermediaries to form reproductive relations with others;[30] an animal may engage in sexual relationships with self-directed movement and more or less consciously at that; the human being develops its subjectivity in relation to its organic givenness and becomes self-conscious as a sexuate subjectivity. Indeed, for Irigaray, the difference between human sexes is above all "a difference in relational identity."[31] While the human being is sexually differentiated like other organisms, this organic situation becomes a question of developing one's subjectivity and linguistically articulated identity in relation to other subjects—a question of how one engages organic determination through identification with or as a sex (or not). For the human being, the question of sexual difference includes what one understands one's sexuate determination to mean for living one's life and how one makes connections with sexuate others accordingly. It also includes the ways that sexual difference can go unthought, erased, or denied as real or ontologically significant.

As Irigaray writes in *To Be Born*, directly invoking Hegel, sexual difference for the human being "is both the place and the mediation which permits the passage of nature and spirit, the one into the other, in each individual, and in this way ensure a real link between one individual and another."[32] Taking spirit in the roughly Hegelian sense of embodied and self-conscious individuals and the institutions they form, Irigaray looks to explain a threshold that is at once natural *and* spiritual—that is, an infrastructure of life itself through which the human being develops its identity as limited and relational. Following Irigaray's warning against invoking nature as a mere immediacy,[33] we may reject claims to pure access to the body outside of its various social and technological mediations. From conception to death, the human body is imbued with social/symbolic meaning and mediated with technologies that transform embodiment. I cannot but think of my body as mediated through social/symbolic meaning and technologies in relation to others. Given this dynamic mediation, sexual difference for the human being is never one-sidedly natural or "spiritual" but rather a site of exchange for the development of subjectivity.

Nevertheless, from the Irigarayan perspective, these meanings and technologies are themselves constrained by morphological differences and bodily capacities that ground the possibility of social and biological (re)production. That we are sexually differentiated is a *necessary* condition on which the human being, and thus all other identities that are products of human history, depends. Historically, the organic structure of sexual difference—particularly the difference between male and female sexes, whose characteristics can be developed and distributed in various ways, opening the human being beyond a reductive dimorphism[34]—has enabled or undergirded the very emergence of this threshold into spirit. Simply put, there could be no human history without sexual difference, through which generational reproduction and individual development have been made possible.

Note the change in verb tense in these previous sentences. One might ask: So what if human history is founded on sexual difference? So what if, up until now, the human being *has* made "effective connections" through sexuate otherness? To push the issue a final time, might the uniquely spiritual existence of the human being engender a more radical split from the relational, sexuate mode of being governing much of life? What if the subject seeks to "develop" their subjectivity by attempting to overcome sexual difference and sexuate embodiment itself? In other words, can the social relations of the human being retroactively "dissolve" their own presocial conditions of possibility by overcoming the limit of sexual difference? Is this retroactive causal power not precisely the unique power of human spirit—that is, to declare itself free of the causes that have conditioned it?

In response to these questions, I emphasize that the natural-spiritual threshold of sexual difference cannot be collapsed without destroying what it means to be human. A danger lies, for Irigaray, when the human power for conceptual abstraction "forgets"—often under the violence of androcentric cultural logics—how sexuate determination and relationality always already structure the possibilities of *embodied* subjectivity. Indeed, an account of human life requires not only concern for commonly shared structures of consciousness but also for sexuate differences incarnated in the finitude of the body.[35] The human being cannot be without the body that "already represents an objectivity," Irigaray writes, insofar as sexual differentiation is a necessary condition for subjectivity.[36] Thus, when thinking through the possibility of technologies that strive to overcome the finitude of the organic body or through the discourses that deny the irreducibility of sexual difference for the being of the human being, we must remember that sexual difference is not merely a reproductive relationship, nor is it something closed off from future development or to new forms that may challenge how it has functioned historically. Once more, reproductive relations between sexes would remain a genealogically irreducible condition of all future human life, regardless of any attempt to "overcome" this condition in actuality. Yet, fundamentally, these relations point to the way that sexual difference involves an ontological relationality to forms of sexuate otherness that one embodies simply by existing with a sexually differentiated morphology. Given that humanity is irreducible to one sex/form of sexuate morphology, any singular human being *must* relate to the structure of sexual difference and thus express it through some kind of embodied, morphological determinateness.

In order to underscore the dynamism of embodiment, it is necessary to return to the ways in which sexual difference may be open to possible future expressions in view of the mediations between sexuate morphology and various social and technological forces. Following Irigaray's insights, a nuanced sexual ontology ought to recognize how the dialectic between organic determination and social/symbolic mediations operates distinctly across historical epochs, grounds various social expressions and identities, and compels various transformations and developments of the sexuate body. Depending on social, historical, and technological conditions, there may be opened or foreclosed routes by which the human subject can relate to its own sexuate embodiment and to sexuate others.[37] In particular, certain corporeal technologies provide the clearest opportunities for transfiguring the structures of sexual difference. First, the technologies of sexual transition reveal the extent to which morphology is subject to development in historically variant ways, perhaps in the future transforming primary sex characteristics in ways not yet available today. Second, the reproductive technologies previously discussed may engender possibilities for a monosexual human existence or otherwise transform the means of generational reproduction away from heterosexual copulation. Third, future transhumanist technologies may offer possibilities for recombining male and female characteristics or for bringing forth new forms of sexuate embodiment not yet imagined.

Irigaray has not written about these kinds of technologies directly, and I cannot explore any of them in sufficient depth here. However, suffice it to say that, in *all* of these cases, sexual difference remains or would remain an irreducible condition of human existence. While I engaged the question of reproductive technologies earlier, I add now that transhumanist technologies and future transition technologies would in no way dissolve our sexuate nature. Regardless of whether technologies bring about new kinds of embodiments or enable greater traversal/transition between sexes, none of these possibilities would render us nonsexuate. They would simply shift the relations between distinct sexuate morphologies that are irreducible to each other in their characteristics. Nor would they destroy the specificities of male and female sexes (as what they embody or not, thus in irreducible ontological relationality to which they are differentiated or not). Hence, regardless of how one is positioned in relation to the male/female distinction, and however these relations change in the future, Irigaray's point holds: the body carries with it a morphologically incarnated, ontological relationality to sexuate otherness, such that one sex/form of sexuate morphology can never exhaust all that is or can be "*the* human."[38] Any pretension to overcome sexual difference would require ignoring the embodied nature of subjectivity, suturing analysis so far from the structures of life itself that there is no organic body left for which to account. To erase this most basic aspect of our existence is to be left with nothing discernably human at all—and this holds for *any* sexuate being.

Conclusion

In this chapter, I have developed an account of sexual ontology that has engaged the question of possibility in two senses: first, in terms of the negativity according to which any one sex/form of sexuate morphology is limited and relational; and second, in terms of the way that this relational structure can open a multiplicity of lived expressions and enable beings to develop in their singularity. In the course of analysis, I have examined how sexual difference is an irreducible structure of much of life without rendering this condition into something static, immutable, or closed off to historical transformations. By laying out the complexities of this account, I have argued against a reading of Irigaray's philosophy as unattuned to this dynamism while also rebuffing a nominalist dispersal of sexual difference. Reconciling these commitments lies in understanding the historical dynamism of the expressions of sexual difference, alongside the ways that these expressions incarnate an irreducible, ontological relationality to distinct sexes/forms of sexuate morphology.

The theme of the future(s) of sexual difference opens fecund ground for Irigaray's work, given her account of its natural-historical emergence and development. The underside of recognizing the historical dynamism of this structure involves the precarity of the future, including the kinds of violence that can be done to sexual difference, whether by technologically manufacturing a monosexual society, or by perpetuating androcentric logics that ignore the importance of sexual difference to life, or by bringing life to extinction, and so on. The issues I have raised in this chapter aid in thinking through the irreducibility of sexual difference as an ontological condition of much of life, and most importantly of the human being, in view of such precarity. Given the dynamism of her account of the relational, sexuate mode of being, Irigaray's critique of cultural and philosophical neutrality remains urgent. As an ontology that need not rely on decontextualized and static notions of sex, it is able to respond to denials of the ontological nature of sexual difference and of the mutability of lived embodiment. Thus, with nuance, it is able to engage the precarity of the future of sexual difference and the various ethical problems that arise therefrom. Perhaps Irigaray's greatest lesson is that we may no longer consider these problems as if we ourselves were outside of sexual difference.

Acknowledgments

I thank Jennifer Carter, Mary Rawlinson, the anonymous reviewers, and the editors of this volume for their extensive comments on drafts of this essay. I also note that there are a number of thematic overlaps between this chapter and another article I have written on Deleuze and Guattari's sexual ontology. However, these topics are engaged under different conceptual apparatuses and in relation to different concerns in the secondary literature. See: James Sares, "The Schizoanalysis of Sex: Toward a Deleuzean-Guattarian Sexual Ontology," *philoSOPHIA: A Journal of transContinental Feminism* 10, no. 1 (2020): 47–70.

Notes

1. My account is intended to be expansive. Organisms that change sex over their lives may embody distinct sexuate morphologies over time or at the same time. Yet, it still holds that a determinate difference between sexes prevents any "one" involved in this difference from being "whole" or representing the organism simpliciter. Similarly, hermaphroditic organisms can still fall under this analysis, insofar as one sexuate *part* of that being does not exhaust what that being is as a *whole* and thus sexual difference is contained *within* themselves. Organisms with life stages lacking developed sex characteristics, may be considered differentiated vis-à-vis the possible sexes they can develop (or not). Finally, a similar idea may even apply to individuals that lack certain sex characteristics in otherwise sexually differentiated species, their being differentiated, in this very lack, in relation to that which they are not. However, I leave it open to debate whether such individuals should be considered "sexuate" in that lack or simply related to sexual difference negatively. Other complications will be made clear later.

2. Two terminological clarifications are in order. First, I refer to "sexuate beings" broadly as those that exist in some relation to sexual differentiation. I prefer "sexuate" to "sexed," insofar as the former better implies not merely a passive condition but also a lived embodiment/expression. However, note that Irigaray often uses the term "*sexuate* difference" with more specific reference to the relationality developing the sexuate subjectivity of the human being. Also note that, out of another personal preference, I use the terms "*sexual* ontology" and "*sexual* difference" throughout this essay. Second, at times, I use the term "sex" alone for stylistic variation with these points in mind. I also use "form of sexuate morphology" alone, for instance, when underscoring how these differentiated morphologies can be found together or in different combinations in individuals, in order to bracket whether these cases may be classified as additional sexes. Generally, my concern in this essay is with how distinct forms of sexuate morphology structure the being of all sexuate beings *in some way*, regardless of further complications with categorization and taxonomy.

3. In contemporary philosophy of biology, species are now often understood in terms of genealogies and homeostatic property clusters, the latter Ingo Brigandt defines as "a cluster of many properties that are more or less correlated, where a kind member need not possess all of these properties" (or possess them in precisely the same way or to precisely the same degree). See: Ingo Brigandt, "Philosophy of Biology," in *The Bloomsbury Companion to the Philosophy of Science*, ed. Steven French and Juha Saatsi (London: Bloomsbury Academic, 2014), 249. This definition avoids the problem of species essentialism in view of the complications presented by evolutionary theory. There may be contestations over where to draw species distinctions, but again, I am not concerned with the complications of taxonomy in this essay.

_4. This is not a metaphysical claim about (in)determinism in nature, which I bracket in this essay. Rather, I underscore how sexuate embodiment is open to reconfiguration, development, and divergent expressions over time and across/within individuals.

5. Given that I am developing an account through Irigaray's philosophy, I follow her in leaving aside outer world skepticism as it involves the natural reality of sexual difference and historical skepticism as it involves the emergence and development of human history. Putting Irigaray's work in conversation with these philosophical issues may be left to future work.

6. Irigaray ILTY, 36. Irigaray might be read as identifying life with sexual difference here, though I disagree with making such an identification given the existence of asexual organisms.

7. Irigaray SG, 107.

8. Irigaray TBB, 3.

9. Elizabeth Grosz, *Becoming Undone: Darwinian Reflections on Life, Politics, and Art* (Durham, NC: Duke University Press, 2011), 101.

10. Grosz, *Becoming Undone*, 101.

11. Grosz, *Becoming Undone*, 100.

12. The qualification "at least," to which I refer again later in this essay, allows us to encompass in our analysis organisms like fungi with multiple mating types. Also, I leave open whether organisms with two sexes in addition to a hermaphroditic form would count as having three distinct sexes, or whether it is better to understand hermaphroditic organisms as internalizing "the two" in themselves. In either case, even truly hermaphroditic organisms like certain plants exhibit sexual difference of "the two" in their distinct *parts*.

13. Grosz, *Becoming Undone*, 102.

14. On the one hand, sexuate exceptions may include organisms that can *also* reproduce asexually, for instance, by budding or by parthenogenesis. On the other hand, this analysis may not apply to *exclusively* parthenogenic beings whose species is "exhausted" by one sex/form of sexuate morphology. In these cases, we must question the genealogies of these beings, such that sexual difference

may be an indirect or genealogical condition of their being. Otherwise, we may accept that these beings do not *currently* fall under the sexuate mode of being in the full sense.

15. Grosz, *Becoming Undone*, 147.

16. Irigaray TBB, 38–39.

17. See also, for instance, Rachel Jones's emphasis on the importance of conceiving sexual difference ontologically in terms of how sexually distinct children relate to the mother, even in utero. Rachel Jones, *Irigaray: Towards a Sexuate Philosophy* (Cambridge: Polity, 2011), 160–198.

18. Stephen Seely, "Does Life Have (a) Sex? Thinking Ontology with Irigaray and Simondon," in *Feminist Philosophies of Life*, ed. Hasana Sharp and Chloë Taylor (Montreal: McGill University Press, 2016), 117.

19. Seely, "Does Life Have (a) Sex?," 115.

20. See, for instance, ILTY, 103; SFO, 58; Catherine Malabou and Ewa Ziarek, "Negativity, Unhappiness or Felicity: On Irigaray's Dialectical Culture of Sexual Difference," *L'Esprit Créateur* 52, no. 3 (2012): 11–25; Laura Roberts, *Irigaray and Politics: A Critical Introduction* (Edinburgh: Edinburgh University Press, 2019), 101–102; and Gail Schwab, "Sexual Difference as a Model: An Ethics for the Global Future," *Diacritics* 28, no. 1 (1998): 76–92.

21. We might even say that any life created by future human technologies would depend on sexual difference genealogically, given their emergence from *our* activities.

22. Alison Stone, *Luce Irigaray and the Philosophy of Sexual Difference* (Cambridge: Cambridge University Press, 2006), 224–229.

23. Irigaray TBB, 3. Although Irigaray invokes Heidegger's *Gestell* in this reference, note that her understanding sexual difference as "frame" does not invoke calculative and instrumental reason but rather is used in the sense of an organic structure of life itself.

24. I use the term "distribution" to refer to how various elements of sexuate embodiment—for instance, genital morphology and chromosomes—may not align in what are "typical" ways for that species, despite these characteristics being differentiated in relation to distinct sexes/forms of sexuate morphology.

25. Irigaray herself leaves this insight open in writing that "the natural is *at least* two." Irigaray ILTY, 35, original emphasis.

26. Ruthanne Crapo, "The Way of Love: Practicing an Irigarayan Ethic," unpublished doctoral dissertation, Vrije Universiteit Amsterdam, 2016, 108.

27. See: Jane Gallop, "Quand nos lèvre s'écrivent: Irigaray's Body Politic," *Romanic Review* 74 (1983): 77–83; and Margaret Whitford, *Luce Irigaray: Philosophy in the Feminine* (New York: Routledge, 1991).

28. I thank Jennifer Carter for emphasizing this point to me over many conversations.

29. Irigaray and Marder, TVB, 79.

30. Irigaray and Marder, TVB, 79.

31. Irigaray KW, 127.

32. Irigaray TBB, 4.

33. Irigaray SG, 3.

34. We may be concerned to do justice to the existence of intersex and trans phenomena, especially as they can involve morphological or chromosomal divergences from the designated "normativity" of male and female sexes. Nevertheless, these complications do not dissolve the reality of male and female sexes, nor the reproductive logic by which that difference emerges and predominates. Moreover, intersex individuals incarnate characteristics of the two and are thus engendered always in relation to them, while transition often occurs from one of these given determinations to/toward another in various relevant aspects. However, I also emphasize a need to be open to and respect a multiplicity of sexuate embodiments, challenging Irigaray's claim that humanity is "composed of women and men and of nothing else." Irigaray ILTY, 47. For a discussion of how Irigaray's philosophy might apply to trans narratives, see: Danielle Poe, "Can Luce Irigaray's Notion of Sexual Difference Be Applied to Transsexual and Transgender Narratives?," in *Thinking with Irigaray*, ed. Mary C. Rawlinson, Sabrina L. Hom, and Serene J. Khader (Albany: State University of New York Press, 2011).

35. Regardless of whether separating consciousness from the body is possible, a mere consciousness or thinking program is not an embodied *human being*. For Irigaray, at least, who does not deny the external reality of materiality, the sexuate body is the inextricable condition of possibility for a distinctly *human* subjectivity as such.

36. Irigaray TBT, 21.

37. On this point, I bracket judgment as to whether Irigaray, at times, problematically attributes certain gender expressions, relations to nature, and linguistic tendencies as "belonging" archetypally to one human sex, and whether these attributions need be read as inevitable or rather as an entrenched *historical* condition open to future change (which accords with my interpretation). For a discussion of this issue, see, for example, Morny Joy, "Autonomy and Divinity: A Double-Edged Experiment," in *Thinking with Irigaray*, ed. Mary C. Rawlinson, Sabrina L. Hom, and Serene J. Khader (Albany: State University of New York Press, 2011), 234.

38. I add that, even if an individual were engineered to lack certain sex characteristics, or somehow to approach a kind of sexual "neutrality" (how and if this might be possible, while still being human, I bracket here), such a form of embodiment would still not be all that the human being *can be*, in virtue of *not* being other sexes. Again, I leave open in what sense even these individuals would be "sexuate" or just related to sexual difference negatively as a whole.

Bibliography

Brigandt, Ingo. "Philosophy of Biology." In *The Bloomsbury Companion to the Philosophy of Science*, edited by Steven French and Juha Saatsi, 246–267. London: Bloomsbury Academic, 2014.

Carter, Jennifer. Email message to author, June 29, 2018.

Crapo, Ruthanne. "The Way of Love: Practicing an Irigarayan Ethic." Unpublished doctoral dissertation, Vrije Universiteit Amsterdam, 2016.

Gallop, Jane. "Quand nos lèvre s'écrivent: Irigaray's Body Politic." *Romanic Review* 74 (1983): 77–83.

Grosz, Elizabeth. *Becoming Undone: Darwinian Reflections on Life, Politics, and Art*. Durham, NC: Duke University Press, 2011.

Jones, Rachel. *Irigaray: Towards a Sexuate Philosophy*. Cambridge: Polity, 2011.

Joy, Morny. "Autonomy and Divinity: A Double-Edged Experiment." In *Thinking with Irigaray*, edited by Mary C. Rawlinson, Sabrina L. Hom, and Serene J. Khader, 221–244. Albany: State University of New York Press, 2011.

Malabou, Catherine, and Ewa Ziarek. "Negativity, Unhappiness or Felicity: On Irigaray's Dialectical Culture of Sexual Difference." *L'Esprit Créateur* 52, no. 3 (2012): 11–25.

Poe, Danielle. "Can Luce Irigaray's Notion of Sexual Difference Be Applied to Transsexual and Transgender Narratives?" In *Thinking with Irigaray*, edited by Mary C. Rawlinson, Sabrina L. Hom, and Serene J. Khader, 111–129. Albany: State University of New York Press, 2011.

Roberts, Laura. *Irigaray and Politics: A Critical Introduction*. Edinburgh: Edinburgh University Press, 2019.

Sares, James. "The Schizoanalysis of Sex: Toward a Deleuzean-Guattarian Sexual Ontology." *philoSOPHIA: A Journal of transContinental Feminism* 10, no. 1 (2020): 47–70.

Schwab, Gail. "Sexual Difference as a Model: An Ethics for the Global Future." *Diacritics* 28, no. 1 (1998): 76–92.

Seely, Stephen. "Does Life Have (a) Sex? Thinking Ontology with Irigaray and Simondon." In *Feminist Philosophies of Life*, edited by Hasana Sharp and Chloë Taylor, 108–128. Montreal: McGill University Press, 2016.

Stone, Alison. *Luce Irigaray and the Philosophy of Sexual Difference*. Cambridge: Cambridge University Press, 2006.

Whitford, Margaret. *Luce Irigaray: Philosophy in the Feminine*. New York: Routledge, 1991.

Part III

Divine Women

Chapter Six

A Theology of Lips

Beyond the Wounding of Desire

Wesley N. Barker

In "Bodies That Matter" Judith Butler notes that conceiving the material-discursive relation of lived bodies as an either/or proposition oversimplifies the dynamism of the space that constitutes their limits at any given time.[1] Butler's work has inspired queer and feminist theories of performativity that have emphasized the discursivity of materiality in order to unshackle the body from essentialist binds. The last few years in global politics, however, have increasingly borne witness to the limits and dangers of discourses that are not held accountable to how living and nonliving things materialize. From #BlackLivesMatter to COVID-19 life and death consequences to disparities that result from how prediscursive materialities materialize are apparent, raising questions about the agency matter has in its appearances in and to the world.

It is precisely in regard to the question of discourse and its relationship to the materiality of bodily life that the work of Luce Irigaray's writing, especially her invocation of religious language, remains useful for thinking about "new ways for bodies to matter."[2] Within the saying and unsaying of feminine desire vis-à-vis her mimetic use of fleshy language, Irigaray's writing evokes a territory at the limits of philosophy—a space that explicitly invites exploration of religious language. In Irigaray's early works in particular, Christian theology provides Irigaray with a vocabulary that holds flesh and radical alterity together. This essay therefore reads the ethical dimensions of desire evoked in Irigaray's language of lips in relation to Irigaray's appropriation of Christian theological imagery and concepts. The essay concludes by examining Irigaray's invocation of lips crossing in *An Ethics of Sexual Difference* to shift focus away from the association of desire with *either* penetrative wounding *or* impenetrable touching, and toward a notion of desire as a continuous incarnation of the ambiguities of eros found in the generative slippage between flesh and word.

Mimesis as a Framework for Rethinking Desire, Discourse, and Flesh

A former student of famed theorist Jacques Lacan (1901–1981) at his Freudian School in Paris, Irigaray draws heavily on linguistic adaptations of psychoanalysis to articulate the relationship between desire, representation, ethics, and subjectivity. In Lacan's theory of subjectivity, one becomes a subject through the process of negotiating the symbolic realm for representing one's desires. The becoming subject enters into linguistic relations in an attempt to unite the imaginary realm of the symbolic with the Real of desire, recovering a lost condition of wholeness.

In keeping with her training in Lacanian psychoanalysis, Irigaray reads women's desires as mediated through a masculine symbolic such that women can only speak their desires mimetically, distanced from their desires by a language that is not their own. Irigaray writes, "And when *she* is obliged to be 'clear,' in the traditional mode of the clarity of truth, she tries to do 'as well as,' 'like' that which has already been produced of the world."[3] By this logic, the feminine is not the language of women; the feminine is the language through which women mimic masculine discourse. Or, as Irigaray suggests in the final set of interview questions in *This Sex Which Is Not One*, women engage in "masquerading," veiling themselves in a femininity that occludes their own desires.[4]

Somewhat ironically, this discourse of psychoanalysis that describes the alienation of the subject from its desires provides Irigaray with a theoretical foundation for constructively thinking about the slippage between discourse and flesh. In her early writings, Irigaray employs mimesis to exploit the misrecognition within the representational function of language, harnessing the imaginary to expose its limits.[5] Because the feminine in language does not belong to a female imaginary, women's miming does not produce an exact copy. Mimesis actually reveals the difference within language that is always already part of the reductive movement to sameness. Pressing the limits of real and imagined in the distance and difference created by an imperfect copy, Irigaray uses mimesis to cultivate the possibility of a truly sexually differentiated desire—one that could ground a female imaginary and the conditions therein of an alternate way of becoming a subject. Irigaray explains this strategic significance of mimesis thus:

> To play with mimesis is thus, for a woman, to try to recover the place of her exploitation by discourse, without allowing herself to be simply reduced to it. It means to resubmit herself—inasmuch as she is on the side of the "perceptible," of "matter"—to "ideas," in particular to ideas about herself, that are elaborated in/by a masculine logic, but so as to make "visible," by an effect of playful repetition, what was supposed to remain invisible: the cover-up of a possible operation of the feminine in language.[6]

Insofar as mimesis requires "woman" to "resubmit herself" to a particular framework of what is "perceptible," Irigaray suggests mimesis disrupts the sort of inside-outside dichotomies that would allow for woman to stand outside of discourse. The feminine in language does not describe a condition of the feminine as an inescapably totalizing reality; the feminine can be used mimetically to provoke a space of difference of an othered desire apart from that reality.

Irigaray insists that the strategic success of mimesis requires a woman to willfully embed herself in the masculine structures that render things perceptible. Irigaray suggests that a new, "feminine syntax" might be the solution to this "masquerade of femininity."[7] Significantly, she suggests that this feminine syntax would be "deciphered" in terms of the "gestural code of women's bodies."[8] Here Irigaray distinguishes between the undifferentiated feminine within masculine language and a feminine that would differentiate itself by disrupting the order of sense-making in language. Irigaray suggests that the "feminine syntax" would be a differentiated feminine that harnesses the significatory capacity of flesh to gesture toward an othered desire. This feminine syntax would be "difficult to 'read'" and hard to "hear" presumably because—by virtue of both its embodiedness and otherness, this feminine syntax is unrepresentable within a masculine economy of signification.[9]

Because the possibility of a differentiated feminine exists outside the logic of identity of a masculine economy, Irigaray's rhetoric of maternity, of wombs, and of lips is always under contestation in her texts. Judith Butler reads this disruptive quality of Irigaray's work, arguing that Irigaray's mimetic use of the seemingly essentialist tropes of maternity disrupt classical—especially Platonic—concepts of matter that render the feminine a formless receptacle. Referring to Irigaray's use of the maternal to critique Plato's notion of origins, Butler writes, "This textual practice is not grounded in a rival ontology, but inhabits—indeed, penetrates, occupies, and redeploys—the paternal language itself."[10] This fleshy rhetoric necessarily evokes the sense-making of language all the while refusing to represent anything that system recognizes.

Reading the radical scope and undertaking of Irigaray's mimesis as Butler does, one finds that the visceral and bodily language in Irigaray's writings does not describe a condition of the feminine as an essential reality. Rather, Irigaray's fleshy language evokes a particular understanding of reality and a possibility of desire that has not yet been articulated. As Elizabeth Grosz suggests, in Irigaray's work mimesis adopts expectations "to such an extreme degree that the end result is the opposite of compliance."[11] The result, Grosz writes, is that Irigaray's mimesis "unsettles the system by throwing back to it what it cannot accept about its own operations."[12] Mimicry thus becomes an embodiment of disruption rather than a passive resignation to repeat and abide by the strictures that limit the feminine. The ambiguity that mimesis fosters opens a space for reading Irigaray beyond herself, toward an indeterminate future that prevents her theory from falling irretrievably back into the economy of sameness.

Mimetic Lips, Speaking *of* Desire

Irigaray's fleshy language cultivates ethical possibilities emerging from the tensions surrounding the speaking of feminine desire. One of the most famous examples of this involves her language of lips. The sensuously disruptive lips make appearances throughout her work, including in the early work of *Speculum* (1974 in French, 1985 in English) and, not insignificantly, in *Elemental Passions* (1982 French, 1992 English). More prominently these lips appear in the essay "When Our Lips Speak Together" (*This Sex Which is Not One*, 1977 in French, 1985 in English). In this evocative piece, Irigaray invokes the language of lips—of the female genitals and of the mouth—moving between pleasure and speech, in pleasure and speech, appropriating the mimetic condition of the feminine to disrupt the sameness of the masculine economy of desire.

Irigaray begins the essay as though conversing directly with her reader. Using the first-person plural and second-person singular pronouns, "we" (*nous*) and "you" (*tu*), respectively, she involves the reader. Repeatedly invoking forms of the "same" (*même*, *mêmes*) Irigaray suggests that "we" are caught up in a reductive mode of communication in which to speak (*parler*) will "reproduce the same history."[13] In this way, she claims the prevailing language of humankind is one that reduces everything to sameness.

The initial "we" in the text is the "we" of men and women speaking together; however, a few lines down, changes in the participle endings indicate that the *we* now references a feminine "we."[14] By virtue of her new address, Irigaray banishes the male interlocutor of her first paragraph. His absence coincides with the creation of space for Irigaray's feminine interlocutor to emerge and speak freely. The now feminine "we" becomes her dialogical interlocutor. A female other, or a "you" from whom Irigaray has been distanced through masculine language, becomes her addressee. But the presence of this female interlocutor is troubled. Irigaray's tone creates a scene of love and heartache familiar to her readers. As though summoning this woman from a place of exile, she beckons her new interlocutor to "come back" (*reviens*).[15] It is as though the "I" and "you" that could create a feminine "we" have been involuntarily separated, and their reunion elicits a memory that cannot help but bear the scars of their split.

Here lips speak a play of presence and absence that is also a play of literal and figurative bodies in space and time. "How can I touch you," Irigaray asks this female lover, "if you're not there?"[16] This female body Irigaray addresses is in one sense disembodied, at once present in the language of the feminine and absent because that feminine belongs to a language of sameness that does not speak the desires of her literal body. Amid the play of presence and absence, the reader loses sight of what the feminine "is" in a way that challenges the prioritization of a singular, authoritative presence behind the sign.

Irigaray deepens the sense of the interlocutor's involuntary estrangement from her body, likening her disappearance to a bodily sacrifice at someone else's altar. Irigaray writes, "Your blood has become their meaning."[17] The language of blood (*sang*) and sense (*sens*)—which I will revisit later—is striking here. It resonates with other references that Irigaray makes to the ways the sacrifice of women's embodied desires has been the occasion for language to rise to the level of transcendence. For instance, in *An Ethics of Sexual Difference*, Irigaray writes, "Language . . . feeds on blood, on flesh."[18] The phrasing in *Ethics* and in the beginning of "When Our Lips Speak Together" imagines masculine language (*langage*) as cannibalistic.[19] In this sense, the flesh and blood of woman has figuratively nourished "le langage." I propose that for Irigaray, *le langage* feeds on the fleshiness of *the feminine* tongue (*la langue*) in a way that silences *the feminine* and keeps women from speaking (*parler*).

After suggesting that the making of meaning is part of a debt owed to woman as the feminine other who gives language the difference it needs to make sense, Irigaray continues to invoke the language of blood, bodies, and sacrifice. However, these subsequent invocations of blood and sacrifice in Irigaray's use of the lips do not reinscribe women's desires in the sameness of (masculine) language by reducing women to reproduction or objects of men's pleasure. Irigaray does not let the lips passively await slaughter for the pleasure of man and his God. Through their refusal to be reduced to the reductive sense-making of *le langage*, the lips speak out against the erroneous depiction of their passive participation in the masculine economy of sameness. Irigaray writes, "We are not lacks, voids awaiting sustenance, plenitude, fulfillment from an other. By our lips we are women: this does not mean that we are focused on consuming, consummation, fulfillment."[20] The lips are not reducible to their role as other and/or as mother to a masculine system of exchange.[21]

Immediately following the paragraph in which Irigaray declares that women are not "lacks" or "voids," her tone shifts again. She transitions from a rhetorical accusation of the "absent" male interlocutor to an erotic invitation to her female interlocutor. This play of presence and absence is part of what Maggie Berg has identified as a "desire for that which is proximate and close—the self or female lover—rather than desire for the lost and displaced mother."[22] The erotic relationship between Irigaray and her female interlocutor will come into focus as we move forward in this analysis.

Irigaray writes, "Kiss me. Two lips kiss two lips, and openness is ours again. . . . Between us, the movement from inside to outside, from outside to inside, knows no limits. It is without end. These are exchanges that no mark, no mouth can ever stop."[23] Irigaray is ostensibly engaging in the dynamism and limitlessness of the mutual touching between the women as speaking subjects and objects of one another's pleasure—as the "You/I."[24] In this mutuality of the eros of the lips (hers and her interlocutors'), Irigaray rejects the association of women's pleasure with reproduction and with being the other of a masculine subject. But linguistically, some ambiguity persists in the text about the gender of the erotic encounter here.[25] The gender-neutral language read alongside the play of presence and absence of the male interlocutor—who remains at play in the background of this affair—disrupts the certitude about who is and can be part of this erotic encounter that disrupts the masculine subject-object distinctions. It is precisely this sort of ambiguity afforded by mimesis that enunciates Irigaray's criticism of the singularity of phallogocentric desire and occasions her effort to reimagine the relationship between ethics, desire, and subjectivity.[26]

And in an overt refusal of linearity, the dynamic and disruptive lips gesture to a rethinking of the relationship between desiring bodies and the very discourse that alienates them. Irigaray deploys the fleshy, voluptuous, sensuous language of the lips in an at times *utter*ly confounding manner, resisting both the disembodiedness and linearity of sense-making. For instance, in the self-titled essay of *This Sex Which Is Not One*, Irigaray invokes both classical Greek philosophical distinctions between matter and form and Freudian psychoanalytic notions of the morphology of subjectivity in an erotic refusal that is never a simple reversal. Irigaray writes, "And if woman takes pleasure precisely from this incompleteness of form which allows her organ to touch itself over and over again, indefinitely, by itself, that pleasure is denied by a civilization that privileges phallomorphism."[27] Here Irigaray suggests that masculine discourse, which is constituted through a rendering of women as shapeless matter or "nonthematizable materiality," then denies women the pleasure that their indeterminate or "nonthematizable materiality" might provide.[28]

Invoking the language of labia, vulva, and womb, Irigaray articulates the reduction of women to procreative sex *and* refuses that reduction of her desire.[29] With multiple sites of pleasure, women find pleasure with or without sex, with or without procreation.[30] Against the singularity of the phallus, the multiplicity of the lips inspires a subjectivity that defies reduction to sameness, rejecting a notion of desire oriented in relation to a single organ. The lips disrupt the linearity of sense-making, insisting instead upon a fluidity of expression of desire, opening previously foreclosed possibilities for ethical relation between the sexes within and through language. Though the lips of the mouth typically mark the doorway to speech and labial lips present the passageway of reproduction, for Irigaray, the possibility of language and sex, sexuality and subjectivity, come from the touching of these lips that are always "at least two."[31] As Irigaray claims, "For in what she says, too, at least when she dares, woman is constantly touching herself."[32]

In yet another example, the passage quoted earlier from "When Our Lips Speak Together" demonstrates Irigaray's use of the feminine to refuse the reduction to sameness as a question of both ethics and desire.[33] In an early translation of "When Our Lips Speak Together" in the journal *Signs*, Carolyn Burke writes the following footnote about the play between blood and meaning/sense given in Irigaray's statement, "Your blood becomes their meaning." According to Burke, "The play on *sang* ('blood') and *sens* ('meaning,' 'sense') extends the analogy between sexuality and writing. Blood is at once metaphorical and literal, a source of female sense and sexuality."[34] As previously noted, embedded in Irigaray's play between *sang*, *sens*, and sacrifice is the notion that the blood of the feminine interlocutor's difference is sacrificed for the sake of the masculine world of meaning-making; yet Irigaray's move to allow feminine blood to conflate with meaning ultimately resists the determinacy of that sacrifice.

Thus it is no accident that the reader senses, or makes meaning from, the materiality or fleshiness of Irigaray's writing. In these visceral invocations, Irigaray probes the depths of sacrifice to relocate an othered desire. Indeed, as the lips begin to speak and an other way of knowing emerges, Irigaray writes, "Wait. My blood is coming back. From their senses. It's warm inside us again. Among us. Their words are emptying out, becoming bloodless, Dead skins. While our lips are growing red again."[35] Meaning in the text manifests through the senses, stimulated by Irigaray's erotic language of the sensations of feminine lips and the implication that the readers who partake in this meaning-making do so as kissers and lovers of those lips. This meaning is tied to the becoming of a desire signaled by reinvigorated lips—whose blood has returned to them through the mimetic manipulation of language and a different way of knowing, sensing, and meaning. Irigaray's deliberate transition from the language of sacrifice to pleasure will inform my move toward an indeterminate incarnate desire rather than wounded desire as it regards her allusions to Christian theology.

Irigaray plays with the space between the discursive and material bodies using the fleshiness of rhetoric to allow space for thinking erotically, maintaining the space that prevents two from being collapsed into one, ensuring one reach for the other without grabbing hold.[36] Because lips touch without being absorbed into oneness they serve as a physical representation of relation without assimilation, of reaching without grasping the limits of the other. Heralding the indeterminacy of the lips, Irigaray writes, "This self-touching gives woman a form that is in(de)finitely transformed."[37] The lips open to the alterity of space enfolded in flesh such that the lips are never just lips; they are never just entrances or exits, conditions of speaking or silence; they are thresholds of flesh and thought—of anticipating the other, whether outside or within the self, in all its uncertain wonder. In *This Sex Which Is Not One*, Irigaray interweaves the reference to lips with women's pleasure and the possibility of women's sexuality writing, "Her sexuality, always at least double, goes even further: it is *plural*."[38] As more than two, the lips frame the space for a plurality of pleasure; lips thus frame a space of othered desire modeled on the indeterminacy of eros rather than in reduction to sameness; these lips are ethical. It is precisely by virtue of their invocation of desire as embodied alterity that these lips also invite theological reflection.

Irigaray and Theology: A Wounded Eros

Irigaray's own dialogue with religious discourse is both sustained and explicit, from *Speculum*, *Marine Lover*, and *Sexes and Genealogies* to *Between East and West* and *To Be Born*. Philosophers and theologians alike have explored the complexities of Irigaray's invocations of language of transcendence, of flesh, of the divine, and so on, for decades. Her use of such terms is always already entangled with the philosophical, ethical, and psychoanalytic genealogies of her thinking; it is no wonder that her work continues to present an inexhaustible source of inquiry beyond the bounds of disciplinary thinking.

Discussions of Irigaray in Christian theological circles over the last few decades have concentrated on how her work disrupts metaphysical divisions that prioritize transcendence over immanence.[12] Irigaray's notion of the "sensible-transcendental" as emerging, contra Freudian morphology of the subject, through the "morpho-logic" of women's writing has provided feminist theologians a significant framework for rethinking Christological concepts such as Incarnation and for reinterpreting accounts by/about women mystics in the Christian tradition.[39]

Irigaray mimes the Christian tradition using explicit references to Christological language—incarnation, parousia, and the cross—to expose the ways the feminine has been used in elaboration of a God of and for men and to simultaneously use this revelation of her occlusion to articulate a way of knowing and being through sexual difference. As Ada Jaarsma writes, "The story of the incarnation in Irigaray's work does not occupy a foundational role that excludes other stories, traditions, or practices, but rather constitutes a narrative site at which to glimpse complex inter-related problems of Irigaray's project."[40] In what follows, I examine Irigaray's miming of the European Christian, and particularly French Catholic, tradition as she moves between theology and philosophy, psychoanalysis and ethics. I will argue that "playful crossing" engenders what one might call a theology of lips that explicitly refuses "proper" or narrow understandings of what theology should be and how it should function in the world.

Because it is inherently problematic to reduce the countless theological debates across geographically and historically diverse communities to a "Christian tradition," and because I am not interested in making a claim about right belief, I will borrow those dimensions of the language of incarnation that seem most normative in the context of Irigaray's French-Catholic background. Further still, without complete "fidelity to a single discourse,"[41] I read the Incarnation from a literary rather than a theological perspective, as I cannot, in the time and space of this essay, address the centuries of debate about the status of the Incarnation (as though they are ever settled by doctrine). I therefore offer a depiction of incarnation that supports the very critique of the Incarnation that Irigaray provides in order to highlight what the lips attempt to accomplish in her work.[42]

Within the context of Irigaray's mimetic use of incarnational language, there are two specific places I consider where the lips relate directly to the question of the relationship between discourse and matter as an erotic space: the first is in *Speculum* and the second is in *Ethics*. In both of these examples, Irigaray seems to tap into the ambiguities of the Christian theological tradition when it comes to interpreting the relationship between word and flesh and human and divine in the "Word-made-flesh" of the Incarnation.[43]

In *Speculum*'s "La Mystérique," Irigaray appropriates the voice of the thirteenth-century female mystic Angela of Foligno (ca. 1248–1309), situating the sensible flesh and the transcendental divine elicited by the wounds of Jesus in relation to the embodied eros of Angela's feminine lips. Consistent with Irigaray's citational practices in her mimetic writing, Irigaray reimagines and redeploys the specificity of Angela's experience to mime the history of interpretation of women's mystical (here) experience (not unlike what she does with Antigone, Echo, et al.). Ann-Marie Priest emphasizes that "La Mystérique" "uses many classical mystical images (drawn overwhelmingly from Angela) in depicting mystic union."[44] Similarly, feminist philosopher of religion Amy Hollywood emphasizes that Irigaray's use of the Christian mystical tradition muddles the historical specificity of primary texts and the experiences of individual mystics.[45] That there are three epigraphs from three different mystics—Meister Eckhart, John Ruysbroeck, and Angela of Foligno—at the outset of Irigaray's essay evidences these claims.[46] Therefore, in miming Angela's meditation on the wounded body of Christ, Irigaray simultaneously mimes the Christian mystical tradition. While this ambivalence about the mystical tradition understandably frustrates those invested in doing careful historical theology, I will focus on how Irigaray uses the language of wounds and lips within a broader disruption of the word-flesh relationship that she probes in miming the mystics.

In a stark example of miming that draws attention to the status of the lips in Irigaray's work, Irigaray elicits the vulvic nature of Christ's wounds (*vulnus*), especially the wound of his side, which Angela famously kisses in a meditation found in the collection of her writings, commonly referred to as the *Book* (*Il libro*) (1248–1309). Irigaray writes:

> And she never ceases to look upon his nakedness, open for all to see, upon the gashes in his virgin flesh, at the wounds from the nails that pierce his body as he hangs there, in his passion and abandonment. And she is overwhelmed with love of him/herself. In his crucifixion he opens up a path of redemption in her fallen state.
>
> Could it be true that not every wound need remain secret, that not every laceration was shameful? Could a sore

> be *holy*? Ecstasy is there in that glorious slit where she curls up as if in her nest, where she rests as if she had found her home—and He is also in her. . . . In this way, you see me and I see you, finally I see myself seeing you in this fathomless wound which is the source of our wondering comprehension and exhilaration. And to know myself I scarcely need a "soul," I have only to gaze upon the gaping space in your loving body.[47]

Irigaray suggests that the mystic recognizes herself in the wounds of Christ. But these are not the wounds of any man; they are the wounds of a God-man. Read mimetically, this God-man of the metaphysical tradition has wounded Angela by mediating her access to the divine through a masculine symbolic.

Yet there is another more complicated reading acting invariably in the same moment. In Irigaray's essay, the mystic relates to Christ's suffering by seeing herself in him and him in her. But this is not a reductive identification that results in an annihilation of human flesh so often associated with the ascent of the soul. Irigaray's depiction of the ecstatic union insists on the irreducibility of Christ and the mystic's coupling. Consistent with Irigaray's lips in *This Sex* this is a mystical union signaled by the simultaneous relationality and irreducibility of their two fleshes. Put differently, the two touch continuously without ever being reduced to one. To borrow from Irigaray's language in *Ethics*, the two create an open-ended envelope for each other, a space where the other can dwell and yet move freely in relation to their desires. "*La Mystérique*" insists on this openness by playing with theological notions of the wound of Christ as a symbol of his passion as well as the vulvic image of "openness" that expresses the desire of a female imaginary.[48]

In the passage quoted earlier, the *vulnus* and the vulvic are the marks of bodies wounded by a discursive tradition, but whose wounds become the possibility of their ecstasy, their mystical, thoroughly enfleshed pleasure. Irigaray describes the intense love that the mystic experiences as she gazes upon his wounds. The wounds are revealing—they are part of his nakedness. The "gashes in his virgin flesh" suggest that the wounds attest to his innocence.[49] The language of "virgin flesh" reminds the reader that, consistent with the theological tradition's insistence on Christ's sinlessness, these wounds are not the consequence of guilt or sin. The language of virgin flesh also echoes with Irigaray's earlier lines that he is "that most female of men."[50] In the theological tradition for explicating salvation, the sinlessness of Christ provides a rational basis for the redemptive power of his sacrifice. Irigaray writes, "In his crucifixion he opens up a path of redemption in her fallen state."[51] But the power of this meditation on the wounds of Christ will not be redemption for sin; it will be an interrogation of her fallenness.

Irigaray immediately follows this identification of the crucifixion and redemption with two rhetorical questions: "Could it be true that not every wound need remain secret, that not every laceration was shameful? Could a sore be *holy*?"[52] The scene of love has moved beyond agapeic love for Christ's sacrifice. In keeping with the notion that the multiplicity of feminine desire rejects making sense in language as ever a singular endeavor of a male body, the play between *vulnus* and vulva dances erotically at the limits of pleasure and pain, fullness and lack, openness and secrecy.

In addition to the mystic's rhetorical rejection of the shamefulness attributed to women's flesh, her questions mirror the wound of Christ, interrogating the phallogocentric myth of the sacred and profane that differentiate what is holy from what is shameful. The slippage between *vulnus* and vulva figures the site of this contestation. As Kathryn Stockton writes in her intriguing literary interpretation of this text, "Woman's 'slit,' here pronounced 'glorious,' mirrors Christ's 'fathomless wound.' The wound itself acts as mirror(s), enabling 'woman' to reflect upon her material folds."[53]

The vulvic imagery enters the conversation as a question of sexual difference that will transform the annihilation of the feminine self, an annihilation that must happen in an ecstatic union with a masculine God. Rather than a penetration of one into another that results in the annihilation of difference between the human self and the divine other, here ecstasy is one of mutual touching. And this mutual touching is the possibility of her self-recognition becoming, through her own desire, "*outside of all self-as-same*."[54] The play between the *vulnus* and the vulvic in the previously quoted passage both mimics and disrupts theological moralizing of feminine desire that would depict women as dangerously carnal by virtue of their open genital and oral lips—yet without the promise of fulfillment in the form of transcendence typically afforded matter. This is an erotic coupling of two bodies whose slits attest to their mutual transcendence. Irigaray transforms the *vulnus*/vulvic relationship into a sensible-transcendental erotic coupling that plays upon the fleshiness of Christ's wound in order to share in the fleshy lips of women's "nonthematizable materiality" (à la Butler) or "material opacity" (à la Irigaray).[55] In this erotic coupling of *vulnus* and vulva, their fleshy "slits" attest to their mutual transcendence, such that the specificity of their flesh is irreducible and yet never fixed.

The fleshiness of the mystic and Jesus's mutual ascent is a reminder that eros is an embodied desire of irreducibly differentiated flesh and spirit. Taking on the mystic's voice, Irigaray writes, "But if the Word was made flesh in this way, and to this extent, it can only have been to make me (become) God in my jouissance, which can at last be recognized."[56] Irigaray's mystic suggests that meditation on Christ's wounds will give her access to self-knowledge that will also be, for her body, a mark of redemption and not sin.

Eros without Penetration?

Although the interplay of the *vulnus* and vulvic disrupts associations of women's sexuality with woundedness—of women with carnality and carnality with sin—in a way that restores eros to the incarnation, this play remains risky. In *Acute Melancholia*, Hollywood notes Irigaray's shift away from associating the lips with Christ's side wound, due to precariousness of associating feminine desire with woundedness more broadly. Citing Irigaray's critique of Lacan in *Marine Lover of Friedrich Nietzsche*, Hollywood notes that Irigaray dissociates the penetrative attributes of Christ's wound from the vaginal in order to "reject an understanding of the female sex as wound-like."[57]

Hollywood then argues that Irigaray's abandonment of the penetrative quality of wounds as irredeemably threatening to women's subjectivity proves shortsighted. She claims that Irigaray's rejection of penetrative space results from Irigaray's insufficiently critical adoption of the psychoanalytic framework. In this view, Irigaray's abandoning of the penetrative quality of wound casts the othered desire of woman as exclusively anti-penetrative, thus conceding to a framework that associates penetration as belonging exclusively to the masculine sex. Hollywood suggests that Irigaray's turn away from the wound reinforces Butler's criticism that Irigaray's lips present a "rigorously anti-penetrative eros of surfaces."[58] By the logic of Butler's critique, Irigaray's erotic scene is not just anti-penetrative; its identifications are sexed, such that even if one wanted to explore possibilities for rethinking the penetrative apart from a heterosexual matrix, it is now impossible by virtue of this sexing. However, Hollywood adds that the mystical texts themselves destabilize "gender positions" so as to exceed reductions of penetration to the masculine and anti-penetration to the feminine.[59] By Hollywood's reading, Irigaray has missed the potential radicality of the tradition itself and therein missed an opportunity for thinking beyond the limits of the heterosexual matrix. To dissociate the language of penetration from heteronormative desire, Hollywood draws on medieval devotional literature and art to locate spaces of difference that imagine Christ's wounds apart from a fatalistic notion of penetration that she thinks Irigaray is attempting to avoid. She concludes, "Perhaps the Christ of '*La Mystérique*' is better read as refusing gender binaries than as feminized and so as refusing the distinctions Irigaray herself continues to desire, even as she calls for their radical reimagining."[60] I agree with Hollywood that this tension exists in Irigaray, but I will insist that it is not just the wounding in "*La Mystérique*" that can disrupt binaries; this disruption is available in the lips, the labia, the boundaries themselves that constitute the threshold of *vulnus*/vulva. Put simply, the radicality of desire that Hollywood suggests is available by thinking the *vulnus*/vulva in relation to the tradition is also offered, I would argue, in Irigaray's later readings of the lips.

Indeed, the power of the mimetic work of Irigaray's writing—of the writing that the lips foster—rests in its appropriation-as-refusal of binaries of interior and exterior of a masculine time and space of the subject and its becoming. Reading Irigaray's mimesis as a radical philosophical, linguistic, theological, and ethical endeavor, I argue that the eros of the lips cannot be reduced to *either* surfaces *or* wounds, nor can it be said that the lips are *either* exclusively anti-penetrative *or* penetrative.

The lips provide an eroticism that redefines the inside-outside that marks the language of surface and penetration.[61] I want to rethink the lips and the radicality of touching by revisiting the remaking of materiality and alterity that the eros of the lips invokes. I therefore propose turning to the previously described embodied alterity of Irigaray's eros that the mimetic lips elicit to consider how the eros of flesh and language transcends the language of wounding.

Crossing Lips: Beyond a Wounded Eros

In "When Our Lips Speak Together," Irigaray claims that love does not demand wounding. Playing with the autoeroticism of the lips and the possibility of love of self and love of other outside the phallic economy, Irigaray writes, "I love you: body shared, undivided . . . There is no need for blood shed, between us. No need for a wound to remind us that blood exists."[62] The suggestion that there is no need for a bleeding wound is to suggest that pleasure, not reduction, is the possibility of life. The pleasure that would be a jouissance of the lips of feminine desire is not reducible to a particular notion of the feminine, or of her flesh. What's more, read in relation to "The Power of Discourse and the Subordination of the Feminine" (the interview also published in *This Sex*), this pleasure of the lips is perhaps the " 'elsewhere' of feminine pleasure" found only at the price of *crossing back through the mirror that subtends all speculation.*"[63]

Irigaray is explicit that the purpose for articulating this " 'elsewhere' of feminine pleasure" would be to disrupt the logic of identity given in the specular economy of the masculine symbolic. Exposing those "conditions under which systematicity"[64] emerge and potentially "threaten[ing]" the logic of the system will require a recrossing or "*crossing back*" (*retraversée*).[65] This crossing back is precisely what mimesis continuously performs, and it is insofar as Irigaray's mimetic lips engender an erotic space capable of holding word and flesh together in this " 'elsewhere' of feminine pleasure" that they are worth revisiting apart from the language of a fatalistically wounded eros. Furthermore, if as Irigaray writes, the " '*elsewhere' of female pleasure* might rather be sought first in the place where it sustains ek-stasy in the transcendental . . . where it serves as security for a narcissism extrapolated into the 'God' of men," the lips are especially worth revisiting as the figure of "*crossing back through the mirror*" of Christian theology.[66]

In 1984's *An Ethics of Sexual Difference* (1984 French, 1993 English) Irigaray's lips call forth theology, ethics, and the horizon of feminine desire in a way that challenges the relationship of eros to wounding. In *Ethics* Irigaray evokes God, the lips, and incarnation at multiple points in the text; bringing these terms together in the chapter "Sexual Difference," she reimagines the space and time of sexual difference apart from the masculine discourse of metaphysics, thus emphasizing the space of the lips' eros beyond the language of a wound.

Irigaray contends that prevailing images of a Father-God posit the divine as "the immutable spokesman of a single sex" such that women have been left without access to a "horizon . . . of the gods."[67] Because her notion of ethics is aligned with criticisms of self-sameness in both its philosophical and psychoanalytic manifestations, the very possibility of a non–self-same ethic requires the remaking of the world apart from the singular. An ethics of sexual difference, she says, requires a remaking of space and time, of transcendence and immanence, such that women could create their own places to inhabit, places that would have their own borders, their own horizons, their own limits, and therein access to a new horizon of other gods.

This "remaking of immanence and transcendence" occurs, Irigaray says, via "the threshold of the *lips*."[68] The "the *lips*," she writes, "are strangers to dichotomy and opposition. Gathered one against the other but without any possible suture, at least of any real kind."[69] Here, lips figure a relation both within the self and between self and other that does not collapse into sameness, and the horizon of their touching without collapsing has a spatial and temporal reality that literally and figuratively reimagines immanence and transcendence in relation rather than in opposition. Irigaray continues, "In this approach, where the borders of the body are wed in an embrace that transcends all limits . . . each one discovers the self in that experience which is inexpressible yet forms the supple grounding of life and language."[70] The lips call to an ethical horizon at the threshold of an irreducible difference of desire that separates as it connects them, that gives them boundaries as they give contours to each other. Lips link the concreteness of flesh in all its senses with the indeterminacy of transcendence, refusing to reduce word to flesh or flesh to word.

After invoking the threshold of the lips and their capacity to reshape immanence and transcendence and reimagine the horizon of the divine, Irigaray sets off the following in parentheses:

> (Two sets of lips that, moreover, cross over each other like arms of the cross, the prototype of the crossroads *between*. The mouth lips and the genital lips do not point in the same direction. In some way they point in the direction opposite from the one you would expect with the "lower" ones forming the vertical.)[71]

Irigaray's lips conjure images of female genitals and the mouth, suggesting that feminine desire is sexual, symbolic, and irreducible to either. That the relationship between desire and representation emerges from the crossing of lips is telling.

The lips of pleasure and speech figured in the cross could seem like dis-membered body parts, suggesting a sacrifice wherein women's bodies are deprived access to the difference of their desire. And while alienation from one's own desire is a familiar trope in Irigaray's mimetic use of the feminine, the lips "crossing over each other like arms of the cross" connect this alienation from self with alienation from the divine.[72] In the Christian tradition, this alienation is intensified by Jesus's maleness, which comes to represent a troubling mark of Christ's *universal* humanity, heightening the invisibility of feminine genital lips and the silence of lips of orality.[73] In Christian theology, the Incarnation links the Logos of creation to the Logos of Salvation. The Gospel of John opens with the verse, "In the beginning was the Word and the Word was God and the Word was with God" (John 1:1, New Revised Standard Version). The theological concept of Incarnation and its doctrinal formulations are founded upon this statement. Echoing the introductory words in Genesis, the Word that will become flesh a few verses later in John 1:14 is explicitly linked to the Logos that creates the world. The notion of the word becoming flesh in the male Jesus who then dies to offer salvation for humanity makes man inseparable from this divine economy. The possibility for salvation, which in most Christian traditions involves bodily resurrection, is tied to this male body, the incarnation of a masculine logos of creation. Inasmuch as the cross is synonymous with sacrifice in Christianity, the lips reveal a veiled erasure of feminine desire concomitant with the becoming of a masculine God. These lips represent a sacrificed other, silenced and displaced from the logos of creation and the discourse of world-making.

But such a reading potentially returns lips to the language of wounding sacrifice that undermine the eros lips have engendered through their remaking of the space and time of transcendence and immanence. Returning then to the passage in *Ethics*, I suggest the crossing of the lips invites another reading. Irigaray's lips reappear from this sacrifice, resurrected in a space between—literally, parenthetically—transforming the sacrifice into an affirmation of othered desire, a desire that refuses the Oedipal desire for oneness of a masculine model of the subject. This othered feminine desire becomes the condition for resurrecting/

reimagining the division between immanence and transcendence that mark the distinction between the material and discursive realms. The sexed specificity *and* indeterminacy of the lips allow Irigaray to reframe the cross's image of sacrifice as an ethical image of incarnate otherness emerging through the irreducible alterity of eros rather than through the singularity of a wound.

Irigaray's evocative lips play upon the slippage between the discourse and materiality that the Word-made-flesh of Christian language of the Incarnation enables by virtue of its occlusion of the body of woman—an overt sexing of the materiality of flesh that matters and dematerialization of woman's desire. In Irigaray's miming of this part of Christian tradition, she re-traverses the space and time of the Incarnation to reimagine the relationship between word and flesh. Mimetically drawing on the disruptive force of sexed material/visceral imagery to play upon the relationship between matter and language, she is "crossing back through the mirror" of the specular economy to articulate the " 'elsewhere' " of female pleasure."[74] Here, the lips as cross and/or crossing gesture toward the incarnation of an othered/elsewhere desire disrupt the binaries of the space-time of metaphysics, refiguring the space and time of incarnation differently.

Horizontally, the lips refuse the linearity of time and the telos of representational language; vertically, they refuse the hierarchy of space that prioritizes spirit over matter, word over flesh. The "lower" genital lips of sexual pleasure here are replacing the verticality of the phallus, upsetting the orientation of a world that separates and hierarchizes the heavenly over the terrestrial, the symbolic over the concrete. The lips of the mouth, which are above the lips of the genitals, point horizontally, articulating the horizon of desire that emerges through this resignification.

In her reconstructed cross, Irigaray refigures the sacrificed God-man of metaphysics through an image of lips that touch and speak differently by virtue of a space between them, such that their borders constitute horizons of othered desire. Though this language involves a reification of binaries on one level, I would argue that, read mimetically, the lips exceed the limits of those binaries. The lips reconstruct the cross through an othered fleshy desire that she understands as being in a process of becoming; therefore, lips are constitutive of the cross itself as an incarnation that crosses over metaphysical distinctions of terrestrial and heavenly, a body suspended across space and time. The lips reconstruct a different sort of cross, an intermediary space. Thus, in the image of a cross, the mimetic lips re-traverse the masculine logic of the Christian tradition to offer a different incarnation, one that holds the relationship of word and flesh together in a different space-time of the "'elsewhere' of feminine pleasure."

Moreover, I would argue that these lips crossing are not inscribed in the penetrative versus anti-penetrative logic; these lips cross through and over one another as a radical touching. Perhaps the crossing lips mark that "ceaseless exchange" that "increases indefinitely from its passage in and through the other" of the multiplicity of woman's pleasure that disrupts the economy of sameness.[75] Perhaps their *traversée* is constitutive of their *croix*; their crossing and moving through one another constitutes their word-flesh dynamic of incarnation as an "elsewhere." Here the lips are neither bleeding wounds nor impenetrable surfaces; they are marked more by their behavior than some fixed idea of their matter. The lips begin to reconstitute, close, and go past the gap that they create in and through their crossing.[76] Irigaray's crossing lips in *Ethics* insist on incarnation as an interval of eros, refusing the wounding singularity of Christology marked by the reduction of time, space, and maleness of the Incarnation in a particular telos.[77] The lips instead create the contours that transform that space by suspending incarnation in a different temporality—one that refuses to put off the incarnation's value in a future and/or in a transcendental other.

Though the in-between spaces that constitute the limits of the lips are not unlike wounds, the ethical dimensions of Irigaray's erotic lips are not reducible to a disembodied desire for some radically other transcendent. Irigaray's lips offer a theological dimension to flesh and a sexed fleshiness of theological alterity. The connection between heaven and earth is no longer represented by the singularity of an arguably disembodied phallic signifier. Instead, this link is represented by the multiple folds in female genital lips—lips that challenge notions of a disembodied movement between heaven and earth. Lips' mutual touching might also be a penetration with tongue (*la langue*) and lips, invoking a pleasure without wounding. In the crossing lips, the border between one and the other and between one and the same is now reframed as an interval of time and space made possible by the erotic space of two, which are always more than two, reaching toward each other, touching, without grabbing hold. The lips are absolutely fleshy, and the specificity of this flesh shapes the contours of the space between them that constitute their crossing.

By virtue of the layers of those touching folds that confound the space of inside and outside, lower lips of feminine desire figure the vertical stretching between transcendence and immanence as an extension upward and downward, inward and outward—giving depth and dimension, giving flesh to the body on the cross, refusing to allow the specificity of its flesh to become a disembodied, masculine universal. In this fleshy resignification of Christian language of Incarnation and Crucifixion, lips perform nothing short of the resignification of the order of the universe: a resurrection that would redeem a world constructed through the annihilation of the feminine other.

The specular economy that enables the "'God' of man" also attributes transcendence to language and immanence to matter. This is the space-time of the cross that Irigaray's lips must re-traverse or penetrate in order to articulate an "'elsewhere' of feminine pleasure."[78] In the interval created by their rhetoric, I contend that the lips offer the type of "playful crossing" that Irigaray states in "The Power of Discourse" would refigure such distinctions between language and matter.[79] I argue that Irigaray's lips are probing the Christian Incarnation to embody the interval of uncertainty and tension between word and flesh without hierarchy. If it would take a "playful crossing, and an unsettling one, which would allow woman to rediscover the place of her 'self-affection.' Of her 'god,'" could Irigaray's lips offer up a different sort of divine, and therein a different *theo/logia*?[80] Could we read the lips crossing as laying claim to their nonthematizable materiality as a site of possibility or, as Stockton so provocatively suggests, for Irigaray embracing "their material opacity" as the rupture onto/into a "God" who is "also a crack, a lack, a gap—a fracture we need for the sake of new pleasures?"[81]

This theology of lips (perhaps?) conceives an eros that holds flesh and radical alterity together in a way that the God-man of the Christian Incarnation cannot. Beyond the time and space of the historical specificity of the incarnation, this theology of lips marks embodied tension of desire at the limits of word and flesh, or discourse and matter, where bodies struggle to see and be seen without reifying the specular economy. To borrow from Butler's analysis of the distinctly nonphallogocentric materiality of Irigaray's feminine, Irigaray's lips constitute "a nonthematizable materiality" precisely because they refuse the binaries of metaphysics.[82] Perhaps a desire belonging to an "nonthematizable materiality" allows the possibility for thinking *through* sexual difference to get beyond sexual difference.

In the introduction to *Ethics*, Irigaray remarks that thinking through sexual difference would be the "salvation" of "our time," reminding her reader that beyond philosophical critique or rhetorical play, the lips are the incarnation of an ethical possibility.[83] The lips return later in the text to express a desire that is ethical in its refusal to be singular: They refuse to be *either* material *or* transcendental. Irigaray's lips crossing mimic the Christian cross to reorder the relationship between immanence and transcendence, insisting instead that incarnation is partial—always open even as it may be sealed, always changing even in its specificity. The lips' rhetorical capacity to resignify the incarnation is inextricably bound to this irreducible relationship between pleasure/genitals and speech/mouth that indicates a differentiated desire. The lips may be rhetorical, but if they're not really lips, if it's not really flesh, then the ethical force of her writing is lost. It is this embodied alterity in the space of writing that evokes an eros irreducible to its potential wounding.

Eros and Incarnation: Toward a Theology of Lips

In the space between rhetoric and flesh, the embodied alterity of the lips engenders a nonphallogocentric logos of an other sort of a non-metaphysical transcendence. Here, the lips are an invitation to lived reality at the crossroads of what is imagined and what is real. Because the lips are mimetic and bound to a discourse of sexual difference that is itself a repetition of sameness and difference, they invite meditation on the gap where their fleshy edges intimately meet. To borrow Anne Carson's imagery, the space of reaching without grasping, of touching without holding, desire without consuming, ensures the desire the lips evoke is erotic.[84]

Rather than a gaping space of wounded desire of the feminine, the lips in *Ethics* dis-assimilate the feminine by speaking flesh to desire, by incarnating an other desire through a disruptive mimesis that recasts the relationship between language and matter. An emphasis on the crossroads of the lips insists that lips are erotic—sexual and signifying, but reducible to neither. They are erotic in that their borders are themselves constituted by the space between them, a space that is always radically touching. The lips, mimetically read as the crossroads of signification and flesh indeterminately entangled in the becoming of subjects, give new depth and dimension to the cross—the incarnate desire of the lips on the cross prioritize the ambiguity of difference in eros rather than woundedness. The crossing lips figure an incarnation suspended in radical alterity, embodying that occluded space upon which the binary logic of inside and outside, of heaven and earth, of subject and object are constructed.

As a rhetorical and material terrain for exploring the contours of this in-between space, the lips mark the pleasures of flesh becoming words in speech, insisting that incarnation is not simply a descent of the divine to the human but an ascent of the human to the divine. That she uses these lips, a certain flesh-made-word, to turn to the word-made-flesh of incarnation is an invitation to recall that bodies are sites where flesh and signification are bound up with one another in the sameness and difference of the space-time of living.

Bodies live, die, and are resurrected where flesh and signification meet. The coding of flesh into bodies—old bodies, young bodies, black bodies, male bodies, female bodies, transgender and cisgender bodies, able bodies, disabled bodies—has real effects, even if that coding is impermanent, dynamic, and to some extent arbitrary. In this context, returning to Irigaray is compelling because, as the lips reveal, her work operates in the tension between the material and the discursive, between the present and the future that these living, flesh and blood bodies inhabit.

Most significantly, this irreducible space of desire constituted by the lips neither fetishizes the wounding that can accompany the experiences of living amid this tension, nor does it close off, or suture, every hole as though it were a wound. A theological ethics of the lips would be one that reflects upon the intertwining of flesh and signification as reaching for one another in the sweet bitterness of eros rather than the deep wounding of a desire resolved in the separation of the soul from its body or the annihilation of the self in becoming divine.

Notes

1. Judith Butler, "Bodies That Matter," in *Engaging with Irigaray: Feminist Philosophy and Modern European Thought*, ed. Carolyn G. Heilbrun and Nancy K. Miller (New York: Columbia University Press, 1994), 141–173. Butler notes that this now famous essay that was first published in the eponymous book was originally written for the volume on Irigaray.

2. Butler, "Bodies That Matter," 145.

3. Irigaray ESD, 138, emphasis added.

4. Irigaray TS, 134–135.

5. Mimesis is a strategy most evident in Irigaray's early works of the 1970s–1990s. *Speculum of the Other Woman*, *This Sex Which Is Not One*, and *An Ethics of Sexual Difference* offer especially sustained adoptions of mimesis that expose the tensions between the ideality of differences and their veiling in a discourse that drives toward singularity. Mimesis also functions constructively in

these works, linking the multiplicity of women's desires with inconsistencies and disruptions in language that confound the drive toward singularity of meaning. Irigaray's later works are increasingly less mimetic and are more ostensibly critical and constructive political projects; however, meditative and poetic dimension persists in Irigaray's writings to press the limits of meaning-making, even when not explicitly a mimetic adoption of the feminine. I view the progression of Irigaray's work as varied but continuous, mostly in concert with Maria Cimitile and Elaine Miller's evaluation of Irigaray's writings. Cimitile and Miller frame their edited volume *Returning to Irigaray* with an attention to debates about conceptual and stylistic shifts in Irigaray's writings. Their introduction astutely suggests that interpretations of continuity and/or discontinuity in Irigaray's body of work are testaments to the limits of our own philosophical positions, positions that lack the capacity to imagine other worlds with Irigaray. See the introduction to Maria C. Cimitile and Elaine P. Miller, *Returning to Irigaray: Feminist Philosophy, Politics, and the Question of Unity* (Albany: State University of New York Press, 2007), 1–23.

6. Irigaray TS, 76.

7. Irigaray TS, 134.

8. Irigaray TS, 134.

9. Irigaray TS, 134–135.

10. Butler, "Bodies That Matter," 158.

11. Elizabeth Grosz, *Sexual Subversions: Three French Feminists* (Winchester, MA: Unwin Hyman, 1989), 113.

12. Grosz, *Sexual Subversions*, 113.

13. Irigaray TS, 205.

14. Irigaray TS, 205. In the French text, this shift is signaled by the past participle "es" endings indicating feminine dialogical partners of I/you and we/us. Carolyn Burke suggests that the shift disrupts the "subject-object paradigm." Carolyn Burke, "Irigaray through the Looking Glass," *Feminist Studies* 7, no. 2 (Summer 1981): 300.

15. Irigaray TS, 206.

16. Irigaray TS, 205.

17. Irigaray TS, 205.

18. Irigaray ESD, 127.

19. In French *le langage* is masculine, refers to language in the sense of expression in words, and is different from one's tongue (*la langue*) as in one's national language, speech (*la parole*), or discourse (*le discours*). Irigaray is playing on the absence of a feminine language from which to express feminine desire that is implicit in masculine gendering *langage* when she says, "If we keep on speaking the same language (*langage*) together, we're going to reproduce the same history." Irigaray TS, 205.

20. Irigaray TS, 209–210.

21. Irigaray TS, 208–209.

22. Maggie Berg, "Irigaray's Contradictions: Poststructuralism and Feminism," *Signs* 17, no. 1 (1991): 67.

23. Irigaray TS, 210.

24. Irigaray TS, 210.

25. Irigaray TS, 210. The French uses the *tu* form with present tense verbs such that endings do not clearly signal the interlocutor's gender at this point in the text.

26. Berg, "Contradictions," 66.

27. Irigaray TS, 26.

28. See Butler's suggestion that woman constitutes and yet is excluded from the form/matter binary in "Bodies That Matter," especially, 155.

29. See Irigaray TS, 26–29.

30. Irigaray TS, 28.

31. Irigaray TS, 28.

32. Irigaray TS, 29.

33. Irigaray TS, 205.

34. In the 1980 English debut of *Quand nos lèvres se parlent* in *Signs*, Carolyn Burke translates the line "Ton sang devenu leur sens" as "Your blood translated to their senses" (*Signs* 6, no. 1 [Autumn 1980]: 69); however, the later translation by Catherine Porter reads, "Your blood becomes their meaning." Burke's translation lends itself to the poetic reading of Irigaray's work and language, but I prefer Porter's translation here because it captures the language of sacrifice more clearly. Irigaray TS, 205.

35. Irigaray TS, 212.

36. In her 1987 interview with Alice Jardine, published in the English translation of *Je, Tu, Nous*, as "Writing as a Woman," Irigaray insists the lips act as a reclamation of the body as the foundation of differentiated, sexed subjects. Irigaray JTN, 58–59.

37. Irigaray S, 233.

38. Irigaray TS, 28.

39. For Irigaray's depiction of morpho-logic, see Irigaray JTN, 59. The need for a new morphology ties back into Irigaray's critique of metaphysical distinctions of form/matter that are constructed on the occlusion of the feminine that constitutes its logic. Leading theologians who have explicitly used Irigaray's deconstruction of metaphysics in their own constructive projects include Ellen Armour, Sarah Coakley, Serene Jones, Morny Joy, Catherine Keller, and the late philosophers of religion Pamela Sue Anderson and Grace Jantzen. The inexhaustibility of the question of incarnation in Irigaray's work is evident in more recent critiques offered by Anne-Claire Mulder and Emily A. Holmes, among others. Furthermore, constructive theologians and/or religion scholars are not the only ones who have been interested in incarnation, as is evidenced by Gail Schwab, Peta Hinton, and Kathryn Stockton.

40. Ada S. Jaarsma, "Irigaray's *To Be Two*: The Problem of Evil and the Plasticity of Incarnation," *Hypatia* 18, no. 1 (Winter 2003): 48.

41. Irigaray TS, 30.

42. I will capitalize Incarnation when referring to the specific incarnation of Jesus as Christ and theologies of that incarnation in the Christian tradition. I will not capitalize incarnation when referring to it more generally.

43. The verse that foregrounds the theology of Incarnation is from the Gospel of John, which reads, "The Word became flesh" (John 1:14, New Revised Standard Version).

44. Ann-Marie Priest, "Woman as God, God as Woman: Mysticism, Negative Theology, and Luce Irigaray," *Journal of Religion* 83, no. 1 (January 2003): 19. Priest's meditation on the language of lips in "La Mystérique" emphasizes the mystical experience, and the experience of woman, as that of saying the unsayable.

45. Hollywood is quite critical of Irigaray's appropriation of the mystics as narrowly and a-historically focusing on the "divinized body." Amy M. Hollywood, "Beauvoir, Irigaray, and the Mystical," *Hypatia* 9, no. 4 (Fall 1994): 160–161.

46. Carole Slade explains how the last epigraph comes from Angela of Foligno, "Last Letter," which itself belongs to a larger set of writings, *Instructiones*. Carole Slade, "Alterity in Union: The Mystical Experience of Angela of Foligno and Margery Kempe," *Religion and Literature* 23, no. 3 (Autumn 1991): 109–126.

47. Irigaray S, 199–200, ellipsis original.

48. See Irigaray's suggestion that space for men and women needs to be reimagined in ESD, 11–12. See also her engagement with Spinoza on the relationship of space to the ethics of "God." Irigaray ESD, 83–94.

49. Irigaray S, 200.

50. Irigaray S, 199.

51. Irigaray S, 200.

52. Irigaray S, 200.

53. Kathryn Stockton, "'God' between Their Lips: Desire between Women in Irigaray and Eliot," *Novel* (Spring 1992): 354. Stockton accurately depicts the ambiguity of pleasure that the lips evoke apart from their mediation by the mystical scene of heterosexual love.

54. Irigaray S, 200, emphasis original.

55. Butler, "Bodies That Matter," 155; Irigaray TS, 179.

56. Irigaray S, 200.

57. Hollywood, *Acute Melancholia*, 172.

58. Butler, "Bodies That Matter," 158; Butler in Hollywood, *Acute Melancholia*, 172.

59. Hollywood, *Acute Melancholia*, 187.

60. Hollywood, *Acute Melancholia*, 188.

61. Butler, "Bodies That Matter," 158.

62. Irigaray TS, 206.

63. Irigaray TS, 77. See also Butler's discussion of the relationship between this " 'elsewhere' of female pleasure" and matter in Irigaray's reading of Plato's portrayal of the feminine and the form/matter binary in "Bodies That Matter," especially 149–165, emphasis original.

64. Irigaray TS, 74.

65. Irigaray TS, 77.

66. Irigaray TS, 77, emphases original.

67. Irigaray ESD, 17.

68. Irigaray ESD, 18.

69. Irigaray ESD, 18.

70. Irigaray ESD, 18–19.

71. Irigaray ESD, 18.

72. Irigaray ESD, 18.

73. In renaissance art, the *ostentatio genitalium* (showing of genitals) represents a fixation on Jesus's maleness, which, as Leo Steinberg suggests in his *The Sexuality of Christ in Renaissance Art and in Modern Oblivion*, restores the potentiality of human sexuality. In Steinberg's depiction, the maleness of Christ affirms the form/matter binary as belonging to a masculine logic. Steinberg's emphasis on the textuality of images contributes to thinking through the relationship between flesh and signification in Irigaray. Steinberg claims images offer a subtlety of representation that words alone do not. I contend Irigaray invokes the materiality of flesh in her writing to create fleshy words that play with the space between the real and the specular. Leo Steinberg, *The Sexuality of Christ in Renaissance Art and in Modern Oblivion*, second ed. (Chicago: University of Chicago Press, 1996).

74. Irigaray TS, 77.

75. Irigaray TS, 31.

76. Irigaray's lips on the cross take on the mediating quality of mucous, membranes, and angels. Gail Schwab suggests a connection between the lips and angels from the point of view of how essential their fleshiness in Irigaray's writing is to their unique mediating function. See Gail M. Schwab, "Mother's Body, Father's Tongue," in *Engaging with Irigaray: Feminist Philosophy and Modern European Thought*, ed. Carolyn G. Heilbrun and Nancy K. Miller (New York: Columbia University Press, 1994), 351–378. This connection between lips, angels, and mucous as gesturing to the importance of interval thinking in Irigaray's project is also suggested when Irigaray refers to the lips as "the threshold that gives access to the *mucous*." Irigaray ESD, 18.

77. For a discussion of matter as potentiality in Aristotelian notions of form and matter and Irigaray's critique of such concepts, see Rebecca Hill, *The Interval: Relation and Becoming in Irigaray, Aristotle, and Bergson* (New York: Fordham University Press, 2012). See also Butler's discussion of form/matter in both Plato and Aristotle in "Bodies That Matter," especially 149–161.

78. Irigaray TS, 77.

79. Irigaray TS, 77.

80. Irigaray TS, 77.

81. Stockton, "'God' between Their Lips," 353. Stockton borrows from Irigaray's reference to "material opacity" in TS, 179.

82. Butler, "Bodies That Matter," 155.

83. Irigaray ESD, 5.

84. Anne Carson, *Eros the Bittersweet: An Essay* (Princeton, NJ: Princeton University Press, 2016), 171.

Bibliography

Berg, Maggie. "Luce Irigaray's Contradictions: Poststructuralism and Feminism." *Signs* 17, no. 1 (Autumn 1991): 50–70.

Burke, Carolyn. "Irigaray through the Looking Glass." *Feminist Studies* 7, no. 2 (Summer 1981): 288–306.

Butler, Judith. "Bodies That Matter." In *Engaging with Irigaray: Feminist Philosophy and Modern European Thought*, edited by Carolyn G. Heilbrun and Nancy K. Miller, 141–173. New York: Columbia University Press, 1994.

Carson, Anne. *Eros the Bittersweet: An Essay*. Princeton, NJ: Princeton University Press, 2016.

Grosz, Elizabeth. *Sexual Subversions: Three French Feminists*. Winchester, MA: Unwin Hyman, 1989.

Hill, Rebecca. *The Interval: Relation and Becoming in Irigaray, Aristotle, and Bergson*. New York: Fordham University Press, 2012.

Hollywood, Amy M. *Acute Melancholia and Other Essays: Mysticism, History, and the Study of Religion*. New York: Columbia University Press, 2016.

Hollywood, Amy M. "Beauvoir, Irigaray, and the Mystical." *Hypatia* 9, no. 4 (Fall 1994): 158–185, esp. 160–161.

Jaarsma, Ada S. "Irigaray's *To Be Two*: The Problem of Evil and the Plasticity of Incarnation." *Hypatia* 18, no. 1 (Winter 2003): 44–62.

Priest, Ann-Marie. "Woman as God, God as Woman: Mysticism, Negative Theology, and Luce Irigaray." *Journal of Religion* 83, no. 1 (January 2003): 1–23.

Schwab, Gail M. "Mother's Body, Father's Tongue." In *Engaging with Irigaray: Feminist Philosophy and Modern European Thought*, edited by Carolyn G. Heilbrun and Nancy K. Miller, 351–378. New York: Columbia University Press, 1994.

Slade, Carole. "Alterity in Union: The Mystical Experience of Angela of Foligno and Margery Kempe." *Religion and Literature* 23, no. 3 (Autumn 1991): 109–126. http://www.jstor.org/stable/40059491.

Steinberg, Leo. *The Sexuality of Christ in Renaissance Art and in Modern Oblivion*, second ed. Chicago: University of Chicago Press, 1996.

Stockton, Kathryn. "'God' between Their Lips: Desire between Women in Irigaray and Eliot." *Novel* 25, no. 3 (1992): 348–359.

Chapter Seven

Hailing Divine Women in Godard's *Hail Mary* and Miéville's *The Book of Mary*

Tessa Ashlin Nunn

"And it came to pass, that, when Elizabeth heard the salutation of Mary, the babe leaped in her womb; and Elizabeth was filled with the Holy Ghost. And she spake out with a loud voice, and said, Blessed art thou among women, and blessed is the fruit of thy womb."[1] Mary hailed Elizabeth. Elizabeth hailed Mary. Mary's speech permeated Elizabeth. The Christian religion at times calls for or upholds practices and ideologies that oppress women. And yet, Mary and Elizabeth's mutual recognition and communication model a love to and for women.

In this essay, I use Luce Irigaray's notions of the feminine divine to examine representations of the female gender in Anne-Marie Miéville's short film *The Book of Mary* (*Le Livre de Marie*) and Jean-Luc Godard's feature-length *Hail Mary* (*Je vous salue Marie*). Supposedly, Miéville and Godard directed these films separately without any intention to create a combined project. Yet, since their premiere in 1985, the two works are always projected jointly, with *The Book of Mary* preceding *Hail Mary*. Both films, set in Switzerland during the 1980s, construct a loose narrative around a character named Mary. In Miéville's film, a young girl learns that her parents plan to divorce and then spends time with each of them separately. In *Hail Mary*, the eponymous virgin is in constant conflict with her boyfriend Joseph who, having ended his relationship with his girlfriend Juliette, wishes to have complete control over Mary. After Gabriel announces her immaculate conception, Mary struggles to convince Joseph as well as her doctor that she is still a virgin. The couple weds and raises Mary's son until he runs away to tend to his Father's affairs. Interspersed through the central plot, the film depicts a separate narrative about an Eve-like character and her sexual adventure with a science professor, who advocates intelligent design. Although only *Hail Mary* engages with explicit biblical references, I study these films as separate attempts to recount the story of a young woman or girl who *could* have had an experience like that of the Virgin Mary.

By asking how women's divineness, as Irigaray sketches it, can be perceived in cinema, this essay reconsiders how women see their gender in films. For Lucy Bolton, the emphasis on seeking cultural signs to enable women to symbolize their desires is what makes Irigaray's psychoanalytic theory useful for feminist film theory. Relying less on Irigaray's psychoanalytic work, I draw on her concepts of the divine, in addition to her work on the sexual marketplace, to model a viewing practice in which the spectator actively probes films for signs of women's divineness. This search begins by looking for loving relations between on-screen mothers and daughters. Then, I examine the films' representations, or the absence of representation, of sociability among women instead of rivalry upholding women's symbolic status as exchange objects in the sexual market. Finally, I explore how the films portray autonomous women, meaning women who love themselves as they love others and women acting as creators instead of reproductive apparatus to be conquered. Maintaining the desire to see positive images of women, this method of analysis demonstrates that viewers have the choice to recognize women as loving, creative members of the female gender, even when films represent them as silent orifices through which men perpetuate the human race.

By actively seeking positive images of the female gender, spectators can honor women either as they appear in a film or in what the film represses. In Laura Mulvey's theory of female spectatorship, women oscillate between masculine and feminine positions, causing them to identify passively with the objectification of female characters. A search for the divine in cinematic portrayals of women, however, urges moviegoers to love themselves as they affirm favorable representations and dismiss negative representations.[2] By identifying with female characters as members of their gender community but not reflections of a limited definition of *woman*, female viewers can escape overidentifying with how women appear on screen. According to Mary Ann Doane's essay "Film and the Masquerade," this process of overidentification pushes women toward becoming the projected images, even when they represent negative role models.[3] In an Irigarayan approach to cinema, as Bolton has demonstrated, the film analyst avoids mastery of the filmmaker or spectator, letting them both simply be.[4] While it is possible to criticize Godard for producing a twentieth-century revamping of patriarchal perspectives on Christianity or to read *The Book of Mary* as a revisionist telling of the Marian myth, my intention is to examine how these films subvert or confirm traditions suppressing representations of divine women.

The Book of Mary: A Mother-Daughter Story

For Irigaray, to address oppression founded on sexual indifference, reconsidering the role of sexual difference in religion is fundamental. "To posit a gender, a God is necessary: *guaranteeing the infinite*."[5] The God-figure acts as a *horizon* allowing one to become, meaning to move infinitely toward a defined state of wholeness.[6] Seeking a feminine ideal, Irigaray reads Christian scripture to find a space for divine women, whom she identifies as women faithful to themselves, their sex, and their mothers. In Christianity, men endeavor to emulate God the Father and Christ the Son, while women, according to Irigaray, are left without any feminine divine models, namely women to admire and follow. Prevented from becoming toward an infinite horizon, woman is "fixed in the role of mother through whom the *son* of God is made flesh."[7] She is a divine instrument but not a divine woman. Irigaray does not claim to identify what the divine is or should be. Rather, she delineates "the structural possibility or necessity of the divine" elaborating the "ontological possibility of the divine as an existential-hermeneutic condition."[8] Instead of imposing its will on women, this malleable concept of the divine provides a horizon toward which women can develop their individuality in communication with other women as well as "a mirror to reflect women's own beauty back to themselves as an identity value."[9]

Mother-daughter relationships are paramount in rethinking sexual difference in religion. For Irigaray, a woman cannot become divine if she does not acknowledge her mother's divine potential. Patriarchal societies render this task difficult by dissuading women and girls' recognition of their mothers, as demonstrated in Irigaray's critique of Freud's theory on femininity.[10] Revaluing Christianity's feminine genealogy in her later essays, she turns to the Virgin Mary as a possible model for women's divine becoming. Asking why biblical women receive so little public attention, Irigaray's essay "Equal to Whom?" proposes that, due to men's rule over symbolic systems, images of holy women remain sparse. This dearth, she contends, dissuades admiration for female genealogies.

While I agree that women should discover or rediscover their gender's spiritual and religious history, I question if Christian iconography's sexual indifference stems from a paucity of representation. A plethora of paintings and monuments depict biblical women in both holy and secular spaces. Yet, these images seldom illustrate autonomous women striving toward their own ideal. As Irigaray points out in the essay "Divine Women," Western tradition "presents and represents the radiant glory of the mother, but rarely shows us a fulfilled woman," limiting portraits of women to "either mother (given that a *boy* child is what makes us truly mothers) or woman (prostitute and property of the male)."[11] So that women can reassert themselves "as women who not only give birth to children but who are also creators of cultural representations and symbols," it is imperative to produce images of women as daughters of mothers and as daughters loving *to* their mothers.[12] In *An Ethics of Sexual Difference*, Irigaray writes, "Women must love one another as mothers, with a maternal love, and as daughters, with a filial love. Both of them. In a female whole that, furthermore, is not closed off."[13] Without a representation of the divine made in their image that reflects a bidirectional love for their genealogy, women lack an ideal serving as the goal toward which they strive to become.

In his attempt to recreate Mary's story, Godard left out her mother and joined a long tradition of remaining oblivious to the mother of the Holy Mother. While religious writings emphasize father-son relationships, the only Christian text mentioning her family is the apocryphal Gospel of James. In Godard's film, Mary's lineage is limited to her father and her son. When the angel Gabriel comes to announce her pregnancy, he searches for her at her father's gas station. Later, after the baby's birth, Mary, Joseph, and the son go to her father's home where a woman leads Mary inside, while her father and Joseph discuss an economic alliance. The woman, too young to be Mary's mother, is the only woman in the film with whom Mary speaks. Cradling the child, the woman thanks Mary "pour toutes les femmes" (for all women). This scene exemplifies how Mary's virginal conception of the son overshadows her faithfulness to herself and her openness to the word of the Other (which I will discuss later in this essay). The woman is grateful to Mary for serving as the instrument through which God the Father acted. Both in the film and in Christianity at large, men and women venerate Mary as a virgin and the mother of Jesus but rarely as an autonomous woman.

In contrast to Godard's inscription of the Virgin in a masculinist history, Miéville links a child named Mary to a feminine genealogy and a cinematic aesthetic respecting the nonvisual. Through black shots and silence separating the different scenes, the cinematography alludes to a maternal ontology by evoking the invisible and the unheard. According to Irigaray, men favor the visible because it marks their exit from the womb and confirms their victory over the maternal.[14] Furthermore, Western cultures relegate female sexuality, like female genitals, to the invisible, the dark continent. For this reason, exploring the "non-visual ways of relating to the world and to other people" on screen is essential for analyzing films in relation to Irigaray's work.[15] The emptiness of the black screen confesses *The Book of Mary*'s failure to show a totality, whereas the nature shots inserted throughout *Hail Mary* attempt to connect the film to a universal knowledge of what exists, even when no one is looking.

The Book of Mary begins with the mother's story as both parents discuss their need for a separation. The film places the spectator in a sonorous experience with sounds of nature (flowing water and bird cries) as the opening credits appear on a black background. The disconnection between the visual and auditory fields continues in the first shot as we see Lake Geneva while hearing, in the voice-over, both the sound of birds and Mary's parents. During the early shots of the couple's conversation, the sound and the image are out of sync until the mother disagrees that she is on an equal footing with her husband. In an abrupt moment of harmonization, the aural and optical fields come together. By renouncing the role her husband assigned her, she becomes a subject that speaks.

In the couple's separate attempts to define and demonstrate love, the father turns to reason, understanding love as a question of logic; the mother, however, apprehends love as an undefinable element to be invented. Their inability to communicate love to one another elucidates a keystone in Irigarayan theory: hindered communication between the two sexes. The husband, whose voice is heard first, takes on the voice of God, the voice guaranteeing the social order that reduces women to property, excludes them from "between-woman sociality," and prevents "intersubjective exchanges" between the two genders.[16] In this sequence, the husband defends his frequent absences and situates love within an exchange system by contending that love does not always imply investing; sometimes it means saving, as if only one individual determines how love moves between two people. The scene's cinematographic and communicative discords accentuate a failure to speak "to *one another*," which Irigaray defines as a nonhierarchical, intersubjective model that, through mutual listening, "opens up a present in order to construct a future."[17]

Claiming not to experience reciprocity in her marriage (now that she too works outside the home), the wife suggests a need to build an identity in which she can situate herself as both a woman and a mother. To validate her role as a caregiver, she attempts to distinguish "un travail de mère" (a mother's job) and "une affaire de femme" (a woman's issue), but only concludes that she no longer needs to be subjugated and desires to see clearly. When the family is later seated at the breakfast table, the wife protests against their current trajectory of imitating expectations and expresses her desire to invent. Her husband responds, "Les femmes inventent peu. Même l'âme, c'est un homme qui l'a inventée" (Women are rarely inventive. Even the soul, it's a man who invented it). In line with Irigaray's argument, in *I Love to You*, that women's construction of their subjectivity is the groundwork for communication between the sexes, both the husband and wife need creative license before they can love each other. The film frames the couple's separation as a vital step allowing the mother to become a creative subject (hinted at when she engages in craftwork while her husband moves out) and a speaking subject who creates her own soul.

Miéville's short offers a positive maternal figure, who seeks her autonomy and values her genealogy. For Irigaray, love for the female gender and divineness first develop in women's love for their mothers, which transforms them into "daughter-gods."[18] Through her love for her autonomous mother, freed from masculine laws, a woman cherishes herself as her mother's creation and a member of her gender. Mary's actions attest to a visceral affection for her mother. In a bathtub together, Mary licks her mother's shoulder as if she wanted to appreciate and know her beyond the visible, reconnecting with her as a first life source and provider of nourishment. Mary asks her mother to describe how she was when she was younger. Acknowledging Mary's penchant for these stories, her mother praises this mother-daughter history as "le plus fort souvenir d'amour" (the strongest memory of love). Adding that it is difficult to rediscover this strength while moving forward, she urges Mary to prolong this force by learning to give and receive. This advice aligns with Irigaray's notion of mothers and daughters exchanging objects in an effort to be "defined as female I ⟷ You."[19] When the exchange object is history, a woman's maternal genealogy empowers her as she communicates it.

At her father's home, Mary becomes a vessel to be filled with already determined information, not a subject with whom the parent shares love and encourages inventive efforts. Studying her geometry lesson, Mary forms a V-shape with her hands and defines it as an angle. When she denies that her father's inverted V, formed with his hands, is also an angle, he enforces the law of binaries making the possibility of the V dependent on the existence of the inverted V.[20] Instead of copying the triangles he draws, Mary refuses to follow his instructions and covers the notebook with her hand. She cannot name or determine what a triangle is, only the father has naming power. Later, eating an apple, of which she offers a bite to her father, Mary seems to take on an Eve-like role. Yet, in contrast to Eve, Mary satisfies her curiosity with her own creativity. Refusing her father's reason, she interprets the world through a frame of multiplicity as she compares music to a conversation in which people simultaneously agree and disagree. She imitates such a conversation until her father silences her. Repressing her access to language, he peels away her subjectivity. Although Mary sits on her father's lap in this shot, filmed straight on, neither of them look at each other. Despite having the veneer of familial love, the father-daughter relationship is founded on subjugation and rigid rules. Nothing is exchanged between the two as the father distributes knowledge and the daughter is expected to receive it without protest.

After the parents' separation, their two homes become divergent spaces in which Mary experiences her body and language. In contrast to her father's seemingly windowless, urban apartment, the maternal household opens onto a panorama of Lake Geneva. At her mother's home, Mary engages in imaginative play and, unlike her seated positions in the apartment, she moves about freely. Traveling between the living room and the lakeside balcony, she improvises a dance expressing diverse sentiments, in a way mimicking her verbalization of music as a conversation conveying accord and dissension. After she finishes the dance by collapsing on the floor, her mother enters and asks if she is tired or dead. Mary despondently responds that she is dead because nothing remains the same. Trying to console her, the mother reminds her that everything must become, which means everything must change. As she caresses her child, the mother remarks that the verb "to love" (*aimer*) is in her name (*Marie*). This emphasis on change and the fluidity of language as a basis for love resonates with Irigaray's observation that "to regulate and cultivate energy between human beings," we need "language that facilitates and maintains communication."[21] Love—an exchange in which both subjects give and receive—necessitates an ethic of language in which both subjects can become without controlling the other.

Language remains fluid in the film's ambiguous ending that hints at a change in Mary's relationship to her origin. In the final scene, Mary says goodbye to her mother as she leaves on a date. Once her mother has left, Mary sings Beethoven's "Für Elise" waving a knife as if it were a baton. She stops, looks at her boiled egg, and tells it:

> Ce sera tuer dans l'œuf l'organisation de l'Europe. Il faut absolument étouffer cette affaire, dans l'œuf. D'ailleurs, on ne fait pas d'omelette sans casser des œufs. Alors . . . je sais pas, moi. Je sais vraiment pas quoi dire. Va te faire cuire un œuf. Ça me paraît la seule solution.

> It would be nipping the unification of Europe in the bud. This affair absolutely must be smothered, from the beginning. Anyway, we can't make an omelet without breaking eggs. So . . . I don't know. I really don't know what to say. Get lost! That seems to be the only solution.

The sequence finishes with a close-up shot of the broken egg and then abruptly transitions to *Hail Mary*. David Sterritt reads this final scene as an opening into Godard's film that foreshadows the round images punctuating the feature length, such as the moon, basketballs, and Mary's pursed lips. Moreover, Sterritt emphasizes the egg's symbolic connection "to the feminine (through its Origin)" and "to procreation (through its primary purpose)."[22] For Cynthia Erb, the ending creates "a figural birth" to Godard's film.[23] What interests me is not so much the object, or what follows the final shot, but the egg's necessary destruction. This enigmatic ending suggests that the egg must be destroyed, in the same way that the daughter must separate from her maternal origin, exit childhood, and become something. Perhaps Miélville's Mary could only experience reciprocal love for her mother during the period when she was independent from men.

Although the film contains no explicit scriptural reference, the title, *Le Livre de Marie* (*The Book of Mary*), underscores a biblical lacuna. It cannot refer to knowledge or representations of the Virgin Mary as a child because, with the exception of one apocryphal text, this knowledge and these representations do not exist. Miélville, therefore, creates a possible representation of a mystery. The film suggests that to become a divine woman, capable of inspiring divine love, Mary must have learned to love within a reciprocal exchange.

Hail Mary: A Story of Men

Cinema, like religion, offers an understanding of the world constructed by those who create and diffuse it. *Hail Mary* associates the filmmaking process with the creation of life by intelligent design through the character of the professor who seemingly proposes that "cinematic meaning is produced by a director who stands in relation to his creation as God does to life."[24] As S. Brent Plate contends in *Religion and Film: Cinema and the Re-creation of the World*, both cinema and religion are forms of worldmaking that order the cosmos to instruct viewers or followers how to see time and space.[25] Inspired by Plate's theory, I argue that films and religion are likewise systems of *peoplemaking* that present characters to teach how to think about gendered persons. Commending some characters and disparaging or ignoring others, cinema and religion shape how spectators or believers perceive people as positive or negative models.

The story of Mary and Joseph, as man and woman, remains rare in cinema. As Godard said to an Italian reporter, "Cinema has dealt with God, Cecil DeMille gave him a long beard, Jesus frequently appeared on screen, but no one has told the story of Mary and Joseph."[26] While Mary is the main character of *Hail Mary*, the film focuses on the men around her and their attempts to define her. By limiting women to their relationships with men, it relies on a myriad of sexist traditions.

The Catholic community certainly did not appreciate Godard's version of Mary's life and her sacred motherhood. When John Paul II condemned it as hurtful to Christians, *Hail Mary* became the first film openly criticized by a pope. In response to protests across the globe, several countries banned or attempted to ban the film for its nude and sexualized virgin.[27] In my view, such critiques miss the point. We should see Mary as a sexual/sexuate, loving being. Who is she beyond the recipient of the Holy Ghost, the container of the son, and the mother of Jesus?

We also need representations of Mary as a woman among women. Apart from linking Mary to the redemption of Eve's sin, the film fails to show Mary's place in a female community. She exists as Joseph's girlfriend, her father's daughter, and her son's mother, but never as a daughter or a friend to other women. Although she plays on a women's basketball team, she never talks to the other players. Placing her among men, Godard limits her interactions with women to competitive encounters. In the essay "Divine Women," Irigaray maintains that women without a god cannot communicate or commune with other women because they lack a horizon to share.[28] The absence of female relationships in the film reveals Mary's disbelief in a god. She does not aspire to a divine horizon, even if her body is the site of a divine action. Unable to recognize her belonging to a gender community, Mary cannot recognize any divine ontology or her capacity to be the origin of a divine child. Consequently, she is confined to the role of an instrument.

In the opening scene, Joseph and his ex-girlfriend Juliette restrict the female gender to containers in which men enter and out of which children emerge; in other words, women are reduced to a silent hole. With the camera focused on Joseph eating, Juliette establishes the theme of associating women with their orifices by declaring: "Tout ce qui sort de ma bouche, ça devient de la merde" (Everything that comes out of my mouth becomes shit). Joseph consumes nourishment through his mouth while Juliette equates her speech to abject waste. After he advises her to simply stop speaking, she proposes marriage as a solution to their failing relationship, offering to sacrifice herself in what Irigaray qualifies as the rite through which men establish societies—the exchange of silent women.[29] Juliette then generalizes all women as desiring to have a baby. Seemingly without intending to challenge patriarchal practices, she performs an estranged form of femininity as a masquerade by limiting women to motherhood and treating her body as an exchange object. A disinterested Joseph responds, "Les hommes croient qu'ils entrent dans une femme" (Men believe that they enter in a woman). The film repeatedly returns to this view of men's relation to women's vaginas, suggesting that penetration erases the memory of being born out of a woman.

Instead of celebrating their gender, the female characters in *Hail Mary* confirm and perpetuate male characters' symbolic dominance by belittling women's speech and treating themselves as exchange objects. Joseph mediates an antagonistic relationship between Mary and Juliette, who talk about each other to Joseph, but they never talk to each other. In their inquiries regarding each other, they recognize their common situation as objects managed by men and uphold this situation through their rivalry. Within the sexual market system, women become objects of exchange ensuring the symbolic order, without gaining access to it or receiving payment in symbolic form. That is to say, women's "silent" but "productive" bodies regulate social relations between men and create societies' infrastructures, "without being recognized as a force of production."[30]

Conforming to the Western traditions that limit women to mothers, virgins, or prostitutes, the film opposes the sexual value of the virginal and then maternal Mary to women who are neither virgins nor wives nor mothers, namely Eva and Juliette. Joseph scorns Juliette, and Eva's professor-cum-lover abandons her, because, like prostitutes, they lack the pure exchange value of a virgin and the use value of a mother. As Irigaray shows in "Women on the Market," in an exchange market determining women's value, women and men never positively acknowledge sexual difference and establish ethical relations based on this difference. Furthermore, this absence of recognition distances women from each other by weakening any affinity they may have among themselves as members of the same gender, thereby minimizing the possibility of female friendships. Due to the film's emphasis on their positions within the sexual market, the three main female characters exist only in relation to men.

While the film includes hardly any dialogue between women, the female characters talk about each other regarding their relationships to men, thereby confirming their existence as always and only exchange objects. At the end of the opening scene, Juliette asks in the voice-over, "Où t'en es avec Marie?" (Where are you with Mary?). The story of Mary and Joseph thus begins. While we do not hear Joseph's response to Juliette's question, the film itself seems to answer it by exposing Joseph's relationship *with* Mary but not her relationship *to* him. Here, I base my differentiation between a relationship *with* and *to* someone on Irigaray's notion of the preposition in "I love *to* you" as a guarantor of two intentionalities.[31] Because the other characters treat Mary as an instrument through which God and men arrive at their ends, no one acknowledges her intentionality.

Women's capacity to create undermines men's capacity to produce only lifeless creations, void of breath. As Mulvey observes, Godard conflates Mary's "enigmatic properties of femininity" and "the mystery of origins, particularly the origins of creativity, whether the creation of life or the creative processes of art."[32] In Godard's earlier films *A Woman Is a Woman*, *A Married Woman*, and *Contempt*, men attempt to decide when and if the female protagonists become pregnant. *Hail Mary* nuances this theme by accentuating the importance of the name. To ensure his symbolic status as father and prevent the development of a maternal genealogy from mother to son, Joseph will accept that the son is not his child as long as the son bears his name; that is to say, as long as the son continues his genealogy. We then learn that the couple is married when Joseph abrasively corrects someone who calls Mary "Mademoiselle." As Irigaray argues, the surname of the husband or the father demarcates "ownership" over the wife and children.[33] Joseph's anger at the stranger demonstrates his desire to maintain an order in which his name holds power. According to Irigaray, man appropriates the other sex to develop a relation to himself as an origin.[34] While the mother and son stand in for Joseph's inability to create a genealogy, Mary does not mark her lineage with her name nor celebrate her creative role as mother.

Instead of establishing her own family line, Mary opposes the first woman—the sinner. Interwoven in the sequences of Mary and Joseph, the story of Eva develops. Searching to fulfill her curiosity, she questions and seduces her professor, who calls her Eve. Denying the possibility of a divine or maternal ontology, the professor uses science and metaphysics to explain human existence. Playing the part of the snake, he poisons her with the name Eve and prevents her from developing her own theory of origins. Eva's sin resides not in her hunger for knowledge but in her renunciation of herself. She commits what Irigaray calls the sin of women: the sin of leaving themselves.[35] Mary is likewise guilty of this sin by allowing others to name her.

A Loving and Speaking Virgin or a Virgin among Men

In Godard's film, Mary acquires a son and a husband whereas the professor leaves Eva to return to his wife and son. Losing herself to another, in abidance with the law of the father, Mary atones for Eva/Eve, who loses herself outside the law. In Irigaray's understanding of Mary's atonement for Eve's sin, the first woman's fault resides in her desire to reduce the divine to knowledge. She wanted to know the unknowable. Mary, in contrast, preserves a "virginal breath" and a relation to life and divine love that neither appropriates nor consumes herself, others, or God.[36] For Irigaray, Mary's breath serves as a "vehicle for love" and grants her autonomy, interiority, and subjectivity. Through her breath and language, Irigaray's Mary loves *to* herself and others. By examining the absence of this virginal breath in *Hail Mary*, I show how consent and reciprocal love serve as the foundation for Irigaray's notions of virginity and conception, which contribute to an understanding of women's divineness instead of reinforcing women's reified status in the sexual marketplace.

Before women can look to Mary as a divine model, they must first appreciate her as a woman. Irigaray proposes two interpretations of the Annunciation and Mary's virginal conception in which Mary conserves her autonomy. In one reading, God's word, produced through breath, serves as a substitute for physical relations between lovers. In her second interpretation, Irigaray understands the Annunciation and Mary's pregnancy as God's announcement through speech and Mary's response leading to the child's conception.[37] In this reading, God and Mary unite through communication as both lovers and loved ones. The Annunciation thus models communication and a belief in the unknown through love: "Mary said 'Yes,' yes to the advent of something not yet appeared, and that she was able to bring into the world. Mary is thus capable of more than the totality of that which already exists."[38] Mary's greatest achievement was her ability to see what was not visible. The Christian tradition, however, tends to limit Mary's lauded deeds to what patriarchal society already expects women to do: remain a virgin until they become mothers.

For Irigaray, Mary's breathing exteriorizes "the redemption of humanity" through the union of God's breath and Mary's virginal breath to create a life.[39] Godard's Mary, in contrast, breathes in fear and suffering, giving no indication of consent. In *Hail Mary*, the cinematography transforms the conception into a scene of anguish and torment. Lying naked on her bed, Mary alternates between slow deep breaths and gasps for air as her body twists into poses resembling Charcot's hysteric women or the *Pietà*. The camera captures her body in voyeuristic low-angle shots before cutting to close-up shots of her pubic region. The emphasis on her suffering in this sequence hints at the Passion of the Christ and, in a way, acknowledges women's pain. Irigaray equates women's suffering to Christ's anguish since both have striven to save the world, yet they endure hardship differently. Yet, contrary to Christ and other masculine religious figures, women receive little recognition for their suffering for others.

Although Mary does not say yes to the Annunciation in the film, unlike Joseph and her doctor, she is able to see what is not there. Having never had sex and having menstruated a few days earlier, she struggles to convince her incredulous doctor that she is indeed a pregnant virgin. In the Gospels, Elizabeth believes Mary by encountering the Holy Spirit through her presence. Never speaking to women about her immaculate conception, Godard's Mary asks men to confirm what she already knows as if their acknowledgment carries more weight than her speech and her trust in herself. Irigaray suggests that communicating among women, "sheltered from men's imperious choices that put them in the position of rival commodities," women "forge a social status that compels recognition."[40] Without such recognition, Mary's lack of confidence in her knowledge and distance from other women maintain her commodity-like situation. She therefore cannot make her knowledge recognizable.

The film focuses on Mary's virginity uniquely in relation to men. For Irigaray, the physical presence of the hymen does not determine a woman's virginity. Rather, her spiritual interiority, which she establishes for herself, and her capacity to welcome "the word of the other without altering it" defines her as a virgin faithful to herself and her gender.[41] Spiritual virginity requires an act of love for both the self and the other. To maintain her virginity, a woman must not lose herself "in the attraction for the other," nor allow the other to rule her.[42] Irigaray describes the woman "capable of virginity" as "capable of keeping an autonomous and free breathing, a breathing which serves not only her survival, but to be and become a human."[43] In this sense, breathing is the movement toward a divine horizon. Unlike the virgin defined by her position in the sexual market, Irigaray's notion of a virgin situates women outside this market. As sovereign subjects instead of exchange objects, women can love their femininity, which they determine for themselves, and maintain their virginity (a sign of their progress toward a divine horizon) safe from penetration.

This Irigarayan concept of virginity is absent from *Hail Mary* because the film reduces women to vaginas through which men affirm their subjectivity. During the Annunciation scene, Gabriel reformulates Joseph's earlier comment about entering women, adding a cyclical element to the birth of man: "N'oublie pas, ce qui entre sort, et ce qui sort entre" (Don't forget: what enters comes out, and what comes out enters). Man leaves his mother to impregnate another woman, from whose womb another man will exit. In the film's final scene, Gabriel sees Mary and hails her: "Je vous salue, Marie." She then gets in a car and hesitatingly traces her lips in the air with a phallic-shaped lipstick. The last shot features a close-up of the hole in Mary's pursed, painted mouth. In effect, the film concludes with Mary as a holy hole.

Connecting Mary's, Eva's, and Juliette's stories, the first and final scenes interrogate the cyclical entering and exiting of women's bodies as an ontological basis for men's existence. Mulvey sees the last sequence as the completion of a cycle in which the "Virgin turns into a whore" as Mary reverts to Eve, "the mother of lust."[44] I, however, view this scene as a continuation of Mary responding to the image of her gender produced and hailed by men. She first acted as a container and an orifice out of which came a child. When her son's departure into the world frees her from being mother-the-nurturer, she once again becomes woman-the-silent-hole.

Mary and the World

While *Hail Mary* denies Mary relations to other women, it links her to the natural universe. Throughout the film, shots of Mary alternate with shots of nature, particularly the moon, grass, and flowing water. On the one hand, these shots give the camera an all-seeing, godlike power. On the other hand, Mary's connection to nature in these montages associates her with what Irigaray calls the feminine task of presiding over nature.[45] Shots of the male characters tend to follow shots of industrialized areas' cacophony and artificial lights. As Irigaray writes, a woman lives "in an interweaving of relations with other subjects or with nature," whereas a man "builds himself his own world: with tools, objects, laws, gods."[46] The film's associations between gender and space suggest that Mary has the task of restoring modern society to a more divine, natural state.

Through the parallel stories of Eva and Mary, the film opposes metaphysical origins to maternal ontology. Feigning knowledge of universal laws, the professor teaches Eva that our origin lies in science and reason.

The professor insists on a separation between the planned development of the world created by intellect and the chance of the natural world. Without any acknowledgment of the maternal, he urges Eva to understand her existence through the scientific origins of the cosmos: "Tu es née de quelque chose, ailleurs, dans le ciel. Cherche, et tu trouveras bien plus que tu n'imagines" (You were born out of something, elsewhere, in the sky. Search, and you will indeed find more than you think). Like the serpent and, in a sense, the father in *The Book of Mary*, the professor seduces Eva by convincing her that he possesses the knowledge she lacks. Later, he contradicts his previous assertions, advising her to believe only in natural laws. His shifting position corroborates with his final remark that men are fickle and cannot be believed. According to Irigaray, claims to the universal pervert nature by contending that it is "easy to explain" and by imposing "norms that kill or mortify life rather than realizing it fully."[47] The film shows that knowledge of origins and the workings of the universe are only enunciations in a system that gives more weight to certain enunciators and ignores others.

Neglect for maternal ontologies stems from a desire to dominate and determine nature. The film's divide between the natural world as the feminine and the tamed world as the masculine supports Irigaray's contention that the human race is split into two tasks, not two genders.[48] Women become *guardians of nature* while men become *guardians of culture*. At the same time, the social valence given to women's role in childbearing reduces women to pure nature. By not showing the birth of Mary's son but alluding to it with a shot of a cow licking a newborn calf, the film accentuates this reduction. Equated to nature, women become a force to be conquered, and their "deliberate human participation" in motherhood is forgotten.[49] Men, however, can deny their origins in nature by relying on industry and tools: they can refute their subjugated role to a creator by creating objects. Moreover, through the father's name, they can reject their maternal (and therefore natural) origin. Guarding and giving value to man-made creations, men seek to become their own creators.

A Feminine Horizon

For Irigaray, if women wish to enter a symbolic order, they must construct one that recognizes sexual difference, positively affirms their belonging to a gender, and esteems their maternal origins. To create a more ethical future, in which women can celebrate their sexual difference and gain full subjectivity in society, women cannot simply destroy current patriarchal systems. They must develop new systems for creating and interpreting cultural signs. By reconsidering women's situation in relation to the divine, Irigaray offers a method for women to positively identify as a gender within sexual difference, a method that is applicable to female spectatorship.

Films like *The Book of Mary* and *Hail Mary* exemplify Western cultures' challenges in representing women as divine. By reading these two films through an Irigarayan perspective, I have modeled how spectators can seek female genealogies and love for the feminine in films that succeed or fail in creating positive images of the female gender. Such a practice encourages viewers to recognize how films show women in communion with each other, loving mother-daughter relationships, and respect for female genealogies. This method of engaging with cinema also urges spectators to acknowledge the gaps in films that reduce women to reproductive objects to be conquered, thereby preventing viewers from accepting these cinematic representations as desirable or normal. The act of looking for positive images of women can cultivate spectators' appreciation of sexual difference, even when these images are absent. Searching for light when cinema represents women as dark holes, spectators can create their own divine horizon.

Notes

1. Luke 1:41–42, King James Version.

2. Laura Mulvey, "Afterthoughts on 'Visual Pleasure and Narrative Cinema' Inspired by King Vidor's *Duel in the Sun* (1946)," in *Visual and Other Pleasures* (London: Palgrave Macmillan, 1989), 29–38.

3. Mary Ann Doane, "Film and the Masquerade: Theorising the Female Spectator," *Screen* 23, no. 3–4 (1982): 74–88.

4. Lucy Bolton, *Film and Female Consciousness: Irigaray, Cinema and Thinking Women* (New York: Palgrave Macmillan, 2011).

5. Irigaray SG, 61.

6. Irigaray ESD.

7. Irigaray SG, 62.

8. Alison Martin, *Luce Irigaray and the Question of the Divine* (Leeds: Maney, 2000), 133.

9. Martin, *Luce Irigaray and the Question of the Divine*, 139.

10. In Freudian psychoanalysis, the young girl's hatred of the mother increases the value of male sexuality. Freud negates any role that the mother could have in representing femininity or reproduction in the eyes of the young girl. Although the mother becomes the girl's object of identification, Freud denies the possibility of femininity developing through mimicry of the mother because this mimicry would suggest that the mother has something desirable to mirror. Irigaray demonstrates that, to avoid presenting the woman as someone who has something, Freud denies the possibility of the girl attempting to represent her origin outside of a phallic ontology. Irigaray S.

11. Irigaray SG, 63.

12. Anne Keary, "Catholic Mothers and Daughters: Becoming Women," *Feminist Theology* 24, no. 2 (2016): 198.

13. Irigaray ESD, 105.

14. Irigaray SG, 50.

15. Bolton, *Film and Female Consciousness*, 50.

16. Irigaray ILTY, 44–45.

17. Irigaray ILTY, 45–46.

18. Irigaray SG, 71.

19. Irigaray JTN, 48.

20. Cynthia Erb astutely interprets this scene as an allusion to the Virgin Mary's exclusion from the Holy Trinity. "The Madonna's Reproduction(s): Miéville, Godard, and the Figure of Mary," *Journal of Film and Video* 45, no. 4 (1993): 45.

21. Irigaray ILTY, 100.

22. David Sterritt, *The Films of Jean-Luc Godard: Seeing the Invisible* (Cambridge: Cambridge University Press, 1999), 174.

23. Erb, "The Madonna's Reproduction(s)," 43.

24. Lisa Trahair, "Belief in Cinema: Jean-Luc Godard's *Je vous salue, Marie* and the Pedagogy of Images," *Angelaki* 17, no. 4 (2012): 194.

25. S. Brent Plate, *Religion and Film: Cinema and the Re-creation of the World* (New York: Wallflower Press, 2008).

26. Translations are my own unless otherwise indicated. Maria Pia Fusco, "Godard: Ma Papa Wojtyla Avra' Visto Il Mio Film?," *La Repubblica*, April 25, 1985, https://ricerca.repubblica.it/repubblica/archivio/repubblica/1985/04/25/godard-ma-papa-wojtyla-avra-visto-il.html.

27. See Maryel Locke, "A History of the Public Controversy," in *Jean-Luc Godard's "Hail Mary": Women and the Sacred in Film*, ed. Maryel Locke and Charles Warren (Carbondale: Southern Illinois University Press, 1993).

28. Irigaray SG, 62.

29. Irigaray JTN, 7–10.

30. Irigaray, "Women's Exile: Interview with Luce Irigaray," trans. Couze Venn, *Ideology and Consciousness* 1 (1977): 71–73.

31. Irigaray ILTY, 103.

32. Laura Mulvey, "Marie/Eve: Continuity and Discontinuity in Jean-Luc Godard's Iconography of Women," in *Jean-Luc Godard's "Hail Mary": Women and the Sacred in Film*, ed. Maryel Locke and Charles Warren (Carbondale: Southern Illinois University Press, 1993), 46.

33. Irigaray S, 83.

34. Irigaray BTI, 357.

35. Irigaray C, 92.

36. Irigaray BEW, 78–89.

37. Irigaray BEW, 52.

38. Irigaray C, 98.

39. Irigaray C, 89.

40. Irigaray TS, 33.

41. Irigaray BTI, 357.

42. Irigaray BTI, 161.

43. Irigaray C, 96.

44. Mulvey, "Marie/Eve," 51.

45. Irigaray SG, 110.

46. Irigaray KW, 151.

47. Irigaray SG, 117.

48. Irigaray SG, 120.

49. Irigaray BTI, 357.

Bibliography

Bolton, Lucy. *Film and Female Consciousness: Irigaray, Cinema and Thinking Women*. New York: Palgrave Macmillan, 2011.

Doane, Mary Ann. "Film and the Masquerade: Theorising the Female Spectator." *Screen* 23, no. 3–4 (1982): 74–88.

Erb, Cynthia. "The Madonna's Reproduction(s): Miéville, Godard, and the Figure of Mary." *Journal of Film and Video* 45, no. 4 (1993): 40–56.

Fusco, Maria Pia. "Godard: Ma Papa Wojtyla Avra' Visto Il Mio Film?" *La Repubblica*, April 25, 1985. https://ricerca.repubblica.it/repubblica/archivio/repubblica/1985/04/25/godard-ma-papa-wojtyla-avra-visto-il.html.

Hail Mary. Directed by Jean-Luc Godard. 107 min. New Yorker Films, 2006. DVD.

Irigaray, Luce. "Women's Exile: Interview with Luce Irigaray." Translated by Couze Venn, *Ideology and Consciousness* 1 (1977): 71–73.

Keary, Anne. "Catholic Mothers and Daughters: Becoming Women." *Feminist Theology* 24, no. 2 (2016): 187–205.

Locke, Maryel. "A History of the Public Controversy." In *Jean-Luc Godard's "Hail Mary": Women and the Sacred in Film*, edited by Maryel Locke and

Charles Warren, 1–9. Carbondale: Southern Illinois University Press, 1993.

Martin, Alison. *Luce Irigaray and the Question of the Divine*. Leeds: Maney, 2000.

Mulvey, Laura. "Afterthoughts on 'Visual Pleasure and Narrative Cinema' Inspired by King Vidor's *Duel in the Sun* (1946)." In *Visual and Other Pleasures*, 29–38. London: Palgrave Macmillan, 1989.

Mulvey, Laura. "Marie/Eve: Continuity and Discontinuity in Jean-Luc Godard's Iconography of Women." In *Jean-Luc Godard's "Hail Mary": Women and the Sacred in Film*, edited by Maryel Locke and Charles Warren, 39–53. Carbondale: Southern Illinois University Press, 1993.

Plate, S. Brent. *Religion and Film: Cinema and the Re-creation of the World*. New York: Wallflower Press, 2008.

Sterritt, David. *The Films of Jean-Luc Godard: Seeing the Invisible*. Cambridge: Cambridge University Press, 1999.

Stone, Alison. "Mother-Daughter Relations and the Maternal in Irigaray and Chodorow." *philoSOPHIA* 1, no. 1 (2011): 45–64.

Trahair, Lisa. "Belief in Cinema: Jean-Luc Godard's *Je vous salue, Marie* and the Pedagogy of Images." *Angelaki* 17, no. 4 (2012): 194.

Part IV

Rethinking Race and Sexual Difference

Chapter Eight

White Supremacist Miscegenation

Irigaray at the Intersection of Race, Sexuality, and Patriarchy

Sabrina L. Hom

Far-right, White Nationalist, and neo-Nazi groups have received increasing attention in past years due to their increasing visibility and influence. The number of hate groups in the United States increased by 30 percent between 2015 and 2019,[1] while J. M. Berger estimates that Twitter accounts belonging to neo-Nazi and white supremacist organizations have increased their number of followers by 600 percent since 2012, growing faster than ISIS.[2] Mark Potok of the Southern Poverty Law Center observed, "In the immediate aftermath of the [2016 U.S. presidential] election, the Southern Poverty Law Center (SPLC) noticed a dramatic jump in hate violence and incidents of harassment and intimidation around the country."[3] Steve Bannon, erstwhile chairman of the alt-right platform *Breitbart*, was a senior advisor to President Trump, while "white nationalist" Richard Spencer held a rally in Washington, DC, where he led a crowd of supporters in a straight-armed salute and a chant of "Hail Trump."[4] The so-called "Unite the Right" rally in Charlottesville in August 2017 turned into a white supremacist race riot that resulted in three deaths and dozens of injuries. In Europe, far-right politicians like Geert Wilders, Marine Le Pen, Nigel Farage, and Norbert Hofer have gained prominence from nationalist and Islamophobic rhetoric, in some cases achieving or approaching significant victories. The ostensive white nationalist goals of "defending" white women's purity while enacting violence against people of color and traitorous white women emerge as a theme motivating acts of violence and terrorism, for example, in the writings of mass murderers Anders Breivik,[5] Dylann Roof, and Elliott Rodger.[6]

White nationalists position themselves rhetorically as the defenders of white civilization and pure white lineage—threatened, they claim, by demographic changes such as immigration and social changes such as integration and increased rates of interracial marriage. The Southern Poverty Law Center provides a brief summary and backgrounding of the term:

> Adherents of white nationalist groups believe that white identity should be the organizing principle of the countries that make up Western civilization. White nationalists advocate for policies to reverse changing demographics and the loss of an absolute, white majority. Ending non-white immigration, both legal and illegal, is an urgent priority—frequently elevated over other racist projects, such as ending multiculturalism and miscegenation—for white nationalists seeking to preserve white, racial hegemony.[7]

White nationalists present themselves as defenders against "white genocide," the destruction of white populations and white culture through violence and rape as well as through demographic change. It is against the paranoid fantasy of "white genocide" that the aforementioned violence is justified, as well as extreme anti-immigration policies. Obviously, there are significant differences between the international collection of alt-right, ethno-nationalist, neo-Nazi, and Euro-fascist groups contained under my label of white nationalism. I do not mean to elide the significant local historical, political, and economic effects that embolden these groups in their contexts. However, these organizations actively build international solidarities, and they are linked by common histories of colonialism and mutually resonant fears over immigration, Islam, and the loss of ethnoracial purity. The rhetoric of racial purity and racial/sexual threat shared by white and ethno-nationalist movements commits them to a shared sexual politics that emphasizes patriarchal control.

While white nationalists argue for the maintenance or creation of separate, pure, white nations and peoples, they are not primarily concerned with reproductive purity but rather with maintaining a racialized apparatus of sexuality that establishes not "purity" per se but rather white male dominance. The appearance of racial "purity" is an aftereffect of the control of white women's sexuality and what JanMohamed calls the "peculiar silence"[8] around white men's sexual contact with nonwhites. This apparatus of racial/sexual control might be called "white male supremacy"[9] or, as Audre Lorde puts it, "racist patriarchy."[10] In order to draw out the logic of racist patriarchy, I'll first look at the curious frequency of what I call "white supremacist miscegenation": instances of white supremacist, neo-Nazi, and ethno-nationalist leaders who engage in interracial sexuality. In the second section, I'll explore how this phenomenon fits into white supremacist ideology and histories of racial/sexual violence. Far from mere hypocrisy, this pattern illuminates the gendered logic of white supremacy, which rests on both the reproductive control of white women and the sexual exploitation of nonwhite women. In my final section, I'll argue that Irigaray's analysis of the reproductive instrumentalization and commodification of women provides a foundation from which to understand the role of white women in white nationalist ideology, but fails to account for racial difference. At the same time, black feminist works illuminate the situation of black women in racist patriarchy, illustrating that apparent contradictions in white supremacist ideology have their origins in the logic of slavery and colonialism. I will juxtapose the work of Irigaray with that of theorists focused on the experiences of women of color, in order to get a fuller picture of "racist patriarchy" that illuminates the role of both white and nonwhite women therein.

White Supremacist Miscegenation

The goals and values of white supremacist movements are often taken at face value, as 1) defined exclusively through the logic of racial difference and hierarchy—as opposed to, say, gender or class politics—and 2) committed to racial purity and segregation. For a nutshell description of their project, we need look no further than what the Anti-Defamation League calls "the most popular white supremacist slogan in the world," the "fourteen words": "We must secure the existence of our people and a future for white children."[11] White supremacists are understood to be defenders of white purity and reactionaries against a paranoid fantasy of white genocide. But both the gender politics and the racial politics of white supremacy are misrepresented on this superficial reading, as is shown by the frequency of "white supremacist miscegenation."

"Miscegenation" is an archaic term for interracial sexuality and marriage; it has an intrinsically pejorative implication, and was coined and popularized by pro-slavery campaigners who used the threat of interracial sexuality to undermine abolitionist and integrationist movements. The term itself originated in an 1863 hoax pamphlet[12] that represented parodically exaggerated support of interracial sexuality in order to discredit the abolitionist movement; the goal of the hoaxer—who was largely successful—was to embarrass abolitionist leaders and to mobilize white fears about interracial sexuality in defense of slavery.[13] I use this term to describe certain forms of interracial sexuality not in order to endorse its virulently racist implications but rather to emphasize an intrinsic tension within white supremacist movements, which simultaneously normalize certain forms of interracial sexuality while gaining power from hyperbolic fears of interracial sexuality. In doing so, I echo the parodic origins of the term and make use of an Irigarayan mimetic practice in order to underline internal tension in the logic of white male supremacy.

In January 2017, Mike Enoch, the podcaster "considered one of the leading figures of the emerging white nationalist movement in America,"[14] was revealed to be a pseudonym of Mike Peinovich, a New York software developer. "Despite making regular jokes about the Holocaust and killing Jews on his podcast, Peinovich is married to" a Jewish woman.[15] Within a few weeks, Peinovich was reported to be making a comeback,[16] and in August 2017 he was a headliner at the "Unite the Right" event in Charlottesville. Richard Spencer, a leading alt-right and white nationalist figure who has spoken of his desire to turn America into a "white ethno-state," has admitted that he favors dating Asian women.[17] Andrew Anglin, founder of the neo-Nazi website the *Daily Stormer*—called the "top hate site in America" by the SPLC[18]—and, along with Spencer and Enoch, the third member of the self-proclaimed "first triumvirate" of the alt-right,[19] posted a now-deleted YouTube video of himself in a Philippine shopping mall with what he described as his Filipina "jailbait girlfriend."[20] Glenn Miller, the homophobic former Klan leader and anti-Semitic mass shooter, was once arrested soliciting sex from "a prostitute who was a black man dressed as a woman."[21] In the words of the SPLC's Mark Potok, "It's the dirty little secret of the white supremacist movement in America: Klan leaders with black girlfriends. A neo-Nazi caught with a black transvestite. A macho skinhead arrested while soliciting sex from Latino men."[22] The most public and committed white nationalists are both loud defenders of white purity and enthusiastic practitioners of miscegenation.

"White supremacist miscegenation" is hardly new; in fact, it continues the tradition of sexual coercion and exploitation of women of color that was part of the fabric of slavery and the Jim Crow South. Thomas Jefferson, the founding father and slaveholder whose "great aversion" to miscegenation was such that he argued freed slaves ought to be deported to the West Indies in order to avoid it,[23] famously fathered several children with his slave Sally Hemings. Strom Thurmond, an American senator who filibustered for more than twenty-four hours in an attempt to maintain legal segregation, was revealed after his death to have fathered a child with an African American woman. Sexual contact between elite white men and black women was omnipresent in the segregated American South, along with the offspring of these relationships. At the same time, white men mobilized to castrate and lynch black men on the merest suspicion of a sexual approach to white women.[24]

I am *not* interested in calling out white nationalists for their alleged hypocrisies. Their ideology is repugnant enough on the face of it that pointing out hypocrisy can hardly do more to discredit them. Instead, I am interested in the deeper patterns and values within a community that consistently produces such couplings at the same time it decries them. What I have called the "instability" or "internal tension" over miscegenation in white supremacist discourse is not a simple matter of hypocrisy, in the ordinary sense of selfishly or lazily falling short of one's stated goals; rather, it indicates that *the stated goals of white supremacy do not align with its internal logic.*

As Charles Mills points out, white supremacy rests on a set of prima facie absurd and contradictory claims, but these claims were and still are treated as authoritative reasons. They are maintained by "epistemologies of ignorance" that render certain evident patterns unnoticed, certain contradictions unchallenged. Indeed, apparent contradictions are in, Mills says, a "symbiotic rather than conflictual relation" once we understand the unwritten rules of raced and gendered domination.[25] Observing apparent contradictions, such as white supremacist miscegenation, does not in itself *subvert* systems of domination, but doing so is necessary to *understand* those systems. The pervasiveness of interracial sexuality among the spokesmen of white purity and ethno-nationalism is one of these often-forgotten patterns that lies in plain sight. Abdul JanMohamed sites the origins of this pattern in slavery, and describes the "peculiar silence" that covers over this contradiction: "white patriarchy's sexual violation of the racial border—the master's rape of the female slave—was an 'open secret.' But this 'common knowledge' could not be permitted to the realm of even a pseudo-scientific discursivity lest it undermine the sociopolitical impermeability of that border, which was of course essential to the very structure of racism and slavery."[26] The silence around white supremacist miscegenation amounts to a site of manufactured ignorance, while overcoming this silence illuminates the central racial/sexual logic of white patriarchy.

The Two Faces of White Patriarchy

In his sociological work on race and sexuality in the United States in the mid-1960s, Calvin C. Hernton noted two common sayings: if a white man expressed support for integration or civil rights, he was met with the retort, "But would you want your sister to marry one?"[27] (meaning a black man; the possibility of interracial sexuality and marriage was commonly raised as an argument against the integration of schools, neighborhoods, etc.). At the same time, white men among their own were known to say "a man is not a man until he has slept with a nigger."[28] Between these two sayings, the two prerogatives—or perhaps imperatives—of white male supremacy emerge: maintaining white control over the reproductive capacities of the white women in the family, along with unimpeded sexual access to women of color. This reflects the racial/sexual order of slavery, where, as JanMohamed points out, within this apparatus "rape, the forceful possession of female slaves by their white masters, is permissible, while any version of the opposite relation, one between a white woman and a black male slave, is strictly prohibited."[29] The suggestion of black men's sexual approaches to or contact with white women, regardless of whether this contact was consensual, was used to justify racist violence "in defense of womanhood."[30] White supremacist discourse creates the ideal of the chaste, pure, all-but-sexless white woman against the image of the hypersexualized black woman who is held responsible for her own exploitation.[31] These two distinct yet deeply interrelated forms of sexual dominance together form the basis of white masculinity.

White supremacists can claim impunity of white male access to women of color *alongside* a discourse of white purity because the duty of ensuring "the existence of our people"—in other words, the reproduction of "pure" white children—is placed on white women. While the role of white women in white supremacist communities is in flux—it's reported that white women are increasingly taking on active roles and leadership positions in some groups, at the same time that other white supremacists like Andrew Anglin have endorsed increasingly overt misogyny, for example, by banning women from creating content for the *Daily Stormer*—white supremacist ideology remains largely traditionalist, situating women as homemakers and mothers of white babies.[32] In their more honest moments, many figures will openly admit to the imperative of controlling women and appropriating their reproductive capacities to the masculine white supremacist project: the French white nationalist and fascist intellectual Guillaume Faye says that "the union of a woman of race X with a male of race Y is much more dangerous for race X than for race Y. For women are the biological and sexual reservoir of a race, a people, a genetic patrimony—not men."[33] The core role of white supremacist women is a "procreative mission"[34]; Lana Lokteff, the white nationalist radio personality, has described matchmaking between white supremacist men and women as a "eugenics process" aimed at "making lots of white babies."[35] Anglin attacked Heather Heyer, the counterprotester killed at the Charlottesville rally of the "alt-right," for being childless, blogging that "a 32-year-old woman without children is a burden on society and has no value."[36] Men are situated as protectors and defenders of white women whose racial purity and reproductive capacities are at the heart of their value; the promise of protection and the specter of the nonwhite rapist are tools to recruit and maintain white women as loyal supporters of white supremacist movements.[37]

The white supremacist preoccupation with the sexual control and reproductive instrumentalization of women has predictably made them hate and fear women's sexual autonomy: the newsletter of the KKK, *The Klansman*, declares that women's liberation, described as a Jewish conspiracy, "more than any other thing is responsible for the zero population growth of the white race."[38] The commitment of white supremacy to male dominance has contributed to a significant crossover between white supremacists and various misogynistic communities of the "manosphere,"[39] like self-identified Men's Rights Activists, Pickup Artists, and Gamergaters.[40] A common complaint of the denizens of these sites is that women (often, specifically white women) have been lured away from traditional values of marriage, family, and chastity by feminism. In a trope so typical we might call it the misogynist's paradox, women are simultaneously attacked for being sexually promiscuous and for being so "stuck up" or otherwise misled as to sexually reject the complainant. One of the young men recruited by this violent mix of misogyny and white supremacy was Elliott Rodger, the "incel" (involuntarily celibate) young mixed-race man who killed six people and, in his "manifesto," described himself as motivated by resentment toward white women who refused to have sex with him and the nonwhite men whom they chose instead. Seeking a less extreme solution to the "problem" of women's liberation than Rodger's, an anonymous community at 4chan aimed to increase "the white birthrate" by creating and popularizing memes depicting cute white babies.[41] On *Breitbart*, then published by Trump advisor Steve Bannon, provocateur Milo Yiannopoulos argued that birth control should be "un-invented."[42] Other initiatives lay bare that the "protection of women" is as empty a goal as "white purity" and the overt goal of white nationalism is to gain control of white women's reproduction. Anglin's *Daily Stormer* has published a post entitled "Female Sexual Choice Must Be Suppressed"[43] and another lengthy post on "stealthing," the act of surreptitiously removing a condom during sex; the post provides an explainer on the many states in which "stealthing" is not illegal, along with a how-to guide, including instructions on how to restrain a woman who becomes suspicious and how to shame her into continuing the resultant unwanted pregnancy.[44]

Another white (male) nationalist strategy in the face of women's increasing resistance to sexual and reproductive control is to seek women who are easier to control. Since white nationalist ideology affords white men impunity of access to nonwhite women, concerns about racial and cultural purity do not limit such access. Manosphere bloggers from the United States, Australia, and Europe frequently advocate traveling to the developing world as an easy way to collect sexual partners, both for commercial sex and because, as exotic foreigners with disposable income, they are perceived as more attractive abroad.[45] White male supremacists are especially drawn to Asian women due to stereotypes that Asian women are more traditional and submissive than "Western" women; the *Daily*

Stormer's Andrew Anglin has explained his interest in "jailbait" Filipina women by saying, "I like young Filipino girls because they are shorter than me and they don't care if I boss them around or if I tell them to shut up. American girls are too problematic."[46] By targeting women who are relatively young, poor, or in some cases already victims of sex trafficking, and by "importing" wives who depend on their husbands for material support, immigration status, and more, white male supremacists can bring their orientalist fantasies of subordinate and easily controlled Asian women closer to reality.

White nationalist figures can simultaneously argue for white male control over white women in the name of racial purity, while also arguing for the utility of seeking nonwhite sexual and romantic partners. This is possible because the duty of reproducing white purity has always been placed upon white women, where it occasions white male control. No such limitation or responsibility exists for white men within this ideology; instead, sex with nonwhite women, particularly those situated as less powerful by age, nationality, or class, also serves to reaffirm his white male value and power. In this instance the Irigarayan mirror that reflects and affirms his worth is marked as different and lacking not only by sex but also by race. The work of feminist philosophers like Irigaray to lay bare the logic of patriarchy and the gendered economy of (re) production make a significant contribution to understanding the aspect of white patriarchy that is focused on the control of white women, but the aspect that is focused on access to nonwhite women—the source of "white supremacist miscegenation" itself—can only be understood through perspectives that center on racialized sexual exploitation.

The Origins of the Race/Gender System: Intersectionality at the Genesis of Gender Inequality

Although Irigaray rarely addresses race directly, her framework is strikingly effective in explaining how white nationalists conceive of *white* women. It is less successful at describing the various roles of nonwhite women. Juxtaposing Irigaray's analysis with that of black feminist scholars illuminates a side of white patriarchy that is omitted from her analysis.

Irigaray's focus on what she calls the "economy of (re)production"[47] illuminates the role of white women in white patriarchy. Irigaray describes women as reduced to a "maternal function" to reproduce the male lineage,[48] and traded as commodities among men,[49] in a process that represses female genealogies[50] and reduces women to object status. Within a logic of the same that exclusively values the (white) male as bearer of the phallus, Irigaray argues, women are valued precisely for their ability to reproduce the phallus, in the form of a son and heir in the father's lineage. Irigaray sums up the way that this reproduction symbolizes a mastery of nature/death, the superiority of the male sex, and as a guarantee of familial wealth:

> The boy child is the sign of the seed's immortality, of the fact that the properties of the sperm have won out over those of the ovum. Thus he guarantees the father's power to reproduce and represent himself, and to perpetuate his gender and his species. What is more, the son, as heir to the name, ensures that the patrimony will not be squandered. And as heir, he enriches the "house" by one more member.[51]

Irigaray's analysis emphasizes the alienation of women from the products of their labor, which are appropriated to the male line, as well as the collapse of women to an undifferentiated "maternal function." This analysis both illuminates the "procreative mission" of (white) women in white nationalist thought and elides the way that the "maternal function" is differentiated through race.

While Irigaray understands the role of women in patriarchy as reproducing her husband's "gender and his species," she leaves out the significance of whiteness. As Anne Goodwyn Jones explains in her analysis of the idealized figure of the Southern white woman, "For white men, this image implied the purity of blood and thus of white patriarchal lineage: white supremacy as well as the male line of succession and inheritance were guaranteed by her chastity and desirelessness."[52] W. J. Cash argues that the regime of control ensuring white women's sexual/racial purity against "miscegenation" is committed to protecting the status of sons vis-à-vis family property: "In their concern for the taboo on the white woman, there was a final concern to the right of their sons in the legitimate line, through all the generations to come, to be born to the great heritage of white men."[53] In Cash's analysis, discursive and economic motivation converge inextricably: the "great heritage of white men" is inherited both in the sense of what Cheryl Harris calls "whiteness as property"[54] and in the more material sense of wealth inherited by legitimate sons. Here, the purity of white women as passive sheathes, or to use Faye's language "reservoirs" of "patrimony," is marked not only by the phallogocentric erasure of any intrinsically female genealogy or sex but also by the positive interpellation of whiteness as a signifier of value.[55]

If, as Cash argues in his account of the racial politics of the Jim Crow South, the lionization of the white Southern woman as reservoir of purity and virtue derives from her role as "perpetuator of that [racial] superiority in the legitimate line," this purity is only legible beside those women who mother the illegitimate line.[56] Patricia Hill Collins points out that the construction of white women's purity was always accomplished against the counterpart of hypersexualized black and mulatto mistresses,[57] who, as property, had no protection against rape and were excluded from the protected "purity" of the white woman.[58]

Nonwhite women are not only a symbolic counterpoint to white purity, but they play a distinct and significant role in the racial/sexual economy of (re)production. Under US slavery, the law of *partus sequitur ventrem* established that all children born to enslaved women were themselves enslaved, and the property of the mother's owner.[59] Harryette Mullen, following the nineteenth-century author and abolitionist Harriet Jacobs, explains that "the function of bourgeois white women is to marry and reproduce heirs, while the function of slave women is to be sexually available to black and white men and reproduce slaves."[60] It is estimated that, despite harsh treatment that led to disproportionately high rates of infant and child mortality among slaves, 5 to 6 percent of slaveowners' profits came from "natural increase";[61] the economic importance of slave reproduction increased after the importation of enslaved people was banned in the United States in 1808. As Adrienne Davis points out, "In the United States, it was enslaved women who reproduced the workforce,"[62] even as white women reproduced the white heirs who would benefit from their labor. It is the specific ways in which American slavery parasitized itself upon the reproductive abuse of enslaved women that leads Davis to note that slavery, "while obviously racially supremacist, was also fundamentally a system of gender supremacy."[63]

The doubling of enslaved women, who reproduce labor and property, with white women, who reproduce whiteness itself in the form of legitimate heirs to the white male patriarch, emphasizes the ways in which legitimate inheritance itself is founded on the former, illegitimate line. The children born to mulatto mistresses and enslaved women were delegitimized not only by the contingent marital status of their parents but by the racial logic of their situation; they could not compete with sons in the legitimate line for inheritances or dilute the family patrimony among many heirs. As Hortense Spillers explains of the paradoxical status of an enslaved woman's child, "The offspring of the female does not 'belong' to the Mother, nor is s/he 'related' to the 'owner,' though s/he 'possesses' it, and in the African-American instance, often fathers it, *and*, as often, without whatever benefit of patrimony."[64] The offspring of enslaved women not only avoided diluting familial wealth but rather added to it, enriching the house, to use Irigaray's terms, by adding not one more member but one more piece of valuable property. The "heritage" and "patrimony" passed through the "legitimate line," then, is materially indebted to a miscegenated illegitimate line.

While the preceding analysis suggests a neat dichotomy of white women, who reproduce white heirs, and nonwhite women, who reproduce labor and property, in practice the economy of (re)production was not so simple. In many instances, particularly in the fluid spaces around colonial frontiers where white women were in short supply and interracial sexuality was often advantageous, it was an open question *which* women were capable of continuing a white lineage. Bonita Lawrence documents that in Canada, indigenous women who married white men were at times conscripted into whiteness by laws that juridically whitened their children and denied both mothers and children the right to First Nations status or to live on reserves.[65] Ann Laura Stoler describes Dutch colonists in the Indies as anxiously maneuvering to educate and discipline the mixed-race children of white fathers into whiteness and Europeanness.[66] Particularly in the Dutch Indies, Stoler describes "a direct line drawn from language acquisition to motherhood to morality,"[67] where the mixed-race children of white colonials were understood as developing a morally and racially degraded character because they were more comfortable speaking their mother's tongue than Dutch. In order to reassert the lineage and language of the father, Dutch officials developed a series of strategies to separate mixed-race children from their mothers and mother tongues by educating them in Dutch language and culture. In Australia, mixed-race children were removed from Aboriginal mothers en masse under the auspices of "protecting the half-breed" from their uncivilized and unsavory mothers;[68] it was hoped that the mixed-race girls in particular might assimilate to whiteness sufficiently to be married off to white settlers. In the instances that nonwhite women were pressed into service in the reproduction of white heirs, this involved an even more dramatic breach of maternal genealogy than that detailed in Irigaray, where the relation of mother to daughter is breached first by Oedipal resentments and then by the daughter's appropriation to her husband's family. In Lawrence's example, this breach in female genealogy cuts the juridically "whitened" mother off from her kin, her ethnicity, and her land; in Stoler's and Jacobs's studies, daughters are cut off from the mother's language or wholly removed from her care.

Just as the analysis of the reproductive instrumentalization of women in the system of private property requires acknowledgment of differences in women's status, so too does analysis of what Gayle Rubin calls the "traffic in women" in which daughters and sisters are given or exchanged as a means of creating alliances between men.[69] While Irigaray and Rubin do not thematize race, these analyses, again, apply exclusively to those women with the status of acknowledged kin: sisters and daughters who have been born or assimilated into the "legitimate" white line. The status of this exchange as the basis of *white* sociality is dramatized in the notoriously racist film *Birth of a Nation* (1915), wherein, after the threat of black male appropriation of white women has been obviated through Ku Klux Klan violence, the divisions of the Civil War are healed as the scions of white Northern and Southern families, formerly opponents in the war, marry one another's sisters. The (re)birth of the United States as a united, white nation is occasioned by the reinscription of white women as tokens of exchange and alliance between white men.

If white women are exchanged as signifiers of kinship and alliance among white men, women of color are trafficked instead as commodities who might be bought, borrowed, or sold without creating ties of affinity. Under slavery, black women were bought and sold as workers and breeders; slaveowners were known to sell their light-skinned mulatto daughters in what was called the "fancy-girl market": a market for light-skinned concubines and sex workers who fetched higher prices than even the strongest male workers.[70] The comparison between white daughters "given" in marriage and mulatto daughters sold to fancy-girl traders emphasizes Spillers's observation that the unkinning of enslaved persons is key to their transformation into property[71] and serves as an important reminder that, contra Irigaray and Rubin, women are commodified in very different, race-stratified markets.

Irigaray's analysis does leave open the space, albeit unspoken, to consider the wide range of ways in which racialized women are valued "on the market." Irigaray points out that "commodities among themselves are thus not equal, nor alike, nor different. They only become so when they are compared by man,"[72] a comparison that grounds the abstraction of money as a signifier of exchange value. This imposition of monetary value, of course, describes enslaved women *better* than their white counterparts, but one might say that the hyperbolic value placed upon white women in the economy of white patriarchy is that they are priceless, or those whose exchange is not based on money. The frequent emphasis on the *golden* hair of white women and girls who are coded as desirable speaks to the specific investment of the white woman's body with value. In the film *King Kong* (1933), which is generally interpreted as a heavy-handed racial allegory,[73] the blonde character Ann Darrow travels to a remote island, where a native chief offers her companions six native women in exchange for the "golden woman." Irigaray speaks of the woman's body "transformed into gold to satisfy his autoerotic, scoptophiliac, and possessive instincts"[74] by imprinting it "with the value of the phallus-penis" as the token of recognition and exchange among men. We should note that this particular site in the sexual economy is symbolically marked out for a "golden woman" who is marked not only by the phallus but also by the "golden" signifier of whiteness. While, as in the example from *King Kong*, an exchange value can perhaps be established between white and nonwhite women, the signifier of whiteness marks out certain women as part of a rarefied economy.

Irigaray's neglect of women of color is not unusual in philosophical accounts of the origins and workings of patriarchy. In *The Origin of the Family*, Friedrich Engels argues that the institution of the modern family originates from the accumulation of private property. Speculating about earlier systems in which men and women had sex freely, or in which men and women paired for reproduction but the right of the mother to the child (being, after all, a connection that is far more easily verified) superseded that of the father, Engels postulates that men instituted patriarchal control over women and children in order to ensure that their property would be inherited by children of their own bloodline.[75] Susan Okin echoes this argument in *Women in Western Political Thought*, arguing that norms confining women to the household and controlling their sexuality are rooted in the desire to ensure the paternity of heirs.[76] As mentioned earlier, Rubin, following Lévi-Strauss, argues that gender inequality is rooted in the "traffic in women," whereby men build political and economic relationships with one another by "giving" their sisters and daughters to other men in marriage; this traffic, and the edifice of human society that it enables, is founded on the incest taboo, which forbids men from marrying their own kinswomen. These analyses all confine themselves to accounts of those women who are counted as kin and as mothers of legitimate heirs.

Irigaray's own focus on wives and their role in reproducing a legitimate patriarchal lineage seems to follow from her debt to Marx and Engels in her analysis of the commodification of women.[77] Engels, who frequently mentions enslaved people and writes about historical contexts (like ancient Greece and Rome) where slavery is common, does not consider slaves to be among the "women" whose status he is exploring: for example, Engels writes that "in the heroic age we find the woman already being humiliated by the domination of the man and by competition from girl slaves"[78]—evidently, the "women" of whom he writes are "free" women, not the "girl slaves." Men's sexual access to enslaved women is Engels's evidence for the "one-sidedness of monogamy," but his analysis by necessity says nothing about those "girl slaves" whose role is *not* to produce legitimate heirs or to perform monogamy. The role of those women who are classed (and, in our historical moment, raced) to *not* produce legitimate heirs is both whitewashed—sexually exploited women are "competing" for men—and omitted from analysis. It is these marginalized women who must be recentered in feminist analysis.

Just as many white feminists have implicitly treated white women as the generic or universal, the analysis of patriarchy itself has often focused only on one aspect: the workings of patriarchy to create "pure" and "legitimate" white lineages. As is shown in the history and the present predominance of white supremacist miscegenation, white patriarchy is also centrally concerned with sexual and reproductive access to nonwhite women, although this aspect of white patriarchal sexuality is less openly acknowledged.

Centering nonwhite women in analyses of patriarchy is a means to correct for the focus of much foundational feminist work, including Irigaray's, on a generic "woman" who is implicitly raced as white. Furthermore, by emphasizing the double action of white patriarchy to produce both pure white legitimate lineages and also to produce highly profitable but unacknowledged racially impure lineages, the feminist analysis of white patriarchy can make sense of the phenomenon of "white supremacist miscegenation." The nature and role of patriarchy in white nationalism is central to its ideology, its justifications, and its strategies of recruitment: feminist analyses have been and will be significant in resisting its spread. Irigaray's thought alone does not contain all of the resources needed to work through issues of white nationalism, but Irigaray scholars can build on her work by recognizing its shortcomings in terms of race. Through a juxtaposition with black feminist thought, Irigaray's account of phallogocentrism helps to illuminate the contemporary ideology of white nationalism and to demonstrate its roots in white patriarchy.

Notes

1. "Hate Groups Reach Record High," Southern Poverty Law Center, https://www.splcenter.org/news/2019/02/19/hate-groups-reach-record-high, accessed October 24, 2019.

2. J. M. Berger, "Nazi vs. ISIS on Twitter: A Comparative Study of White Nationalist and ISIS Online Social Media Networks." George Washington University Program on Extremism, February 2016, https://extremism.gwu.edu/sites/g/files/zaxdzs2191/f/downloads/Nazis%20v.%20ISIS.pdf, accessed October 24, 2019.

3. Mark Potok, "The Year in Hate and Extremism," *Southern Poverty Law Center: The Intelligence Report*, February 15, 2017. https://www.splcenter.org/fighting-hate/intelligence-report/2017/year-hate-and-extremism, accessed July 1, 2019.

4. Daniel Victor and Liam Stack, "Stephen Bannon and Breitbart News, in Their Words," *New York Times*, November 14, 2016, https://www.nytimes.com/2016/11/15/us/politics/stephen-bannon-breitbart-words.html, accessed July 1, 2019; Joseph Goldstein, "Alt-Right Gathering Exults in Trump Election with a Nazi-Era Salute," *New York Times*, November 20, 2016, https://www.nytimes.com/2016/11/21/us/alt-right-salutes-donald-trump.html, accessed July 1, 2019.

5. I am indebted to Ellen Mortensen of the University of Bergen for pointing out this aspect of Breivik's ideology.

6. Jane Clare Jones, "Anders Breivik's Chilling Anti-feminism," *Guardian*, July 27, 2011. https://www.theguardian.com/commentisfree/2011/jul/27/breivik-anti-feminism, accessed July 1, 2019.

7. "Extremist Profiles: White Nationalist," Southern Poverty Law Center, https://www.splcenter.org/fighting-hate/extremist-files/ideology/white-nationalist. Accessed July 1, 2019.

8. Abdul R. JanMohamed, "Sexuality on/of the Racial Border: Foucault, Wright, and the Articulation of 'Racialized Sexuality,'" in *Discourses of Sexuality: From Aristotle to AIDS*, ed. D. C. Stanton (Ann Arbor: University of Michigan Press, 1995), 104.

9. Danielle Paquette, "The Alt-Right Isn't Only about White Supremacy. It's about White Male Supremacy," *Washington Post*, November 25, 2016. https://www.washingtonpost.com/news/wonk/wp/2016/11/25/the-alt-right-isnt-just-about-white-supremacy-its-about-white-male-supremacy/, accessed July 1, 2019.

10. Audre Lorde, "The Master's Tools Will Never Dismantle the Master's House," in *This Bridge Called My Back*, ed. Gloria Anzaldúa and Cherríe Moraga (Albany: State University of New York Press, 2015), 94.

11. Anti-Defamation League, "Fourteen Words," *ADL Hate on Display Hate Symbols Database*, https://www.adl.org/education/references/hate-symbols/14-words, accessed July 1, 2019.

12. David G. Croly, *"Miscegenation": The Theory of the Blending of the Races, Applied to the White Man and the Negro* (New York: Dexter, Hamilton, 1864).

13. Sidney Kaplan, "The Miscegenation Issue in the Election of 1864," *Journal of Negro History* 34, no. 3 (1949): 284; 295ff.

14. Times of Israel Staff, "White Supremacist Outed for Having Jewish Wife," *Times of Israel*, January 17, 2017, https://www.timesofisrael.com/white-supremacist-outed-for-having-jewish-wife/, accessed July 1, 2019.

15. Daniel Sugarman, "Neo-Nazi Blogger Revealed to Be Married to a Jewish Woman." *Jewish Chronicle*, January 18, 2017, https://www.thejc.com/news/world/neo-nazi-blogger-revealed-to-be-married-to-jewish-woman-1.430845, accessed July 1, 2019.

16. Sam Kestenbaum, "Neo-Nazi Podcaster Mike Enoch Is Back—Despite Jewish Wife," *Forward*, January 31, 2017, https://forward.com/news/361659/neo-nazi-podcaster-mike-enoch-is-back-despite-jewish-wife/, accessed July 1, 2019.

17. Josh Harkinson, "Meet the White Nationalist Trying to Ride the Trump Train to Lasting Power," *Mother Jones*, October 27, 2016, https://www.motherjones.com/politics/2016/10/richard-spencer-trump-alt-right-white-nationalist/, accessed July 1, 2019.

18. Kevin Hankes, "Eye of the Stormer," *Southern Poverty Law Center: The Intelligence Report*, February 9, 2017, https://www.splcenter.org/fighting-hate/intelligence-report/2017/eye-stormer, accessed July 1, 2019.

19. Southern Poverty Law Center, "Andrew Anglin," https://www.splcenter.org/fighting-hate/extremist-files/individual/andrew-anglin, accessed July 1, 2019.

20. "Andrew Anglin Does the Philippines Jailbait-Style," *Liveleak*, video file, https://www.liveleak.com/view?i=53b_1426403408, accessed July 1, 2019.

21. Steve Daniels, "I-Team: Alleged Kansas KKK Shooter Glenn Miller Caught with Black Raleigh Prostitute, Was in Witness Protection," *ABC 11 Eyewitness News*, April 24, 2014. https://abc11.com/archive/9514949/, accessed July 1, 2019.

22. Mark Potok, "Sex, Lies and White Supremacy," *Southern Poverty Law Center: The Intelligence Report*, 2015, https://www.splcenter.org/fighting-hate/intelligence-report/2015/sex-lies-and-white-supremacy, accessed July 1, 2019.

23. Elise Lemire, *Miscegenation: Making Race in America* (Philadelphia: University of Pennsylvania Press, 2002), 27.

24. Kris DuRocher, "Violent Masculinity: Learning Ritual and Performance in Southern Lynchings," in *Southern Masculinity: Perspectives on Manhood in*

the South since Reconstruction, ed. C. T. Friend (Athens: University of Georgia Press, 2009), 55.

25. Charles W. Mills, "Racial Liberalism," *PMLA* 123, no. 5 (2008): 1380.

26. JanMohamed, "Sexuality on/of the Racial Border," 104.

27. Calvin C. Hernton, *Sex and Racism in America* (New York: Doubleday, 1965), 20.

28. Hernton, *Sex and Racism in America*, 6.

29. JanMohamed, "Sexuality on/of the Racial Border," 101.

30. Angela Y. Davis, *Women, Race and Class* (London: Penguin, 1983), 195.

31. Patricia Hill Collins, *Black Feminist Thought: Knowledge, Consciousness, and the Politics of Empowerment* (London: Routledge, 2008), 129; Adrienne Davis, "Don't Let Nobody Bother Yo' Principal: The Sexual Economy of American Slavery," in *Sister Circle: Black Women and Work*, ed. S. Harley (New Brunswick, NJ: Rutgers University Press, 2002), 114.

32. "White Supremacists Feud Over the Racist Gender Gap," *Anti-Defamation League Blog*, April 16, 2016, https://www.adl.org/blog/white-supremacists-feud-over-the-racist-gender-gap, accessed July 1, 2019.

33. Guillaume Faye, "The Race-Mixing Imperative," *Altright.com* (blog), https://altright.com/2016/09/20/the-race-mixing-imperative/, accessed July 1, 2019.

34. Jessie Daniels, *White Lies: Race, Class, Gender and Sexuality in White Supremacist Discourse* (London: Routledge, 1997), 41.

35. Flavia Dzodan, "Alt-Feminism and the White Nationalist Women Who Love It," *Medium.com*, March 7, 2017, https://medium.com/this-political-woman/alt-feminism-and-the-white-nationalist-women-who-love-it-f8ee20cd30d9, accessed July 1, 2019.

36. Suzannah Weiss, "Hate Site Criticizes Charlottesville Victim's Weight and Childlessness," *Glamour*, August 15, 2017, https://www.glamour.com/story/daily-stormer-heather-heyer-mocking-article, accessed July 1, 2019.

37. Kathleen Blee, *Inside Organized Racism: Women in the Hate Movement*. Berkeley: University of California Press, 2003.

38. Daniels, *White Lies*, 120.

39. "Misogyny: The Sites," *Southern Poverty Law Center: The Intelligence Report*, March 1, 2012, https://www.splcenter.org/fighting-hate/intelligence-report/2012/misogyny-sites, accessed July 1, 2019.

40. Aja Romano, "How the Alt-Right's Sexism Lures Men into White Supremacy," *Vox*, December 14, 2016, https://www.vox.com/culture/2016/12/14 13576192/alt-right-sexism-recruitment, accessed July 1, 2019.

41. Robyn Pennacchia, "Hey, White Ladies! 4Chan Wants to Meme Some Babies into Your Womb!" *Wonkette*, January 14, 2017, https://www.wonkette.com/hey-white-ladies-4chan-wants-to-meme-some-babies-into-your-womb, accessed July 1, 2019.

42. Abby Ohlheiser, "The 96 Hours That Brought Down Milo Yiannopoulos," *Washington Post*, February 21, 2017, https://www.washingtonpost.com/news/

the-intersect/wp/2017/02/21/the-96-hours-that-brought-down-milo-yiannopoulos/, accessed July 1, 2019.

43. David Futrelle, "'Female Sexual Choice Must Be Suppressed,' Daily Stormer Demands," *We Hunted the Mammoth* (blog), April 6, 2017, http://www.wehuntedthemammoth.com/2017/04/06/female-sexual-choice-must-be-suppressed-daily-stormer-demands/, accessed July 1, 2019.

44. David Futrelle, "Daily Stormer to White Dudes: Slip Your Condoms Off to Impregnate White Women against Their Will!" *We Hunted the Mammoth* (blog), May 19, 2017, http://www.wehuntedthemammoth.com/2017/05/19/daily-stormer-to-white-dudes-slip-your-condoms-off-to-impregnate-white-women-against-their-will/, accessed July 1, 2019.

45. Neetzan Zimmerman, "Pickup Artists Put Together Map Rating 'Easiness of Girls by Country,'" *Gawker*, October 17, 2013, https://gawker.com/pickup-artists-put-together-map-rating-easiness-of-gir-1447203167, accessed July 1, 2019.

46. Ben Garrison, "Ben Garrison's Exclusive Interview with Andrew Anglin," *Rogue Cartoonist* (blog), August 29, 2015, http://roguecartoonist.blogspot.com/2015/08/ben-garrisons-exclusive-interview-with.html, accessed July 1, 2019.

47. Irigaray S, 110.

48. Irigaray S, 95–96.

49. Irigaray, "Women on the Market" in TS.

50. Irigaray SG, 2; Irigaray S, 221ff.

51. Irigaray S, 74.

52. Anne Goodwyn Jones, "The Work of Gender in the Southern Renaissance," in *Southern Writers and Their Worlds*, ed. C. Morris and S. Reinhardt (Baton Rouge: Louisiana State University Press, 1996), 49.

53. W. J. Cash, *The Mind of the South* (New York: Alfred A. Knopf, 1941), 116.

54. Cheryl Harris, "Whiteness as Property," *Harvard Law Review* 106, no. 8 (June 1993): 1707.

55. For further discussion of whiteness as a master signifier that grafts itself onto the phallic economy, see Kalpana Seshadri-Crooks's *Desiring Whiteness*. The relationship of whiteness to the phallus in Irigaray is also discussed in Sabrina L. Hom, "Between Races and Generations: Materializing Race and Kinship in Moraga and Irigaray," *Hypatia* 28, no. 3 (2013): 419–435.

56. Cash, *Mind of the South*, 116.

57. Collins, *Black Feminist*, 129.

58. Davis, "Don't Let Nobody Bother Yo' Principal," 114.

59. Davis, "Don't Let Nobody Bother Yo' Principal," 108.

60. Harryette Mullen, "Optic White: Blackness and the Production of Whiteness," *Diacritics* 24, no. 2/3 (1994): 81.

61. Dorothy Roberts, *Killing the Black Body: Race, Reproduction, and the Meaning of Liberty* (New York: Vintage, 1998), 21.

62. Davis, "Don't Let Nobody Bother Yo' Principal," 109.

63. Davis, "Don't Let Nobody Bother Yo' Principal," 119.

64. Hortense J. Spillers, "Mama's Baby, Papa's Maybe: An American Grammar Book," *Diacritics* 17, no. 2 (1987): 74.

65. Bonita Lawrence, "Gender, Race, and the Regulation of Native Identity in Canada and the United States: An Overview," *Hypatia* 18, no. 2 (2003): 3–31.

66. Ann Laura Stoler, *Carnal Knowledge and Imperial Power: Race and the Intimate in Colonial Rule* (Berkeley: University of California Press, 2010), 119ff.

67. Stoler, *Carnal Knowledge and Imperial Power*, 121.

68. Margaret D. Jacobs, *White Mother to a Dark Race: Settler Colonialism, Maternalism, and the Removal of Indigenous Children in the American West and Australia, 1880–1940* (Lincoln: University of Nebraska Press, 2009), 72.

69. Gayle Rubin, "The Traffic in Women: Notes on the 'Political Economy' of Sex," in *Deviations: A Gayle Rubin Reader* (Durham, NC: Duke University Press, 2011).

70. Davis, "Don't Let Nobody Bother Yo' Principal," 116; Pamela Bridgewater, "'Ain't I a Slave?' Slavery, Reproduction Abuse, and Reparations," *UCLA Women's Law Journal* 14, no. 1 (2005): 117.

71. Spillers, "Mama's Baby, Papa's Maybe," 74.

72. Irigaray TS, 177.

73. James Snead, *White Screens/Black Images: Hollywood from the Dark Side* (London: Routledge, 2016), 8.

74. Irigaray S, 115.

75. Friedrich Engels, *The Origin of the Family, Private Property and the State*, trans. Alick West, corrected by Mark Harris (Marx/Engels Internet Archive, 1993, 1999, 2000), 2:3.

76. Susan Okin, *Women in Western Political Thought* (Princeton, NJ: Princeton University Press, 2013), 44.

77. Irigaray S, 120–124; TS 170ff.

78. Engels, *The Origin of the Family, Private Property and the State*, 2:4.

Bibliography

"Andrew Anglin Does the Philippines Jailbait-Style." *Liveleak*. Video file. https://www.liveleak.com/view?i=53b_1426403408. Accessed July 1, 2019.

Anti-Defamation League. "Fourteen Words." *ADL Hate on Display Hate Symbols Database*. https://www.adl.org/education/references/hate-symbols/14-words. Accessed July 1, 2019.

Berger, J. M. "Nazi vs. ISIS on Twitter: A Comparative Study of White Nationalist and ISIS Online Social Media Networks." George Washington University Program on Extremism, February 2016.

Blee, Kathleen. *Inside Organized Racism: Women in the Hate Movement*. Berkeley: University of California Press, 2003.

Bridgewater, Pamela. "'Ain't I a Slave?' Slavery, Reproduction Abuse, and Reparations." *UCLA Women's Law Journal* 14, no. 1 (2005): 89–162.

Cash, W. J. *The Mind of the South*. New York: Alfred A. Knopf, 1941.

Collins, Patricia Hill. *Black Feminist Thought: Knowledge, Consciousness, and the Politics of Empowerment*. London: Routledge, 2008.

Croly, David G. *"Miscegenation": The Theory of the Blending of the Races, Applied to the White Man and the Negro*. New York: Dexter, Hamilton, 1864.

Daniels, Jessie. *White Lies: Race, Class, Gender and Sexuality in White Supremacist Discourse*. London: Routledge, 1997.

Daniels, Steve. "I-Team: Alleged Kansas KKK Shooter Glenn Miller Caught with Black Raleigh Prostitute, Was in Witness Protection." *ABC 11 Eyewitness News*, April 24, 2014. https://abc11.com/archive/9514949/. Accessed July 1, 2019.

Davis, Adrienne. "Don't Let Nobody Bother Yo' Principal: The Sexual Economy of American Slavery." In *Sister Circle: Black Women and Work*, edited by S. Harley, 103–127. New Brunswick, NJ: Rutgers University Press, 2002.

Davis, Angela Y. *Women, Race and Class*. London: Penguin, 1983.

DuRocher, Kris. "Violent Masculinity: Learning Ritual and Performance in Southern Lynchings." In *Southern Masculinity: Perspectives on Manhood in the South since Reconstruction*, edited by C. T. Friend, 46–64. Athens: University of Georgia Press, 2009.

Dzodan, Flavia. "Alt-Feminism and the White Nationalist Women Who Love It." *Medium.com*, March 7, 2017. https://medium.com/this-political-woman/alt-feminism-and-the-white-nationalist-women-who-love-it-f8ee20cd30d9. Accessed July 1, 2019.

Engels, Friedrich. *The Origin of the Family, Private Property and the State*. Translated by Alick West, corrected by Mark Harris. Marx/Engels Internet Archive, 1993, 1999, 2000.

"Extremist Profiles: White Nationalist." Southern Poverty Law Center. https://www.splcenter.org/fighting-hate/extremist-files/ideology/white-nationalist. Accessed July 1, 2019.

Faye, Guillaume. "The Race-Mixing Imperative." *Altright.com* (blog). https://altright.com/2016/09/20/the-race-mixing-imperative/. Accessed July 1, 2019.

Futrelle, David. "Daily Stormer to White Dudes: Slip Your Condoms Off to Impregnate White Women against Their Will!" *We Hunted the Mammoth* (blog), May 19, 2017. http://www.wehuntedthemammoth.com/2017/05/19/daily-stormer-to-white-dudes-slip-your-condoms-off-to-impregnate-white-women-against-their-will/. Accessed July 1, 2019.

Futrelle, David. "'Female Sexual Choice Must Be Suppressed,' Daily Stormer Demands." *We Hunted the Mammoth* (blog), April 6, 2017. http://www.wehuntedthemammoth.com/2017/04/06/female-sexual-choice-must-be-suppressed-daily-stormer-demands/. Accessed July 1, 2019.

Garrison, Ben. "Ben Garrison's Exclusive Interview with Andrew Anglin." *Rogue Cartoonist* (blog), August 29, 2015. http://roguecartoonist.blogspot.com/2015/08/ben-garrisons-exclusive-interview-with.html. Accessed July 1, 2019.

Goldstein, Joseph. "Alt-Right Gathering Exults in Trump Election with a Nazi-Era Salute." *New York Times*, November 20, 2016. https://www.nytimes.com/2016/11/21/us/alt-right-salutes-donald-trump.html. Accessed July 1, 2019.

Hankes, Kevin. "Eye of the Stormer." *Southern Poverty Law Center: The Intelligence Report*, February 9, 2017. https://www.splcenter.org/fighting-hate/intelligence-report/2017/eye-stormer. Accessed July 1, 2019.

Harkinson, Josh. "Meet the White Nationalist Trying to Ride the Trump Train to Lasting Power." *Mother Jones*, October 27, 2016. https://www.motherjones.com/politics/2016/10/richard-spencer-trump-alt-right-white-nationalist/. Accessed July 1, 2019.

Harris, Cheryl. "Whiteness as Property." *Harvard Law Review* 106, no. 8 (1993): 1707–1791.

Hernton, Calvin C. *Sex and Racism in America*. New York: Doubleday, 1965.

Hom, Sabrina L. "Between Races and Generations: Materializing Race and Kinship in Moraga and Irigaray." *Hypatia* 28, no. 3 (2013): 419–435.

Jacobs, Margaret D. *White Mother to a Dark Race: Settler Colonialism, Maternalism, and the Removal of Indigenous Children in the American West and Australia, 1880–1940*. Lincoln: University of Nebraska Press, 2009.

JanMohamed, Abdul R. "Sexuality on/of the Racial Border: Foucault, Wright, and the Articulation of 'Racialized Sexuality.'" In *Discourses of Sexuality: From Aristotle to AIDS*, edited by D. C. Stanton, 94–116. Ann Arbor: University of Michigan Press, 1995.

Jones, Anne Goodwyn. "The Work of Gender in the Southern Renaissance." *Southern Writers and Their Worlds*, edited by C. Morris and S. Reinhardt, 41–56. Baton Rouge: Louisiana State University Press, 1996.

Jones, Jane Clare. "Anders Breivik's Chilling Anti-feminism." *Guardian*, July 27, 2011. https://www.theguardian.com/commentisfree/2011/jul/27/breivik-anti-feminism. Accessed July 1, 2019.

Kaplan, Sidney. "The Miscegenation Issue in the Election of 1864." *Journal of Negro History* 34, no. 3 (1949): 274–343.

Kestenbaum, Sam. "Neo-Nazi Podcaster Mike Enoch Is Back—Despite Jewish Wife." *Forward*, January 31, 2017. https://forward.com/news/361659/neo-nazi-podcaster-mike-enoch-is-back-despite-jewish-wife/. Accessed July 1, 2019.

Lawrence, Bonita. "Gender, Race, and the Regulation of Native Identity in Canada and the United States: An Overview." *Hypatia* 18, no. 2 (2003): 3–31.

Lemire, Elise. *Miscegenation: Making Race in America*. Philadelphia: University of Pennsylvania Press, 2002.

Lorde, Audre. "The Master's Tools Will Never Dismantle the Master's House." In *This Bridge Called My Back*, edited by Gloria Anzaldúa and Cherríe Moraga. Albany: State University of New York Press, 2015.

Lynskey, Dorian. "The Rise and Fall of Milo Yiannopoulos—How a Shallow Actor Played the Bad Guy for Money." *Guardian*, February 21, 2017. https://www.theguardian.com/world/2017/feb/21/milo-yiannopoulos-rise-and-fall-shallow-actor-bad-guy-hate-speech. Accessed July 1, 2019.

Mills, Charles W. *The Racial Contract*. Ithaca, NY: Cornell University Press, 1999.

"Misogyny: The Sites." *Southern Poverty Law Center: The Intelligence Report*, March 1, 2012. https://www.splcenter.org/fighting-hate/intelligence-report/2012/misogyny-sites. Accessed July 1, 2019.

Mullen, Harryette. "Optic White: Blackness and the Production of Whiteness." *Diacritics* 24, no. 2/3 (1994): 71–89.

Ohlheiser, Abby. "The 96 Hours That Brought Down Milo Yiannopoulos." *Washington Post*, February 21, 2017. https://www.washingtonpost.com/news/the-intersect/wp/2017/02/21/the-96-hours-that-brought-down-milo-yiannopoulos/. Accessed July 1, 2019.

Okin, Susan. *Women in Western Political Thought*. Princeton, NJ: Princeton University Press, 2013.

Paquette, Danielle. "The Alt-Right Isn't Only about White Supremacy. It's about White Male Supremacy." *Washington Post*, November 25, 2016. https://www.washingtonpost.com/news/wonk/wp/2016/11/25/the-alt-right-isnt-just-about-white-supremacy-its-about-white-male-supremacy/. Accessed July 1, 2019.

Pennacchia, Robyn. "Hey, White Ladies! 4Chan Wants to Meme Some Babies into Your Womb!" *Wonkette*, January 14, 2017. https://www.wonkette.com/hey-white-ladies-4chan-wants-to-meme-some-babies-into-your-womb. Accessed July 1, 2019.

Potok, Mark. "Sex, Lies and White Supremacy." *Southern Poverty Law Center: The Intelligence Report*, 2015. https://www.splcenter.org/fighting-hate/intelligence-report/2015/sex-lies-and-white-supremacy. Accessed July 1, 2019.

Potok, Mark. "The Year in Hate and Extremism." *Southern Poverty Law Center: The Intelligence Report*, February 15, 2017. https://www.splcenter.org/fighting-hate/intelligence-report/2017/year-hate-and-extremism. Accessed July 1, 2019.

Roberts, Dorothy. *Killing the Black Body: Race, Reproduction, and the Meaning of Liberty*. New York: Vintage, 1998.

Romano, Aja. "How the Alt-Right's Sexism Lures Men into White Supremacy." *Vox*, December 14, 2016. https://www.vox.com/culture/2016/12/14/13576192/alt-right-sexism-recruitment. Accessed July 1, 2019.

Rubin, Gayle. "The Traffic in Women: Notes on the 'Political Economy' of Sex." In *Deviations: A Gayle Rubin Reader*. Durham, NC: Duke University Press, 2011.

Seshadri-Crooks, Kalpana. *Desiring Whiteness*. Abingdon: Routledge, 2002.

Snead, James. *White Screens/Black Images: Hollywood from the Dark Side*. London: Routledge, 2016.

Southern Poverty Law Center. "Andrew Anglin." https://www.splcenter.org/fighting-hate/extremist-files/individual/andrew-anglin. Accessed July 1, 2019.

Spillers, Hortense J. "Mama's Baby, Papa's Maybe: An American Grammar Book." *Diacritics* 17, no. 2 (1987): 65–81.

Stember, Charles H. *Sexual Racism: The Emotional Barrier to an Integrated Society*. New York: Elsevier, 1976.

Stoler, Ann Laura. *Carnal Knowledge and Imperial Power: Race and the Intimate in Colonial Rule*. Berkeley: University of California Press, 2010.

Sugarman, Daniel. "Neo-Nazi Blogger Revealed to Be Married to a Jewish Woman." *Jewish Chronicle*, January 18, 2017. https://www.thejc.com/news/world/neo-nazi-blogger-revealed-to-be-married-to-jewish-woman-1.430845. Accessed July 1, 2019.

Times of Israel Staff. "White Supremacist Outed for Having Jewish Wife." *Times of Israel*, January 17, 2017. https://www.timesofisrael.com/white-supremacist-outed-for-having-jewish-wife/. Accessed July 1, 2019.

Victor, Daniel, and Liam Stack. "Stephen Bannon and Breitbart News, in Their Words." *New York Times*, November 14, 2016. https://www.nytimes.com/2016/11/15/us/politics/stephen-bannon-breitbart-words.html. Accessed July 1, 2019.

Weiss, Suzannah. "Hate Site Criticizes Charlottesville Victim's Weight and Childlessness." *Glamour*, August 15, 2017. https://www.glamour.com/story/daily-stormer-heather-heyer-mocking-article. Accessed July 1, 2019.

"White Supremacists Feud Over the Racist Gender Gap." *Anti-Defamation League Blog*, April 16, 2016. https://www.adl.org/blog/white-supremacists-feud-over-the-racist-gender-gap. Accessed July 1, 2019.

Zimmerman, Neetzan. "Pickup Artists Put Together Map Rating 'Easiness of Girls by Country.'" *Gawker*, October 17, 2013. Accessed July 1, 2019. https://gawker.com/pickup-artists-put-together-map-rating-easiness-of-gir-1447203167. Accessed July 1, 2019.

Chapter Nine

Justice in an Unjust World

The Politics of Narration in Luce Irigaray and Frank Miller's *Sin City*

Mary C. Rawlinson

> In our time, we are fascinated by infinite subtleties involved in the manufacture, commerce, and ownership of property. Yet, we know practically nothing about the commerce between people. We are so alienated by goods, money, economic exchanges in the narrow sense, that we are in danger of losing our most basic physical and moral health.
>
> —Luce Irigaray, *Thinking the Difference*

> Once you got everybody agreeing with what they know in their hearts ain't true, you got 'em by the balls.
>
> —Senator Rourke in Frank Miller's *Sin City*

> It is not a fragrant world, but it is the world you live in.
>
> —Raymond Chandler, *The Simple Art of Murder*

Irigaray's Apocalyptic Tone

As Derrida remarks, philosophers regularly strike an apocalyptic tone, and Luce Irigaray is no exception.[1] Across a variety of texts, Irigaray advances a narrative of disaster to counter narratives of progress in philosophy, science, and politics. In the mad dash for profit and power, humans have created a world that is inimical to their health and happiness: too fast, too loud, too anonymous, too violent to generate and sustain community and a self-realizing agency. Science treats nature as a resource to be exploited and turns it into a lethal force, opening up a history of nuclear dread and climate disaster. Irigaray frequently exposes the collusion of science and capital in the "destruction of the sensible world that threatens us with individual and collective death, physical and spiritual annihilation."[2] She anticipates the urgency of climate change, as well as the threats to agency and community posed by the speed and distractions of contemporary media.[3]

Under the narrative of nature as war, the discourse of rights turns nature into property and opens a history of border wars.

> What does it mean that our culture is threatened with destruction? Of course, there are the obvious threats posed by war, since warfare is the only way of assuring international equilibrium—or so we are informed by the media, whose economy might bear investigation.
>
> . . . So the death machines are traded around with vast capital expenditures, and all to keep the peace, or so they tell us.[4]

Man's fraternal economies originate in a myth of nature as violence and install sovereign power as a necessary check on man's natural violence. Within this scenario, fictions of equality operate to erase both differences among men and the subjection of women.

> Claims that men, races, sexes, are equal in point of fact signal a disdain or a denial for real phenomena and give rise to an imperialism that is even more pernicious than those that retain traces of difference. Today it is all too clear that there is no equality of wealth, and claims of equal rights to culture have blown up in our faces. All those who advocate equality need to come to terms with the fact that their claims produce a greater and greater split between the so-called equal units and those authorities or transcendences used to measure or

> outmeasure them. Whether we like it or not these authorities are still called capital, or profit, and God(s), Man/Men.[5]

As Irigaray argues, claims of equality are not only empirically false, they also serve to erase sexual difference, as if the story of man already included the story of woman, as if sexual difference made no difference in thinking human experience.[6] Either woman is a special case and not relevant to general figures of agency and subjectivity, or she is already subsumed in the narrative of man. Sexual difference, as Irigaray often remarks, must be erased if the logic of the same, the fiction of equality, and the hegemony of the laws of property and sexual propriety are to be maintained.

Thus, Irigaray links the monetizing of experience to the erasure of sexual difference and the subjection of women. The erasure of sexual difference initiates the transformation of singular human beings into units of general classes or "populations."[7] Money serves as the measure of all things or the "universal mediator," as if all values and goods—a pair of shoes, schoolbooks, your child's kidney—could be arrayed on the same scale.[8] Global capitalism and neoliberal ideology turn every relationship into an economic exchange that concentrates wealth, privilege, and power. All of life seems to be subjugated to the "unconditional power of money," so that vivacity and generativity are threatened both globally and in the individual.[9]

In the early 1990s Irigaray diagnoses the imposition of capitalism and industrialization by wealthy countries in developing areas as a new form of imperialism that undermines indigenous forms of economic activity, while creating dependency.

> Often the help which we plan to give to less wealthy countries is a way of imposing industrialization as we know it on them. . . . We know what the limits of industrialization are as regards employment, yet we go on involving other countries in this process and, in this way, win a few more years for an economic regime whose blind alleys should be all too obvious to us.
>
> In my view, it would be fairer politically-speaking to encourage a form of economic development that was appropriate to the environment and culture of a country, in other

> words to promote economic diversity rather than imposing a single and inevitably competitive model.[10]

The global hegemony of capitalism not only preserves privilege and wealth, it amplifies social and economic inequity. The "disproportionate" power of money is

> rarely questioned by democratic regimes even though it inevitably leads to new hierarchies between rich and poor and between affluent and impoverished countries, along with a redistribution system based upon pity and upon appeals to share, which potentially exacerbate loss of human dignity and authoritarian relations between people.[11]

Global capitalism produces and reproduces structural inequity both within and between states. Twenty years before Thomas Pikkety's critique of the structural inequalities of global capital,[12] Irigaray had already interrogated the rhetoric of free markets and distributed growth that justifies capital's hegemony.

The narratives of global capital delegitimize other forms of economic and social relation as naïve or impractical in order to effect this dispossession of the electorate. On the one hand, there is the insistence on the science of the markets, as if capitalism were a fact of nature. On the other, there is the fiction of shared prosperity and the circulation of capital, despite the increasing damming up or concentration of wealth and the constantly ever deepening drought of social and economic inequity. There is the narrative of work rewarded and the reality of privilege advantaged. In the narrative of global capitalism, those who fail deserve to do so. The market culls the weak just as nature does. The poor deserve to be poor. In 2014 the Speaker of the US House of Representatives blamed the economic distress of American workers on their own laziness and desire to "just sit around."[13] Global capitalism finds it impossible to address structural inequity, racism, and gender inequity, because to do so would undermine its central narrative of competition and individual success and its conflation of wealth and virtue.

The hegemony of this narrative of identity under global capital has emerged in tandem with a coarsening of political discourse, at least in the United States, and a strategy on the part of entrenched interests of demonizing political opponents. In 2015 former New York

City mayor Rudy Giuliani suggested that President Obama's upbringing was un-American: "He doesn't love you. And he doesn't love me. He wasn't brought up the way you were brought up and I was brought up through love of this country."[14] The current disregard of truth may seem shocking, but it is the legacy of a long road of irresponsible political speech that has put democratic coalitions in danger when their agency is urgently needed to address the effects of multiple wars and conflict zones, increasing inequity, and climate change.

For Irigaray, new narrative and affective infrastructures of experience will be required to support the collaborative agencies demanded by the urgencies of social inequity and climate disaster:

> Social justice, and especially sexual justice, cannot be achieved without changing the laws of language and the conceptions of truths and values structuring the social order. Changing the instruments of culture is just as important in the medium to long term as a redistribution of goods in the strict sense. You can't have one without the other.[15]

As long as fictions of equality and free markets continue to circulate, it will be difficult to gain a purchase on the structural inequities that these fictions sustain. As long as the facts don't matter, justice will be impossible.

Central to the narrative of Man that Irigaray criticizes is the identification of political community with the fraternity of contract and the right to property, as well as the installation as the subject of ethics and politics of a detached, rational subject whose logical procedures secure the right.[16] Working with the fictions of equality and free markets, the trope of an unsituated, impartial judge masks the reality of structural exclusions and marginalizations along the fault lines of gender and race that mark the narrative of Man.[17]

If Irigaray often strikes an apocalyptic tone, she just as regularly insists that ethics and politics should focus not on property, sexual propriety, or ascribing blame and praise, but on "what is to be done and how to do what is necessary to guarantee the existence of a world that is livable in the future."[18] An essential project in this collaborative activity would be the production of new narratives of human experience other than the story of Man that might better sustain the prosperity of each and all and of Earth on which all life depends.[19]

Despite her frequent focus on language and her emphasis on the need to put into circulation new images of sexual identity and human relationships, oddly Irigaray rarely turns to literature as an ally in her philosophical aims. Of late, she has turned more and more to an emphasis on personal happiness, intimacy with nature, yoga, and other practices that may address spiritual distress but that are unlikely to provide narratives on which to build solidarities.[20] In the introduction of *To Speak Is Never Neutral* (1985/2002), Irigaray identifies philosophy with poetry, and she decries the failure to "salute the poet" in philosophy, in Aristotle or Hegel. At the same time, she expresses skepticism about the "current effervescence centered around literature," and insists on the importance of *her* writing being considered philosophy. The text drops the question of what Plato called philosophy's "old quarrel" with literature, and Irigaray does not pick it up again.[21] Moreover, she does not advance her own project of elaborating new narratives of agency and solidarity as conditions for achieving justice in an unjust world. This task proves to be the central focus of the noir genre of fiction and film.

Liminal Ethics: Noir Crime Fiction as Political Philosophy

> If way to the Better there be, it exacts a full look at the Worst.
>
> —Thomas Hardy, *In Tenebris II*, l. 14

While philosophers often argue that literature supplements philosophy with emotional intelligence and an appreciation of the particular,[22] perhaps, rather than merely serving philosophy in its conventional aims, literature actually challenges the concepts of philosophy—particularly philosophy's concepts of agency and justice. Crime fiction as a genre gives a philosophical account of the conditions of justice and agency. This literature shifts the problem of justice from the articulation of rights among equals to an analysis of the vulnerabilities, concentrations of power, and structural inequalities that make justice elusive and agency difficult. Crime fiction explores the moral claims intrinsic in social relations, as well as the limits of reason in resolving moral ambiguities and conflicting obligations.

My analysis develops three points of critique for ethics and political philosophy:

(1) Just as they purvey a fiction of equality, so, too, ethics and political philosophy tend to locate justice in the mutual recognition or symmetry of fraternity. Each rational agent recognizes the other as the same and respects him on that account.[23] This "logic of the same" produces an idea of justice that reinforces the exclusions of gender and race, while, at the same time, casting moral urgencies as conflicts of rights among equals.[24] Yet, almost any morally charged relation—parent/child, teacher/student, doctor/patient, boss/worker—involves unequal subjects and differentials of power. The concept of fraternity cannot capture these asymmetries. Crime fiction refigures ethical agency in the context of these differences and dependencies, rather than a fiction of equality. It exposes the constitutive role of vulnerability in any ethical relation.

(2) Against the detached subject of moral philosophy, crime fiction demonstrates the dependency of agency on a culture of possibilities, and it situates agency in a world of structural injustice. From Wilkie Collins and Conan Doyle to Carl Hiaasen and Thomas Harris, crime fiction problematizes the inequities of race, class, and gender, revealing how the "Man of reason" takes command of the narrative through a series of exclusions. My reading of crime fiction locates the ethical and political subject in the context of forces of power and capital, where possibilities are distributed unequally, and infrastructures of race and gender abet the concentration of wealth and the proliferation of elite zones of security.

Crime fiction and the noir genre in film explore the *impossible agencies* of those excluded from the culture of possibilities.[25] In an inherently unjust world, law is "the pre-engaged servant of the long purse."[26] Defenseless citizens are either manipulated and abused by the very institutions meant to protect them, or they are forced to live in circumstances that make avoiding violence and crime almost impossible. A philosophical analysis of this genre engages contemporary debates about crime, poverty, incarceration, and the abuse of vulnerable populations—particularly young men of color—by authority, as well as the persistent disempowerment of women.

(3) Against the fictions of equality and moral detachment, the genius of crime fiction and the noir genre film is to recast the problem of moral agency within the reality of a world of "mean streets."[27] The moral problem for the detective, or for any ethical and political agent,

is to discover how to be effective in a world of violence and injustice without being made mean by it. Rather than providing a comfortable experience of "symmetry," the genre provokes this disturbing *krisis* in the reader's thought and feeling.

While moral philosophy is regulated by the false ideal of an unambiguous moral agency, crime fiction demonstrates the ineluctable intertwining of good and evil in the same action or agency. Philosophy would have us believe that right action is always possible, given the rule of reason, but agents are regularly afflicted with impossible choices. Do I stay in Alabama to care for my ailing mother, when doing so means abandoning my family and work in New York? More drastically, do I sell my daughter to feed the rest of my family? Crime fiction captures the true view of what is going on in the impossibility of acting without transgressing some genuine claim.

Crime fiction offers a critique of Kantian ideals of moral purity and demonstrates the liminality of the moral agent.[28] Violence seems necessary to protect the vulnerable from those social and institutional powers that thrive by subverting the law and subjecting the individual. In his liminality, the detective is the violent agent of peace, the unlawful agent of justice, the undomesticated agent of domestic privacy. Is violence essential to justice and moral harm to moral agency?[29]

The philosophical analysis of crime fiction resituates agency in the context of infrastructures of race and gender that enforce inequities, where institutions meant to serve the vulnerable actually reinforce their lack of agency. In an era of public lying and "fake news," it provides a trenchant analysis of the dependence of justice on truth and of injustice on the perversion of truth by power. The genre substitutes an account of the real asymmetries, differences, and dependencies of ethics and politics for the fiction of mutual recognition among equal subjects. And, it challenges philosophy to show a path from structural inequity to the justice of a genuinely shared culture of possibilities without a detour through violence and transgression.

If an ethics and politics centered on the fictions of equality and a detached rational subject seem ill equipped to address the structural injustices of global capital in the era of "fake news," the noir genre of American crime fiction engages just such a world. *Sin City*, Frank Miller's neo-noir film and graphic novels, explores the possibility of agency in an unjust world and develops four essential themes for an analysis of justice under global capital:

1. Justice has an epistemic basis, that is, it depends on truth and on respect for the truth. Injustice flourishes when there are no consequences for the powerful for lying in public speech and when "fake news" gains as much traction as an honest free press.
2. Under global capital the very institutions meant to protect the vulnerable actually exploit them. Infrastructures of race and gender perpetuate social, economic, and political inequity and consolidate privilege through the concentration of wealth and the proliferation of elite zones of security.
3. In a world of systemic injustice, the vulnerable rely on liminal figures who do not reflect the fictive moral purity of the subject of moral philosophy. The detective and the other avatars of justice in the world of the noir genre always find themselves faced with compromised and compromising choices. Often it appears necessary to resort to violence to protect the vulnerable, as if violence were necessary to justice.
4. *Sin City*, like the noir genre in general, explores various forms of collaboration across race and gender. Perhaps these collaborations could produce solidarities capable of addressing injustice in a time of money and fake news. Perhaps *Sin City* answers Irigaray's apocalyptic call for new narratives of human agency capable of sustaining each and all.

Sin City: Justice, Truth, and New Narratives of Collaboration

The film *Sin City* appeared in 2005, directed by Robert Rodriguez and Frank Miller, with Quentin Tarantino as "guest director." The seven-volume series of graphic novels by Miller, on which the film is based, appeared as a series of stories from 1991 to 2000 and in a collected edition by Dark Horse Press in 2005. The directors set out to hew as closely as possible to the dialogue and look of the graphic novels.[30]

Critics refer to *Sin City* as a *neo*-noir film largely for technical reasons, due to the use of digital imagery and special effects as well as its explicit references to comic book heroes.[31] As Andrew Spicer remarks, "Any attempt at defining film noir solely through its 'essential' formal components proves to be reductive and unsatisfactory because film noir, as the French critics asserted from the beginning, also involves a sensibility, a particular way of looking at the world."[32] This is no less true for neo-noir works like *Sin City*.[33] Indeed, Miller himself explicitly identifies the "spooky" black and white "look" of his noir graphics and his frequent use of shadows and blinds with the techniques that are typical of film noir. At the same time, Miller insists that these technical gestures are "metaphors for the torment, or the rage, or the self-hatred, or the despair the characters are going through."[34] They embody a "particular way of looking at the world."

Not only in its digital effects but in its style, narrative, and character, *Sin City* adheres closely to the definition of noir in Raymond Chandler's classic study, "The Art of Murder." Its heroes and heroines are common people. As Chandler remarks, the noir genre "gave murder back to the kind of people that commit it for reasons, not just to provide a corpse."[35] The film and graphic novels situate crime and violence within their real social, economic, and political conditions of emergence. "Their characters lived in a world gone wrong. . . . The law was something to be manipulated for profit and power. The streets were dark with something more than night."[36] Like Irigaray, the noir genre ties this moral darkness and violence to the unconditional power of money and the subjection of women.

In this "world gone wrong" justice requires that agents be willing to sacrifice their own moral purity to protect the vulnerable. "Violence did not dismay them," remarks Chandler; "it was right down their street."[37] A realist about power and inequity, the noir hero knows that resistance will provoke a violent response by the ruling elite, and he must be ready to meet it. At a time when the law is the "servant of the long purse,"[38] the noir detective serves as the extralegal agent of justice.

As Chandler argues, the noir hero couples this hard-bitten realism with "heart." In the noir genre, the detective deploys affect as well as acumen.[39] He displays emotional intelligence as well as the capacity for love. Feelings provide evidence for his analysis just as reasons and facts do. Quintessential noir heroes such as Philip Marlowe and Sam Spade, perhaps surprisingly, exhibit just the capacity for love and the appreciation of the other in her singularity that Irigaray makes essential to human relationships and political life.[40]

While the noir hero's fierce sense of injustice moves him to act, there is nothing utopian in his thinking. Indeed, his milieu, like Basin City, appears to be a place without a future.[41] The community has been afflicted by a neglect of the public good, and public space has become a claustrophobic warren of violent ghettos. It is always dark, and life is both fragile and cheap.

"The realist in murder," Chandler argues, "writes of a world in which gangsters can rule nations and almost rule cities."[42] The stories of *Sin City* occur amid the radical corruption of politics, the church, and the police, as well as a pervasive violence and sexualization of women. "It is not a fragrant world, but it is the world you live in."[43] No less apocalyptic in tone than Irigaray, the noir genre similarly depicts a world in which the institutions meant to protect the vulnerable exploit them, a world of structural injustice built on the twin powers of concentrated wealth and violence against women.

Chandler articulates the moral principle on which justice depends in the noir genre: "Down these mean streets a man must go who is not himself mean, who is neither tarnished, nor afraid."[44] The heroes of *Sin City* exhibit the noir hero's combination of acumen and heart as well as his capacity to engage with violence to protect the vulnerable. Like the heroes of crime fiction, the heroes of *Sin City* are the unlawful agents of justice, the undomesticated guardians of domestic security, and the violent servants of peace in an absurd and corrupted world.

Sin City, however, develops a theme that appears in the noir genre but is overshadowed there by the critical narrative of the femme fatale.[45] In *Sin City*, agency always requires a collaboration across sexual difference. Each hero is paired with an equally strong and honorable heroine. While women are especially vulnerable in a culture of sexual exploitation, *Sin City* represents women not merely as victims to be rescued, but as powerful agents of resistance, capable of protecting themselves and their communities.

Moreover, in *Sin City* these collaborations also transgress racial differences. The tight community of women that run Old Town, Basin City's zone of prostitution, are of multiple races, and the alliance of equals between Dwight, who is white, and Gail, the African American leader of Old Town, proves to be one of the most powerful and effective in the film. At one point, Dwight remarks with passion that Gail will always be his woman, "always and never." Miller himself parses the scene: "Rather than try to dominate and possess Gail, Dwight realizes that the woman he loves will always belong to herself as much as she belongs to him."[46] Gail may be a femme fatale,[47] but Dwight is in no way afraid of her sexuality, nor does he seek to control it. His passion belongs to her freedom. While the noir genre often valorizes the figure of the lone detective, *Sin City* explores the extralegal, extra-institutional collaborations and communities across race and sexual difference that may be a condition for justice in an unjust world, as well as the trust and heart necessary to sustain that collaboration and community.

Sin City comprises six parts. Two short vignettes begin and end the film. In each, the same hit man assassinates a beautiful woman. Within this frame, three stories are presented. The first is broken into two parts, which begin and end the sequence. Each story involves extreme violence against women, including sexual torture, murder, and cannibalism. All three stories focus on how the collaboration between the hero and heroine succeeds in achieving some measure of justice in this inherently corrupted and violent world.

In the first story, Detective Hartigan has tracked down a vicious sexual sadist and serial murderer, who turns out to be Junior Roark, the son of Senator Roark. When Hartigan attempts to capture Junior and rescue his latest victim, "skinny little Nancy Callahan," Hartigan's own crooked partner shoots him, but not before Hartigan has effectively castrated Junior with a gunshot to the groin. Hartigan survives long enough to protect Nancy until other police arrive. As he loses consciousness, the story breaks off.

The second story involves Kevin, a cannibalistic serial killer who is preying on the women of Old Town while protected by his patron, Cardinal Roark, the even more powerful and more evil brother to the senator. The Cardinal's narrative justifies his indulgence: "they're all whores." Kevin kidnaps young women and chops them up, eating them piece by piece. A beautiful hooker named Goldie recruits the hero Marv, an ugly brute sometimes given to delusions, who nevertheless displays the noir hero's honor and mission. Kevin, preternaturally stealthy, kills Goldie while she is in bed with Marv, and Marv vows, as she knew he would, to avenge her killing. He succeeds in eliminating both Kevin and the Cardinal, but he is captured and executed after confessing to the murders of the women himself, because the police and judicial authorities, who are nothing more than Roark's henchmen, threaten to harm his mother.

In the third story Dwight, a convicted murderer, has just returned to his old life after acquiring a new face. He's visiting Shellie, the barmaid from Kadie's Club Pecos, when a corrupt cop named Jackie Boy, who likes to beat women, stops by with his crew. Dwight, hiding in the bedroom, hears Jackie threatening Shellie and runs him off. Before Shellie can warn him that Jackie is a cop, Dwight goes in pursuit because "they're going to hurt a woman." He teams up with his "warrior woman" Gail, the leader of Old Town, where "women are the law." Organized crime as well as the police respect the women's self-governance, as long as they confine their authority to the precincts of Old Town. Dwight, Gail, and the women of Old Town kill Jackie Boy and his goons, using Becky, the youngest girl, as a lure. In killing a cop, the women effectively violate the truce that has protected them. The mob captures Gail and announces the immediate takeover of Old Town. During her interrogation, Gail learns that there is a "snitch" in Old Town. Dwight and the women of Old Town stage a counterattack and eliminate the mobsters. Gail has shown a particular maternal care for Becky, who in turn is regularly worrying about her own mother. Becky turns out to be the snitch, and she is the victim of the hit man in the final vignette closing the film.

Prior to that concluding scene, however, the film returns to the story of Hartigan and "skinny little Nancy Callahan." Hartigan wakes up in a hospital bed surrounded by IVs with Senator Roark at the foot of his bed threatening to kill him. But in fact, the plan is to convict Hartigan of Junior's crimes. Roark's goons try to beat a confession out of Hartigan, but he resists. Convicted anyway, Hartigan is imprisoned for eight years. During that time, he receives regular letters from "skinny little Nancy Callahan," who calls herself Cordelia and addresses him as Galahad. With the integrity and constancy of Lear's Cordelia, she reaches out to Hartigan's purity of heart. After eight years, Nancy/Cordelia's letters suddenly cease. After a few months, Hartigan receives an envelope containing the little finger of a young woman. Hartigan assumes that Roark's agents have found Nancy. He confesses to Junior's crimes and is released. He tracks Nancy down at Kadie's Club Pecos, where Goldie picked up Marv. "Skinny little Nancy Callahan" turns out to be the voluptuous young woman, played by Jessica Alba, who dances on a pedestal above the bar and whom we have already seen in the second and third stories.

Nancy recognizes him and is overjoyed to see the man she has loved since childhood, but Hartigan suddenly realizes that he has put her in danger: Roark has released him so that Junior can follow him to Nancy. Hartigan and Nancy flee together, but they are captured by Junior's goons, who leave Hartigan naked with a noose around his neck and his toes perched on the edge of a chair. He nearly succumbs but, with an immense act of will, manages to free himself. Junior, who "likes to hear them scream," has taken Nancy to the Roark family farm, where we also see Kevin the cannibal. Junior has strung Nancy up and is whipping her, but she "stays strong," refusing him the screams he desires. Hartigan succeeds in rescuing her, killing Junior and the goons in the process, but he realizes that she will never be safe as long as he is alive. He sends Nancy back to Basin City, and in this unjust world Hartigan tries to find justice: "an old man dies, and a young woman lives." Then he shoots himself. Righting the logic of generations, the old man does not survive his Cordelia.

Nancy appears in all three stories and provides the central figure of female agency in the film. She has survived with not only her virginity intact, but also her integrity and her agency. Nancy does not work the streets like the other girls but has used her talent as a dancer to install herself above that traffic: no one touches Nancy. Nancy survives because she trusts Hartigan and because he proves trustworthy, but also because of her own agency, because she "stays strong" and refuses to gratify Junior by screaming.

Each story details the evil of institutions—political, ecclesiastical, and legal—that cannot be trusted, but the story of Hartigan and Nancy focuses in particular on the intrinsic connection between justice and truth. Injustice flourishes when false narratives hold sway. As the despicable Senator Roark asserts, "Power don't come from a badge or a gun; power comes from lying—lying big and gettin' the whole damn world to play along with you." This collusion of power and false narratives points not merely to error or mistaken belief, but to a more pernicious form of false consciousness. Roark lectures Hartigan: "Once you got everybody agreeing with what they know in their hearts ain't true, you got 'em by the balls." The audacity of power lies in its ability to rewrite reality, to install a fake narrative, even when those determined by it do not believe it. The ability to sustain a wide gap between public narrative and material reality provides a measure of power.[48] Lying in public speech and spreading fake news has long been a strategy of autocrats and tyrants. As Homer remarked, "Rumor is the messenger of Zeus."[49] *Sin City* projects the dark outcome of cruel leaders who lie to maximize their own power and profit.

To possess the truth, to expose the fake narrative to the glare of reality, puts life at risk: "Tell anyone the truth," Roark threatens Hartigan, "and they're dead." The just man takes the place of the criminal: Hartigan rescues Nancy but is convicted of Junior's crimes, just as Marv kills the monster preying on the girls of Old Town only to be forced to confess to the crimes himself. The agent of justice even endures being falsely cast as unjust for the sake of justice.[50]

The ethical principles that guide these heroes' pursuit of justice reflect the unfragrant conditions of their agency. As Marv states, "It's wrong to hurt girls," and it's right to repay Goldie's generosity by punishing her killer. Dwight tells Gail that he's intent on killing Jackie and his goons, "because they deserve it, and not for revenge or because it will make the world a better place." The noir hero's anti-utopianism does not undermine his commitment to justice, nor is his violence personal. At the same time, these heroes exhibit the real complexities and ambivalences of moral agency. Far from being "one dimensional characters" who exhibit a "simplistic opposition between good and evil"[51] or a "moral polarization" that fails to capture the "ambivalence" of film noir,[52] the three male leads of *Sin City* are flawed and full of self-doubt and self-interrogation, at the same time that they adhere steadfastly to the moral principle of protecting the vulnerable from exploitation. After his release from prison, Hartigan goes in search of Nancy, but in doing so, he puts her in danger. Dwight means to stop Jackie from abusing women, but his precipitous action puts those very women in danger. All three explicitly doubt their own perceptions and struggle to know how to realize their commitments to justice. They figure the real exigencies of moral action in a "world gone wrong."

The intergenerational collaborations across race and sexual difference that address justice in an unjust world can only be sustained by trust and truth. Becky betrays Gail's trust, thereby endangering all the women of Old Town. So she must be eliminated, as she is in the closing hit: her betrayal makes collaboration impossible and puts the community at risk. At the same time, the agents of justice can tell the difference between the material realities of injustice and public lying or fake news. They give voice to the vulnerable in narratives that expose inequity and undermine the consolidation of power. Transgressing differences of race, sex, and generation, the noir heroes and heroines of *Sin City* form a community of truth and trust that sustains them all in a time when violent injustice is pervasive and, as Hartigan laments, "the truth don't matter like it ought to." The narrative not only reinforces Irigaray's critique of life under global capital, but also answers to her call for new narratives of solidarity and collaboration capable of sustaining a "livable future."

Notes

1. Jacques Derrida, "Of an Apocalyptic Tone Recently Adopted in Philosophy," *Oxford Literary Review* 6, no. 2 (1984): 3–37.

2. Irigaray SG, 146. On the way in which capital proves to be anti-life, see also SG, 187.

3. See, for example, Irigaray DB, 163.

4. Irigaray SG, 186. Cf. Arundhati Roy, "War Is Peace," in *The Algebra of Infinite Justice* (London: Flamingo/Harper Collins, 2002). In the essay "Come September" in the same volume, Roy remarks:

> What the free market undermines is not national sovereignty, but *democracy*. As the disparity between rich and poor grows, the hidden fist has its work cut out for it. . . . Today Corporate Globalization needs an international confederation of loyal, corrupt, preferably authoritarian regimes in poorer countries, to push through unpopular reforms and quell the mutinies. It needs a press that pretends to be free. It needs courts that pretend to dispense justice. It needs nuclear bombs, standing armies, sterner immigration laws, and watchful coastal patrols to make sure that it's only money, goods, patents, and services that are globalized—not the free movement of people, not a respect for human rights, not international treaties on racial discrimination or chemical and nuclear weapons, or greenhouse gas emissions, climate change or, god forbid, justice.

Roy's analysis of the nexus of threats that afflict human existence under global capital is remarkably consonant with Irigaray's. For both it is essential to see how all these threatening powers are intertwined: war, social inequity and labor exploitation, gender and racial injustice, environmental and climate exploitation, fake news, all reflect the subjugation of life to the interests of global capital.

5. Irigaray SG, vi.

6. Note Irigaray's inclusion of race here and her tacit recognition of intersectionality. This is one of many points in her work where she demonstrates, against charges of white heteronormativity, that the thought of sexual difference,

Irigaray's thought, opens space for the articulation of other exceptions to the narrative of Man. Western philosophy produces the figure of a generic, detached, purely rational subject, at the same time that it subjects each and all to the laws of property and sexual propriety as a means of creating social order and the possibility of productive labor. Irigaray demonstrates over and over again how that generic subject has always already been marked male and white and compliant with the laws of property and sexual propriety, while the others are themselves rendered his property. There are solidarities here to be nurtured.

7. At this point Foucault's analysis of "biopower" usefully supplements and is supplemented by Irigaray's thought of sexual difference. As Foucault demonstrates, the transformation of singular human beings into units of a population facilitates power in managing them to maximize wealth and security. For an attempt to "marry" Foucault and Irigaray at just this point, see, Mary C. Rawlinson, *Just Life: Bioethics and the Future of Sexual Difference* (New York: Columbia University Press, 2016), preface and chapter 2.

8. Irigaray ILTY, 50.

9. Irigaray JTN, 76. The failure to address climate change illustrates the sacrifice of life to money and Irigaray's insistence that humans' relation to nature as property has put all life in danger. Agribusiness and its allied processed food industry threaten not only the climate, but the individual. Its commodity farming reduces biodiversity and relies on fertilizers and other inputs, that is, on pollutants made from fossil fuels. It markets addictive foods, high in fat and sugar, contributing directly to a global obesity epidemic. Human health is sacrificed to capital. See, Mary C. Rawlinson, "The Climate of Food: Justice, Truth, and Structural Change," in *Food, Environment, and Climate Change: Justice at the Intersections*, ed. Erinn Cuniff Gilson and Sarah Kenehan (London: Rowman & Littlefield, 2018), 91–118.

10. Irigaray DB, 159.

11. Irigaray ILTY, 50. Peter Buffet also implicates the "charitable-industrial complex" in global social and economic inequity. Members of foundation boards try to solve problems with their right hand that they have themselves created with their left. Peter Buffett, "The Charitable-Industrial Complex," *New York Times*, July 26, 2013. On the way wealthy states use aid to other countries as a means of managing overproduction, see also Rawlinson, *The Climate of Food*, 91–118.

12. Thomas Pikkety, *Capital in the Twenty-First Century*, trans. Arthur Goldhammer (Cambridge, MA: Harvard University Press, 2014), 237–469.

13. Jonathan Weisman, "Why Is Unemployment So High? Lazy Americans, Boehner Says," *New York Times*, September 22, 2014.

14. Darren Samuelson, "Giuliani: Obama Doesn't Love America," *Politico*, February 18, 2015, https://www.politico.com/story/2015/02/rudy-giuliani-president-obama-doesnt-love-america-115309, accessed March 1, 2015. The remark

foreshadowed the continued coarsening of public discourse under the forty-fifth president of the United States.

15. Irigaray JTN, 22.

16. "Man" refers to the fiction of a disinterested, purely rational subject produced by Western philosophy.

17. The theoretical construct of the "original position" is the latest installment in the history of figures of the Man of reason. See John Rawls, *A Theory of Justice* (Cambridge, MA: Harvard University Press, 1971). Advanced as a point of departure for making decisions about the justice of policies or actions, the figure ignores the real operation of power as well as the dependence of decision-making on being situated. The approach treats injustice as either the effect of an individual intention or an unintended, accidental consequence of an otherwise fair system. It is akin to the drawing-room mysteries that Raymond Chandler decries for treating injustice as an aberrant disruption of an otherwise fair and rational order.

18. Irigaray DB, 96.

19. For more than three decades Irigaray has argued that human survival and human flourishing depend on a fundamental change in humans' relation to nature and to other animals. See, for example, "The Right to Life," in Irigaray JTN, 75–81. See also, Irigaray TD, 16: "Mankind has generally put property ahead of life. Men care little about living matter or its cultural economy. Men's society is built upon ownership of property. Life itself is treated like a commodity, productive capital, and possessed as a tool of labour, but not as the basis of an identity to be cultivated."

20. Indeed, Irigaray's recent writing on her relation to nature explicitly contrasts her affinity for and her nourishing relation to nature with her alienation from the human. See, for example, TVB. She seems to have abandoned the political. Even her recent work on pedagogy seems more focused on the personal relation of mentoring than on pedagogy as a progressive political practice.

21. See Plato, *Republic*, 607b.

22. See, for example, Martha Nussbaum, *Poetic Justice: The Literary Imagination and Public Life* (Boston: Beacon Press, 1995), or Elaine Scarry, *On Beauty and Being Just* (Princeton, NJ: Princeton University Press, 1999).

23. Scarry argues that symmetries of beauty in art lead us to the idea of justice as the "symmetry of fraternity."

24. See, for example, Irigaray's critique of the politics of the same in ILTY, 38–41.

25. See Chester Himes's studies of the impossibility of being a black man in America, for example, in the character of Johnny Perry in *The Crazy Kill* (New York: Vintage Crime, 1989). Much of the detectives' effort in this novel focuses not on the murder but on doing what they can to prevent Perry's destruction. Perry's very agency has put him at risk given the racist culture of

possibilities that excludes him from the narrative position. See also Thomas Harris's analysis of the impossibility of female agency in the character of Clarice Starling in *Hannibal* (New York: Delacorte Press, 1999). Clarice discovers that she cannot be herself within the law.

26. Wilkie Collins, *The Woman in White* (New York: Penguin, 1981), 33. Originally published 1860 by Harper and Brothers, New York.

27. Raymond Chandler, *The Simple Art of Murder* (New York: Vintage Books, 1988), 18. Originally published in 1944 in *Atlantic Monthly*.

28. See Mary C. Rawlinson, "Liminal Agencies: Literature as Moral Philosophy," in *Literature and Philosophy: A Guide to Contemporary Debates*, ed. David Rudrum (London: Palgrave Macmillan, 2006), 129–141.

29. I do not pretend to answer this question in this essay. Crime fiction puts philosophy on notice that it is in need of an answer.

30. Frank Miller, *Sin City*, 8 vols. (Milwaukie, OR: Dark Horse Books, 2005). *Sin City*, directed by Frank Miller, Robert Rodriguez, and Quentin Tarantino, produced by Elizabeth Avellán (Austin, TX: Troublemaker Studios, 2005). Certain images from the novel are reproduced almost exactly in the film: Nancy dancing on the bar, Roark's face as he torments Hartigan, Hartigan's suicide. The latter fades into the cartoon from the book.

31. For example, Marv, the hero of the second story, frequently jumps from tall buildings with his coat flying open behind him like a superhero's cape.

32. Andrew Spicer, *Film Noir* (London: Longman, 2002), 25. The definition of the noir genre remains highly contested. The term *film noir* was coined in the mid-forties by the French film critic Nino Frank. See his "Un nouveau genre 'policier': L'aventure criminelle," *L'ecran français* 61 (August 1946), which clearly remarks the kinship between film noir and crime fiction. The term became a standard part of the critical lexicon in France after the publication of Raymond Borde and Étienne Chaumeton, eds., *Panorama du film noir américain (1941–1953)* (Paris: Minuit, 1955). See also Spicer, *Film Noir*, 1–26.

33. The distinction between noir and neo-noir proves hard to sustain on anything other than technical grounds. Some critics have argued that neo-noir is distinguished by a foregrounding of social issues like race, class, and gender, which are only latent in noir, but this just ignores central noir authors like James M. Cain and Chester Himes, whose work explicitly investigates just these issues. See, for example, Jerold J. Abrams, "Space, Time, and Subjectivity in Neo-Noir Cinema," in *The Philosophy of Neo-Noir*, ed. Mark T. Conard (Lexington: University Press of Kentucky, 2007), 7–20. Nor is the critique of capitalism new to neo-noir fiction and film, as evidenced by any number of stories by Dashiell Hammett and Chandler analyzing money and power in Los Angeles. See James Naremore, "A Season in Hell or the Snows of Yesteryear?," preface to the English translation of *Panorama of American Film Noir (1941–1953)*, ed. Raymond Borde and Étienne Chaumeton, trans. Paul Hammond (San Francisco: City Lights Books,

2002), vii–xxi; or Jeanne Schuler and Patrick Murray, "'Anything Is Possible Here': Capitalism, Neo-Noir, and *Chinatown*," in *The Philosophy of Neo-Noir*, ed. Mark T. Conard (Lexington: University Press of Kentucky, 2007), 167–181. In the words of Naremore, Borde and Chaumeton had already identified noir film as an "antigenre that reveals the dark side of savage capitalism. . . . Noir produces a psychological and moral disorientation, an inversion of capitalist and puritan values, as if it were pushing the American system toward revolutionary destruction." See also Erik Dussere, *America Is Elsewhere: The Noir Tradition in the Age of Consumer Culture* (London: Oxford University Press, 2014), 22.

Some scholars question whether noir is a genre at all, and perhaps the debate over genre is not particularly clarifying. See Mark T. Conard, "Nietzsche and the Meaning and Definition of Noir," in *The Philosophy of Film Noir*, ed. Mark T. Conard (Lexington: University Press of Kentucky, 2006), 7–22. Informed by Irigaray's apocalyptic critique of injustice, the reader cannot miss the continuities between the noir fiction of Cain, Chandler, and Hammett and the neo-noir graphic novels and film *Sin City*. The aim in all three literatures is to right a "world gone wrong." Indeed, I would argue, these themes of justice and injustice define the mystery and detective genre from the very beginning in Poe and Collins throughout its development in noir fiction.

34. Frank Miller and Roberto Rodriguez, *Frank Miller's "Sin City": The Making of the Movie* (Austin: Troublemaker, 2005), 16.

35. Chandler, *Simple Art of Murder*, 14.

36. Raymond Chandler, *Trouble Is My Business* (New York: Vintage, 1988), 2. Originally published 1939 in *Dime Detective*.

37. Chandler, *Simple Art of Murder*, 14.

38. Collins, *Woman in White*, 33. In 1860 Collins had already diagnosed the problem of the corruption of the law by money and privilege in much the same terms that Chandler employs in "The Simple Art of Murder." In a world where cities and nations are ruled by "gangsters" and, as Chandler observes, "a judge with a cellar full of bootleg liquor can send a man to jail for having a pint in his pocket," justice requires an extralegal agency, just as it did in Collins's *The Woman in White*.

39. Edgar Allan Poe, who introduces the figure of the detective, renders him passionless and defined by his acumen, by his ability to sort the essential from the inessential just as the philosopher does. Dupin is not engaged in human affairs outside of his detection. See, for example, Poe, "Murders in the Rue Morgue," in *Complete Tales and Poems* (Edison, NJ: Castle Books, 2002), 117–140. The noir hero, on the other hand, couples reason with feeling in both life and his detection.

40. See, for example, Irigaray TBT, 109. In *The Big Sleep*, for example, Marlow takes each member of the Sternwood family as a "singular sensibility, thought, and truth."

41. The town depicted in *Sin City* is named Basin City; the "B" and "a" have fallen off the sign marking entry into the town.

42. Chandler, *Simple Art of Murder*, 17.

43. Chandler, *Simple Art of Murder*, 17.

44. Chandler, *Simple Art of Murder*, 18. Commenting on the noir hero's "range of awareness" and capacity for "adventure," Chandler avers that "if there were enough like him, the world would be a very safe place to live in, without becoming too dull to be worth living in."

45. The role of the femme fatale in the noir genre has been badly overrated. For every seductive Cora Smith (*The Postman Always Rings Twice*) or Phyllis Dietrichson (*Double Indemnity*), there is a maternal Mildred Pierce (in the film of the same name) or a genuinely loving Mrs. Rutledge (*The Big Sleep*). It is not even remotely plausible to say that either Marlowe or Spade needs "to control women's sexuality in order not to be destroyed by it," as Janey Place writes in "Women in Film Noir," in *Women in Film Noir*, ed. E. Ann Kaplan (London: British Film Institute, 1999), 49. Certainly, the heroes of *Sin City* are empowered by their relationships with women and by their respect for them. The women of *Sin City* may be femmes fatales, but they are morally discerning in their choices of victims and fully allied with male agents of justice. As Julie Grossman argues in *Rethinking the Femme Fatale in Film Noir: Ready for Her Close-Up* (New York: Palgrave Macmillan, 2009), "An overemphasis on the 'femme fatale' has not only resulted in a misreading of many film noir movies, but has fed into cultural and critical obsessions with the bad, sexy woman, which inevitably become prescriptive and influence cultural discourse about female agency in counterproductive ways" (5). Such readings miss entirely the long history in crime fiction of trenchant critiques of gender as well as capital. Such critiques go back to the first detective novel in English, Wilkie Collins's *The Woman in White*, which displays the evils of nineteenth-century English laws governing marriage and property as well as the necessity to justice of collaborations across sexual difference.

46. Miller and Rodriguez, *Frank Miller's "Sin City,"* 46.

47. I should say that she knows how to *play* the femme fatale. For Gail, "femme fatale" refers to a strategic tool, not an identity.

48. "Power largely consists in the ability to make others inhabit your story of their reality, even if you have to kill a lot of them to make that happen. In this raw sense, power has always been very much the same everywhere; what varies is primarily the quality of the reality it seeks to create: is it based more in truth or in falsehood, which is to say is it more or less abusive of its subjects?" Philip Gourevitch, *We Wish to Inform You That Tomorrow We Will Be Killed with Our Families: Stories from Rwanda* (New York: Picador, 1999), 181.

49. *The Odyssey of Homer*, trans. Richard Lattimore (New York: Harper Colophon, 1967), 282.

50. Speaking truth to power in Russia or China or Saudi Arabia might easily result in death. So far in the United States, it results only in being fired or being trolled. Of course, the latter can be life-threatening.

51. Doug Keesey, *Neo-Noir: Contemporary Film Noir from "Chinatown" to "The Dark Night"* (Harpendon, UK: Kamera Books, 2010), 44.

52. Brian McDonnell and Geoff Mayer, *Encyclopedia of Film Noir* (Westport, CT: Greenwood Press, 2007), 381.

Bibliography

Abrams, Jerold J. "Space, Time, and Subjectivity in Neo-Noir Cinema." In *The Philosophy of Neo-Noir*, edited by Mark T. Conard, 7–20. Lexington: University Press of Kentucky, 2007.

Buffett, Peter. "The Charitable-Industrial Complex." *New York Times*, July 26, 2013.

Chandler, Raymond. *The Simple Art of Murder*. New York: Vintage, 1988. (Originally published 1944 in *Atlantic Monthly*.)

Chandler, Raymond. *Trouble Is My Business*. New York: Vintage, 1988. (Originally published 1939 in *Dime Detective*.)

Collins, Wilkie. *The Woman in White*. New York: Penguin, 1981. (Originally published 1860 by Harper and Brothers, New York.)

Conard, Mark T. "Nietzsche and the Meaning and Definition of Noir." In *The Philosophy of Film Noir*, edited by Mark T. Conard, 7–22. Lexington: University Press of Kentucky, 2006.

Derrida, Jacques. "Of an Apocalyptic Tone Recently Adopted in Philosophy." *Oxford Literary Review* 6, no. 2 (1984): 3–37.

Dussere, Erik. *America Is Elsewhere: The Noir Tradition in the Age of Consumer Culture*. London: Oxford University Press, 2014.

Frank, Nino. "Un nouveau genre 'policier': L'aventure criminelle." *L'ecran français* 61 (August 1946): 8–10.

Gourevitch, Philip. *We Wish to Inform You That Tomorrow We Will Be Killed with Our Families: Stories from Rwanda*. New York: Picador, 1999.

Grossman, Julie. *Rethinking the Femme Fatale in Film Noir: Ready for Her Close-Up*. New York: Palgrave Macmillan, 2009.

Harris, Thomas. *Hannibal*. New York: Delacorte Press, 1999.

Himes, Chester. *The Crazy Kill*. New York: Vintage Crime, 1989. (Originally published 1959 by Avon, New York.)

Keesey, Doug. *Neo-Noir: Contemporary Film Noir from "Chinatown" to "The Dark Night."* Harpendon, UK: Kamera Books, 2010.

Lattimore, Richard, trans. *The Odyssey of Homer*. New York: Harper Colophon, 1967.

McDonnell, Brian, and Geoff Mayer. *Encyclopedia of Film Noir*. Westport, CT: Greenwood Press, 2007.

Miller, Frank. *Sin City*. 8 vols. Milwaukie, OR: Dark Horse Books, 2005.

Miller, Frank, and Roberto Rodriguez. *Frank Miller's "Sin City": The Making of the Movie*. Austin, TX: Troublemaker, 2005.

Miller, Frank, and Roberto Rodriguez, dir. *Sin City*. Austin, TX: Troublemaker Studios, 2005.

Naremore, James. "A Season in Hell or the Snows of Yesteryear?" In *Panorama of American Film Noir (1941–1953)*, edited by Raymond Borde and Étienne Chaumeton, translated by Paul Hammond, vii–xxi. San Francisco: City Lights Books, 2002.

Nussbaum, Martha. *Poetic Justice: The Literary Imagination and Public Life*. Boston: Beacon Press, 1995.

Pikkety, Thomas. *Capital in the Twenty-First Century*. Translated by Arthur Goldhammer. Cambridge, MA: Harvard University Press, 2014.

Place, Janey. "Women in Film Noir." In *Women in Film Noir*, edited by E. Ann Kaplan, 35–54. London: British Film Institute, 1999.

Poe, Edgar Allan. "Murders in the Rue Morgue." In *Complete Tales and Poems*, 117–140. Edison, NJ: Castle Books, 2002.

Rawlinson, Mary C. "The Climate of Food: Justice, Truth, and Structural Change." In *Food, Environment, and Climate Change: Justice at the Intersections*, edited by Erinn Gilson and Sarah Kenehan, 91–118. London: Rowman & Littlefield, 2018.

Rawlinson, Mary C. *Just Life: Bioethics and the Future of Sexual Difference*. New York: Columbia University Press, 2016.

Rawlinson, Mary C. "Liminal Agencies: Literature as Moral Philosophy." In *Literature and Philosophy: A Guide to Contemporary Debates*, edited by David Rudrum, 129–141. London: Palgrave Macmillan, 2006.

Rawls, John. *A Theory of Justice*. Cambridge, MA: Harvard University Press, 1971.

Roy, Arundhati. *The Algebra of Infinite Justice*. London: Flamingo/Harper Collins, 2002.

Samuelson, Darren. "Giuliani: Obama Doesn't Love America." *Politico*, February 18, 2015. https://www.politico.com/story/2015/02/rudy-giuliani-president-obama-doesnt-love-america-115309. Accessed March 1, 2015.

Scarry, Elaine. *On Beauty and Being Just*. Princeton, NJ: Princeton University Press, 1999.

Schuler, Jeanne, and Patrick Murray. "'Anything Is Possible Here': Capitalism, Neo-Noir, and *Chinatown*." In *The Philosophy of Neo-Noir*, edited by Mark T. Conard, 167–181. Lexington: University Press of Kentucky, 2007.

Spicer, Andrew. *Film Noir*. London: Longman, 2002.

Weisman, Jonathan. "Why Is Unemployment So High? Lazy Americans, Boehner Says." *New York Times*, September 22, 2014.

Part V

Environments of Relational Difference

Chapter Ten

Artificial Life, Autopoiesis, and Breath

Irigaray with Ecological Feminism and Deep Ecology

Ruthanne Crapo Kim

Sexuate Difference and Feminist Ecologies

In the age of the Anthropocene, ecological feminism is a growing area of specialization in the field of environmental ethics, arguing that the patriarchal domination of women and other social groups are parallel to man's exploitation of "nonhuman nature"; thus, both must cease in order to gain ecological stability.[1] Rosemary Radford Ruether suggests that the views of feminism and environmentalism[2] mutually reinforce one another in that they both involve the development of worldviews and practices that are not based on models of dominance.[3] As global climate change correlates to human activity, environmental degradation affects disproportionately the human lives of women, children, and colonized people, as they bear the cost of the rich world's consumption.[4] This degradation includes the life cycles and behaviors of nonhumans and the people whose global identities are situated as closest to these nonhumans and their systems—namely, those deemed women.[5] Yet, few women worldwide possess significant political say about these things, even though their occupations and livelihood remain intricately connected to ecological elements formerly understood as "common,"[6] such as water or air.[7] The principal strategy to undo this dominance has been to demonstrate how interconnected all living beings are, often implying a monist correction to a dualist worldview.

Irigaray's ethics of sexuate difference—out of which an ecological ethics[8] can be developed—offers a philosophical account arguing the priority of ontology as a necessary condition for our ability to realize our elemental material interconnections. She theorizes energy, breath, and interior space, arguing that we must rethink these invisible processes in order to reveal the passage between nature and culture.[9] Important to her ontology is an asymmetrical dualism where one finds belonging in difference, respecting variations of biology,[10] morphology, and relational attachment. Thus, a twoness not split from the same whole is postulated in order to displace appropriative power relations. I read her formulating a phenomenological perspective to the environmental debate, questioning an unthought androcentric transcendentalism wherein sexuate sameness permits binary opposition to remain invisible. She writes,

> What distinguishes a human being from other living beings is the ability to create *invisibility* rather than to make appear, to render visible. . . . The respect of the invisibility of the other, this hospitality given to the other . . . in oneself—in one's own body, and one's own breath, one's own mind or soul—, corresponds, for me, to a human becoming, a human being.[11]

In these words, Irigaray delineates two kinds of invisibility: 1) a social phenomenon where, by means of abstraction, we minimize the visible into a reductive resource and blind[12] ourselves to the material volume of other; 2) an unseen elemental proximity[13] within and outside of us,[14] often signified in Irigaray's work as breath. She defines the human beyond a social animal, a being capable of respecting the invisible in one's self and the other and overcoming the subsequent abstract reduction of the world within oppositional valuation. Instead, we are elemental beings—we commune with an elemental world and share a first community and moral obligations with air, water, soil, darkness and light, cold and heat.[15] Irigaray's intervention has been to rethink these elements as capable of "speaking" or "dialoguing" with us, revealing without enclosing their being. She is radical in that she perceives their difference without signaling what it is, creating an ethical demand that we co-adapt our desire, intentionality, and existence with irreducible elemental others.

Irigaray's work aligns with ecofeminism in that she dismantles how differences have been used to identify "a lack" that women supposedly suffer and could in varying degrees be said of animals, plants, and rocks. Typically, the lack pertains to cultural abilities that men in the Western world historically and philosophically champion: rationality, language, physical dominance, technological prowess, private property, and a free market. As Timothy Morton argues, "One way to undo this mischief is to combine the biocentric ecofeminists with the radical thought of the French feminists. The reason to admire Irigaray in particular, and employ her thought in an ecological sense, is that her use of paraconsistent logic provides an excellent foundation for thinking ecological beings."[16] Her work takes aim at the groupings women, animals, plants, and rocks and how we conceal their capacity to differentiate, a differentiation at odds with the prevailing Western cultural system, what Morton calls "Agrilogistics."[17] Irigaray highlights the concealment of the onto-psycho-political enframing[18] of Being and its sexuation. While scholars acknowledge the diversity of life beyond dimorphic constructs,[19] I suggest that Irigaray's project helps us conceive of a rupture from morphological sameness—a necessary first gesture.

Plumwood: A Monological Ratiogenic Culture

Irigaray does not name herself an ecofeminist. However, I observe ecofeminist Val Plumwood's theorization resonates with several critiques Irigaray posits and I trace Plumwood in order to delineate key areas of synergy and difference between them. Plumwood cites a "rationality of monologue termed monological" where humans are the only subjects and actors in the world and nature is the background, the substratum upon which humans act. She says, "It [the monological] recognizes the Other only in one-way terms, in a mode where the Others must always hear and adapt to the One, and never the other way around . . . [the monological] block[s] mutual adaptation and its corollaries—negotiation, communication and perception of the Other's limits and agency."[20] Plumwood critiques rationalism as a monologic that privileges the abstract, pure, permanent, mathematical, universal over the contextual, local. She suggests that those committed to rationalism utilize economic dominance, the "chief mark of neo-liberalism" whose intensity, duration, and global reach are now unprecedented.[21] This global economic system recognizes little value in preserving original natural resources such as wild fish or other genetic stock. Instead, rationalists seek bioengineered organisms or systems with shorter reproductive cycles in order to fulfill market slots, remaking the world into a more rational form. She writes,

> The failure to recognize the *limits* arising from other living beings and systems is a product of a monological and deeply human-centered view of humans and of nature. . . . [A] colonizing system [differentiates] between a privileged, hegemonic group awarded full agency status who are placed at the centre and excluded peripheral groups who are denied agency and whose contribution is discounted, neglected, denied, or rendered *invisible*.[22]

I observe a striking parallel between Plumwood and Irigaray in that they both note a monological system and the need for ethical limits guided by other living beings and systems. They reject "active" form over "passive" matter,[23] and they attend to what has been rendered invisible. Additionally, they warn against present ecological solutions within which rationalism blinds us from perceiving how to situate human life in an ecological and embodied reality—Irigaray calls these solutions artificial and Plumwood calls them ratiogenic. Both are concerned with a false genesis of sustainable life and reflexive thinking about life. Plumwood describes ratiogenic or "reason-generated" logic as one that uses the heroic tropes of scientific management and technological innovation to rescue us with neo-liberal market forces from the consequences of anthropogenic climate change.[24] Both trace a reading[25] of Aristotle's analogous account of human generation as the father (male) providing the form and the mother's (female) providing the matter.[26] This formative division creates an opposition where men become consumers and property owners of matter because they are efficient reshapers of the material world. Women and their corollaries—animals, plants, and rocks—become producers, growers, and property. They are the generative material substances of consumption. While Plumwood calls this a human/nature opposition, Irigaray stresses the twoness that we must ontologically account for when theorizing form and matter, situating an asymmetrical dimorphic structure with differing corresponding relationships to nature, which is also *two*, a feature I later develop.[27]

Freya Matthews: Nature as One

Biocentric deep ecologist Freya Matthews also breaks apart the binary opposition between nature and culture by analyzing the natural/artificial. She defines nature as not a thing but a *process* of letting things unfold in their own way—"a pattern of gradual but continuous change—a pattern of ageing and decomposition followed by spontaneous reconstitution into new forms. . . . what happens to things when we let them be."[28] Artifice is then a human redirection of the given world toward abstract, idealized ends.[29] In this, she takes apart "nature" as the real and authentic over "artifice" as crafted human creativity. She argues that human ecological ethics ought to conform with nature as process and minimize artifice that attempts to deny our interconnected ecological selves.[30] Matthews also reveals the deep ecologist bind—by identifying humans as "natural" one may wrongly conclude that whatever humans do is natural, and if natural, then morally justified. Matthews turns to ecological feminists to amend the deep ecologist's commitment to the interconnected thesis that humans are one with Nature. She explains that ecofeminists argue interconnectedness, not as a whole (holistic biocentrism) but as individuals interconnected as family, elemental kin to other natural beings in process; as such, each family has its own moral pursuits and capacity for shared compassion.[31] It is as individuals we feel concern for others, thus, it is the differentiation of an irreducible moral ambivalence that creates both the protection of kin and gives us access to a shared interconnection. Matthews notes the helpful work of ecofeminists to reveal how oppositional dichotomous thinking informs similar distinctions between matter and form.[32] I contend that Irigaray's work clarifies the elemental kinship between humans and nonhumans and formulates an irreducibility without incommensurability, resituating dichotomies outside of oppositional logics. Her self-affection offers a way to return subjects back to themselves in order to clarify the limit of human beings, a critique both Plumwood and Matthew herald. However, Irigaray's limit also reveals an important metaphysical chasm among beings and the need for ethical proximity. As such, her work challenges a persistent "unity" in ecofeminist and deep ecologist conceptions of Nature, particularly the assumption that the flow, the iterative[33] process of Nature is discernable, self-evident, and One. Her elemental account of Nature with sexuate difference reveals the structures by which many conceptions of monism and dualism remain bound to sameness.

Irigaray: Nature as Two—Multiplicity ad Infinitum

Irigaray's commitment to the realness of material elements, rhythms or circulations, and their forgotten status convinces Alison Stone to posit Irigaray's work as committed to a realist essentialism[34] or elemental materialism.[35] Stone reads Irigaray as suggesting that humans have access (not just perceptible access à la Kant) to the given world and we must reckon with the sameness/difference binary as organizing our corporeal perceptions and dialectical reasoning of culture/nature as active (abundance)/passive (lack). Indeed, sexual difference is a force so voluminous that Stone, along with others,[36] concludes one may theorize beyond Irigaray's sexual dimorphism in order to fulfill the radicality of her critique. Elizabeth Grosz suggests that Irigaray's account of bodily variation creates an eruption of differences and that to acknowledge sexual difference as universal does not equate to positing it as the most relevant aspect to a being's identity.[37] In sympathy with this critique of a greater scope of difference, where difference does not collapse into an oppositional relation to sameness, I argue sexual difference theory is useful in that it permits difference to remain asymmetrical to the same. As more than two, difference remains distinct, rather than a plurality of the same. Therefore, I do not read a bounded heterosexism as the event horizon of Irigaray's work and insist her work is capable of being read beyond sexual dimorphism.[38] The temptation may be to make difference itself the master signifier, another variant of monism as difference. Instead, Irigaray theorizes a mediated proximity[39] where wonder between beings transforms present identity relations,[40] refiguring lack, and difference reveals a nonsublating limit. The limit, a generative, nondetermined futural possibility, opens a specificity regarding this nonstatic other. The two evolve without fusion or opposition.[41] Instead, subject positions remain open, transformative unfolding, becoming, incalculable, and irreducible. Her project questions how we formulate rankings, comparisons, and abstractions systemically—all is suspect without a culture of being *at least* two.[42]

This transformative confounding signifies an indeterminate becoming and relates to ecological ethics in that nature as sexed is no longer fixed or oppositional: "The living world gives itself its own forms. . . . forms of the living that it is, gives us back the perspective and the perception of a volume which is, moreover, in permanent *evolution*."[43] Returning to Grosz's critique, she suspects ecofeminists—and I suspect deep ecologists—theorize Nature as ordered with a telos discernable via human reasoning; they theorize it as an immanent being or a One.[44] Irigaray's work on nature is distinctive in that she situates nature as *evolutionary* becoming, with capacity for a futural, nonunifying, unfixed, elemental movement.[45] Breathing that consciously utilizes air to animate the material body into "alive, subtle, changing, and even shareable flesh,"[46] furthers the evolution of the natural human. In a well-known passage, Irigaray insists the natural is at least two—male and female, writing, "Nature is not *one*. . . . limit is therefore inscribed in Nature itself. . . . This two inscribes finitude in the natural itself. No one nature can claim to correspond to the *whole* of the natural."[47] Additionally she writes, "Now the matter is living, and it already has form(s) and aim(s); the form can be shaped, but not ex nihilo, and not only according to our intentions; we are both making and made and we cannot anticipate and decide on the final destination of the work."[48] In these words, she is sympathetic to the deep ecologist's insistence to understand nature with an immanence of its own. However, she is closest to Heidegger's phenomenological position: to insist on an unrepresentable notion of Being[49] as an ontological twoness, refounding any former conceptions of Nature as reducible to utilitarian calculations, locatable telos, or irrelevant abstraction. She posits the irreducibility of animals and plants, and like the *féminin*, refuses to enclose what they are or will be.[50] However, an "artificial" life system conceals this unrepresentable twoness. In the next sections, I develop both Irigaray's critique of artificial life systems and the intervention she suggests to reveal this falsity—a gesture she calls self-affection. I clarify how a process of poiesis as self or auto-affection[51] and breathing are ontological and spiritually practiced conditions for intersubjective relations with plants, animals, and other nonhumans. I utilize the term *autopoietic*[52] to convey both the self-affection and the making that these terms imply, and I elaborate the way this concept identifies more than one world via which we conceptualize subjectivity.

Artificial Life

The word *artificial* derives its meaning from the notion of artifice, chicanery, or deception. Irigaray selects this term and other variants—manufacture, fabricate, clone—to signify lesser copies of mirrored or parallel worlds that deceive us from real material life. An artificial universe is fabricated through the annihilation of feminine difference.[53] Nietzsche declared woman herself to be an artifice, or untruthfulness, yet Irigaray contests that woman is not the artifice—a world blind to difference is. Indeed, one may easily read Irigaray's mimetic techniques, disrupting the masculinist voice she reads in philosophy and psychoanalysis, as a practice meant to reveal such copying.

When reading Irigaray's criticism of artificial life, one may assume she also takes on the natural/artificial binary. Yet, if one reads her structure as a refounding rather than a polarization, then both remain necessary and their axes are not oppositional. I suggest that Irigaray's nature can be figured like Matthews's process, as a *movement* rather than a thing, but a movement of at least two. As such, sexuate difference confounds the end or telos. Natural entities cannot be contained or teleologized and thus ecological ethics must continuously evolve, respecting nature as movement, living growth, and decay. She criticizes human ecological thinking and its concomitant culture as failing to respect the realness of another's movement and to remember and love its own living growth. A person must cultivate breathing with one's own growth, a living not abstract autonomy.[54] As such, human ecological thinking requires an ethical limit in order for reproduction/production to yield difference and living growth. This difference is incalculable, unlocatable, and beyond a singular telos.

However, instead of living growth, we cultivate artificial life systems. She writes, "A culture in the masculine has mimicked life, just as a man mimicked through cloning. Neither the logos nor an only masculine God have really transcended the natural world. They have artificially replicated it for lack of having found it to express a *movement* of nature."[55] Her ecological ethics reveals what halts the movement of life—blind domination and annihilation of difference. As Matthews puts it, "The aim . . . is not so much reduce our impact as to make that impact *generative* for nature."[56] What is generative, Irigaray posits, is sexual difference. The twoness of reality is an unrepresentable coursing throughout the universe whose flourishing yields fecundity. Plumwood, Matthews, and Irigaray reveal that ecological thinking continues to conceive of nature as a thing rather than a process, a product of our own manipulation in order to conceal our immanence.

Irigaray's contribution to this conversation is to theorize nature as a *process* without telos or anthropomorphic organization; it is relentless movement rather than essence, whereby years of species adaption, elimination, and violence yield an uncontainable and temporally discernable reality. Artifice conceals difference as human attempts to deceive themselves of the plenitude of these processes and their complex evolutions. From this perspective, artificial processes are not wrong in and of themselves; they can function within the framework of sexual difference if they continue the movement of nature as process and respect the limits, which yield difference in all its incalculable fecundity. Therefore, I read Irigaray's ecological ethics beyond a facile condemnation or aversion to biotechnology, genetic modification, trans-post-human identities, or the queering of the natural. Instead, it opposes domination or annihilation of difference, difference potentially made possible through these activities or processes.[57] Irigaray speaks of this artifice gone wrong:

> The worst crime of humans, in my opinion, is that of appropriating for their own profit what is indispensable for the life of all. . . . through making use of air or of plants, that are critical to purifying the air, in order to realize or produce things that are not essential for life. . . . We ought to reappraise any human fabrication from such a view point, so that anything can be approached as a kind of tool at someone's disposal without considering the effect of its use upon all the living beings.[58]

The idea of belonging to no one, but essential for all has been a hallmark of ecofeminist theorization.[59] However, Irigaray does not end human fabrication; she questions for whom our fabrications, clones, or duplicates are in service. Her touchstone is all the living beings. If nature and woman share a similar subordination to man, then both may be used to surround and nourish him like a pseudo-environment.[60] An important feature of Irigaray's work is that there is no unified Whole between two existences. The between is "fluid, free . . . neither mastered nor enclosed by any particular world. . . . not reducible to a name, to an object, to any totalization."[61] We will need a culture of difference to engender space that respects the scope of difference that exists in our world. She writes, "It is not in the name of our Western logical principle that we will succeed in coexisting at a world level, for then we would only be cultural colonizers who impose our rules and values on others instead of *evolving* ourselves. In our times, to recognize the real in its diversity is more crucial than obeying our traditional logic."[62] Thus, she signifies the real beyond opposition to the fake, an authentic, real belonging for each subject. Fakery denies the alterity of the real each inhabits. Duplicating, manufacturing, or replicating signify methods to engender without difference and without real proximity for alterity. Her insistence for two genders is more than a call for political equity; it is a demand for the conditions of ontological difference that give us the ability to examine life and offer truth statements about it. She argues for difference at every level and an expansion of difference—natural and spiritual, individual and collective.[63] In order to safeguard this difference, it is necessary to respect ourselves as living beings and we need to cultivate a self-affection that refuses to perceive the self as everything or nothing.[64]

Autopoiesis, Self-Affection, and Breath

Domination results, Irigaray contends, when we fail to cultivate our own self-affection, the formation and ex-istence of "one's own world."[65] She suggests that more than one world exists, or that present human reality is two.[66] Rebecca Hill and Stephen Seely note that Estonian biologist Jakob Uexküll's conception of life-world (*Umwelt*)—a notion that abandons a single objective world and instead postulates life-worlds (*Umwelten*) or milieus figured as a subjective spatiotemporal "dwelling-world" within which an organism senses and perceives—may enlarge Irigaray's conception of "one's own world."[67] I note this rejection of a single objective unifying world and connect briefly this point to Maturana and Varela's observation of autopoiesis. Maturana and Varela define autopoiesis as a system capable of reproducing and maintaining itself; they specify, "The space defined by an autopoietic system is self-contained and cannot be described by using dimensions that define another space."[68] In Irigarayan terms, an autopoietic life-system requires its own linguistic-temporal system whereby it makes sense of its existence. The autopoietic system returns to its own growth, "to an open temporality linked to life, the *mover* of which is the desire for living and for sharing life more than for dominating it through abstract and arbitrary laws. Sharing life in difference brings an additional energy that a human being needs to ensure its growth."[69] Maturana and Varela note the diversity of autopoietic systems and evolutionary reproduction made possible through proper autopoietic unities—in other words, a living sexuate singularity is necessary for Irigaray's sharing of worlds. This world sharing, "confrontation with difference," could be the next natural-spiritual evolution; however, it pivots on an awareness that a singular entity's world does not correspond to all of the real, an ethical limit she calls the negative.[70] Irigaray's self-affection or poiesis is autopoietic in two senses: 1) it individuates a sexuate identity for difference to emerge from the self-same, and 2) it resists a metaphysics that postulates a single objective environment (neutral or neutered). Her work clarifies the ecological consequence from such a faulty metaphysical neutered oneness. Therefore, an intervention to return a subject back to its own belonging and origin (its sexuate living identity) is necessary and such an intervention she calls self-affection.

Irigaray first signals the concept of self-affection in *Speculum* and later indicates how her notion of "two lips" expresses a basic self-affection for the feminine.[71] However, throughout *In the Beginning*, *To Be Born*, and an "Interview: Cultivating a Living Belonging," she develops and clarifies this gesture. I highlight this gesture as an ecologically ethical one—it prevents human anthropocentrism from creating affection by using the other to build our environment. She clarifies the need for her natural-spiritual gesture of self-affection due in part to the failure of Westerners to cultivate self-affection, particularly in man.[72] In *To Be Born* she observes that the trope of Narcissus, typified by psychologist and psychoanalyst Henri Wallon and Jacques Lacan, relies on specular identification to individuate the self,[73] divorcing the child from the living environment, from others, and even the self.[74] This mirrored individuation inverts and fails to grow the subject and the subject's relation to others. As Lenart Škof notes, Irigaray's self-affection moves beyond other philosophical notions of the same expression in that her dialectical gesture both safeguards the subject while radicalizing the transcendence of the other.[75]

Škof and Marder both note that Irigaray, like Feuerbach and Nietzsche, turns to the Vedic and Buddhist traditions, engaging important concepts from these traditions such as attentiveness, compassion, and silence.[76] For example, she cites the Buddha in contemplation as an example of communing with oneself without essence, religious authority, or logical procedure to define that self.[77] She theorizes an interior not split from the exterior, as Škof notes, "a sanctuary in ourselves—a place for the advent of pure breath, which will be the first sign of compassion and love."[78] Engaging active silence, self-affection often employs the middle voice;[79] it may be beyond words, a poetic-poiesis or a remaking one's own self instead of an external object. Without this making of ourselves, social or cultural gatherings rely on a weak unconscious act of group breathing. By ignoring sexuate difference, we fail to put limits on our world horizon and to make room for other beings "not me."[80] We then interact with others and refrain from rendering them into materials available to us to build our world; they are falsely proximate to us.[81] Without self-affection, we reject the dialogical-dialectical relationship for a monological exchange. Distinguishing self-affection from autoeroticism, she describes the first as an antidote to solipsistic individualism, technological and capitalist fatalism, and assimilation into an anonymous neutrality—as "necessary for being human as bread . . . the first condition of human dignity."[82]

However, before bread, she instructs, our first food of life was air.[83] "Breathing," she writes, "corresponds to the first autonomous gesture of the living human being."[84] Breathing is therefore a conscious act whereby people take charge their own lives, cutting their own umbilical cord.[85] Unlike Kant's abstract, universal laws, Irigaray's primordial breath is ontological and existential and forms the basis of our autonomy as a living being in process. She explains, "The breath is necessary. . . . Indispensable for life, breath is also the means, the medium to accede to spiritual life, as an irreducible dimension of human subjectivity."[86] Breath is that which is capable of individuating beings and the condition of passage between these asymmetrical alterities. It is the return to what we breathe—elemental air—that interconnects and clarifies the kinship between disparate beings. Breathing as a spiritual practice embodies rhythmic dialogical movement, approaching the transcendent other and returning to the air or energy of immanent self-affection. A built unnatural transcendence outside of nature "prevent[s] us from dwelling in our own life, our own living environment, and from cultivating and sharing them. . . . the elaboration of a specifically human manner of dwelling within oneself or in the world."[87] Breath as speaking facilitates our capacity to give a language to a world of our own. Breath as silence and listening allows us to relinquish our codes, rules, and preestablished truths, so we can relate without colonizing another spatiotemporal world.[88]

While Plumwood calls for a dialogical interspecies ethics, Irigaray calls for the spatial conditions necessary to do so, namely, that we must cultivate a spatial environment or third place.[89] Irigaray theorizes an interval between, a double envelope, yielding place without substituting the other as place.[90] Thinking about the interval will not prepare humans to release the vice-grip of Platonic form over matter. Instead, we must practice this respect between us. Environmentalists and deep ecologists note the correlation between practices of intentional or attentive breathing and ecological respect. For example, emerging studies reveal that people who practice mindfulness, often facilitated by breathing and guided imagery, display pro-environmental behaviors and that this practice may mitigate racial or ethnic bias.[91] In an Irigarayan sense, breathing consciously limits and protects beings, creating an interior reserve of breath that safeguards others from a consuming self. It frees other people and the environment from being the construction materials needed to build a dominating world of sameness.

Conclusion

In this essay, I traced Irigaray's ethics of sexuate difference, highlighting its eco-phenomenological capacity to refigure material reality and the implications for safeguarding biodiversity. I placed her work in conversation with ecofeminists and biocentric deep ecologists, clarifying her claims of self-affection, breath, and critiques of artificial life as they relate to environmental thinking. All three—Plumwood, Matthews, and Irigaray—insist on a communicative exchange rather than a scientific deliberation. Instead they disclose an animus toward shared realizations and new cultural practices necessary to release the dogmatism of analytical reason alone. They assert a moral rapprochement of ends that fails to cultivate a capacity to enlarge our perception of nonhuman beings. However, Irigaray's project differentiates nature as two, a movement or process rather than essence—without telos or enclosure—and an anticipated incalculable futural becoming. In situating her self-affection as a poiesis of human making, I suggested Irigaray's prescient need for human cultivation, which contrasts sharply against a fabricated, unified world where the environment serves as a neutered backdrop. Therefore, her sexuate ethics offer ecological limits and normative guides that urge humans to relate to other beings with differentiated proximity in order to share the diversity of worlds we inhabit.

Notes

1. Karen J. Warren, "The Power and Promise of Ecological Feminism," *Environmental Ethics* 12 (1990): 127. Warren notes that the capacity to consciously

and radically change the community, a capacity many philosophers agree humans possess and that animals, plants, and rock lack in varying degrees, determines and justifies the moral superiority of humans over the latter, particularly identifying men as human and women as closer to animals, plants, and rocks.

2. Irigaray C, 74. It is notable that Irigaray does not call herself a feminist and denies attributing to herself any label with an -ism, which would include environmentalism.

3. Rosemary Radford Ruether, "Ecofeminism: Symbolic and Social Connections of the Oppression of Women and the Domination of Nature," in *Ecofeminism and the Sacred*, ed. Carol J. Adams (New York: Continuum, 1993).

4. Greta Gaard, "Ecofeminism Revisited: Rejecting Essentialism and Re-placing Species in a Material Feminist Environmentalism," *Feminist Formations* 23, no. 2 (2011): 26–53; Delicia Dunham, "On Being Black and Vegan," in *Sistah Vegan: Black Female Vegans Speak on Food, Identity, Health, and Society*, ed. A. Breeze Harper (New York: Lantern Books, 2010), 42–46; V. Rukmini Rao, "Women Farmers of India's Deccan Plateau: Ecofeminists Challenge World Elites," *Environmental Ethics: What Really Matters, What Really Works*, ed. David Schmidtz and Elizabeth Willott (New York: Oxford University Press, 2012), 194–201; Kristin Shrader-Frechette, *Environmental Justice: Creating Equality, Reclaiming Democracy* (New York: Oxford University Press, 2002), 3–18.

5. Gita Sen, "Women, Poverty, and Population: Issues for the Concerned Environmentalist," in *Feminist Perspectives on Sustainable Development*, ed. W. Harcourt (London: Zed, 1994), 215–225.

6. Garrett Hardin, "The Tragedy of the Commons," *Science* 162 (1968): 1243–1248.

7. Bonnie Mann, "World Alienation in Feminist Thought: The Sublime Epistemology of Emphatic Anti-essentialism," *Ethics and the Environment* 10, no. 2 (2005): 45–74; Greta Gaard and Lori Gruen, "Ecofeminism: Toward Global Justice and Planetary Health," *Society and Nature* 4 (1993): 1–35. According to Gaard and Gruen, women produce approximately 80 percent of global food supplies and for this reason are most severely affected by food and fuel shortages and water pollution.

8. When asked if she would enfold ecological ethics within her work on sexuate difference, she replies that "sexuation is the first biodiversity to be taken into account, and this will allow us to respect all the other diversities without identifying ourselves with them" (Irigaray I, 110).

9. Irigaray TBA, 217–226.

10. Irigaray uses the term *biology* to help us rethink, not reify, how we socially and culturally mark and value biology associated with sex. See Rachel Jones, *Irigaray: Towards a Sexuate Philosophy* (Malden, MA: Polity, 2011), 4–6.

11. Irigaray BTE, 147.

12. Irigaray S, 361; ESD, 70; TBT, 45. Irigaray's critique of Western philosophy's reliance on the ocular is well documented in *Speculum* and her critique of

the visible often accompanies evidence revealed in touching, particularly within the morphology of a woman's body where her body touches itself. This touching within is an invisible quality that undermines the blind spot of sameness or the "substance" granted to those that we touch externally and visibly.

13. Krzysztof Ziarek, "Proximities: Irigaray and Heidegger on Difference," *Continental Philosophy Review* 33 (2000): 142–143. It is beyond the scope of this essay to work out all Irigaray means by the notion of "proximity" and I refer the reader to Ziarek's essay. Ziarek situates Irigaray's use of proximity as the following: "The idea of proximity in Irigaray's work signifies an attempt to produce a transition from the 'monosexual' culture to a culture of sexual difference, to remap relations between the sexes in terms of a transformative event, which transpires beyond the power formations that regulate social life."

14. Irigaray TBT; C, 114; FA, 62; TVB, 29. Within a person, the invisible is an interiority or touching of myself; she often signifies the inside/outside or between invisible as air, not a void or substance, or background; I read her description of air more like an unseen weft that holds us together and makes possible a passage between.

15. Irigaray SFO, 106; TBA, 218.

16. Timothy Morton, "This Biosphere Which Is Not One: Towards Weird Essentialism," *Journal of the British Society for Phenomenology* 46, no. 2 (2016): 144.

17. Timothy Morton, "This Biosphere Which Is Not One," 141–155; Val Plumwood, "Human Vulnerability and the Experience of Being Prey," *Quadrant Magazine* 39, no. 3 (March 1995): 29–35. Morton defines Agrilogistics as the logistics that underpins the Agricultural and then Industrial Revolutions, which were predicated on an unexamined logic—meant to control human anxiety about food scarcity—and a metaphysics of presence or a human desire to be inside rather than outside this logistic infrastructure. I interpret Val Plumwood's essay, "Being Prey," to engage a similar opposition between conceptions of prey and predator. Morton signifies this paradoxical bind as the Ouroboros, a snake eating its own tail. The more humans act, motivated or based on a fear, escape death, the more the repercussions of this fear destroy humans (and others).

18. Martin Heidegger, "On the Essence and Concept of *Physis* in Aristotle's *Physics B, I*," in *Pathmarks*, ed. William McNeill (Cambridge: Cambridge University Press, 1998); Helen Fielding, "Questioning Nature: Irigaray, Heidegger and the Potentiality of Matter," *Continental Philosophy Review* 36 (2003): 1–16; I note Irigaray's crisscrossing dialogue with Heidegger's meditation on enframing or *Gestell*, a notion revealing a world-ordering system where technical know-how makes possible the forgetting of being.

19. Jussi Lhtonen, Hanna Kokko, and Geoff A. Parker, "What Do Isogamous Organisms Teach Us about Sex and the Two Sexes?," *Philosophical Transactions of the Royal Society B* 371, no. 1706 (12 September 2016): 1–12, https://doi/10.1098/rstb.2015.0532. For example, current research on sexual difference delineates isogamy reproduction, a system where all the gametes are

morphologically similar, or have not been divided into dimorphous male and female gametes, which vary principally in size (the system known as anisogamy). Although humans are part of the larger anisogamous group, scientists suggest a proliferation of isogamous organisms exist and anisogamous organisms may all derive from isogamous ancestors. Other differences in bacterial cells' chemistry (positive or negative) or phenotype gene expression can create sexual difference; however, no morphological variation is present.

20. Val Plumwood, *Environmental Culture: The Ecological Crisis of Reason* (New York: Routledge, 2002), 19.

21. Plumwood, *Environmental Culture*, 24.

22. Plumwood, *Environmental Culture*, 26, 29, italics mine.

23. Plumwood, *Environmental Culture*, 179. She notes several post-Cartesian projects committed to recovering the body in the mind and the mind in the body and nature; she cites Irigaray especially as recovering a conception of "speaking matter," a project she states can restore the intentionality stripped from the material sphere and locate an alternative basis for a nonreductive account of continuity between mind and nature.

24. Plumwood, *Environmental Culture*, 26. Plumwood does not attack science or technology at large. However, when economic systems dominate scientific findings and technological solutions, the facts are often underestimated, viewing natural resources as "inessential" or "replaceable."

25. Sophia M. Connell, *Aristotle on Female Animals: A Study of the "Generation of Animals"* (Cambridge: Cambridge University Press, 2016); Emanuela Bianchi, "Sexual Topologies in the Aristotelian Cosmos: Revisiting Irigaray's Physics of Sexual Difference," *Continental Philosophy Review* 43, no. 3 (2010): 373–389. Not all theorists read Aristotle's work as a negative treatment of female nature and suggest these writers offer a wider interpretation of his works.

26. Plumwood, *Environmental Culture*, 30; Irigaray EP, 1; ESD, 12; TS, 174 fn. 3; VB, 76.

27. Irigaray ESD, 47; Irigaray; SFO, 7.

28. Freya Matthews, "Letting the World Grow Old: An Ethos of Countermodernity I," *Worldview: Environment, Culture, Religion* 3 (1999): 125.

29. Freya Mathews, "Letting the World Grow Old," 121.

30. Freya Matthews, "Towards a Deeper Philosophy of Biomimicry," *Organization and Environment* 24, no. 4 (December 2011): 366.

31. Freya Matthews, "Relating to Nature: Deep Ecology or Ecofeminism?" *Trumpeter* 11, no. 4 (Fall 1994): 162.

32. Susan Griffin, *Made from This Earth: An Anthology of Writings* (New York: Harper & Row, 1982); Val Plumwood, *Feminism and the Mastery of Nature* (London: Routledge, 1993); Matthews, "Relating to Nature," 165.

33. Matthews, "Towards a Deeper Philosophy of Biomimicry," 370. In a section detailing reflexivity as signifying a certain freedom without separation

from nature, she offers the term *iterative* universe as better than a dualistic universe, capturing the sense in which we operate in a physical and mental universe where repetition is revealed. She writes that such iterativity is not incompatible with unity, "but instead reproduces that unity at different levels of abstraction."

34. Alison Stone, *Luce Irigaray and the Philosophy of Sexual Difference* (New York: Cambridge University Press, 2006). Stone takes on the charge of essentialism and uses the phenomena of rhythm and fluidic circulation to posit a metaphysics of realism whereby temporal movement constitutes nature as an unfixed force.

35. Alison Stone, "Irigaray's Ecological Phenomenology: Towards an Elemental Materialism," *Journal of the British Society for Phenomenology* 46, no. 2 (2015): 117–131.

36. Rebecca Hill, "Milieus and Sexual Difference," *Journal of the British Society for Phenomenology* 46, no. 2 (2015): 132–140. Hill argues that Irigaray's critique privileges human sovereignty, a feature particular to male subjectivity. Thus, to reject the reign of the absolute male subject, one must also reject any system whereby human anthropocentrism remains intact and conceals other milieus.

37. Elizabeth Grosz, *Becoming Undone: Darwinian Reflection on Life, Politics, and Art* (Durham, NC: Duke University Press, 2011), 106–107.

38. See note 18; Stone, "Irigaray's Ecological Phenomenology, 127–130; Emily Anne Parker, "Irigaray's Critique of 'The Body': An Ironic Illustration of Biocentrism," paper presented at the ninth conference of the Luce Irigaray Circle: Horizons of Sexual Difference, Brock University, St. Catharines, ON, June 14, 2018, 1–18; Emily Anne Parker, "Introduction: From Ecology to Elemental Difference," *Journal of the British Society for Phenomenology* 46, no. 2 (2015): 92 fn. 19. Parker (2015, 2018) explicates and challenges Irigaray's sexual ethics with broader notions of sexual diversity and its implications for eco-phenomenology. Irigaray posits natural biological, morphological, and relational difference between men and women as a project of sexuate belonging. She poses this belonging to formulate differing relations of space and time, contrasting a woman's cultivation of interiority for hospitality and a man's cultivation or projection and exteriority toward objects and dwelling. She suggests that quickly formulated desire projects toward the beyond or the future, rather than the present and our coexistence. I find this dimorphic sexuate belonging problematic in that these differences are meant to signify *how* the elemental or material world interacts with sexuation, not codify this humanly perceived bio-morpho-relational difference. To posit sexuation as *the* difference could be anthropocentric if it remains linked to sexuation as dimorphic, wherein sexual difference may also be chemical, phenotypical, and invisible or amorphic in bacterial cells. Given the alterity of difference in the uni-multi-verse, human sexuation itself is more voluminous than dimorphism,

such as asexual, trans, crip, queer, belongings; additional differences may be microbial, multicellular, and their complex interactions.

39. Irigaray WL, 67; C, 26. Air is the element that mediates imperceptibly both literally and figuratively in her work, able to cross the threshold between worlds and universes of different subjects.

40. Ziarek, "Proximities," 153. Ziarek states, "Irigaray's descriptions of the proximity between the sexes, of the exchanges in which lines of identity do not become congealed so that there is "neither one nor two," elaborate such a new language of relation—a futural disposing of what is into a relatedness without power."

41. Irigaray TBA, 217.

42. Irigaray DB, 6; TS, 21, 26, 143, 207; ILTY, 128. I read being at least two as threshold for multiplicity and an intervention to the Oneness that pervades Western metaphysics, a Oneness that slips into duplicates and mirrored copies (or bioengineered improvements) of the One. For generative fecundity to appear she insists that there must be at least two, which I read as a being "neither one nor two," or an "irreducible two," a transformation of positionality beyond opposition. I question if other cultures not plagued by the Oedipal legacy of phallic logic will need such an intervention. Thus, I read her being two as a universality particular to what ails Western thinking; thus, it is not a global intervention. However, given that Western peoples and cultures may be disproportionately responsible for ecological harm to other living beings and systems, then her critique may be prescient.

43. Irigaray BTE, 146, italics mine.

44. Matthews, "Letting the World Grow Old," 120–121. Matthews argues that Nature knows best and that this logic is self-evident and self-realizing—immanent laws of their own unfolding. To be fair, Matthews relies heavily on a Taoist framework, and the enigma of the Tao, one could argue, refutes a closure of meaning. What I find helpful in Irigaray's work is that she offers a way to conceive of this metaphysical space between beings.

45. Irigaray TBB, 4; IB, 91. While many agree that nature evolves, Irigaray's evolutionary becoming challenges assumptions about the intelligibility and progressive linear direction of evolutionary processes.

46. Irigaray TBA, 220.

47. Irigaray ILTY, 35, italics mine.

48. Irigaray TVB, 76.

49. See Nancy J. Holland, introduction to *Heidegger and the Problem of Consciousness* (Bloomington: Indiana University Press, 2018). Holland notes Heidegger's claim that Dasein constantly reckons with both the physical and mental experiences of human perception. Thus, an internal experience of dealing with beings mediates external perception of the world. In other words, the

world is not a neutral given to which we have pure, unmediated access. Irigaray's analysis adds that dasein is more than one.

50. Irigaray I, 110. When asked about animals and plants, she states, "I cannot answer in the name of animals or plants because I am a human, and I want to respect their own world."

51. Irigaray WL, xiv–xv. She calls this gesture auto-affection in this work in 2002 and then in IB, in 2013, she uses the expression "self-affection." I use these terms interchangeably.

52. Matthews, "Towards a Deeper Philosophy of Biomimicry," 368. Matthews also notes that the use of the term *autopoiesis* is often used to convey self-actualization.

53. Irigaray IB, 129.

54. Irigaray TBA, 217.

55. Irigaray IB, 82, italics mine.

56. Matthews, "Towards a Deeper Philosophy of Biomimicry," 367.

57. Martin H. Krieger, "What's Wrong with Plastic Trees," *Science* 179, no. 4072 (February 1973): 446–455, https//doi/10.1126/science.179.4072.446. Krieger makes a similar argument that what is natural isn't necessarily better or worse; it may be rare and as such its valuation receives economic ranking. However, such ranking does not indicate something is inherently better or worse and humanly designed "artificial" environments may be necessary to reduce harm and protect ecological spaces.

58. Irigaray I, 111–112.

59. Vandana Shiva, *Water Wars: Privatization, Pollution, and Profit* (Berkeley, CA: North Atlantic Books, 2002; 2016), 19–38. Shiva argues water as sacred rather than a commodified thing. She notes cultural practices of hospitality that recognize the shared dependence of protoplasmic cells upon this constituent element.

60. Irigaray ESD, 105.

61. Irigaray IB, 104.

62. Irigaray BNW, 292, italics mine. I underscore my reading of Irigaray's ecological ethics as evolutionary momentum.

63. Irigaray ILTY, 62. Irigaray describes difference as the motor of the dialectic's becoming. By renouncing death as sovereign master, we give our care toward the expansion of life.

64. Irigaray I, 111.

65. Irigaray I, 109–110; IB, 158, 159, 160; BNW, 257.

66. Irigaray SW, xiv–xv.

67. Hill, "Milieus and Sexual Difference," 137; Stephen D. Seely, "From the *Gestell* of Modern Technology to the *Umwelt* of Sexual Difference: Life and Metaphysics in Heidegger, Irigaray, and Uexküll," PhiloSOPHIA annual meeting,

Penn State, May 2014. For further reading see Jakob von Uexküll, *A Foray into the Worlds of Animals and Humans, with "A Theory of Meaning,"* trans. Joseph D. O'Neil (Minneapolis: University of Minnesota Press, 2010).

68. Humberto Maturana and Francisco Varela, *Autopoiesis and Cognition: The Realization of the Living* (Dordrecht, Holland: D. Reidel, 1973; 1980). 89. I note that critics denounce Maturana and Varela's work as radically constructivist or a solipsistic epistemology. It is beyond the scope of this essay to defend their supposition wholly, but I note the usefulness of their observations and contend that Irigaray's metaphysics postulates both a world in which engendering is made possible within one's own subjectivity as well as a metaphysics of difference in which life systems can relate as proximate beings in relation.

69. Irigaray BNW, 290, italics mine.

70. Irigaray BNW, 293.

71. Irigaray S, 133; C, 66.

72. Irigaray IB, 159.

73. W. E. B. Du Bois, *The Souls of Black Folk: Essays and Sketches* (Chicago: A. C. McClurg, 1903), 3. I note Du Bois's double consciousness as a refractive sense of individuation whereby Black people see themselves through the eyes of White people. They do not see themselves in their own specular image. Such a standpoint epistemology reveals the limit of the mirror-stage as a universal stage of development. Instead, the mirror-stage corresponds to a certain cultural position of power.

74. Irigaray TBB, 40.

75. Lenart Škof, "Breath as a Way of Self-Affection: On New Topologies of Transcendence and Self-Transcendence," *Bogoslovni vestnik* 77, no. 3/4 (2017): 580.

76. Škof, "Breath as a Way of Self-Affection," 577–587; Michael Marder, "Afterword—Cultivating Natural Belonging: Luce Irigaray's Water Lily," in *BNW*, 297–313; Irigaray TBB, 17. While critique of Irigaray's broad use of these traditions exists, both Škof and Marder suggest an effective engagement by Irigaray with these concepts and practices.

77. Irigaray TBB, 17.

78. Škof, "Breath as a Way of Self-Affection," 582.

79. Irigaray I, 110.

80. Irigaray ILTY, 35.

81. Irigaray BNW, 258. She describes others as "disappearing into the construction of the world that surrounds us."

82. Irigaray T, 230.

83. Irigaray BNW, 254.

84. Irigaray BNW, 253.

85. Irigaray BNW, 254.

86. Irigaray BTE, 144, 149.

87. Irigaray SFO, 103, 104.

88. Irigaray BNW, 258. She clarifies, "Silence is a word of welcome to the one who comes towards us from beyond the horizon that has been opened but also closed by our language."

89. Irigaray VG, 66; SW, 7; TBB, 57.

90. Irigaray ESD, 49–55.

91. Nicole Barbaro and Scott M. Pickett, "Mindfully Green: Examining the Effect of Connectedness to Nature on the Relationship between Mindfulness and Engagement in Pro-Environmental Behavior," *Personality and Individual Differences* 93 (April 2016): 137–142; Jason Lillis and Steven C. Hayes, "Applying Acceptance, Mindfulness, and Values to the Reduction of Prejudice: A Pilot Study," *Behavior Modification* 31, no. 4 (July 1, 2007): 389–411; Adam Lueske and Bryan Gibson, "Mindfulness Meditation Reduces Implicit Age and Race Bias: The Role of Reduced Automaticity of Responding," *Social Psychological and Personality Science* 6, no. 3 (November 24, 2014): 284–291; Jessica R. Graham, Lindsay M. West, and Lizabeth Roemer, "The Experience of Racism and Anxiety Symptoms in an African-American Sample: Moderating Effects of Trait Mindfulness," *Mindfulness* 4, no. 4 (December 2013): 332–341.

Bibliography

Barbaro, Nicole, and Scott M. Pickett. "Mindfully Green: Examining the Effect of Connectedness to Nature on the Relationship between Mindfulness and Engagement in Pro-Environmental Behavior." *Personality and Individual Differences* 93 (April 2016): 137–142.

Dunham, Delicia. "On Being Black and Vegan." In *Sistah Vegan: Black Female Vegans Speak on Food, Identity, Health, and Society*, edited by A. Breeze Harper, 42–46. New York: Lantern Books, 2010.

Du Bois, W. E. B. *The Souls of Black Folks: Essays and Sketches*. Chicago: A. C. McClurg, 1903.

Fielding, Helen. "Questioning Nature: Irigaray, Heidegger and the Potentiality of Matter." *Continental Philosophy Review* 36 (2003): 1–16.

Gaard, Greta. "Ecofeminism Revisited: Rejecting Essentialism and Re-placing Species in a Material Feminist Environmentalism." *Feminist Formations* 23, no. 2 (2011): 26–53.

Gaard, Greta, and Lori Gruen. "Ecofeminism: Toward Global Justice and Planetary Health." *Society and Nature* 4 (1993): 1–35.

Graham, Jessica R., Lindsay M. West, and Lizabeth Roemer. "The Experience of Racism and Anxiety Symptoms in an African-American Sample: Moderating Effects of Trait Mindfulness." *Mindfulness* 4, no. 4 (December 2013): 332–341.

Griffin, Susan. *Made from This Earth: An Anthology of Writings*. New York: Harper & Row, 1982.

Grosz, Elizabeth. *Becoming Undone: Darwinian Reflection on Life, Politics, and Art*. Durham, NC: Duke University Press, 2011.

Hardin, Garrett. "The Tragedy of the Commons." *Science* 162 (1968): 1243–1248.

Heidegger, Martin. "On the Essence and Concept of *Physis* in Aristotle's *Physics B, I*." In *Pathmarks*, edited by William McNeill, 183–222. Cambridge: Cambridge University Press, 1998.

Hill, Rebecca. "Milieus and Sexual Difference." *Journal of the British Society for Phenomenology* 46, no. 2 (2015): 132–140.

Holland, Nancy J. *Heidegger and the Problem of Consciousness*. Bloomington: Indiana University Press, 2018.

Jones, Rachel. *Irigaray: Towards a Sexuate Philosophy*. Malden, MA: Polity Press, 2011.

Krieger, Martin H. "What's Wrong with Plastic Trees?" *Science* 179, no. 4072 (February 1973): 446–455. https//doi/10.1126/science.179.4072.446.

Lhtonen, Jussi, Hanna Kokko, and Geoff A. Parker. "What Do Isogamous Organisms Teach Us about Sex and the Two Sexes?" *Philosophical Transactions of the Royal Society B* 371, no. 1706 (September 12, 2016): 1–12. https://doi/10.1098/rstb.2015.0532.

Lillis, Jason, and Steven C. Hayes. "Applying Acceptance, Mindfulness, and Values to the Reduction of Prejudice: A Pilot Study." *Behavior Modification* 31, no. 4 (July 1, 2007): 389–411.

Lueske, Adam, and Bryan Gibson. "Mindfulness Meditation Reduces Implicit Age and Race Bias: The Role of Reduced Automaticity of Responding." *Social Psychological and Personality Science* 6, no. 3 (November 24, 2014): 284–291.

Mann, Bonnie. "World Alienation in Feminist Thought: The Sublime Epistemology of Emphatic Anti-essentialism." *Ethics and the Environment* 10, no. 2 (2005): 45–74.

Marder, Michael. "Afterward—Cultivating Natural Belonging: Luce Irigaray's Water Lily." In *BNW*, 297–313.

Maturana, Humberto R., and Francisco J. Varela. *Autopoiesis and Cognition: The Realization of the Living*. Dordrecht, Holland: D. Reidel, 1972; 1980.

Matthews, Freya. "Letting the World Grow Old: An Ethos of Countermodernity I." *Worldview: Environment, Culture, Religion* 3 (1999): 119–137.

Matthews, Freya. "Relating to Nature: Deep Ecology or Ecofeminism?" *Trumpeter* 11, no. 4 (Fall 1994): 159–166.

Matthews, Freya. "Towards a Deeper Philosophy of Biomimicry." *Organization and Environment* 24, no. 4 (December 2011): 364–387.

Morton, Timothy. "This Biosphere Which Is Not One: Towards Weird Essentialism." *Journal of the British Society for Phenomenology* 46, no. 2 (2016): 141–155.

Parker, Emily Anne. "Introduction: From Ecology to Elemental Difference." *Journal of the British Society for Phenomenology* 46, no. 2 (2015): 89–100. https://doi.org/10.1080/00071773.2014.960746.

Parker, Emily Anne. "Irigaray's Critique of 'The Body': An Ironic Illustration of Biocentrism." Paper presented at ninth conference of the Luce Irigaray Circle: Horizons of Sexual Difference, Brock University, St. Catharines, ON, June 14, 2018, 1–18.

Plumwood, Val. *Environmental Culture: The Ecological Crisis of Reason*. New York: Routledge, 2002.

Plumwood, Val. *Feminism and the Mastery of Nature*. London: Routledge, 1993.

Plumwood, Val. "Human Vulnerability and the Experience of Being Prey." *Quadrant Magazine* 39, no. 3 (March 1995): 29–35.

Rao, V. Rukmini. "Women Farmers of India's Deccan Plateau: Ecofeminists Challenge World Elites." In *Environmental Ethics: What Really Matters, What Really Works*, edited by David Schmidtz and Elizabeth Willott, 194–201. New York: Oxford University Press, 2012.

Ruether, Rosemary Radford. "Ecofeminism: Symbolic and Social Connections of the Oppression of Women and the Domination of Nature." In *Ecofeminism and the Sacred*, edited by Carol J. Adams, 15–23. New York: Continuum, 1993.

Sen, Gita. "Women, Poverty, and Population: Issues for the Concerned Environmentalist." In *Feminist Perspectives on Sustainable Development*, edited by W. Harcourt, 215–225. London: Zed, 1994.

Shiva, Vandana. *Water Wars: Privatization, Pollution, and Profit*. Berkeley, CA: North Atlantic Books, 2002; 2016.

Shrader-Frechette, Kristin. *Environmental Justice: Creating Equality, Reclaiming Democracy*. New York: Oxford University Press, 2002.

Škof, Lenart. "Breath as a Way of Self-Affection: On New Topologies of Transcendence and Self-Transcendence." *Bogoslovni vestnik* 77, no. 3/4 (2017): 577–587.

Stone, Alison. "Irigaray's Ecological Phenomenology: Towards an Elemental Materialism." *Journal of the British Society for Phenomenology* 46, no. 2 (2015): 117–131.

Stone, Alison. *Luce Irigaray and the Philosophy of Sexual Difference*. New York: Cambridge University Press, 2006.

Uexküll, Jakob von. *A Foray into the Worlds of Animals and Humans, with "A Theory of Meaning."* Translated by Joseph D. O'Neil. Minneapolis: University of Minnesota Press, 2010.

Warren, Karen J. "The Power and Promise of Ecological Feminism." *Environmental Ethics* 12, no. 2 (1990): 125–146.

Ziarek, Krzysztof. "Proximities: Irigaray and Heidegger on Difference." *Continental Philosophy Review* 33 (2000): 133–158.

Chapter Eleven

She Speaks in Threes

Irigaray, at the Threshold between Phenomenology and Speculative Realism in Teaching Architecture

Michael Lucas

Introduction

Luce Irigaray's critique of Western thinking has contributed to a legacy of subsequent critical examinations of multiple forms of sexism, bias, and privilege across many canons. But more than criticism, her work has informed and transformed thinking in a constructive way inside and across design disciplines. This essay draws on Irigaray's work on language, air, breath, and the *third space* to rethink critical pedagogical practice in the architectural studio. Reading Irigaray alongside Graham Harman on flattened ontologies, I argue that there is a pedagogical benefit to students involved in a sexuate[1] embodied and inductive practice of encounter and discovery in the process of design and making, beyond mere idealist/object form and weak uncritical functionalism.[2] This essay will look at Irigaray's work on *speech*, proposed as a form of transcendence from imposed norms, and *forgetting*, illustrated in her critique of Heidegger in *The Forgetting of Air: In Martin Heidegger*,[3] where she proposed an unconcealment of immanence. Speech and forgetting are linked by the idea of breath, where air, body, and others are bound within one network, and where Irigaray's notion of a *third space* becomes a zone for exploring what each brings. These themes will be read against Graham Harman's *flattened ontology* with its dismantling of hierarchies, and in his idea of the *quadruple* aspects of *objects*, with dynamic concealment and unconcealment. These two seemingly divergent thinkers share a threshold around forms of disclosure and discovery that has richly benefited a pedagogy initiated by the author for a *beginning* design studio sequence[4] in architecture. In this pedagogy students benefit from projects involved across an embodied and inductive process of immanence via direct encounter and discovery, and transcendence from idea to realized work via a process of design and making. I evidence the value of this pedagogical practice by looking at the diverse solutions brought forward by a cohort of students from this embodied process of desire to know through the work, versus replicating precedent, or via uncritical conventional outcomes. This becoming of the beginning designer is enabled by the studio functioning as a variant of Irigaray's concept of *interval*, "a mutation in the perception and conception of *space-time*, our inhabitation of *places*, and the different *envelopes of identity*";[5] a space where one may feel safe investigating the assumptions of the world loosened within one's own cultural roots, engaging one's own questions, and in interrogating the real in a very physical manner as idea, matter, form, nature. In such a space personal and design culture are put into *play*. The pedagogy and studio/shop/campus setting provide a provisional answer to a question about architecture and world building posed by philosopher and architect Andrea Wheeler: "What if it could strengthen our sense of self and reality? What if it could build the horizon for a radically different existential condition? Giving us back to a real perception of our bodies and potential for our senses?"[6]

Triple Spaces, Tripled Speech

In the architectural profession, one can see male privilege in the first discovered theoretical texts, of the Roman, Vitruvius, and through da Vinci's *Vitruvian Man*, where graphic proof via Euclidian circle and square corresponding with proportions of the male body sought to link *man* and nature. Even with the advent of modernism in architecture, and its postwar dominance across written and built discourse, there remained a control and conformity via the organization of the three-dimensional grid, bringing forth a homogenous sameness that spoke to universals imposed, with annihilation of difference in landscape, building, and designer. The urban grid erased memory, and the skyscraper as emerging new building type continued the object-male-power metaphor. Architecture until the beginnings of the twenty-first century continued to be almost exclusively male-dominated and driven.

Despite this historic momentum, with critical social reflection in the 1960s/1970s, women fought for equal access to the workplace, including architecture. When Irigaray wrote *This Sex Which Is Not One*[7] in 1977, many of the larger American architectural programs had less than 10 percent female enrollments. Today, that figure exceeds 50 percent at many American institutions.[8] Clearly, Irigaray was part of an awakening that inspired many women to question artificial limits within the received world, limits in development across a lifetime in career, as well as gaining access to speech about, and control over, their bodies. Irigaray noted:

> We have to reject all the great systems of opposition on which our culture is constructed . . . fiction/truth, sensible/intelligible, empirical/transcendental, materialist/idealist. All . . . function as exploitation and a negation of a relation at the beginning and of a certain mode of connection between the body and the word for which we have paid everything.[9]

The male morphology has not always dominated space, and some Irigaray interpreters look back to the Platonic idea of *chōra* and interpret important female metaphors applicable to earlier understandings of space. In particular, Sue Best suggests one may read in *Timaeus* that Plato inaugurates space as female-gendered *chōra*, variously used in passive and active metaphors of womb/receptacle of mother, of basket sorting its contents, and as relation between things, variously ideal and material.[10] Irigaray's unique embodied thinking has had a major influence on philosophers and designers who provide a useful parallel with Irigaray's work into architectural theory and practice. Agrest, Conway, and Weisman's collection *The Sex of Architecture*[11] brought together a diverse coalition on what gender meant to architecture. Gail Weiss's *Perspectives on Embodiment*,[12] and Elizabeth Grosz's *Volatile Bodies*[13] and *Architecture from the Outside*,[14] confirmed embodied feminist approaches that stood in opposition to dualism.

The body for Irigaray is sexuate, she notes: "The most important intention of my work . . . is to try to make possible a culture of two subjects . . . wherein humans can overcome their animal instincts or primitive attractions through love, through words, through dialogues, cultivating the difference between men and women."[15] Importantly, Irigaray appeals to simultaneously lived and new relational realities across two rich subjectivities, one of which has been silenced. Irigaray focuses criticism on the cultural hierarchies that sustain blind assimilation, a false sense of singularity, and produce mere replicants. Two sexuate embodiments may intertwine in a third mode of possible encounter, dialogue, and negotiation. Irigaray uses the architectural metaphor of room to describe this set of possible spaces:

> We need, so to speak, at least three rooms in order to live together, to dwell together—her room, his room, and the room opened by desire between them: a third room. It is necessary to try to partly materialize, I have not said to always render visible, the three rooms.[16]

This triad of spaces respects the unique embodiment of each with their own space but opens possibilities in the third space due to the nature of encounter versus a hierarchy of imposition. This critical insight into respect, opportunities for growth, and optimism for a better future situation also literally grounds the idea of the studio space as important to our pedagogical practice.

The body recovered by Irigaray is holistic in the senses and contemplates new forms of engagement and time in a negotiated world. Cathryn Vasseleu shows how Irigaray, at the point of sensation, bridges one's vision and haptic natures as linked, and rails against the idea of optics as objective: "Irigaray argues that without the sense of touch seeing would not be possible. The indeterminacy of the body in touch is the basis of an erotically constituted threshold of immersion in the visual."[17] Touch enables our original engagement with others and the world from birth, substantiates and affirms attributes, and initiates discernment across media of light, air, and materiality in design. Touch precedes speech and has been brought to the center of many recent discussions of phenomenology in design.[18] Sensory qualities of touch, taste, and smell ground the world in different ways than concepts and words can, and reveal a world easily hidden in an ocular-centric virtual space. Our pedagogical practice relies upon touch as a major form of negotiation and resistance to imposition of concepts and form, unconcealing new understandings and qualities inherent within the otherness of materials.

Irigaray for Architects (2007), Peg Rawes's interpretation of Irigaray's thinking toward architecture, identifies themes such as *sexed* subjects,[19] fluid matter and space, and the impact of alternate geometries. Her reading of Irigaray posits that beyond the objectness of built things, we must also consider one's relation with the work in real time, the psychic aspects of spatial and haptic experience, testing and creating memory, sensation, duration, and above all the particular sexuate embodiment one brings into relations. Her work indicates that an engendered body matters. In Rawes's thinking, space became less the geometric absence/void than an alternate fluid-like medium filled with light and thermal sensation. Materials, especially emerging materials and new technologies from fashion and space suits to ships and aircraft, allowed material aspects of form and bodily proportion to be expanded. With this thinking and practice, function, a critical topic emerging from modernism, left its conventional, simplistic, and industrial one-size-fits-all definition and was required to address existential issues of self, becoming, and desire, all driven by difference in engendered embodiment.[20]

Nonhierarchical relationships between subjects underpin Irigaray's claims for an ethical theory of sexuate subjects and sexuate spaces. This concern for the negative impact of hierarchy is a common point between Irigaray and Graham Harman that I will link later; each sees the historic momentum of hierarchies of all kinds as limiting frameworks. Architecture, unlike the philosophic project, is situated, grounded in time and space and achieved, and includes myriad forms of representation as well as textual representation. Irigaray's thinking may be read as suggesting to the designer they utilize the medium of architecture to deepen the attentiveness to the multiple and possible subjective and intersubjective realities in the human condition. In Andrea Wheeler's words:

> Doubling subjectivity would mean a double truth . . . a different sort of poetic dwelling, a different way of speaking . . . the exchange between these two subjectivities creates a third language, which unfolds between two modes of speaking; a language we still do not know, and is yet to be created.[21]

This is a critical idea for studio: that the relationships enabled via these embodied studio pedagogical practices creates a third form speech, full of rich ideation, within and through the design process and outcomes, emerging from respectful negotiation with a myriad of design challenges.

Irigaray and Heidegger share creative wordplay, which is the representational textual media of philosophy, to unconceal these sedimented hierarchies. Irigaray's interpreters also use novel means, and the work that inspired this essay is Jane Rendell's musings on Irigaray's multiples:

> This "speaking" subject, speaks in between.
>
> From this place on the threshold between the two, it is possible to consider both, to be attentive to the concerns of theory and at the same time consider modes of practice; to be attentive to modes of practice and at the same time reconsidering new theoretical insights.
>
> She speaks in threes.
> 1 and 1 is three.
> 11 threes.
> Her speech is tripled.[22]

The tripled speech is recognition of immanence hidden between false either/or dichotomies: between theory and application; thought and built work; form and space; concept and experience; designer and constructor. This speech is the offspring of Irigaray's grounding in pairs and negotiated third space as it frees the things, objects, topics, and concepts from singular or binary traps. Tripleness allows an emergence of exploration of multiple realities, the spatial ranges between false opposite points or limits. The architectural project is not one of reaching a singular analytically deductive perfection of form so much as cultivating and renewing a concept of care and thriving for self, for others, and for a world filled with new unique forms of otherness in the between that multiplies possibilities versus reduction to norms. This requires recognizing simultaneous worlds, networks linking ideas, and possibilities emerging from that concealment. As a result, as architectural thoughts, metaphors, processes, and forms are liberated, the practice allows exploration of interrelationships between concept, conceiver, context, method, material, and reflection on built manifestation.

Importantly, architectural design, and that pedagogy that teaches designers to design, requires recognition of that third form of speech, beyond self, but as dialogue with human or material otherness. One rarely designs for oneself. One designs for another, and the process and experience of discerning and testing that intersubjective realm is crucial. One designs for a present, but also a future, so intergenerational forms of speech need to be opened as relation to future others for exploration. One designs as intervention in a larger vibrant ecological world. As Wheeler notes, "From this arrangement, an eco-phenomenology respectful of sexuate difference in architecture, one which takes into account the necessity of return to one's self, to one's nature and particular sexuate belonging, then the space is allowed for each [to be in charge of dwelling, while] coexisting and sharing with the other(s) as different."[23]

Speech, Breath, Air

> The gift gives itself—the infinity of a sensible *hypokei-menon*, without boundary or distinctive trait, with no "proper" being, no singular body, no physical *physis*. A passage that abolishes the break between the physical and the metaphysical by constituting a "ground," earth, and mother other than she or they—still physical and alive. . . . The gift gives itself without breaking into the reserve store if she who will never come back has become, at present, a sensible transcendental always already and nevermore there.[24]

Irigaray's gift opens a transcendental arc from ideas emerging to things becoming, where the desire is to become, to establish the legitimacy of difference through a new concrete situation. This mirrors what is possible for the designer, if encouraged and placed in a context where such thinking and testing is possible.

Existential phenomenology underlies Irigaray's work and as such speech plays a fundamental role as a link between thought and the actionable design media of architecture: materiality, movement, light, space, and resultant time. In the awakening of the sensible transcendental self, one becomes aware of how many situations are not like those past and this originary engagement is capable of a new naming, meaningful to self, free from a previous conceptual tangle. This dwelling in the possible is the opening to a realm that design pedagogy reaches for. Irigaray critiques language that conceals lived woman in-and-of-herself apart from the categories produced by the hegemony of the phallic. Irigaray's *The Forgetting of Air in Martin Heidegger* exposes the forgotten element of woman in Heidegger's later thought within this phenomenological light. In his later work, language is *the* preeminent experience of Being; it is in language that Being envelops us. While Heidegger revolutionizes the questioning of Being, his lack of attention to the question of sexuate difference makes his thought vulnerable to his own critique. Commentators such as Maria Cimitile posit Heidegger poses language to be a central component of our experience of Being.[25] This is especially true in his examples of how language exposes, enables, and restricts forms of dwelling.

It is through her critique of his philosophy that Irigaray distinguishes her *ethics of sexual difference* from Heidegger's philosophy of *ontological difference*. By virtue of this *distance* Irigaray is able to express her relation to Heidegger in ethical terms: to show her gratitude to him, yet voice her disagreements with him. Speech is coupled with breath, which is embodied and personal but also shared; these become metaphors for ideas and thinking. The optic transparency of air means it is overlooked by Heidegger in favor of the metaphor of earth, and his use of grounding. While sky figures as one of Heidegger's fourfold, Irigaray accuses him of forgetting the importance of air, and in doing so, forgetting the speech of the other (woman), an act enabled by breath.

Irigaray creates a new place for her speech without a total denial of Heidegger's: "I am trying . . . to re-open everything he has constructed by taking me inside, putting me outside, . . . where I cannot live, move, breathe. I am trying to re-discover the possibility of a relation to air. Don't I need one, well before starting to speak?"[26] Irigaray's speech provides one with the challenge of thinking through Heidegger's interpretation of the pre-Socratic Greeks in his later philosophy; air offers the passage into Heidegger's thought. The four elements of earth, air, fire, and water provide the starting point for pre-Socratic philosophy, but Cimitile notes Heidegger fails to fully account for the element of air as both the condition for the possibility of Being and as the feminine element.[27]

For Irigaray, air evades any exploitative efforts from humanity to make it a commodity. Air is necessary for living and an element that, to live, we all must share: "Is there a dwelling more vast, more spacious, or even more generally peaceful than that of air? . . . The excess of air is so immediately 'evident' and so little 'apparent' that he did not think of it."[28] Here the metaphor of air may be seen as expanding in scale and complexity into eco-phenomenological connectional aspects within the whole of the environment. This allows commentators like Wheeler to extend this idea of forgotten air into forgotten care for the environment, which creates challenges for requisite new obligations for architecture as environmental design.[29] This unites architecture with larger scale and temporal ecological issues beyond current sustainability toward regenerative thinking in play with forces of otherness.

Having established the remembered air, Irigaray returns to Heidegger's fourfold, and the importance of this nexus:

> The air it provides between her and him is animated by fire and currents, by winds, by desire, with a movement going from one to the other, as well as from the lowest to the highest of the body and the universe, from the most material to that which is most subtle in the micro- and macrocosm.[30]

Dwelling is no longer the image of the consuming flame in the traditional hearth built of stone from the earth; it is open to atmosphere, affect, space, and mood. Irigaray also pairs air with the more tangible qualities of light in an almost architectural manner:

> Light comes about only in virtue of the transparent levity of air. Light presupposes air. No sun without air to welcome and transmit its rays. No speech without air to convey it. . . . The extent of space, the horizons of time, and all that becomes present and absent within them are to be found gathered together in air as in some fundamental thing.[31]

Thinking about air in this way allows for vibrant, ethereal materialism that is fluid, dynamic, open to change, alterity, and varying opacity. This renewed fourfold of light and air invites feminine metaphors as Connor notes "the open, fluid, abundant space of the female . . . of the difference between a closed or appropriative use of space and a relation to space that is itself open and relational."[32] Teaching design, exploring designs, and realizing designs that engage this triple speech in the third space provide one part of a new explorative path for beginning designers. Irigaray brings the young designer to a threshold with new thinking, but it is enriched when looked at in tandem with critiques of other aspects of Heidegger's thinking in a speculative realist approach developed by Graham Harman.

Speculative Realism

While Irigaray's sexuate subjectivity has been engaged within architectural discourse for over twenty years, speculative realism is a philosophical construct where architectural concepts, formal organizing principles, representations, materials, and associated phenomena are considered nonhierarchical equals in a *flattened* ontology, open to speculative mining and alchemy. Graham Harman, one of the key philosophers in speculative realism, performs a novel reading of Heidegger's ideas of tools as revealing the world and how our framing of situations and things both reveals and conceals aspects of the real. But this is more than a different reading of Heidegger's idea of instrumental thinking expanded into the ontology of self via the very tools one uses, or as Harman calls it, *tool-being*.[33] Harman further elaborates on this dance in and out of concealment by establishing his own fourfold, one of *quadruple objects*. Harman replaces what he sees as the problematic term *things* with the more open-ended term *objects*. Anything can be an object, and Harman's objects include aspects far beyond tradition materialist objects. Harman embraces aspects of Latour's *actor-network theory* in positioning networks as objects,[34] DeLanda's *assemblage theory*,[35] and accepts certain conditions of *correlationalism* as developed by Quentin Meillassoux.[36] Harman suggests all systemic structured thinking can only give access to limited aspects of the real, where both holistic monism and separated isolated objects are extremes of idealism. Husserl's *return-to-the-things-themselves* and Heidegger's *Ereignis* (the clearing for coming into view) both fall short in an impossible search for a totalizing subjective correlation. One can't know anything in and of itself; one must always qualify knowledge in terms of its relation to our particular social, textual, biological positions, among others. One's understanding is a provisional, temporal glimpse, one that is real but transitory and partial. Steven Shaviro summarizes Harman's thinking as, "I do not come to know a world of things outside myself. Rather, I discover—which is to say I feel—that I myself, together with things that go beyond my knowledge of them, are all alike inhabitants of a 'common world.'"[37] Harman abandons the authority of the phenomenological project as too hegemonically anthropocentric. He would claim it impossible for the embodied designer to ever map a complete or objective understanding of what is real. Harman may concur with Irigaray in the sense that our thrownness clouds all judgment of the real, and we suffer from the deeper understanding of the richness and possibilities in the world, and self, because of it. Both invite the opportunity to reinvestigate the things that have been concealed by structures, codifications, and hierarchical ordering.

A Flattened Ontology

Key to Harman's work is an interpretation and application where ideas-as-things, relations-as-things, and the nature of things themselves exist within a flattened ontology. Manuel DeLanda explains:

> While an ontology based on relations between general types and particular instances is hierarchical, each level representing a different ontological category, an approach in terms of interacting parts and emergent wholes leads to a flat ontology, one made exclusively of unique, singular individuals, differing in spatiotemporal scale but not in ontological status.[38]

Flattening is counterintuitive to designers who think in spatial terms, and where in visual software *flatten* means loss of editing, nuance, and further experimentation with layers. Harman's flattening means the loosening of the defining hierarchy of conceptual structures themselves such that new possibilities for connectedness might occur. Objects under flattening are capable of recombinant object forms, networks, and new relations; qualities of objects appear, and objects meld into new assemblages and relations. Creativity places new objects in relation as well as new forms, formerly hidden aspects of realities of things and between objects.

Harman's Quadruple Objects

Architectural design usually conceives of *things* engaged in space and time. Harman suggests *all* things are better understood as *objects*, but objects that have a simultaneous quadruple nature as *real objects*, *sensual objects*, *real qualities*, and *sensual qualities*. Between each is tension that conceals and unconceals aspects of the objects. While this is beyond the scope of this essay to fully elucidate, Harman suggests time is the name for the tension between sensual objects and their sensual qualities, space as the tension between concealed real objects and the sensual qualities associated with them.[39] This tension between sensual objects and their real hidden qualities is a striking development tied to the difficulties in what Husserl called *Eidos* (i.e., form/type).[40] Harman explains "the duel . . . underway in hidden real things, between its multitude of hidden features . . . has always been called its essence, and this aspect of the real is entirely withdrawn from human access."[41] Within this kinetic nature of a thing, Harman suggests there is endless speculation and depth for continued philosophical exploration. Importantly, for the embodied designer new explorations open across the whole conceptual, organizational, formal, material, and phenomenological media of architecture.

A Pedagogy at the Threshold between Irigaray and Speculative Realism

Irigaray's sexuate embodiedness opens a relational network of things, bodies, and *betweens* to acknowledge and place into practice via negotiation. The circular engagement of a sense of personhood, the initiation of thought and bodily actions, and the relation to setting and place reinforce identity and affirm (or negate) values and the signification of selves, actions, or places. Their intertwined movement is continual, although across one's development the velocities of encounter and legacies of memories may change. This is a constant process of self-work and occurs explicitly as well as tacitly in the construction and reconstruction of one's world. Sue Best calls attention to how this aspect of Irigaray's work is complementary to Derrida's ideas of deconstruction:

> What Derrida terms "an originary synthesis not preceded by any absolute simplicity" . . . neatly correlates with Irigaray's notion of "a relation at the beginning." While differences between body and concepts may be thought of as things, their mutual dependence is suppressed, or, as Irigaray puts it, "the connection is negated and yet exploited."[42]

For the designer this is critical; the embodied designer and their particular sexuate subjectivity and embodiment is a unique source for unconcealing, and creativity. Individual designers as embodied subjects discern different actionable aspects and qualities from the hidden reserve within specific situations. This is significant, as the history of architecture has tended toward *master* narratives, especially surrounding the authority of geometry and its relationship to the body. Architectural commentator Steven Connor recognizes this attempt at imposition and totalization:

> It is Descartes's coordinated grid which really makes good the idea of absolute space: space which is entirely uniform and absolutely unaffected by everything that takes place within it . . . also nothing in it that is not susceptible to rule and ratio. Absolute, given space governed the scene . . . until non-Euclidean geometries began to multiply and relativize spaces in the later nineteenth century.[43]

The abstract geometric field in architecture is one of stark contrast to the Irigarayan feminine metaphors of lived experience within immersive voids versus as static objects. The embodied world as experienced seems to stand apart from traditional architectural ordering systems that marginalize difference and eliminate it to support larger formal constructs.

Inherent in an embodied realist design philosophy would be a responsibility to not only subjective sexuate difference but also empathy for nonhuman reality—open to new materialism, eco-phenomenology, and effects of complex hyperobjects in the world. It means ideas as things themselves must be reaccommodated. As phenomenology is largely based on human valuation and experience as an exclusive mechanism, phenomenology, like objectivist science, has limitations. The ability to project and speculate, without a prejudiced end product, is also a key to developing creativity. Speculative realism provides an actionable path for a designer's return to the things themselves. Rather than phenomenology engaging a complete or completed world, it allows for a far richer world to reveal itself from a continual becoming.

A foundational concept of *embodied* design is learning through the work itself. The feel and sense of engagement with the work adds tacit forms of knowledge, allows for rethinking through continuing reflection on and through the work. The concept of interrogating the real rejects architectural intervention as onto tabula rasa and builds from an assumption of accessible, inductive, phenomenologically led revealing and unconcealing. While recognizing a vivid givenness to any situation at entry, the speculative aspect places all things, assemblages, relations, and boundaries as open to interrogation by the embodied designer. Irigaray's sexuate difference makes this last claim explicit. The studio is not only a place of respect but a place for negotiation between past self, self-becoming, self and peers, self and media of architecture. Each has forms of resistance that challenge, beckon, and deny a linear flow of uncritical historic momentum.

While this is my overly reductive and cursory summary of what I think Irigaray and Harman may contribute to the lived part of the design process, it sets itself at the threshold of network theory via the enmeshed nature of existence. In design this is an idea that goes back to an earlier generation looking at the existential phenomenological situation. Architectural theorist Christian Norberg-Schulz quotes Jacob von Uexküll to illustrate architecture as a relational nesting: "Like the spider with its web, so every subject weaves relationships between itself and particular properties of objects; the many strands are woven together and finally form the basis of every subject's very existence."[44]

This interwoven subjectivity in architecture and environmental design eclipses a mere teaching of forms and requires a design pedagogy of embodiment, one that offers the opportunity to build upon the specific grounding brought by a particular student into a situation. A pedagogy of discernment across a project's inherent diversity of groundings produces a diversity of initial lateral solutions, versus a false objectivity or norming. Design work proceeds in real time, welcoming insight of past experiences, immediacy, and the possible, and organic growth via experiences as forms of knowledge from iterative processes and judgments. This version of design for beginning students situates carefully constructed project-based grounds and outcomes in and around real things, issues, materials, and situations. It first develops the student's creative, qualitative judgment, versus merely teaching architecture as a technical discipline. The resultant work speaks for itself, rather than being substantiated by a precedent or reference; the work and students each become through the process of design and exchange in the studio.

Embodied Interrogations of the Real

This method and the three following examples of projects are inspired from phenomenological, feminist, and speculative realist roots, and provide a means to describe and enable projects and learning situations where alternate, simultaneous realities may be developed from the resistances and surplus within the givenness of an available situation, augmented by the use of representations. This pedagogy includes inquiry at full-scale, fabrication of materials and assemblages, gathered for qualities and resultant experiential phenomena. The philosophical sources, while introduced at a cursory level in project prompts, work largely behind the project activities interface.

For a beginning designer, the threshold between Irigaray and Harman is one of creative exploration in bringing forth, capable of rehabilitating the Greek poiesis. Aesthetician Derek Whitehead develops this aspect:

> *Poiesis* . . . may enable practitioners in the varying art forms, and aestheticians who reflect upon them, to come to a deeper sense of how artworks work: that they realize themselves inter-dependently of the formative conditions of their inception. . . . The *poietic* act may be seen in those undercurrents of artistic activity . . . wherein the artist, the artwork, and the receiver of such a work are brought forward in all the features of their self-presentation.[45]

This pedagogy requires the encouragement and harnessing of the student's own glimpses of the realities present in the design situation recognized by them, as in the process they are in their own form of poesis, becoming designers. It is a process of testing, iterations, and discernment across many aspects of the real. It requires Irigaray's third space where the studio serves as an interval between things, and where things are open to disclosure as Harman describes in the dance of appearances, through the negotiation of a student aware of self, architectural ideas, and thingness of material, space, light.

This pedagogy is not linear or deductive. It is not based on seeing design as mere problem solving. It is not about replicating projects from a canon. It has an aspect of alchemy, testing, and negotiation within it. The studio allows a particular knitting of design elements into a real, across concepts as things, representations as things, iterations, and in the case of this studio, realizations. Irigaray provides one metaphor of this freedom and transcendence for the beginning designer via the angel: "The angel is that which unceasingly passes through the envelope(s) or container(s), goes from one side to the other, reworking every deadline, changing every decision, thwarting all repetition."[46] The angel is this freedom of exploration of the real encouraged by the optimism driving the process, the forgotten air that appears suddenly through the making, the speech now heard from voices freed to speak and hear others. The angel also metaphorically drives Harmon's autopoiesis of nonhuman agents into play within the studio setting and into the work itself.

The curriculum establishes bodies of knowledge that students must engage and outcomes that must be achieved. Outcomes are typically linked to evidence of cognitive skills, which according to versions of the continuing evolution of Bloom's taxonomy span a series of verb-based capacities, from a basic remembering, through understanding, applying, analyzing, evaluating, and creating.[47] The highest level, creating, is especially daunting to many beginning students who have entered design from traditional academic backgrounds privileging what developmental psychologist Howard Gardner terms verbal-linguistic and logical-mathematical intelligences versus visual-spatial, naturalistic, or kinesthetic intelligences possibly more beneficial in design.[48] Key areas that require reconsideration are *qualitative judgment*, which has a broad index of success versus a singular correct answer; *play*, culturally conditioned to be viewed as nonproductive; and *error*, which in prior education is often associated with failure. Almost all design curricula start with a project-based pedagogy via a studio/laboratory experience that allows evidence via the observation of students in process, and the work produced as evidence of outcomes. Where curricula will differ within professional programs is in topical sequence, pedagogy in the studio, and discernment of outcomes relative to external professional standards, particularly those associated with professional degree status and periodic program review.

FALL: BEGINNING WITH SEEING AND MAKING

The first studio objective is providing opportunities for the student to reestablish immediacy with the world—become aware of one's surroundings and see anew. The beginner typically sees via conventionally framed typologies: buildings, building types, wholes, subject-things with names. These typologies differ from and inhibit a more fine-grained phenomenal analysis, such as the intervals and spaces between things, and qualities of light, surfaces, and textures. The beginner typically sees from a fixed point without movement or time, versus an immersive space where one's position changes, and sensations create a feel of the space and composite elements and media. Bachelard understands this challenge in *Poetics of Space* as a positive form of forgetting:

> Non-knowing is not a form of ignorance but a difficult transcendence of knowledge. . . . a sort of pure beginning, which makes its creation and exercise in freedom. . . . The entire life of the image is in its dazzling splendor, in the fact that an image is a transcending of all premises of sensibility.[49]

Seeing (Slowly)

Seeing through sketching is a time-honored way of achieving hand, eye, and heart in one place at the same time. Embodied seeing, via hand with pencil or pen, places one within a setting and literally draws one into a situation by slowing time. Sketching requires mindfulness and attentiveness to detail, seeing form, surfaces, voids, and shade, via a struggle to get fine-muscle control of a representational instrument. The instrument has a nature that is also learned by the way it marks and interacts with the paper surface being engaged. Tool becomes active extension of the body. While the experience and quality of the sketch do not fully gather what is drawn, they are a personal description beyond the capability of words or the photograph; each media carries its own form of memory and subjective fact.

Coupled with the initial sketching is photography. While a quality sketch, even a good gestural sketch, may take minutes, the photograph is accomplished in seconds. There is a framing of object to edge, a choice of formal internal composition, awareness of the contribution of light and contrast. The image is obtained, and recognition of intuitive compositional elements, apart from subject, may be discussed and tested. Soon, photos are acquiring the mindfulness of the sketches.

Making: UFO (Uninhibited Formal-spatial Operations)

The images of the early weeks become processed with the use of digital software and altered images become templates for the beginning of three-dimensional studies. Images are no longer retained for symbols—not looked at as objects with a name but a set of 2D formal lines, tones, fields and reassessed for the new reality of what is contained in them as compositional grounds. The images provide a graphic field that is physically acted upon by the student, inspired by verbs from Richard Serra's *Verb List*: cut, trim, fold, roll, and other actions, and leading to a three-dimensional deconstruction/reassemblage.[50] Gradually, findings take on their own compositional opportunities apart from the source, and compositions become spatial. This happens across multiple iterations to achieve works that the student judges as satisfying in 3D, and at the scale of the hand. Projects are removed from grounding on tabletops by hanging, and interior volumes and surfaces become developed by the additions of internal, battery-operated LED lights. The paper UFO has one appearance in the sunlight and another in the darkened studio at night—with twenty-five and eventually seventy-five iterations taking flight. Form and appearance are recognized as temporal, changing with lighting and other qualities of the space they are in.

Ultimately, the work collectively impacts space and time via a group installation of the cohort's almost three hundred suspended and LED-lighted UFOs, works of these uninhibited operations, timed to coincide with the university family visitation weekend. The circle of engagement of place-as-received to place-as-impacted by the design work creates a welcomed sense of achievement by the students individually and collectively as agents of change, with their diverse set of findings having tangible outcomes, verifiable by faculty, and the understanding that design is an open form of research.

In this simple manner, a subtle rift is open between the object-world and the newly encountered designed world, which includes the subjectivities of the individual students and intersubjectivities of the cohort. This vicarious causation is the grounds of the recombinative and creativity. As Harman explains: "Vicarious causation is not some autistic moonbeam entering the window of an asylum. Instead, it is both the launching pad for a rigorous post-Heideggerian philosophy, and a fitting revival of the venerable problem of communication between substances."[51]

WINTER: REAL-IZATION AND paraSITE

Building up in scale from hand-sized objects and adding material complexity beyond paper and LED light, the paraSITE project expands the student phenomenal interrogations with an in-situ, full-scale realization and installation.[52] The title playfully yet purposefully simultaneously suggests a parasitic relationship between new work and existing conditions, a notion that all architectural designs have sites already filled with possibility, and implication of the parametric, suggesting multiple metrics

Figure 11.1. UFOs at week-five Family Weekend installation. Courtesy of the author.

as forms of analysis. Assigned locations in studio-building corridors, stairs, and grounds are the settings for studies. New embodied aspects look to students discerning subtle or surprisingly hidden phenomena, or latent experiences to be revealed through their interventions. The 1970s brutalist concrete frame building has corridors surrounding a massive covered exterior three-level stair court used for passage as well as social gatherings. Voids between stair runs, spaces external to, and above and below railings, areas above in cavities of the structure are companion sites. The settings are also easily experienced as part of kinetic, dynamic flows and networks—the dramatic way the structure is lighted in the winter natural light across the day, the way the various portions of the space and structure channel wind vortexes, and the capacity of site locations to be seen from other areas within as well as from dramatic distances away feed into the sense of impact and responsibilities to the work. Students also are cued to see the social fabric of the building—the movement of crowds between classes, the places students choose to pause with a phone or coffee, the places to merely catch one's breath outside of studio.[53]

Sites are recorded with images, video, and representations executed in hand drawings and in virtual digital models. Projects are conceptualized, alternatives are multiplied due to the collective subjectivities of the team members, allowing consideration of possibilities no individual student would be capable of doing. Initially modeled at a smaller scale, full-scale prototypes are developed in shops, which include sewing machines, welding, and vacuum forming. The resistance of materials to arbitrary formal imposition, material weight, aesthetic and performative impact are all discovered in real time. Gravity, physics, and body scale are requisite to inform design. Importantly, error in concept or prototype is another opportunity for iteration and pause for reflection and judgment. The qualitative shine, mechanics of percussive sounding, the shape for grasp of hand are manifest. The billow of fabric, splaying of sunlight into colors, the continued study of the materiality of shadow are all advancements.

One joy for the faculty and older students is seeing an assigned site have dramatically differing concepts and solutions across several years of student cohorts as the lateral subjectivities are recognized and built upon. The creative acts include ethereal pieces such as an upper-level roof deck edge with exquisite metal armature linked to a handrail above a three-story concrete façade flanking the entry to the College of Business. The frame was overlaid with large six-inch-thick sheets of ice that in the glistening sun created long sensuous markings on the tall wall, with later sounds of the crashing shards that fell safely onto a concrete roof below, creating a memorable event as much as an artifact.

Spring: Dwelling within the Air

David Abram suggests this flesh-of-the-world described by Merleau-Ponty enters the designer as breath, like light seen into the eye, but also radiant and felt on the skin.[54] Environmental patterns suggest networks of cause and effect that transcend phenomenological analysis. Timothy Morton cautions some objects of elusive nature defy description, calculation, and even conceptualization. He terms these *hyperobjects* and describes them as variously *interobjective*: formed by relations between more than one object; *phased*: occupying scalar dimensional spaces beyond ones humans can normally perceive; *nonlocal*: massively distributed in time and space such that their totality cannot be realized locally; *molten*: so massive as to refute their being fixed or consistent; and *viscous*: adhering to any other object, no matter how hard an object tries to resist.[55] Moving full-scale work into the realm of nature calls for engaging the temporal ranges of environmental phenomena, a need for resilient structure and materiality for possible wind or rain, tests for certainty of anchorages on a slope and in mud, and the delivery of anticipated dwelling with others into a world of environmental vectors.

Building upon working with others, and making toward realization, the task is a small, mobile, temporary space for dwelling with a group of peers, over a duration of several days, and within the setting of the headlands of a small canyon, literally dwelling-with through something anew, between earth and sky. Temporality is multifold: What is the time of the canyon? How will the diurnal cycle of the sun, frequent fog, dew, possible rain, and potential thirty-mile-per hour winds affect the experience? What crawling, grazing, slithering, flying others may be encountered as the work impacts their canyon homes, and what level of interaction is sought or avoided? How does the intervention speak to welcoming others, of spending the time together, and what levels of privacy are sought? Planning how to assemble the work onsite without available electricity, how to move the components only with the capacity of the team to take it approximately two miles from the studio and shop locations on campus also focus design solutions.

The project, which now includes a similar parallel community college competition in adjacent canyon areas, and is aligned with the college open house for admitted students, has developed a Woodstock-like event status drawing thousands of visitors. Students test lightweight systems that now must carry the weight of multiple people and provide possibility of envelope and closure. The way materials are carried and assembled in the field has created novel responses of giant wheels rolled, slings, stretchers, and backpacks. The route from campus to canyon has become parade-like, with cheering parents, older mentor students, alumni, and faculty. The final tests are in the inhabitation, and the return of materials for recycling. Building a building is impossible due to myriad constraints imposed, yet in developing a sense of community, a sense of dwelling with the canyon, an embodied design succeeds in myriad ways, due to the pedagogy that relies on difference in speech and taking in the canyon air.

Conclusion: Thinking, Speaking, Making at the Threshold

In this essay I have argued for a pedagogy for design that challenges many conventional assumptions and tropes about the push of historic

Figure 11.2. Students adjust tension in their cable-assisted tube steel dwelling, with hand-made hammocks hung within the volume and capacity to add a lightweight top for fog, rain, or cold. The headlands of Poly Canyon annually contain the projects of almost three hundred undergraduate beginning design students in this three-week project culminating their first twenty-two weeks on campus. Courtesy of the author.

momentum and continuity, a nostalgic calcified sense of place, and the privileged formalism embedded in design today. Irigaray's work on the history of metaphysics and the sexuate subject provides an important critique of male-dominated Western culture and, by extension, the architectural profession. In pointing out that Heidegger's work on the fourfold forgets the air, she does not deny his existential-phenomenological project but calls for a broadening of its capacity to deliver a vibrant, meaningful world. Irigaray's metaphor of speech, the third room of encounter, and breathing provide inroads into air, sky, and the expanded horizon of eco-phenomenology, within a design context of care. Her metaphor of multiples hiding between, and indeed dependent on, aspects of sexuate difference have direct application in design pedagogy for beginners. The speculative realism espoused by Harman similarly looks at the disruption and flattening of hierarchies but, in doing so, outlines a real world hidden to traditional phenomenology with its own sense of becoming, which is difficult to align with static models of Being. This thinking has inspired a design pedagogy for beginners where in direct engagement with the media of architecture via projects, and each other, students embrace emerging multiple disclosed *reals* in works that have a broad set of formal, material, and spatial manifestations, each tuned to embodied subjectivity and discernment of phenomena of project location and situation by each designer. The pedagogy rests within a network of Irigarayan third spaces, the studio, the shop, the canyon, each of which allow for sharing difference in student desires discovered through the work, in collaboration and with their own becoming.

Notes

1. For the purposes of this essay, I will use Rachel Jones's argument developed in *Irigaray: Towards a Sexuate Philosophy* (Cambridge: Polity Press, 2011), 217–219, that sexuate difference has an ontological status, versus an ontological difference.

2. In this essay the metaphor of threshold is intentional—Irigaray's claim of ontological sexuate difference does not easily reside with Harman's hostility to placing embodiment in any form as ontological; however, the claim of the essay is that their respective positions, while admittedly in tension, meet at a threshold of radical questioning that affirms similar questioning and explorations of self, agency, and architectural media of the embodied beginning design student

3. Irigaray FA, 5–14.

4. Typically beginning design includes the first year of undergraduate or first semester of graduate school studios in a professional degree program in architecture. Reference the National Conference on the Beginning Design Student: https://www.beginningdesign.org, accessed March 16, 2020.

5. Irigaray ESD, 7. See also: Rebecca Hill, *The Interval: Relation and Becoming in Irigaray, Aristotle and Bergson* (New York: Fordham University, 2012), 1–3.

6. Andrea Wheeler, "Heidegger, the Fourfold and Luce Irigaray's *To Be Born*: An Architectural Perspective," in *Towards a New Human Being*, ed. Luce Irigaray, Mahon O'Brien, and Christos Hadjioannou (London: Palgrave Macmillan, 2019), 85.

7. Irigaray TS.

8. The author's University of Cincinnati 1979 graduating cohort in architecture included six women and over one hundred men. The Association of Collegiate Schools of Architecture shows a constant increase in female graduates and trending parity in graduating cohorts. Faculty still reflect a male dominance by a 2:1 ratio. See https://www.acsa-arch.org/resources/data-resources/acsa-atlas/, "Professor Rank Shows the Largest Gender Gap (2017)," accessed March 2, 2020.

9. Elaine Baruch and Lucienne J. Serrano. *Women Analyze Women: In France, England and the United States* (New York: New York University Press, 1988), 159.

10. Sue Best, "Sexualizing Space," in *Sexy Bodies: The Strange Carnalities of Feminism*, ed. Elizabeth Grosz and Elspeth Probyn (New York: Routledge, 1995), 183.

11. Diana Agrest, Patricia Conway, and Leslie Kanes Weisman, eds., *The Sex of Architecture* (New York: Abrams, 1996).

12. Gail Weiss and Honi Fern Haber, eds., *Perspectives on Embodiment: The Intersections of Nature and Culture* (New York: Routledge, 1999).

13. Elizabeth Grosz, *Volatile Bodies: Toward a Corporeal Feminism* (Bloomington: Indiana University Press, 1994).

14. Elizabeth Grosz, *Architecture from the Outside: Essays on Virtual and Real Space* (Cambridge, MA: MIT Press. 2001).

15. Irigaray in Andrea Wheeler, "Love in Architecture," *Paragraph* 25, no. 3 (2002): 114. Irigaray is here responding to the paper by Wheeler.

16. Irigaray in Wheeler, "Love in Architecture," 115.

17. Cathryn Vasseleu, *Textures of Light: Vision and Touch in Irigaray, Levinas and Merleau-Ponty* (New York: Routledge 1998), 12.

18. Examples include architectural design in Juhani Pallasmaa, *The Eyes of the Skin* (Chichester: John Wiley & Sons, 2005) and Sylvia Lavin, *Kissing Architecture* (Princeton, NJ: Princeton University Press, 2011), craft and material resistance in Richard Sennett, *The Craftsman* (New Haven, CT: Yale University Press, 2008), as well as more conceptually challenging positions on agency and matter by philosophers such as Diana Coole, *New Materialisms: Ontology,*

Agency, and Politics, ed. Diana Coole and Samantha Frost (Durham, NC: Duke University Press 2010), 92–115.

19. Peg Rawes, *Irigaray for Architects* (New York: Routledge, 2007), 25. Rawes term *sexed* subjects and spaces may be criticized as an essentialization of Irigaray's sexuate. Irigaray develops the term *sexuate* to avoid confusion about sex and sexuality in sexual difference.

20. Rawes, *Irigaray for Architects*, 33–61. This chapter in the book is entitled "Passages and Flows" and is an extended discourse on these particular ideas.

21. Wheeler, "Love in Architecture," 110–111.

22. Jane Rendell, *Site-Writing: The Architecture of Art Criticism* (New York: I. B. Tauris, 2010), 27.

23. Wheeler, "Heidegger, the Fourfold and Luce Irigaray's *To Be Born*," 87.

24. Irigaray FA, 94.

25. Maria Cimitile, "The Horror of Language: Irigaray and Heidegger," *Philosophy Today* 45 (January 2001): 71.

26. Irigaray FA, 28–29.

27. Cimitile, "The Horror of Language," 71.

28. Irigaray FA, 8, 40.

29. Andrea Wheeler, "A Future Invested in Sustainability: Sustainable Architecture and Education in the Midwest through the Ethical Philosophy of Luce Irigaray," *Journal of Sustainability Education* (March 2017), http://www.susted.com/wordpress/content/a-future-invested-in-sustainability-sustainable-architecture-and-education-in-the-midwest-through-the-ethical-philosophy-of-luce-irigaray_2017_03/.

30. Irigaray KW, 132.

31. Irigaray FA, 166–167.

32. Steven Connor, "Building Breathing Space," lecture, Bartlett School of Architecture, March 3, 2004, http://www.stevenconnor.com/bbs/, accessed December 12, 2018.

33. Graham Harman, *Tool Being: Heidegger and the Metaphysics of Objects* (Chicago: Open Court, 2002).

34. Graham Harman, *Towards Speculative Realism* (Winchester, UK: Zero Books, 2010), 71–92. Harman's position on Latour draws primarily from Latour's *Science in Action* (Cambridge, MA: Harvard University Press, 1987) and *We Have Never Been Modern*, trans. Catherine Porter (Cambridge, MA: Harvard University Press, 1991).

35. Harman, *Towards Speculative Realism*, 170–173. Harman interprets Manuel DeLanda's work, particularly on realism, in *A New Philosophy of Society: Assemblage Theory* (London: Continuum 2006).

36. Harman, *Towards Speculative Realism*, 199–201. In his reading of Meillassoux, *After Finitude* (London: Continuum 2008), Harman critiques Meillassoux's correlationalism as taking autonomy away from possible objects.

37. Steven Shaviro, *The Universe of Things: On Speculative Realism* (Minneapolis: University of Minnesota Press, 2014), 3.

38. Manuel DeLanda, *Intensive Science and Virtual Philosophy* (New York: Bloomsbury, 2013), 47.

39. Graham Harman, *The Quadruple Object* (Washington, DC: Zero Books, 2011), 20–50.

40. Harman's essay does not quote Husserl directly, but the primary examples of *Eidos* derive from Mediation Four, part 34, of Husserl's *Cartesian Meditations: An Introduction to Phenomenology* (Dordrecht, Holland: Kluwer Academic, 1999), 69–71.

41. Harman, *The Quadruple Object*, 100–101.

42. Best, "Sexualizing Space," 189.

43. Connor, "Building Breathing Space."

44. Christian Norberg-Schulz, *Existence, Space and Architecture* (New York: Praeger, 1974), 9. Norberg-Schulz is quoting from von Uexküll's original 1956 German text now translated, *A Foray into the Worlds of Animals and Humans: With a Theory of Meaning*, trans. Joseph D. O'Neil (Minneapolis: University of Minnesota Press 2010), 4.

45. Derek Whitehead, *Poiesis and Art-Making: A Way of Letting-Be*, http://www.contempaesthetics.org/newvolume/pages/article.php?articleID=216, accessed March 16, 2020.

46. Irigaray ESD, 16.

47. Lorin W. Anderson and David R. Krathwohl et al., *A Taxonomy for Learning, Teaching, and Assessing: A Revision of Bloom's Taxonomy of Educational Objectives* (New York: Longman, 2001).

48. Howard Gardner, *Frames of Mind: The Theory of Multiple Intelligences* (New York: Basic Books, 2011).

49. Gaston Bachelard, *The Poetics of Space*, trans. Maria Jolas (Boston: Beacon Press, 1964), xxxii.

50. Richard Serra, *Verb List* (New York: Museum of Modern Art, 1967–1968), https://www.moma.org/collection/works/152793, accessed December 12, 2018.

51. Graham Harman, "On Vicarious Causation," *Collapse* 2 (March 2007): 187–206.

52. The paraSITE project was developed by colleagues Brian Kelly and Brent Freeby. The author as coordinator expanded access to it to all three hundred beginning design students in architecture and architectural engineering. It has undergone continued refinement by Michael Lucas (coordinator 2009–2013), James Bagall, Angela Brocco, Ryan Brockett, Kevin Dong, Brent Freeby, JoAnn Moore, Humberto Norman, Bryan Ridley, Ed Saliklis, Carmen Trudell (coordinator 2013–2014), Jermaine Washington, Emily White (coordinator 2015–2017 and 2018–2020), Keith Wiley (coordinator 2014–2015 and 2017–2018), Greg Wynn, and Margarita Yin.

53. The author has given a deeper exposition of one such project in "Violet Light under a Saffron Sky: Creativity, Phenomenology, and Speculative Realism in Beginning Design," in *Promoting Creative Thinking in Beginning Design Studios*, ed. Stephen Temple (New York: Routledge, 2018), 184–197.

54. David Abram, *Spell of the Sensuous* (New York: Vintage, 1996), 225.

55. Timothy Morton, *Hyperobjects: Philosophy and Ecology After the End of the World* (Minneapolis: University of Minnesota Press, 2013), 23–24.

Bibliography

Abram, David. *Spell of the Sensuous*. New York: Vintage, 1996.

Agrest, Diana, Patricia Conway, and Leslie Kanes Weisman, eds. *The Sex of Architecture*. New York: Abrams, 1996.

Anderson, Lorin W., and David R. Krathwohl et al. *A Taxonomy for Learning, Teaching, and Assessing: A Revision of Bloom's Taxonomy of Educational Objectives*. New York: Longman, 2001.

Bachelard, Gaston. *The Poetics of Space*. Translated by Maria Jolas. Boston: Beacon Press, 1964.

Baruch, Elaine, and Lucienne J. Serrano. *Women Analyze Women: In France, England and the United States*. New York: New York University Press, 1988.

Best, Sue. "Sexualizing Space." In *Sexy Bodies: The Strange Carnalities of Feminism*, edited by Elizabeth Grosz and Elspeth Probyn, 181–194. New York: Routledge, 1995.

Cimitile, Maria. "The Horror of Language: Irigaray and Heidegger." *Philosophy Today* 45 (January 2001): 66–74.

Connor, Steven. "Building Breathing Space." Lecture, Bartlett School of Architecture, March 3, 2004. http://www.stevenconnor.com/bbs/. Accessed March 16, 2020.

Coole, Diana. "The Inertia of Matter and the Generativity of Flesh." In *New Materialisms: Ontology, Agency, and Politics*, edited by Diana Coole and Samantha Frost, 92–115. Durham, NC: Duke University Press, 2010.

DeLanda, Manuel. *Intensive Science and Virtual Philosophy*. New York: Bloomsbury, 2013.

DeLanda, Manuel. *A New Philosophy of Society: Assemblage Theory*. London: Continuum, 2006.

Gardner, Howard. *Frames of Mind: The Theory of Multiple Intelligences*. New York: Basic Books, 2011.

Grosz, Elizabeth. *Architecture from the Outside: Essays on Virtual and Real Space*. Cambridge, MA: MIT Press, 2001.

Grosz, Elizabeth. Introduction to *Sexy Bodies: The Strange Carnalities of Feminism*, edited by Elizabeth Grosz and Elspeth Probyn, ix–xv. New York: Routledge. 1995.

Grosz, Elizabeth. *Volatile Bodies: Toward a Corporeal Feminism*. Bloomington: Indiana University Press, 1994.

Harman, Graham. *Prince of Networks: Bruno Latour and Metaphysics*. Melbourne: re.press, 2009.

Harman, Graham. "On Vicarious Causation." *Collapse* 2 (March 2007): 187–206.

Harman, Graham. *The Quadruple Object*. Washington, DC: Zero Books, 2011.

Harman, Graham. *Tool Being: Heidegger and the Metaphysics of Objects*. Chicago: Open Court, 2002.

Harman, Graham. *Towards Speculative Realism*. Winchester, UK: Zero Books, 2010.

Heidegger, Martin. *Basic Writings*. Edited and translated by David Krell. New York: Routledge, 1993.

Heidegger, Martin. *Being and Time*. Translated by Joan Stambaugh. Albany: State University of New York Press, 2010.

Hill, Rebecca. *The Interval: Relation and Becoming in Irigaray, Aristotle and Bergson*. New York: Fordham University, 2012.

Husserl, Edmund. *Cartesian Meditations: An Introduction to Phenomenology*. Translated by Dorian Cairns. Dordrecht, Holland: Kluwer Academic, 1999.

Jones, Rachel. *Irigaray: Towards a Sexuate Philosophy*. Cambridge: Polity Press, 2011.

Latour, Bruno. *An Inquiry into Modes of Existence: An Anthropology of the Moderns*. Translated by Catherine Porter. Cambridge, MA: Harvard University Press, 2013.

Latour, Bruno. *Science in Action*. Cambridge, MA: Harvard University Press, 1987.

Latour, Bruno. *We Have Never Been Modern*. Translated by Catherine Porter. Cambridge, MA: Harvard University Press, 1993.

Lavin, Sylvia. *Kissing Architecture*. Princeton, NJ: Princeton University Press, 2011.

Lucas, Michael. "Revisiting the Transcendental: Design and Matter as Constitutive Categories in Architecture." In *Analecta Husserliana: Yearbook of Phenomenological Research*, vol. 107, edited by Anna-Teresa Tymieniecka, 361–379. Cham, Switzerland: Springer, 2011.

Lucas, Michael. "Triple Grounding." In *Proceedings of the 27th National Conference on the Beginning Design Student*, edited by Lindsey Bahe, Peter Hind, and Brian Kelly. Lincoln: University of Nebraska Department of Architecture, 2011. Contributions to the proceedings listed in this bibliography are available for those interested from the author's archives.

Lucas, Michael. "Violet Light under a Saffron Sky: Creativity, Phenomenology, and Speculative Realism in Beginning Design." In *Promoting Creative Thinking in Beginning Design Studios*, edited by Stephen Temple, 184–197. New York: Routledge, 2018.

Lucas, Michael, Brent Freeby, and Brian Kelly. "Power(Tools): paraSITES Progress." In *Proceedings of the 27th National Conference on the Beginning Design Student*, edited by Lindsey Bahe, Peter Hind, and Brian Kelly. Lincoln: University of Nebraska Department of Architecture, 2011.

Lucas, Michael, and Carmen Trudell. "Four Weeks: UFO (I Want to Believe)." In *Proceedings of the 29th National Conference on the Beginning Design Student*, edited by Eric Oskey, Dennis Playdon, and Lorena Alvarez. Philadelphia: Temple University Department of Architecture. 2013.

Meillassoux, Quentin. *After Finitude: An Essay on the Necessity of Contingency*. London: Continuum, 2008.

Massumi, Brian. *Parables for the Virtual: Movement, Affect, Sensation*. Durham, NC: Duke University Press, 2002.

Morton, Timothy. *Hyperobjects: Philosophy and Ecology After the End of the World*. Minneapolis: University of Minnesota Press, 2013.

Norberg-Schulz, Christian. *Existence, Space and Architecture*. New York: Praeger, 1974.

Pallasmaa, Juhani. *The Eyes of the Skin*. Chichester: John Wiley & Sons, 2005.

Rawes, Peg. *Irigaray for Architects*. Abingdon: Routledge, 2007.

Rendell, Jane. *Site-Writing: The Architecture of Art Criticism*. New York: I. B. Tauris, 2010.

Sennett, Richard. *The Craftsman*. New Haven, CT: Yale University Press, 2008.

Serra, Richard. *Verb List*. New York: Museum of Modern Art, 1967–1968. https://www.moma.org/collection/works/152793. Accessed March 16, 2020.

Shaviro, Steven. *The Universe of Things: On Speculative Realism*. Minneapolis: University of Minnesota Press, 2014.

Toadvine, Ted, and Charles Brown, eds. *Eco-Phenomenology*. Albany: State University of New York Press, 2003.

Vasseleu, Cathryn. *Textures of Light: Vision and Touch in Irigaray, Levinas and Merleau-Ponty*. New York: Routledge, 1998.

Weiss, Gail, and Honi Fern Haber, eds. *Perspectives on Embodiment: The Intersections of Nature and Culture*. New York: Routledge, 1999.

Wheeler, Andrea. "Being-Two in an Architectural Perspective: Conversation between Luce Irigaray and Andrea Wheeler." https://workingwith luceirigaray.files.wordpress.com/2013/11/conversation-between-luce-irigaray-and-andrea-wheeler.pdf. Accessed March 16, 2020.

Wheeler, Andrea. "A Future Invested in Sustainability: Sustainable Architecture and Education in the Midwest through the Ethical Philosophy of Luce Irigaray." *Journal of Sustainability Education* (March 2017), http://www.susted.com/wordpress/content/a-future-invested-in-sustainability-sustainable-architecture-and-education-in-the-midwest-through-the-ethical-philosophy-of-luce-irigaray_2017_03/. Accessed March 20, 2020.

Wheeler, Andrea. "Heidegger, the Fourfold and Luce Irigaray's *To Be Born*: An Architectural Perspective." In *Towards a New Human Being*, edited by Luce Irigaray, Mahon O'Brien, and Christos Hadjioannou, 73–89. London: Palgrave Macmillan, 2019.

Wheeler, Andrea. "Love in Architecture." *Paragraph* 25, no. 3 (2002), https://www-jstor-org.ezproxy.lib.calpoly.edu/ stable/43263700. Accessed March 16, 2020.

Whitehead, Derek. "Poiesis and Art-Making: A Way of Letting-Be." *Contemporary Aesthetics*. http://www.contempaesthetics.org/newvolume/pages/article.php?articleID=216. Accessed March 16, 2020.

Chapter Twelve

Commonality in Breath

Reading Northern Ireland's "Peace Process" through the Material Ontologies of Irigaray and Manning

Ciara Merrick

Introduction: Returning to Breath

Northern Ireland has long been a place of conflict and violence. Ruptured in a synonymous cultural, religious, and political partitioning dating back to the Ulster plantations of the 1600s, modern-day Northern Ireland has been defined by a period of violence commonly known as "The Troubles." Beginning in 1969 with concerns over persistent civil rights abuse, Northern Ireland experienced three decades of war where historic sociospatial partitionings coalesced in a bloody and violent debate over who embodies the natural and innate claim to the territory of Northern Ireland: the Protestant, Unionist, Loyalist community who commonly identify as British, or the Catholic, Nationalist, Republic community who traditionally identify as Irish. The historic signing of the Good Friday Agreement on the 10th of April 1998, marked the beginning of a slow and cautious peace process. Two decades later, Northern Ireland is no longer considered to be in the midst of war: violence is not an everyday experience,[1] the soundtrack to life is not composed from bombs and gunshots, the daily commute no longer includes an invasive stop-and-search routine, pavements are not lined with the living statues of the British military, and a haze of fear no longer clouds the country. The Good Friday Agreement undoubtedly achieved a great deal. Northern Ireland is, however, far from peace.

Despite the implicit agreement within the formal peace process to work to overcome divisions, Northern Ireland continues to be visibly (and invisibly) partitioned: culture, politics, nationality, religion, and territory continue to be codified as Catholic or Protestant, green or orange. Legacies of identity persist as definitional, spaces are constituted through these identities, and everyday life and its imaginaries are overwhelmingly framed by territory and legacy. What is more, the Northern Irish peace process is structured by these identarian frames. Despite its very real achievements, the Good Friday Agreement negotiated a politics of peace devoid of movement and possibility; peace and its possibilities have been reduced to a territorializing stasis that simply maintains "what is," albeit, less violently. Becoming peaceful, then, necessitates the creation of new and alternative horizons. These horizons depend, fundamentally—*elementally*—on more dynamic processes than stasis can realize.

The creation of alternative horizons, in which peace emerges autonomously from structures of violence, requires a return to elemental and ontological commitments. It necessitates a return those dynamic, constituting forces that make possible territorializing identities and their spatiotemporal segregations. In its breadth, Luce Irigaray's work is primarily concerned with the making of a new, alternative ontology. Opposed to the self being engineered through rooted legacies, Irigaray illustrates that it is processual dynamics like air, or more specifically the practice of breathing, that gives life to the body.

Breath is movement. It is exhaled and inhaled. Mixed, and differentially proportioned. It is intensities of gases and rhythms. However, once partitioned, breath loses movement, becomes stale and starved for necessities of exchange. Rooting air in an inherited, territorial politics of stasis denaturalizes breath and forgets its very aerial ecologies. Practices of peace and peace-making need breath; they need living, dynamic spaces of intersubjective exchange and movement, and crucially the unknown possibilities that emerge from them.

Moving with the philosophical thinking of Luce Irigaray, this chapter explores the elemental politics of air, specifically, breath, within the peace-as-stasis condition of contemporary Northern Ireland. Although Irigaray's work is inherently political in nature, she is not commonly read as a political theorist. To elicit the onto-political transformation Irigaray advocates, I find it productive to draw on Erin Manning's philosophical work around the ontological and embodied relationality of movement. Manning's thinking cannot be grounded in the mass Being of identity politics—which she names species—wherein hierarchical separation and its representation engineer borders and boundaries as constitutive. In Manning's thinking, prior to form there is movement, and this movement is always-already relational. Movement is the forever deferral of its own completion; it is an iterative, continual, and dynamic movement that is always making body-world constellations more. It is this more-than of movement that Manning takes as her starting point for advancing an embodied, relational ontology.

For me, Manning's thinking can be drawn upon to emphasize the latent, but undeniable, movement of Irigaray's elemental ontology: the "to-be" of bodily becoming. Furthermore, and to push (or more subtly, shift) Irigaray's thinking "beyond her,"[2] it is in creating a dialogue with Manning that we can begin to conceive of how relationality is at the heart of our to-be: our first breath is rooted not simply in a bounded body but in a constellation of embodied and sensuous relations active prior to representational form. It is important to note that to think ontology and breath, as the living force of vitality, as relational is not to forgo autonomy but, rather, to ground the becoming of autonomy within an ecology of relations. By "ecology" I mean relational, dynamic, and, fundamentally, the mutually constitutive, ontological relations necessary for life and possibility. Animating a spacing in-between Irigaray and Manning, I read breath as an excessive movement of becoming—an elemental and embodied vitality moving within a constellation of relations that are active prior to and within form, which are always-already weaving an ecology of contemporary commonality, including identity and its territories. Here, commonality and consensus are not found in the ubiquitous and ceaseless recognition of mass territorial roots, with an assumption that I not only exist but that you can also be convinced to recognize yourself in my image. Rather, it is an incipient commonality active within a relation of reaching-toward whereby difference and dissensus—"the realization that *I* am not yet"[3]—become in a sharing of breath.

I argue for breathing in a relational space between Irigaray's and Manning's philosophical work, to read the theoretical arguments of material and embodied ecologies of political liveliness through the lens of breath, and, particularly, as they are traced in postconflict Northern

Ireland, and, more narrowly, in Belfast, where territoriality, stasis, and proximity are intimate and fraught. The argument speaks from and with a year of fieldwork in Belfast where, among other spaces, I traced breath in the context of an Irish-language project located in the heart of east Belfast. Moving with an Irigarayan-inspired methodology foregrounding openness, being in-between, and excess, I traced the relational movement of breath in this shared space as an active and sensing observant participant.[4] This ethnographic work was supported through interviews where, by embodying a gesture of listening-to in silence, I encountered the experiences and worlds of other bodies active in this space. The chapter respires with the everyday realities of Belfast, experienced and encountered through this sustained period of fieldwork.

The first part of the chapter takes a critical tone, arguing that territorial politics partitions the self and other through a conditioned object-recognition, which appropriates the living vitality of the self, of the other, and of the relations in-between. The following section moves beyond critique and returns to the living vitality of breath, where the eruption of change, wonder, and enchantment might be born. To move with breath is to animate an alternative horizon that shifts the starting point from definitive mass species rooted in territory to the aerial ecology of speciation, from isolated and determined Beings to the relational ecology of the living and moving to-be. Finally, the chapter embodies the call to become attentive to relations of sharing always-already present by tracing the movement of breath in-between a shared encounter present in east Belfast. To begin to conceive of peace and the activity of peace-making from within an alternative horizon is to become attentive to the unnoticed experiences and encounters that are always-already moving with breath and with the body's own intersubjective blossoming.

Stability: Forgetting Breath

The Troubles have inscribed a profound and distinct territorial legacy upon both Northern Irish space and Northern Irish bodies. Today the city of Belfast is a mosaic of different villages, each with a distinct identity—Catholic *or* Protestant—and each with a defined territorial boundary marked by "peace" walls, flags, graffiti, murals, and painted curbstones. Territorial separation and essentialized identarian frames operate to structure contact in Northern Ireland. In Belfast two people meeting for the first time immediately voice the habitually disciplined question: "Where do you live? What school do you go to?" In this meeting the two bodies engage in a structured dance of recognition as they navigate learned questions, code predefined answers, and recognize their bodies known a priori. If you live on the Newtownards Road, you are Protestant; if you live in west Belfast, you are Catholic. If you speak Irish, you are Catholic, and probably a Republican; but if you play the flute in a marching band, you are Protestant, and, more than likely, Loyalist. If you go to St. Mary's Christian Brothers' Grammar School, you are Catholic, but if you go to Strathearn School, you are Protestant; if your eyes are close together, you must be Protestant; if you pronounce "H" as a breathy "haitch," then you are Catholic; and so on. With these answers the body met is instantly recognized to the destruction of possibility, wonder, and enchantment.

The recognition of codes is the absolute capture of the other's body in time and space. It is the reduction of a living body to a static object. Recognition is an externalization where the other is held to the trauma of their difference, as they vanish within the common of a mass species in which they are recognized as either belonging with "us" or with "them," as the species that is "us" or as the species that is "not-us." The workings of such recognition were made acutely evident in one interview:

> You met these people who were grown adults who had the most bizarre ideas about Catholics if they were Protestants or if they were Catholics they had strange ideas about Protestants . . . So it was like everyone in west Belfast must be like Gerry Adams[5] and then everybody in east Belfast must be like Ian Paisley.[6]

To begin with recognition is to already be recognized as a mass species with a mastery and know-how that imposes form and values upon the other through morality and religion. Irigaray advances the term "standardization from below" to refer to the stable, eternal process by which commonly held truths are passed on to new generations.[7] Recalling the inherited truth by which she habitually recognized the Catholic body, one woman stated: "My mother would have always felt that Catholics couldn't really be trusted; that was the narrative and, so, I made the assumption all Catholics couldn't be trusted." Habitual recognition, through labels such as untrustworthy or dishonest, mark the other's body as a constraining or negative force and, when such recognition is active in an environment characterized by warlike and conflictual competition, hate can be produced.[8] As we tend to seek the elimination of what we hate, it is in engineering perception to recognize and approach this body through hatred that the violent past of Northern Ireland can be located.

While recognition no longer leads to elimination, it continues to produce the other as the known but refused foreign representation, locatable outside our insular and insulating territorial bubble. Prior to its birth, the body is already a "Being" stripped of the potential for blossoming and movement: to begin with recognition is to already be known as a species. The other remains a kind of "mythical creature that lives over there and eats eggs upside down." The persistence of territorial segregation in postconflict Northern Ireland sustains the approach toward the other as an advancement of "seizure, capture, comprehension, all gestures of incorporation, introjection, apprehension in which the other as such vanishes."[9] The outside remains out while all that is inside is kept in: "It's as if . . . in my head I know all my community . . . but I think they were sort of like the unknown because I didn't know those people . . . There were other people there and we kind of missed each other." Recognition eliminates the very presence of the other and, thus, prevents a relation in-between. The very breath of the other is appropriated in a gesture of (external) incorporation that reduces difference to a stable and permanent sameness.

The destruction of the moving, sensing body extends far beyond the witnessed body to also encompass the witnessing body. In *To Be Born* Irigaray argues how in Western society and culture the living, sensing body is disciplined, whether consciously aware or not, to comply with the cultural and moral customs of the milieu in which it exists; the body is defined externally. Discussing the desiring, novel body, Irigaray writes:

> It is so much so that, even at the level of perception, the child will be induced to recognize what it perceives—for example what it sees—instead of being initiated into perceiving by itself. . . . A filter of precomprehension thus precedes its approach to the real. And this paralyzes its energy, especially its sensitive energy, through an a priori perception presumed to be common, through a molding which is considered necessary but cuts it off from its source of life and puts it into

> an artificial ecstasy through an imposed communion with the world, with the other, and firstly, with itself.[10]

The mosaic villages of Belfast, isolated within their bounded territories, have been taught "to think in the concrete, to love with constraint and . . . to be content in bubbles."[11] Rooted within concrete, the territorialized body becomes habitually induced to recognize what it perceives, rather than perceiving, that is to say, *making* by oneself in relation.

Wrest of its incipience, relation as mere recognition is the very destruction of the moving, sensing body. In recognition the air is passive and unregistered, breathed without engagement, wonder, and encounter. Although this atmosphere and the habits it induces may affect the body with a sense of comfort, there is a need to be suspicious of such a culture because, via an internal desire for belonging and safety, the body is numbed, more than often unconsciously, "into an affective embrace of stability and permanence."[12] This embrace is present before the very body it constructs and, thus, the static and permanent body it engineers is always-already known in advance of its very becoming. Self, thus, becomes defined in restriction rather than incipient possibility.

To be defined within restriction is, as Irigaray has argued, to breathe an "already used, not truly pure air."[13] Arrested in the impure air of stasis we form a kind of mass species composed of a collective respiration: to be part of us you need to be breathing the same air as us; this is the only air you know, the only breath you desire.[14] Through this single breath, normative sociality becomes rooted to the same world, the same background, the same ideal, and the same perception, which in turn compels the permanence, dominance, and stasis of the common. Irigaray illustrates how, in this rooting, bodies unite in something that binds them together, where community is not "constituted starting from relations of kinship, from closeness with others, but from the outside, starting with rules."[15] Here, then, the body is embraced by a preconstructed world, where it is compelled to submit to what is already common. Bound to a single, unified species, we are not bodies but engineered robots devoid of autonomy, of freedom, of difference, and of movement; we are denied the very breath through which life is given.

The prevailing and absolute embrace of recognition consigns Northern Irish bodies and relations to the stasis of the eternal now. In this temporal and spatial permanence there is and can be no constitutive differentiation, let alone new emergent possibilities, as everything is predefined in sameness while effectively remaining the same: worlds and bodies, and the relations of separation and sameness both between and within them, are static. During The Troubles, it was common for families not aligned to the dominant identity of the area to be forced out of their homes through intimidation and violence. As one woman remembered:

> Umm, but as I say when The Troubles came that all changed in Bryson Street. I remember one very bad night of violence and the next day my nanny turns to me, I'm only about eight years old or something, and my nanny is taking me down the street by the hand and, you know, being really shocked because people's windows were smashed, and people's furniture and belongings were lying all over the road, you know, where they had fled. And I remember the coal, everybody seemed to move out in coal lorries. Coal lorries came and got people's stuff, you know, and then all of a sudden, umm, there's a lot of houses empty which for us as children it was just a game then, that was, we would then play in the empty houses, you know.

At the time of this interview, in September 2017, the stasis and violence of Northern Ireland was acutely felt when four Catholic families were forced to flee their homes following sectarian intimidation. These families had been living in a cross-community housing development that had been a headline initiative under Stormont's "Together Building a United Community" program, the Executive Office's most recent strategy for improving community relations and building a united and shared society.[16] Binary identity politics territorialize worlds as repetitive play; segregated space sustains the standardized recognition of inherited truths that narrate a feared, untrustworthy, threatening, and immoral other, which in turn sustains the stasis of separation—the other continues to be "missed" and sharing across worlds remains an impossibility. The failure of the "Urban Villages" cross-community housing development highlights the inability of a peace process operating within the constraints of predicative logic to actualize real transformation and build shared worlds.

Peace, in Northern Ireland, needs to become a political question rather than a problem to be managed. The Northern Irish peace process has been, and continues to be, the management of "what is"—the management of the prevailing presence of partitioning prefiguring the territory, living relations, and everyday body of Northern Ireland. Here, the task of the ruling elite resides in maintaining habits, customs, existing rules, and, crucially, a consensus for peace, which acts as a binding substitute for an elemental ecology of sharing. Peace processes are not necessarily instruments of change; they can, literally, embody continuation. Although proceeding through a phase of management may be necessary to reduce the tangible presence of violence before a more transformative peace can be animated, in Northern Ireland the ubiquitous nature of stasis has eternalized the structure of conflict in the immobile binary of two already known species—self or other, us or them, Catholic or Protestant, green or orange—for which there exists no middle position in-between.

Cross-community work has been at the heart of the Northern Irish peace process. Guided by rational logic, this work seeks to establish a single recognition of humanity across partitions: a consensus recognizing one humanity, a sameness, between two opposing species. Not only does such peace-work take defined identity categories as its starting point, but the end point persists as the elimination of difference. To begin from species is, Manning argues, to have already put into place a hierarchy of form—a virtuous self and an immoral enemy—that itself becomes a pathology: "an enclosure that wrests from its protected environment all that does not resemble it."[17] To continue to embed peace in structures of Being that are necessarily violent is to confine peace to the accomplishment of the less-than-violent. Furthermore, with stasis dissolving movements of living, relational vitality, as it currently stands the future of Northern Ireland resides in a further extension of the eternal now.

Movement: Learning to Breathe Again

Considering the plea to begin "with the stuff itself,"[18] I now seek to return to the elemental movement of breath. A return to breath does not simply deconstruct dominant preoccupations with codification and commodification, and the preferences for understanding rather than living.[19] To remain in a place of critique is to remain static. It is to prevent the becoming of the new, of the alternative, and of the novel; it is to prevent difference. An affirmative politics necessitates a movement beyond critique.[20] It compels the creation, invention, and becoming of worlds, bodies, and relations anew: it compels a movement of and with breath. To return to the elemental nature of breath is not to reduce elemental materiality and movement, but rather to create *with* breath as "the organizer for living itself and for the coexistence between living beings."[21] The elemental, then, is a politics of composition and synergy, with breath being the material, and hence political, entanglement of living and relational vitality.

Breath is the originary movement shared by all living bodies. Never appearing while not being imperceptible, breath is "both the invisible and that which makes the visible."[22] Respiring with the whole-body breath inspires the body. It houses and nourishes the body. Breath is the first autonomous gesture of the living body and the emergence of a specific living bodily presence, where Irigaray places "an original potential from which we must start and develop."[23] This potential, as Irigaray explains in *To Be Born*, dwells with the first breath of the newborn:

> Whatever the unknown factors of our conception, we have wanted to be born. Our existence cannot be the outcome of a mere chance, and our will to live clearly manifested itself at the time of our birth. We were the ones who determined its moment. We were the ones who gave birth to ourselves through our first breathing.[24]

With its first breath the body takes root in the very act of breathing that gives life, which gives birth, to the newly born body. This first breath is impossible to appropriate. It is not, nor could it be, a used or impure air. It is, however, a shared air. To return to the elemental is to return to our origins, to our original and relational potential. Origins here lie not in the ceaseless search for natural and innate roots, not with belonging to a mass species of Being. Rather the origin of our birth is a making of incipient possibility. It is this original and relational potential that we return to when we move with breath.

Breathing is not a one-time only act. Breath continues to move. Breath bounces, transmits, and vibrates. It is light and free, the elusive element and the originary excess, the movement of becoming and a moving "nextness" continually giving without measure. While in breath there can be stillness; there can never be stasis. To be living is to be in a perpetual movement of becoming. Irigaray is quick to point out this is not a perpetual becoming of the same; it is not to take root in an air that has already been breathed but a becoming already venturing beyond that which has been known and experienced in life. Being, here, is nothing other than a becoming; we are a to-be.[25] The movement of vitality is the natural belonging of the body. It is in the elemental movement of breath that the body, as a to-be, takes root and gives life, gives movement, toward its own blossoming, growth, and becoming. As movement always-already moving, breath cannot be confined or contained and there will always be spaces where the movement of breath exceeds the dominance of stasis. Such spaces are present throughout Belfast and, while some may be fleeting, others will have a more sustained presence. Whether fleeting or sustained, these spaces dwell at the level of everyday interaction, the banal level at which an affective and transformative, if speculative,[26] politics is played out.

To begin to conceive of peace and the activity of peace-making from within an alternative horizon is to become attentive to unnoticed experiences and encounters in Belfast wherein peaceful sharing is already active. These moments cannot be articulated as a norm. They are, however, mobilized as an embodied and situated invitation to move-with the movement of breath and within the spaces that speculative transformative breathing actualizes. The Irish-language project in east Belfast can be approached as one of these spaces. Traditionally, Irish culture and traditions dwell exclusively in Catholic areas and with the Catholic body. The Irish language is not an object available from a Protestant line of orientation. However, the birth of an Irish-language project in Protestant east Belfast challenges the very construction of this orientation and the predetermined body it engineers, by animating an alternative world respiring and inspiring in breath.

Learning a language consciously connects the body to the movement of its own breath. Irish language is composed of sounds and shapes that cannot be located in the English language. Creating the shape of these sounds necessitates an attention to breath.

Drochdhóigh.

An impossible sound. An unknown word.

droCHGHoy.

A different movement of breath.

> CH: a sound located at the front of the mouth; breath pushes first through the teeth and then through pursed lips before it escapes into the air.
>
> GH: a sound created through breath moving in a circular motion at the back of the mouth; breath starts at the rear of the tongue and, from here, is propelled further back toward the mouth's posterior wall, before moving along the soft palate.
>
> CHGH CHGH CHGH CHGH CHGH CHGH CHGH CHGH
>
> A release of breath though the teeth and pursed lips in a direct, linear inhalation, only to be immediately pulled back to the rear of the mouth, where it does almost a complete rotation touching upon the back of the tongue, before moving to the back of the mouth and, finally, the softness of the roof of the mouth and then release.
>
> droCHGHoy.
>
> An attentiveness to a different movement of breath. A new sound.[27]

An active and embodied encounter with the Irish language animates moments whereby dwelling literally becomes rooted in the aerial practice of breathing. Here the body breathes consciously and moves in, and with, the vitality of its own living in the present;[28] a living beyond or, more precisely prior to, the imposition of, and alignment to, the stasis of external identity constructions. The body, at least in this moment of conscious breath, is not compelled to dwell in a predetermined and inherited Protestant orientation firmly rooted in definitional spaces. Rather, it moves with the sounds and shapes of its own breath, prior to any imposition of meaning or the recognition of form—Irish or British. Attention in this space does not reside in understanding or a singular recognition of humanity but with listening-to and feeling the movement of one's own breath. The body is returned, through the movement and stillness of inhalation, to the original potential of the first birth: to the continually blossoming of the to-be.

To begin with movement rather than stasis is to begin to animate an alternative horizon. Brian Massumi in his prelude to *Always More than One* articulates how Manning moves with the very motion of movement to foreground the awareness that the process of creating is always bigger than the creation.[29] To start with movement is to acknowledge that breath will always exceed the body it brings into becoming. Bodies learning the Irish language move with the different shapes, sounds, and sensations of making, opposed to with an understanding or recognition of Gaelic. Breath, then, shifts attention from the defined and known subject to "the movement of difference that marks the very energies of existence before and beyond any lives or imputed identity."[30] This is a shift from who and what we are to the pre-personal elemental forces forever making the body more-than; to the process Manning names speciation. Speciation cannot be thought as a set of Beings in possession of a linear, causal series of defining characteristics. To think with speciation is to give birth not to a fully formed and recognizable body in the first gesture but to a movement of living vitality. Speciation moves not with bodies but with body-tendings, which Manning conceives as "rhythmic activations of a body-morphing that never precedes the event of their coming into relation."[31]

Breath houses and nourishes the body but it does not remain in the body. Autonomy, Irigaray notes, obliges the recognition that the breath that gifts living is first received "from an other body, from our mother"[32]—the practice of breathing demands the recognition of relationality. Breath is the element shared in-between different worlds, imperceptibly crossing the limits of these worlds.[33] It is a matter of differential practice in which the outside is brought in and the inside is brought out.[34] The inhalation of a conscious practice of breathing[35] cultivates an interiority that is always-already active in the cultivation of the other while, simultaneously and immediately, advancing a return to the interiority from which faithfulness to one's own blossoming is affirmed.[36] The bodies learning Gaelic did not become Irish. Yet, in returning to the movement of their own breath in relation to the sounds and shapes of the other, they were moving with an undeterminable and continual movement of becoming or, in Manning's words, they were moving with the relational event of autonomous body-tending. Breath animates a folding in the middle where the in-between is created as the essential opposition between the internal and the external dissolves and the self and other are put into an intersubjective, relational weaving. As Irigaray voices: "I bear the other within me."[37] What emerges in the speciation of the to-be is beyond the human, object, or territory. What emerges is relation, a relation that precedes the body it animates, a relation of incipient possibility, "an incipient relation that speciates" autonomously.[38] Irigaray herself articulated how "it is in the interlacing of our bodies talking to one another that the transcendental matter, from which our 'to be' takes shape, lies."[39]

Peace cannot continue to be confined to the binary, hierarchical separation of our current horizon of identity politics. A transformative peace must learn to breathe autonomous from, if in relation to, violence. Within an aerial ecology peace is not static; it is not a predefined, negative truth to be accomplished in a vision set forth by the Northern Irish political elite. Rather, peace is something that is woven in action, in-between bodies and worlds in relation. Contrary to annexing peace to a gravitational pull of territorial partitioning, we need to become attentive to the potential of peace already moving with an aerial ecology of breath. It is this shared, aerial ecology of relationality, already active within Belfast, to which we now move.

Sharing: An Aerial Commonality

> By now the Newtownards Road, in the heart of the east Belfast, is a place I am familiar with. Four times a week, I leave the city center via the Queens Bridge and head into east Belfast. Navigating the large triangular junction leading to the Newtownards Road and briefly skirting the gated enclave of Catholic Short Strand, I am once again, and every time, hit with a slight unease. Engraved into the background and looming tall to cast a dark shadow over their territory below, are Harland and Wolff's Samson and Goliath. Men in balaclavas supporting guns stare down from the painted walls as they pick out a target. Blood red poppies draw in your gaze and the Red Hand of Ulster glows proudly. The mark of the letters U, V, and F[40] are visibly branded into the bricks and mortar that bind the east together. I walk alongside abandoned shops that are boarded shut with scenes depicting the faded color of the activity that was once alive. My destination soon

comes into sight—the living green wall standing out among the sea of gloomy, gray concrete. I take the cue to turn right, walk through the entrance into a fluorescently lit building, and hurry up the three flights of steps conscious of the time. While I am normally given a few moments at the top of the stairs to catch my breath as I wait for the door to be opened with a smile and friendly call of "maidin mhaith," today the door is wide open as it welcomes people to the *díanchúrsa*. I move across the threshold.

It's the final session of the day and the four classes—*bunrang a hAon, bunrang a dó, meánrang, ardráng*—are in full swing. In the *bunrang a dó* class we are moving through the different tenses of Irish in relation to the *laethanta na seachtaine*. For some of us this is new vocabulary and, faced with looks of confusion and loss, Seamus slows the pace to spend some time going through the unfamiliar words. As Seamus voices each day in turn, my whole body focuses on listening and following the different sounds before we together attempt to repeat what we had heard: *arís, arís, arís. Dé Luan. Dé Mháirt.* Feeling the sounds moving around the mouth: breath escaping in the sound of "jay," the pursed lips of the "loo," and the pulling back of the mouth to create the "un." *Dé Chéadaoin. Dé Déardaoin.* Sensing which sounds hold a silent presence and what sounds move together to a different tone. Jay EEN yuh. Jay SAH-(t)hurn. Jay DO(m)H-nukh.

As we move with the different shapes of these unfamiliar words, my body faults in a state of surprise. It slowly attunes to another sound, to sounds that have never before touched upon Gaelic tones. The faint rhythmic beat of a drum. Flutes breathing a dancing melody. The disciplined echo of heavily clad feet moving in time. DUM. DUM. D-D-D-D-D-DUM. Tootle-too-too-too-tootle-toooooo—to-to-to—toooo-to-to-tootle-tooo. One . . . two . . . one . . . two . . . one . . . two . . . one . . . two. Sitting still in a classroom in the Skainos center I move to a different world, to a novel space that has not previously been listened to. The two sounds play

> together; they swirl, intermingle, and dance. The air fills. It expands, amplifies, and respires with the growing sounds of the two. Jay EEN yuh. DUM.—(t)hurn. *Dé Chéadaoin.* too-tootle-toooooo—to-to-to. DUM. One . . . loo-un. D-D-DUM. two . . . one . . . two . . . one . . . two. Jay DO(m) H-nukh. Then as quickly as the moment of crescendo, I sense a retreat as the sounds of the drums, flutes, and marching pull back to the Newtownards Road. The Gaelic sounds continue to vibrate in the air—Jay LOO-in, Jay march, Jay KAY-deen, JAY-ar-deen, Jay HEEN-yeh, Jay SA-ha-rin, Jay DOH-nee—yet they feel slightly different.[41]

Encounters are composed from the activity of breathing. Moving with breath, the external sounds of the marching band fold inside to reach toward the internal Gaelic enclave in the middle of east Belfast where the sounds of the Irish language, traditionally quieted and contained within the protective walls of the building, rise up to meet the melody of the flutes, the thunder of the bass drum, and the swagger of the marching beat. Within this aerial folding, the inside and the outside are put into incipient relations in-between. While active at the limit, the in-between is not a defined space limited by borders. The in-between is a space of breath, an elemental movement ungraspable in shape and form, which is neither completely material nor wholly incorporeal. Relations in-between the self and the other move with the event in the presence of its emergence to weave a groundless ground, which Irigaray conceives as "an act of grounding which does not end in any ground."[42] This is not a rooting to territory or predetermined, habitual performances of recognition but the weaving of a shared aerial synergy, which can never be partitioned or isolated as breath is gifted and received without demonstration, and before distinction between giver and receiver.[43] The two touch upon one and other in this shared spacing as the air fills and expands in the constellation of sounds active in-between. As touch always elicits a returning caress,[44] the gesture of reaching-toward is always shared. The response is not necessarily felt or acknowledged in words but, rather, through a returning of touch: an encounter in breath is perceived "not first and foremost from sense to sense but from relation to relation."[45] What is animated in the encounter, then, is a reaching-toward in the fleeting present, a forever moving opening, which is not necessarily closeness or distance but, as Irigaray illustrates, simultaneously both.

The distancing of relationality that Irigaray gives voice to is a double gesture. The first gesture is the withdrawal from the familiarity and comfort of learned codes—an engineered recognition in which noise culturally and politically aligns with a mass common species of orange or green that is always-already named as offensive, feared, external, suspicious, and hated. Opposed to recognizing a violent noise activated in a performance of intimidation seeking to assert our presence in this space opposed to yours, what was encountered was moving sounds or, even, body-tendings active prior to form: the enchantment and wonder of different rhythms, tempos, tones, beats, flows, pulses, and vibrations in a movement of becoming not locatable in form.

To encounter the other, to be alive in a relational communion of air, is to turn one's culture upside down, to reverse the learned codes we have been taught and to break with habit.[46] The mystery and wonder of the encounter "interrupts the system of cross-references of my world, re-opens my horizon and questions its finality" to animate a movement of becoming other than Being or beyond species.[47] In their reaching-toward sounds continued in movement and, here, is the second distancing of the double gesture Irigaray gives voice to: a distancing from the "sensory or sensitive experience, of an empathy or intensely close meeting of the world in the present."[48] The materiality and movement of the encounter cannot be directly associated with an organ or an object a priori. This movement is not the activity of a habitual sense modality wherein there is a risk of paralysis, but what Manning refers to as "amodality": a foregrounding not of "the sense itself but its relational potential" in the present.[49] Movement did not cease, and enchantment was not arrested in an activity of naming, in an attempt to recognize the sounds in a known species. Neither was this fleeting encounter reduced to telling, it almost went unnoticed, unrecognized but for the initial touch of mystery in the first moments of reaching-toward. Instead, there was a letting-be, a silence in which an ecology of body-tendings blossomed.

In our very first breath we are not simply born into the world but, rather, into a constellation of relations from which the to-be of both bodies and worlds takes shape. To encounter the other in the movement of breath folding in-between the internal and the external is not to emerge as a determined and composed human self. A shared encounter of breath is the making of speculative, dynamic worldings that refuses categorization: "Beyond the human, beyond the sense of touch or vision, beyond the object, what emerges is relation."[50] This relation is a constitutive intertwining of differentiation in proximity. It is an ethical relation in-between the self and the other who share in the dissenting commonness of the ontological force propelling them.

In the intimate closeness and distancing of breath we can begin to see fleeting moments of peaceful sharing already active in Belfast. As breath universally intertwines the macro and the micro while, paradoxically, being non-scalable, to become attentive to its movement is to begin to animate an alternative, if speculative, horizon from which to conceive of the politics of peace. The challenge for peace-weaving for the future, then, is to enervate these already active entanglements of shared everyday life into wider ecologies.

Conclusion: Commoning in Breath

In this short offering I have returned to the elemental to trace an alternative horizon from which we can begin to animate shared, peaceful worlds in a movement of incipient commonality. To reach toward another body, to move with a forgotten breath, is not to reinstate commonness. Peace will not be a product of commonality determined a priori. To continue to reduce peace to commonality as it is traditionally understood is to continue to engineer an activity that maintains the stasis of what is. Instead of searching for consensus, the starting point from which to cultivate a sharing of peaceful worlds must be difference and, so, dissensus: the making of incipient possibility. While consensus assumes the universality of the simple preframed position form takes, dissensus arises with the nextness of "movement moving" in the tendings of bodies bodying. To become with other bodies, both human and nonhuman, is not to become these bodies. What is shared in relational becoming, in an ecology of breath, is not subsumed into a singular body or one world. Rather, what is shared is a respect for living vitality in and across difference, for the potentialities and possibilities of other bodies and other worlds that are always-already necessarily different from the capacity and the potential of my body and world.[51] It is the continual becoming and distancing of the first, autonomous breath that is shared. To quote Irigaray: "Air is what is left common between subjects living in different worlds."[52]

Despite the prevailing presence of segregation and partitioning in Belfast, moments of incipient sharing are active throughout the city. These moments respire and inspire in breath. To move with these already active spaces is to realize harmony and peace will not be found in the ceaseless search for territorial roots. Nor can it be found in the engineering of consensus among preframed positions, within a commoning that becomes common—within sameness. Peace in Northern Ireland, and perhaps beyond, needs to return to breath and become attentive to the emerging micropolitical associations that are always-already shaping, if only speculatively, the makings of peace. Political action cannot aim for stability-as-stasis, for the maintenance of what is, but neither can it reside in designing what has never before been experienced. Rather, peace will become with a political action choreographing an opening from which the potential to move beyond, or rather before, form can arise: an opening of the body to the activity of breathing that cultivates its own blossoming in a sharing of dissensus. The commoning of breath is not the common (neutral) ground that peace processes driven by the dominant macropolitical seek to construct, but an incipient commoning "beyond community and commonality":[53] a commonality in breath.

Notes

1. It is, however, important to note that the United Kingdom's decision to leave the European Union in June 2016 potentially threatens the "achievement" of peace in Northern Ireland. Brexit has resurrected agonistic, historical debates and positions regarding the constitutional status of Northern Ireland: Does Great Britain *or* the Republic of Ireland hold the natural, innate claim to the territory of Northern Ireland? Acutely playing into the revival of this question are the implications of the Brexit decision for the border on the island of Ireland. While leaders in the United Kingdom, the Republic of Ireland, and across the European Union have repeatedly stated the desire to avoid a return to a hard border, it has become increasingly questionable how this will be possible in the face of the United Kingdom pursuing a "hard Brexit." There are concerns the return of a hard border poses a threat to peace in Northern Ireland. As the Exiting the European Union Committee has stated: "Many in Ireland are deeply concerned that the introduction of new and visible border check points would provide an opportunity and focal point for those who wish to disrupt the peace and feed a sense in some communities that the Good Friday Agreement was being undermined." Exiting the European Union Committee, *The Government's Negotiation Objective: The White Paper* (London: The House of Commons, 2017), 40, paragraph 112.

2. Margaret Whitford, *Luce Irigaray: Philosophy in the Feminine* (Oxon: Routledge, 1991), 6.

3. Erin Manning, *Politics of Touch: Sense, Movement, Sovereignty* (Minneapolis: University of Minnesota Press, 2007), 14.

4. Nigel Thrift, "Afterwords," *Environment and Planning D: Society and Space* 18, no. 2 (2000): 252.

5. Gerry Adams was the leader of Sinn Féin from 1983 to 2018 and has become almost synonymous with the Catholic community. Allegedly, Adams held a leadership role in the Irish Republican Army.

6. Reverend Ian Paisley was a Loyalist politician and Protestant religious leader who was leader of the Democratic Unionist Party from 197 to 2008. He was the key political figure for the Protestant community during The Troubles and the peace process.

7. Irigaray SW, 65.

8. Harry Bregazzi and Mark Jackson, "Agonism, Critical Political Geography, and the New Geographies of Peace," *Progress in Human Geography* 42, no. 1 (2018): 72–91.

9. Irigaray WL, 150.

10. Irigaray TBB, 63–64.

11. Marijn Nieuwenhuis, "On One Breath All Depend," *Journal of Narrative Politics* 1, no. 2 (2015): 171.

12. Andreas Philippopoulos-Mihalopoulos, "Withdrawing from Atmosphere: An Ontology of Air Partitioning and Affective Engineering," *Environment and Panning D: Society and Space* 34, no. 1 (2016): 151.

13. Irigaray BEW, 74.

14. Philippopoulos-Mihalopoulos, "Withdrawing from Atmosphere," 151.

15. Irigaray BEW, 14.

16. Stormont is a colloquial term referring to the devolved Northern Ireland government, whose parliamentary buildings are located in the Stormont Estate, in Belfast. The Good Friday Agreement established a Northern Ireland government operating under a principle of power-sharing, guaranteeing the representation of both Unionist and Nationalists within the Northern Ireland Executive. The Assembly was first elected in June and, while there has been period of political stability, the Assembly has continually and repeatedly collapsed, forcing the reinstation of direct rule. Between 2007 and 2017 the Assembly and Executive published two policy and strategy frameworks addressing peace: the *Programme for Cohesion, Sharing and Integration* in 2010; and *Together: Building a United Community* in 2013, which is the framework still being implemented today. These documents build on the Good Friday Agreement and set forth the latest vision for peace in Northern Ireland.

17. Erin Manning, *Always More than One: Individuation's Dance* (Durham, NC: Duke University Press, 2013), 188.

18. Mark Jackson and Maria Fannin, "Letting Geography Fall Where It May: Areographies Address the Elemental," *Environment and Panning D: Society and Space* 29, no. 3 (2011): 438.

19. Irigaray and Marder TVB, 191.

20. Bregazzi and Jackson, "Agonism, Critical Political Geography, and the New Geographies of Peace," 80–81.

21. Irigaray and Marder TVB, 31.

22. Marijn Nieuwenhuis, "On One Breath All Depend," *Journal of Narrative Politics* 1, no. 2 (2015): 168.

23. Irigaray and Marder TVB, 76.

24. Irigaray TBB, 1.

25. Irigaray TBB, 101.

26. I borrow the term *speculative* from María Puig de la Bellacasa, who advances a speculative ethics that moves with the unfolding present of the in-between: to theorize from the messy, sensual, affective, and embodied realm of life is to make "ethics [and both philosophy and politics] a hands-on, ongoing process of recreation of 'as well as possible' relations [and worlds] and therefore one that requires a speculative opening about what a possible involves." María Puig de la Bellacasa, *Matters of Care: Speculative Ethics in More than Human Worlds* (Minneapolis: University of Minnesota Press, 2017), 6.

27. Extract from the author's fieldwork journal, March 13, 2019.

28. Elisha Foust, "Breathing the Political: A Mediation on the Preservation of Life in the Midst of War," in *Breathing with Luce Irigaray*, ed. Emily A. Holmes and Lenart Škof (London: Bloomsbury, 2013), 188.

29. Brian Massumi, Prelude to *Always More than One: Individuation's Dance*, Erin Manning (Durham, NC: Duke University Press, 2013), xi.

30. Elizabeth Grosz, *Becoming Undone: Darwinian Reflections on Life, Politics and Art* (Durham, NC: Duke University Press, 2011), 91.

31. Manning, *Always More than One*, 208.

32. Irigaray BB, 218.

33. Irigaray WL, 67.

34. Magdalena Gorska, *Breathing Matters: Feminist Intersectional Politics of Vulnerability* (Linköping: Linköping University Electronic Press, 2016), 28.

35. Conscious breathing, as mobilized by Irigaray, does not refer purely to the rational, logical mind. Rather, to become conscious of our breathing is to awaken the body to the sensual, the practical, the affective and to touch: "In this becoming the body is not separated off from the mental, nor is consciousness the domination of nature by a clever know-how. It is a progressive awakening for the entire body through the channelling of breath from centers of elemental vitality to more spiritual centers: of the heart, of speech, of thought." Irigaray BEW, 8–9.

36. Irigaray WL, xiv.

37. Irigaray SW, 43.
38. Manning, *Always More than One*, 221.
39. Irigaray TBB, 102.
40. UVF stands for Ulster Volunteer Force, an Ulster Loyalist paramilitary that undertook an armed campaign during The Troubles. Despite declaring a cease-fire in 1994 and officially ending its campaign in 2007, the UVF continues to have a visible presence in east Belfast.
41. Extract from the author's fieldwork journal, September 9, 2017.
42. Irigaray WL, 72.
43. Irigaray FA, 48.
44. Irigaray FC, 121.
45. Manning, *Always More than One*, 94.
46. Irigaray and Marder TVB, 42–45.
47. Irigaray SW, 97.
48. Irigaray TBB, 65.
49. Manning, *Always More than One*, 5.
50. Manning, *Always More than One*, 12.
51. Irigaray and Marder TVB, 204.
52. Irigaray WL, 67.
53. Manning, *Always More than One*, 201.

Bibliography

Bregazzi, Harry, and Mark Jackson. "Agonism, Critical Political Geography, and the New Geographies of Peace." *Progress in Human Geography* 42, no. 1 (2018): 72–91.

Butler, Judith. "Sexual Difference as a Question of Ethics: Alterities of the Flesh in Irigaray and Merleau-Ponty." In *Feminist Interpretations of Maurice Merleau-Ponty*, edited by Dorothea Olkowski and Gail Weiss, 107–126. University Park: Pennsylvania State University Press, 2006.

Exiting the European Union Committee. *The Government's Negotiation Objectives: The White Paper*. London: The House of Commons, 2017.

Foust, Elisha. "Breathing the Political: A Mediation on the Preservation of Life in the Midst of War." In *Breathing with Luce Irigaray*, edited by Emily A. Holmes and Lenart Škof, 186–202. London: Bloomsbury, 2013.

Gorska, Magdalena. *Breathing Matters: Feminist Intersectional Politics of Vulnerability*. Linköping: Linköping University Electronic Press, 2016.

Grosz, Elizabeth. *Becoming Undone: Darwinian Reflections on Life, Politics and Art*. Durham, NC: Duke University Press, 2011.

Jackson, Mark, and Maria Fannin. "Letting Geography Fall Where It May: Areographies Address the Elemental." *Environment and Panning D: Society and Space* 29, no. 3 (2011): 435–444.

Manning, Erin. *Politics of Touch: Sense, Movement, Sovereignty*. Minneapolis: University of Minnesota Press, 2007.

Manning, Erin. *Always More than One: Individuation's Dance*. Durham, NC: Duke University Press, 2013.

Massumi, Brian. Prelude to *Always More than One: Individuation's Dance*, Erin Manning, ix–xxvi. Durham, NC: Duke University Press, 2013.

Nieuwenhuis, Marijn. "On One Breath All Depend." *Journal of Narrative Politics* 1, no. 2 (2015): 167–179.

Philippopoulos-Mihalopoulos, Andreas. "Withdrawing from Atmosphere: An Ontology of Air Partitioning and Affective Engineering." *Environment and Panning D: Society and Space* 34, no. 1 (2016): 150–167.

Puig de la Bellacasa, María. *Matters of Care: Speculative Ethics in More than Human Worlds*. Minneapolis: University of Minnesota Press, 2017.

Thrift, Nigel. "Afterwords." *Environment and Planning D: Society and Space* 18, no. 2 (2000): 213–255.

Whitford, Margaret. *Luce Irigaray: Philosophy in the Feminine*. Oxon: Routledge, 1991.

Notes on Contributors

Wesley N. Barker is Associate Professor of Religious Studies at Mercer University. Wesley presents and publishes at the intersections of religion, philosophy, ethics, and feminist thought. She has also published articles on pedagogy and curriculum development. Wesley's current monograph draws on the materiality of alterity in Irigaray's work to theorize an ethics of desire that disrupts the politics of recognition.

Athena V. Colman is Associate Professor of Philosophy at Brock University. Her research and teaching interests include feminist philosophy, contemporary French philosophy, phenomenology, psychoanalysis, critical race theory, and the Frankfurt School. Her publications include work on transfeminism, Fanon, Kristeva, Freud, Lacan, and Merleau-Ponty.

Annu Dahiya recently completed her PhD in the program in literature at Duke University. Her research and teaching foreground feminist and anti-racist philosophies; gender, sexuality, and feminist studies; feminist science and technology studies; and continental philosophy of science. Her dissertation, "The Conditions of Emergence: Towards a Feminist Philosophy of the Origins of Life," tracks the seismic effects the concepts of *matter* and *life* have undergone in twentieth-century continental thought and origins-of-life research and meditates on the empirical findings of science in order to craft a feminist philosophy of life that teases out the ontological and political consequences of these transformations. Her work, thus far, has been published in *Transforming Contagion: Risky Contacts among Bodies, Disciplines, and Nations* (2018) and the *Journal of Bioethical Inquiry*.

Sabrina L. Hom is Assistant Professor of Philosophy at Georgia College in Milledgeville, Georgia, and the coordinator of the Women's and

Gender Studies program there. Her research addresses the intersections of race, gender, sexuality, and kinship. She is a cofounder of the Luce Irigaray Circle.

Ruthanne Crapo Kim is a faculty member in the Department of Philosophy at Minneapolis Community and Technical College. Her main research interests include critical philosophy of race, contemporary continental philosophy, environmental justice, and decolonial studies. She has published articles on creolization and sexual difference, decolonizing pedagogy, and ontological labor in the academy.

Michael Lucas is Emeritus Professor in Architecture at California Polytechnic State University, San Luis Obispo, and former Associate Dean for Academic Affairs with the College of Architecture and Environmental Design. He served as Planning Commissioner in his coastal home of Morro Bay, California, for many years. Michael's research is in the area of human development and spatial concept formation, place, and identity, looking at the juncture of cultural and individual tacit, phenomenological, and intuitive knowing. In addition to his work on embodiment and design pedagogy, his publications on architecture, eco-phenomenology, and environmental ethics have engaged Indigenous situations in North America, as well as Finland, Turkey, and the United Kingdom. His current research is in collaboration with colleagues at the University of Prešov, Slovakia, on UNESCO World Heritage sites in the Carpathian Mountains.

Ciara Merrick successfully defended her doctoral thesis in December 2019 at the University of Bristol, where she was a postgraduate student in the School of Geographical Sciences. Her research puts Luce Irigaray's thinking into a productive, if at times uneasy, dialogue with other feminist thinkers and looks at how everyday encounters animate peaceful and caring relations within and across difference in the context of postconflict Northern Ireland. Ciara participated in the seminar Lucy Irigaray holds with PhD students at the University of Bristol in 2017 and co-led a workshop at the Luce Irigaray: How to Give Birth to a New Human Being? seminar at the Institute for Contemporary Arts.

M. D. Murtagh is a PhD candidate at Duke University in the literature program. M. D.'s work spans twentieth-century continental philosophy, feminist and black feminist theory, and the philosophy of science, especially physics. His dissertation "A Cosmology of Sexual Difference: The Quantum Gravity Matrix and Embryogenesis of the Universe" argues that sexual difference can be conceived beyond sexed bodies, as the very organizing principle of fundamental reality, and that it is possible to reconceive the cosmology of our universe as an embryogenesis (rather than an evolution) in an ongoing and self-differentiating relation with an incorporeal, maternal quantum matrix that theoretical physicists refer to as Hilbert space. M. D. is the 2019 recipient of the Irigaray Circle's Karen Burke Memorial Prize and has been published in *philoSOPHIA: A Journal of Feminist Continental Philosophy*, with an article forthcoming in *Hypatia: A Journal of Feminist Philosophy*.

Tessa Ashlin Nunn is a PhD candidate in Romance Studies at Duke University. Her dissertation, "Writing Women Dance," proposes a concept of grace based on dance scenes in nineteenth-century French novels written by women. Her research interests include feminist thought, film studies, dance history, and nineteenth- and twentieth-century literature. She has published on Francophone films, contemporary French feminism, nineteenth-century literature, and ballet in popular culture.

Mary C. Rawlinson is Professor and Director of Graduate Studies, Department of Philosophy, Stony Brook University in New York. Rawlinson's publications include *Betrayal of Substance: Death, Literature, and Sexual Difference in Hegel's "Phenomenology of Spirit"* (2020), *Just Life: Bioethics and the Future of Sexual Difference* (2016), *Engaging the World: Thinking After Irigaray* (2016), *The Routledge Handbook of Food Ethics* (2016), *Labor and Global Justice* (2014), *Thinking with Irigaray* (2011), and *Derrida and Feminism* (1997). Her next book, *Liminal Ethics*, investigates the idea of justice in crime fiction. Rawlinson was the founding editor of *IJFAB: International Journal of Feminist Approaches to Bioethics* (2006–2016) and Cofounder and Director of the Irigaray Circle (2007–2017). In 2018 she was appointed Senior Visiting Research Fellow at the Institute for Advanced Studies, University College London.

Yvette Russell is Senior Lecturer in Law and Feminist Theory at the University of Bristol Law School. Her research spans the areas of the law and humanities, and her current research looks at how we can productively theorize the end of sexual violence, with reference to feminist philosophy and Indigenous feminisms, and argues that we must situate resistance to sexual violence within a context of revolutionary decolonial politics. Yvette has published widely on law, philosophy, and feminism and is the author (with Joanne Conaghan) of *Sexual History Evidence in Rape Trials* (forthcoming).

James Sares is a doctoral candidate in philosophy at Stony Brook University. His research engages themes in phenomenology, metaphysics, and the philosophy of science.

Brenda Sharp completed her MSc research as a mature student at the London School of Economics and is now a PhD candidate at the University of Winchester. Her current research seeks to explore the relationship between a conception of love and morality in the work of philosopher Iris Murdoch. Brenda's interests lie in the areas of philosophy, political theory, gender politics, theology, and ethics. Brenda has published articles on gender-specific violence in a war situation and the gendered politics of the family.

Index

www.ingramcontent.com/pod-product-compliance
Lightning Source LLC
LaVergne TN
LVHW040201080826
844660LV00001B/61

* 9 7 8 1 4 3 8 4 8 8 4 5 5 *